CHANGE AND RESILIENCE

CHANGE AND RESILIENCE

THE OCCUPATION OF MEDITERRANEAN ISLANDS IN LATE ANTIQUITY

edited by

Miguel Ángel Cau Ontiveros and Catalina Mas Florit

OXBOW | books
Oxford & Philadelphia

Joukowsky Institute Publication 9

General series editor: Prof. John F. Cherry
Joukowsky Institute for Archaeology and the Ancient World
Brown University, Box 1837/60 George Street, Providence, RI 02912, USA

Published in the United Kingdom in 2019 by
OXBOW BOOKS
The Old Music Hall, 106-108 Cowley Road, Oxford, OX4 1JE

and in the United States by
OXBOW BOOKS
1950 Lawrence Road, Havertown, PA 19083

Published by Oxbow Books on behalf of the Joukowsky Institute

Paperback Edition: ISBN 978-1-78925-180-7
Digital Edition: ISBN 978-1-78925-181-4 (ePub)

A CIP record for this book is available from the British Library

Library of Congress Control Number: 2019939197

Printed in the United Kingdom by Short Run Press

Typeset in India for Casemate Publishing Services. www.casematepublishingservices.com

For a complete list of Oxbow titles, please contact:

UNITED KINGDOM
Oxbow Books
Telephone (01865) 241249
Email: oxbow@oxbowbooks.com
www.oxbowbooks.com

UNITED STATES OF AMERICA
Oxbow Books
Telephone (610) 853-9131
Fax (610) 853-9146
Email: queries@casemateacademic.com
www.casemateacademic.com/oxbow

Oxbow Books is part of the Casemate Group

Front cover: Castle of Santueri (Felanitx, Mallorca) (photograph by M. Á. Cau Ontiveros).
Back cover: Mosaic of Balearia found at the Early Christian Church of Son Peretó (Manacor, Mallorca)
(photograph by M. Riera Sureda).

Contents

List of Figures

Acknowledgments

This volume is the result of the international conference *Change and Resilience: The Occupation of Mediterranean Islands in Late Antiquity*, held at the Joukowsky Institute for Archaeology and the Ancient World (JIAAW), Brown University (Providence, Rhode Island, USA), on December 1–3, 2017.

We are most grateful to JIAAW and our colleagues at the Institute, and in particular to its Director, Peter Van Dommelen, for believing in this initiative and providing funding, logistics, and guidance to make the event a reality. We also want to thank Julia Hurley, Evan Levine, Matthew Pihokker, Daniel Plekhov, Ian Randall and Martin Uildriks for helping in the organization of the conference. We are indebted to Sarah Sharpe and Jessica Porter for their excellent organizational help both before and during the meeting.

For non-US or overseas scholars, organizing an event in the USA with many scholars coming from Europe was indeed a challenge and it would never have been possible without the support—apart from that of JIAAW— from several institutions and different units within Brown University. We are most grateful to the Cogut Institute for the Humanities, for a grant from the Humanities Initiative, and to the Dean's Office, for the Charles K. Colver Lectureship grant. We would also like to thank the John Carter Brown Library, and in particular Neil Safier and Tara Kingsley for all their support. The Program in Early Cultures provided not only funds, but also the guidance of John Bodel and Stephen Houston. We are grateful too for contributions from the Department of History, the Haffenreffer Museum of Anthropology, the Department of History of Art and Architecture, the Program in Medieval Studies, and the Department of Religious Studies. Back in Spain, the Catalan Institute for Research and Advanced Studies (ICREA), the Equip de Recerca Arqueològica i Arqueomètrica de la Universitat de Barcelona (ERAAUB), and the Agència de Gestió d'Ajuts Universitaris de Recerca from the Generalitat de Catalunya also supported the initiative. This book is also edited in the framework of the project *Archaeology, Remote Sensing, and Archaeometry: A Multidisciplinary Approach to Landscape and Ceramics from the Roman to the Medieval Period in Mallorca (Balearic Islands) (ARCHREMOTELANDS)*, HAR2017–83335-P, funded by the Ministerio de

Ciencia, Innovación y Universidades, with a contribution from the European Regional Development Fund of the European Commission.

We are, of course, grateful to all the participants and to the contributors to this volume, because they created a fantastic atmosphere that made the conference a gratifying event. We would like to thank David Abulafia (University of Cambridge) for agreeing to be the keynote speaker, and Michael MacCormick (Harvard University) for being willing to close the conference with his concluding remarks. We are also indebted to Sue Alcock, John Cherry, and Peter Van Dommelen for accepting the challenge of being the discussants for the various sessions. We would also like to thank those scholars who presented posters that enhanced the contents of the conference.

As for the present book, we are immensely grateful to John Cherry, General Series Editor of the Joukowsky Institute Publication series, for accepting this volume and for his enormous effort and support all through the editorial process. We are also grateful to Oxbow Books for their willingness to publish the volume.

The conference, and now this volume, represent our final contributions to a nurturing research period at the JIAAW and Brown University. Our immense gratitude goes to Peter Van Dommelen, Ayla Çevik, Felipe Rojas, Sarah Newman, John Cherry, Sue Alcock, Yannis Hamilakis, Robert Preucel, Jonathan Conant, Kevin Smith, and Michele Hayeur, among many others, who were a continuous source of inspiration. We are most grateful to them and the rest of our colleagues at JIAAW and Brown University in general, as well as to our friends in the Summit neighborhood for making our stay in Providence (Rhode Island) an unforgettable scientific and personal experience. We will continue working on Mediterranean islands, trying to solve some of the questions posed by research into the transition from Roman to Medieval, always anchored in intense and rigorous field archaeology, as is proper for our scholarly tradition. In a way, we will remain floating islands of Brown, drifting from and to the shores of the Western Mediterranean.

Providence and Barcelona

Notes on Contributors

David Abulafia has been Professor Emeritus of Mediterranean History at the University of Cambridge since 2000 and a Fellow of Gonville and Caius College, Cambridge since 1974; he later became the Papathomas Professorial Fellow and retired in 2018. He is also a Fellow of the British Academy and a member of the Academia Europaea. He is a maritime historian with a particular interest in Italy, Spain and the rest of the Mediterranean during the Middle Ages and Renaissance. His interest in the meeting of religions in medieval Spain and Sicily led him into the Atlantic. He has published and edited several books on Mediterranean history. One of his most influential books is *The Great Sea: A Human History of the Mediterranean* (2012). The book received the Mountbatten Literary award from the Maritime Foundation and has been translated into many different languages.

Gabriele Castiglia completed his Ph.D. at Pontificio Istituto di Archeologia Cristiana (PIAC), Rome, in 2017 where he is now a teaching assistant. He is currently working, as field director, on Late Antique and Early Medieval archaeological sites in Liguria (Albenga and Costa Balenae), and in Eritrea (Adulis—Northern Red Sea Region) where he is also studying the dynamics of Christianization in the Horn of Africa. His most recent monographs and edited books include *Il Duomo di Siena: Excavations and Pottery below the Siena Cathedral* (2014), and the *Acta XVI Congressus Internationalis Archaeologiae Christianae. Romae (22–28/9/2013). Costantino e i Costantinidi. L'innovazione costantiniana, le sue radici e i suoi sviluppi (2016).*

Miguel Ángel Cau Ontiveros (Ph.D., University of Barcelona, 1997) is a Research Professor at the Catalan Institution for Research and Advanced Studies (ICREA) and director of the Archaeological and Archaeometric Research Group of the University of Barcelona (ERAAUB) (Spain). He specializes in Roman and Late Antique Mediterranean archaeology and in the archaeometry of ceramics. He has worked intensively in the Balearic islands, where he currently directs the excavations of the Roman city of *Pollentia*, the early Christian complex of Son Peretó, and several field and geophysical surveys.

James Crow is Professor of Classical Archaeology at the University of Edinburgh. His research focuses on the archaeology of settlement and frontiers. Over the past 30 years his fieldwork and studies have ranged from Hadrian's Wall in Britain to the eastern Mediterranean, in particular Greece and Turkey from Roman to later Medieval times. Recently, he has focused on Byzantine urban and landscape archaeology, especially the water supply of Constantinople, and on the coastal regions of the Black Sea and the Aegean.

Miljenko Jurković is Professor of Late Antique and Early Medieval art history at the University of Zagreb, where he completed his Ph.D. in 1990. He is Head of the Department of Art History, and Director of the International Research Centre for Late Antiquity and the Middle Ages. He is the founding editor of the academic journal *Hortus Artium Medievalium* (1995) and the series *Dissertationes et monographiae* (2001). Currently, he leads several research projects including the *Corpus architecturae religiosae Europeae—IV–X saec.*; the transformation of historical landscapes on the Quarnero islands; the Early Medieval fortified settlement Guran; and the Early Medieval monastery of St Mary in Bale.

Catalina Mas Florit (Ph.D., University of Barcelona, 2013) is Juan de la Cierva Incorporación Postdoctoral Fellow in the Department of History and Archaeology at the University of Barcelona and former postdoctoral visiting scholar at the Joukowsky Institute for Archaeology and the Ancient World, Brown University. Her research focuses on Late Antiquity, especially in the western Mediterranean with a particular interest in islands and rural areas. She has directed the excavations of the Roman villa of Sa Mesquida (Mallorca, Spain), and the Early Christian complex of Illa del Rei (Menorca, Spain). She is currently writing a book about the transformation of the rural landscape during Antiquity on the island of Mallorca.

Alessandra Molinari is Full Professor of Medieval Archaeology at the University of Rome "Tor Vergata" and defended her Ph.D. thesis in Archaeology in 1994 at the University of Siena-Firenze-Pisa. She is now directing excavations at the Old Cathedral of Arezzo (Tuscany), co-directing with M.O.H. Carver the ERC project "The Archaeology of Regime Change: Sicily in Transition" and is senior researcher in the ERC project "Petrifying Wealth". She recently co-authored the books *L'archeologia della produzione a Roma (secoli V-XV)* (2015) and *Il medioevo nelle città italiane* (2017).

Giorgos Papantoniou (Ph.D., The University of Dublin, Trinity College, 2008) is a member of the Research Training Group 1878 "Archaeology of Pre-Modern Economies" of the Universities of Bonn and Cologne. He has published extensively on ancient Cypriot material culture history, landscape archaeology, ritual, cult, and iconography, including *Religion and Social Transformations in Cyprus: From the Cypriot Basileis to the Hellenistic Strategos* (2012). He is the coordinator of the international network "Unlocking Sacred Landscapes" (http://www.ucy.ac.cy/unsala/).

Philippe Pergola is Directeur de Recherche at the C.N.R.S., Université d'Aix-Marseille (Laboratoire d'Archéologie Médiévale et Moderne en Méditerranée)—UMR 7298; Ecole Doctorale 355 "Espaces, Cultures, Sociétés". He is Professor of Christian Topography. He was Dean and former President of the Pontificio Istituto di Archeologia Cristiana, a member of the Ecole Française de Rome, and President of the Unione Internazionale degli Istituti di Archeologia Storia e Storia dell'Arte in Rome. His research interests are focused on the archaeology and history of Late Antiquity and the Early Middle Ages in the Mediterranean islands, Rome, and Liguria.

Natalia Poulou is Professor of Byzantine Archaeology in the Aristotle University of Thessaloniki, Greece. Her research centers on Byzantine archaeology and architecture, and on urban planning and transformations during the transitional period of Byzantium (seventh to ninth centuries). She is the director of the University's excavation at Loutres, Mochlos (Crete) and a member of the excavations in Philippi; she has also excavated on Samos and Kythera.

Pier Giorgio Spanu completed his Ph.D. in Post-Classical Archaeology at the "Sapienza" University in Rome in 1995. He is currently Professor of Christian and Medieval Archaeology at the University of Sassari. His research interests are mainly focused on Late Antique and Early Medieval archaeology, underwater archaeology and landscape archaeology. He has conducted investigations in Sardinia, Sicily, Morocco, Tunisia and Spain.

Rebecca Sweetman is a Professor of Ancient History and Archaeology in the School of Classics, University of St Andrews, Scotland. Her Ph.D. (University of Nottingham, 1999) was on the Roman and Late Antique mosaics of Crete. Her book, *The Mosaics of Roman Crete* was published in 2013. She has written several articles on globalization and Christianization in the Roman provinces of Greece and has undertaken field projects in the Peloponnese, Cyclades and Crete. She is currently working on a Leverhulme Major Research Fellowship on the religious and economic networks of the Cyclades in the Roman and Late Antique periods.

Christina Tsigonaki (Ph.D., University Paris I, 2002) is Assistant Professor of Early Byzantine Archaeology in the Department of History and Archaeology at the University of Crete, and a research member of the Institute for Mediterranean Studies (Foundation for Research and Technology—Hellas). Her research interests, focusing on the archaeology of the Eastern Mediterranean during the Early Byzantine period, include monumental topography and topography of human activity, landscape archaeology, urbanism, religious and secular architecture, architectural sculpture, and new technologies in archaeological research. Since 2011 she has been the director of the excavation at the Acropolis of Eleutherna (Central Crete) and, since 2017, co-director of the archaeological survey at Mount Oxa (Elounda, East Crete).

Sam Turner (Ph.D. in Early Medieval Archaeology, University of York, 2004) is Professor of Archaeology at Newcastle University. He is currently involved in fieldwork with international teams in the UK, Spain, Italy, Greece and Turkey. His recent books include *Wearmouth and Jarrow: Northumbrian Monasteries in an Historic Landscape* (2013) and *Making Christian Landscapes in Atlantic Europe: Conversion and Consolidation in the Early Middle Ages* (2016). At Newcastle University he directs the McCord Centre for Landscape, an interdisciplinary research centre concerned with the history, heritage, management and planning of landscapes.

Athanasios K. Vionis (Ph.D., University of Leiden, 2005) is Associate Professor in Byzantine Archaeology and Art at the University of Cyprus. He has published extensively on Byzantine/Medieval and post-Medieval material culture and landscape archaeology in the Aegean and Cyprus. His monograph *A Crusader, Ottoman, and Early Modern Aegean Archaeology* was published in 2012 (Archaeological Studies Leiden University 22). He is the director of the Artefacts and Landscape Studies Laboratory (ArtLandS Lab) (http://www.ucy.ac.cy/artlands/en/), and has been collaborating with archaeological projects in Greece (Boeotia, Naxos, the Cyclades, Chios, Achaia) and Turkey (Sagalassos, Çeşme).

Enrico Zanini (Ph.D., University of Pisa, 1996) is currently Full Professor in Methodologies of Archaeological Research at the Department of History and Cultural Heritage in the University of Siena, where he also teaches Late Antique and Byzantine Archaeology. At present, he is Director-in-Chief of two archaeological fieldwork projects: the excavations in the Early Byzantine district of Gortys on Crete (www.gortinabizantina.it) and at the Roman and Late Antique settlement of Vignale (Tuscany) (www.uominiecoseavignale. it). Recent co-edited books include *The Insular System of the Early Byzantine Mediterranean: Archaeology and History* (2013), and *Statio amoena: Sostare e vivere lungo le strade romane* (2016).

Contributor Addresses

David Abulafia
University of Cambridge
Gonville and Caius College
Cambridge CB2 1TA
United Kingdom
dsa1000@cam.ac.uk

Gabriele Castiglia
Pontificio Istituto di Archeologia
Cristiana
Via Napoleone III 1
00185 Rome
Italy
castiglia84@gmail.com

Miguel Ángel Cau Ontiveros
ICREA and Equip de Recerca
Arqueològica i Arqueomètrica de la
Universitat de Barcelona (ERAAUB)
Departament d'Història i
Arqueologia
Facultat de Geografia i Història
c/Montalegre 6–8
08001 Barcelona
Spain
macau@ub.edu

James Crow
School of History, Classics and
Archaeology
University of Edinburgh
Edinburgh EH8 9AG
Scotland
United Kingdom
jim.crow@ed.ac.uk

Miljenko Jurković
University of Zagreb
Faculty of Humanities and Social
Sciences
Department of Art History
Ivana Lučića 3
10000 Zagreb
Croatia
mjurkovic@ffzg.hr

Catalina Mas Florit
Equip de Recerca Arqueològica i
Arqueomètrica de la Universitat de
Barcelona (ERAAUB)
Departament d'Història i
Arqueologia
Facultat de Geografia i Història
c/Montalegre 6–8
08001 Barcelona
Spain
cmas@ub.edu

Alessandra Molinari
Department of History,
Humanities, Culture and Society
Via Columbia 1
00133 Rome
Italy
molinari@lettere.uniroma2.it

Giorgos Papantoniou
Research Training Group 1878:
Archaeology of Pre-Modern
Economies
Abteilung für Klassische
Archäologie
Institut für Archäologie und
Kulturanthropologie
Rheinische Friedrich-Wilhelms-
Universität Bonn
Lennéstr. 1
D-53113 Bonn
Germany
papantog@uni-bonn.de

Philippe Pergola
Pontificio Istituto di Archeologia
Cristiana
Via Napoleone III 1
00185 Roma
Italy
pergola@univ-amu.fr; pergola@
piac.it

Natalia Poulou
Department of History and
Archaeology
Aristotle University of Thessaloniki
Faculty of Philosophy
School of History and Archaeology
54124 Thessaloniki
Greece
npoulou@hist.auth.gr

Pier Giorgio Spanu
Dipartimento di Storia, Scienze
dell'Uomo e della Formazione,
Università di Sassari
Via Zanfarino 62
07100 Sassari
Italy
pgspanu@uniss.it

Rebecca J. Sweetman
School of Classics
University of St Andrews
St Andrews KY16 9AL
Scotland
United Kingdom
rs43@st-andrews.ac.uk

Christina Tsigonaki
Department of History and
Archaeology
University of Crete
University Campus Gallou,
Rethymno 74100
Crete
Greece
tsigonaki@uoc.gr

Sam Turner
School of History, Classics and
Archaeology
Newcastle University
Newcastle upon Tyne NE1 7RU,
United Kingdom
sam.turner@ncl.ac.uk

Athanasios K. Vionis
Department of History and
Archaeology
University of Cyprus
P.O.Box 20537
Nicosia 1678
Cyprus
vionis@ucy.ac.cy

Enrico Zanini
Dipartimento di Scienze Storiche e
dei Beni Culturali
Via Roma, 47
53100 Siena
Italy
enrico.zanini@unisi.it

Foreword

Islands, Change and Late Antiquity

MIGUEL ÁNGEL CAU ONTIVEROS AND CATALINA MAS FLORIT

From Ithaca to Avalon, from Atlantis to Aeolia, islands have been mythical and magical places, with a sense of remoteness and mystery. Islands certainly have a privileged place in the human imagination, often rooted in the mythical Golden Age, or linked to Paradise, the Garden of the Hesperides, or even to imaginary Arcadia, a home to heroes and supernatural beings. All this island magic and mystery has also contributed, in a way, to the construction of a fake idea of the Mediterranean. Islands appear like a ghost in the distance; as a destination to be explored, to be conquered. But islands were also perceived as places of isolation, suffering, and remoteness, and as places used for exile and punishment.

Island archaeology has grown exponentially from the time that islands came to be considered ideal settings for the study of socio-cultural transformations and cross-cultural interaction. The ideas of MacArthur and Wilson (1967) and their theory of island biogeography were soon thereafter adapted to archaeology, with an emphasis on the notion of islands as laboratories (e.g., Evans 1973; 1977; Terrell 1977); their study has subsequently evolved, giving more importance to connectivity and its role in wider seascapes. The focus has often been on prehistory and on processes of first colonization: Cherry (1981; 1985), for example, applied principles of island biogeography to the study of the first colonization of Mediterranean islands. But the idea of islands as isolated and remote places has come under challenge from other theoretical approaches, including postprocessual and postcolonial archaeologies. Islands have now been placed in the wider framework of an archaeology of the seas, emphasizing, among other aspects, connectivity, interaction, and the role of local populations (e.g., Rainbird 1999; 2007; Broodbank 2000; 2013; Horden and Purcell 2000). To a considerable extent, the focus has shifted from biological and geographical models to more culturally-oriented explanations, in the process generating some interesting debates (e.g., Fitzpatrick et al. 2007; Fitzpatrick and Anderson 2008; Terrell 2008). Even if the role of connectivity, and the agency of the humans that colonized, populated or visited islands, have been widely embraced, it nonetheless cannot be denied that not all islands had the same opportunities for connection. In the human imagination, islands still embed a sense of remoteness, isolation, and exoticism—places where time passes slowly.

During the last three decades, growing interest in the human occupation of islands has incited the development of numerous surveys and excavations throughout the entire Mediterranean, and beyond it. The focus has traditionally centered on prehistory and on the colonization of islands. The study of islands, however, can make momentous contributions to the understanding of the Mediterranean Sea across historical periods. The influence of the Braudelian approach, and the idea of the Mediterranean as a coherent object of study, have led to fundamental works in the comprehension of the Mediterranean Sea. Scholars such as Horden and Purcell (2000), MacCormick (2001), Abulafia (2011), and Broodbank (2013) have helped shape our understanding of the history of the Mediterranean. The idea of the Great Sea as an entity, and the notion of transformation, have also been at the center of debate regarding Late Antique history and archaeology. Brown (1971), Cameron (1993), and Wickham (2005), among others, have provided a new dimension to the study of the transition between the Roman era and the Middle Ages, including the Mediterranean and its shores in Late Antiquity. In that scholarly enterprise (not always explicitly), islands have been essential to reconstructing Mediterranean seascapes and, thus, their history.

Island societies, connected to a wider Mediterranean seascape, experienced deep transformations that accord with broader changes in the mainstream of what the Romans termed *Mare Nostrum*, but also moments in which they evolved separately. Late Antiquity was one of those periods of change. The transformation of imperial Roman structures, the consolidation of Christianity, the Barbarian invasions, the fall of Rome, the rise of Barbarian kingdoms, the presence of Byzantium, and the rise of Islam and the Carolingians are just some of the crucial events that shaped the Mediterranean in this long period. Interest in this transitional period has a long history, and the thesis of Henry Pirenne clearly influenced it strongly. The European initiative *The Transformation of the Roman World*, supported by the European Science Foundation in the 1990s, was essential in approaching this period of transition. The volumes published as a result of this initiative soon became standard scholarly references (e.g., Pohl 1997; Hodges and

Bowden 1998; Pohl and Reimitz 1998; Brogiolo and Ward-Perkins 1999; Brogiolo et al. 2000; Pohl et al. 2000; Hansen and Wickham 2000; de Jong et al. 2001; Goetz et al. 2002; Corradini et al. 2003), and these themselves have prompted many further research initiatives. Other works have been essential in understanding the faith of both cities and the countryside, and, more generally, Late Antiquity and the Early Middle Ages (e.g., Hodges and Whitehouse 1983; Durliat 1990; Christie and Loseby 1996; Liebeschutz 2001; Francovich and Hodges 2003; Christie 2004; 2016; Wickham 2005; Ward-Perkins 2006). In recent decades, there has been an explosion of interest in Late Antiquity, and syntheses have appeared in many regions of the Mediterranean.

We co-editors are islanders born and raised on the biggest island of the remotest archipelago in the Mediterranean. We know how important the remains of our past are for our identity. One example is the cyclopean constructions still standing in our beloved Mallorca, just as in Sardinia. As islanders who have migrated to the mainland, we can affirm that that sense of identity has always been there: even some of our traditions are imported to the mainland, having been brought, and somehow artificially imposed, by island communities. Islands are also ingrained in our senses: many islanders can smell the sea and feel its presence, even if it is not in sight. On a daily basis, we experience the fact that islands can also be a concept beyond their physical boundaries. We embrace the idea of floating islands, a kind of metaphor for islander communities abroad. Of course, this idea (or rather idealization) of islands is also the construction of a fake. Yet often how we perceive things is more important than how things really are (if that reality exists).

We know by heart that sometimes "everything must change so that everything can stay the same", to use the words from Tancredi in *The Leopard* (di Lampedusa 1960)—an idea that Dawson (2014) has also used in her book on Mediterranean Islands. But change did happen: it is immutable to existence. After all, change has always been the object of study in archaeology. We have used "change" in the title of this volume because we wanted to explore how and to what extent islands were transformed. Was there change or—better—different episodes of change? What are the reasons behind these transformations? Was change similar in all the islands? How did populations perceive and adapt to this change?

To discuss these issues, we invited a group of scholars to offer a vision of the occupation of islands in Late Antiquity, or better of their transformation, from West to East right across the Mediterranean. The idea was not new, and it took form over the years. Volume XLIV of the *Corso di cultura sull'arte ravennate e bizantina: Le grandi isole del Mediterraneo orientale tra tarda antichità e medioevo*, edited by Luciana Farioli Campanati in memory of Luciano Laurentzi, was an inspiration during the period in Ravenna when we were excavating the church of San Severo in Classe. The idea crystallized there of a volume on the transformation of islands, and not only those of the eastern Mediterranean. Our presence at Brown University in the Joukowsky Institute for Archaeology and the Ancient World, and the academic environment that we found there, gave us the final strength to organize an international conference on this topic and to publish this volume now.

As for the use of the word "resilience" in the title, it was not our intention to force our contributors to apply resilience theory (e.g., Redman and Kinzig 2003; Redman 2005; Faulseit 2016; Bratmöller et al. 2017) in the study of islands in Late Antiquity. The idea, rather, was to highlight that in periods of crisis, societies, like ecosystems, adapt, because resilience, as Folke (2003; 2006) reminded us, "incorporates the capacity of social-ecological systems to cope with, adapt to, and shape change and learn to live with uncertainty and surprise." The main aim of using this term, therefore, was to explore how things changed and what the adaptations were. We wanted to do so nurturing a comparative overview of islands across the Mediterranean Sea, building an archaeological dialogue between the West and the East to outline the transformation of Mediterranean islands as a whole.

Two sessions of the conference adopted a geographical approach, starting in the western and central Mediterranean and travelling to the eastern Mediterranean. A third session gathered papers dealing with phenomena that had a powerful impact on individuals, such as Christianization or the creation of a powerscape with the construction of fortifications.

The papers published here likewise follow a geographical order from west to east, in a journey across the Mediterranean making stops on some of its largest and more significant islands. The volume starts with a contribution from Mallorca in the Balearic Islands by Mas and Cau in which they try to outline the transformation of the island from the Roman to the Medieval period, putting emphasis on changes in the countryside and the role of rural basilicas (Chapter 1). There follows a study on Corsica, where Pergola and Castiglia address both urban and rural transformations by integrating literary and archaeological sources (Chapter 2). Coverage of the western Mediterranean islands is completed with a contribution by Spanu on the problem of the *Barbarikinoi-Barbaricini* that should be identified with the Mauri deported to Sardinia while the island was part of the African *Regnum Vandalorum* (Chapter 3). Molinari rethinks Sicily by focusing on resilience and disruption in her exploration of the transformation or persistence of exchange networks, settlements, and agricultural and ecological systems (Chapter 4). Jurković then offers a synthesis of the Adriatic islands of Croatia concentrating on two recent case studies on the island of Rab and the bigger islands of the Quarnero gulf (Chapter 5).

Moving farther east, Zanini explores the transformation of Crete, using the specific case of Gortyna, and explaining it in the framework of a dialogue between micro-ecological and macro-economic factors (Chapter 6). Tsigonaki deals with the defensive works in cities and major settlements on Crete and how these contributed to the creation of a powerscape within the cities (Chapter 7). Sweetman addresses the Christianization of the Cyclades and their connection with neighboring territories (Chapter 8). Turner and Crow try to understand the impact of religious change in the landscapes of the Early Middle Ages (ca. A.D. 600–900), drawing on their investigations on the island of Naxos (Chapter 9). Poulou synthesizes transformations in the Aegean islands (Chapter 10), while Vionis and Papantoniou use the example of Cyprus to study changes in landscapes and mindscapes (Chapter 11). The volume ends with a contribution by Abulafia that serves the purpose of providing a comparative commentary on the various chapters (Chapter 12).

Overall, we hope that this volume will provide the reader with an overview of the transformations that occurred in the main Mediterranean islands during Late Antiquity, in the passage from the Roman to the Medieval Ages. It is scholars who themselves conduct active fieldwork on the Mediterranean islands who have provided these contributions. Despite the problems of editing a book where English is not the mother-tongue of many of the contributors—a task only made possible thanks to the diligence of John Cherry—we feel that the chapters in this volume contribute to a more diverse and rich debate incorporating other national and local traditions into a wider discussion on the transformation of Mediterranean islands in transition. Whether we have accomplished the aims of the volume only the future will tell.

References

Abulafia, David

    2011   *The Great Sea: A Human History of the Mediterranean*. Oxford University Press, Oxford.

Bradtmöller, Marcel, Sonia Grimm, and Julien Riel-Salvatore

    2017   Resilience Theory in Archaeological Practice: An Annotated Review. *Quaternary International* 446: 3–16.

Brogiolo, Gian Pietro, Nancy Gauthier, and Neil Christie (editors)

    2000   *Towns and their Territories between Late Antiquity and the Early Middle Ages*. The Transformation of the Roman World 9. Brill, Leiden, Boston, Köln.

Brogiolo, Gian Pietro, and Bryan Ward-Perkins (editors)

    1999   *The Idea and Ideal of the Town between Late Antiquity and the Early Middle Ages*. The Transformation of the Roman World 4. Brill, Leiden-Boston-Köln.

Broodbank, Cyprian

2000   *An Island Archaeology of the Early Cyclades.* Cambridge University Press, Cambridge.

2013   *The Making of the Middle Sea: A History of the Mediterranean from the Beginning to the Emergence of the Classical World.* Thames and Hudson, London.

Brown, Peter

1971   *The World of Late Antiquity:* AD 150–750. Thames and Hudson, London.

Cameron, Averil

1993   *The Mediterranean World in Late Antiquity,* AD 395–600. Routledge, London.

Cherry, John F.

1981   Pattern and Process in the Earliest Colonization of the Mediterranean Islands. *Proceedings of the Prehistoric Society* 47: 41–68.

1985   Islands Out of the Stream: Isolation and Interaction in Early East Mediterranean Insular Prehistory. In *Production and Exchange: The Aegean and Eastern Mediterranean,* edited by A. Bernard Knapp and Tamara Stech, pp. 12–29. UCLA Institute of Archaeology Monograph 25. University of California, Los Angeles.

Christie, Neil

2004   *Landscapes of Change: Rural Evolutions in Late Antiquity and the Early Middle Ages.* Ashgate, Aldershot.

2016   *From Constantine to Charlemagne: An Archaeology of Italy AD 300–800.* Routledge, London.

Christie, Neil, and Simon T. Loseby (editors)

1996   *Towns in Transition: Urban Evolution in Late Antiquity and the Early Middle Ages.* Scholar Press, Aldershot.

Corradini, Richard, Max Diesenberger, and Helmut Reimitz (editors)

2003   *The Construction of Communities in the Early Middle Ages:* Texts, Resources and Artefacts. The Transformation of the Roman World 12. Brill, Leiden-Boston.

Dawson, Helen

2014   *Mediterranean Voyages: The Archaeology of Island Colonisation and Abandonment.* UCL Institute of Archaeology Publications 62. Left Coast Press, Walnut Creek, California.

de Jong, Mayke, Frans Theuws, and Carine Van Rhijn (editors)

2001   *Topographies of Power in the Early Middle Ages.* The Transformation of the Roman World 6. Brill, Leiden, Boston, Köln.

di Lampedusa, Giuseppe

1960   *The Leopard,* Collins and Harvill Press, London.

Durliat, Jean

1990   *De la ville antique à la ville byzantine: le problème des subsistances.* École Française de Rome, Rome.

Evans, John D.

1973   Islands as Laboratories for the Study of Culture Process. In *The Explanation of Culture Change: Models in Prehistory,* edited by Colin Renfrew, pp. 517–520. Duckworth, London.

1977   Island Archaeology in the Mediterranean: Problems and Opportunities. *World Archaeology* 9(1): 12–26.

Farioli Campanati, Raffaela (editor)

2001   *XLIV Corso di Cultura sull'Arte Ravennate e Bizantina. Seminario internazionale di studi sul tema: <<Le grande isole del Mediterraneo orientale tra tarda antichità e medioevo>>. In memoria di Luciano Laurenzi.* Edizione del Girasole, Ravenna.

Faulseit, Ronald K.

2016   *Beyond Collapse: Archaeological Perspectives on Resilience, Revitalization, and Transformation in Complex Societies.* Center for Archaeological Investigations, Occasional Paper 42. Southern Illinois University Press, Carbondale.

Fitzpatrick, Scott M., and Atholl Anderson

2008   Islands of Isolation: Archaeology and the Power of Aquatic Perimeters. *Journal of Island and Coastal Archaeology,* 3(1): 4–16.

Fitzpatrick, Scott M., Jon M. Erlandson, Atholl Anderson, and Patrick Kirch

2007   Straw Boats and the Proverbial Sea: A Response to 'Island Archaeology: In Search of a New Horizon', *Island Studies Journal,* 2(2): 229–238.

Folke, Carl

2003   Freshwater for Resilience: A Shift in Thinking. *Philosophical Transactions of the Royal Society London B,* 358: 2027–2036.

2006   Resilience: The Emergence of a Perspective for Social-ecological Systems Analyses. *Global Environmental Change* 16(3): 253–267.

Francovich, Riccardo, and Richard Hodges

2003   *Villa to Village: The Transformation of the Roman Countryside in Italy, c. 400–1000.* Duckworth, London.

Goetz, Hans-Werner, Jörg Jarnut and Walter Pohl (editors)

2002   *Regna and Gentes: The Relationship between Late Antique and Early Medieval Peoples and Kingdoms in the Transformation of the Roman World.* Transformation of the Roman World 13. Brill, Leiden-Boston.

Hansen, Inge Lyse, and Chris Wickham

2000   *The Long Eighth Century: Production, Distribution and Demand.* The Transformation of the Roman World 11. Brill, Leiden-Boston-Köln.

Hodges, Richard, and William Bowden

1998   *The Sixth Century: Production, Distribution and Demand.* The Transformation of the Roman World 3. Brill, Leiden-Boston-Köln.

Hodges, Richard, and David Whitehouse

1983   *Mohamed, Charlemagne & the Origins of Europe: Archaeology and the Pirenne Thesis.* Cornell University Press, Ithaca, New York.

Horden, Peregrine, and Nicholas Purcell

2000   *The Corrupting Sea: A Study of Mediterranean History.* Blackwell, Oxford.

Liebeschuetz, John H. W. G.

2001   *The Decline and Fall of the Roman City.* Oxford University Press, New York.

MacArthur, R.H., and Edward O. Wilson.

1967   *The Theory of Island Biogeography.* Monographs in Population Biology. Princeton University Press, Princeton, New Jersey.

McCormick, Michael

    2001   *Origins of the European Economy: Communications and Commerce AD 300–900.* Cambridge University Press, Cambridge.

Pohl, Walter

    1997   *Kingdoms of the Empire: The Integration of Barbarians in Late Antiquity.* The Transformation of the Roman World 1. Brill, Leiden-New York-Köln.

Pohl, Walter, and Helmut Reimitz (editors)

    1998   *Strategies of Distinction: The Construction of Ethnic Communities, 300–800.* The Transformation of the Roman World 2. Brill, Leiden-Boston-Köln.

Pohl, Walter, Ian Wood, and Helmut Reimitz (editors)

    2000   *The Transformation of Frontiers from Late Antiquity to the Carolingians.* The Transformation of the Roman World 10. Brill, Leiden-Boston.

Rainbird, Paul

    1999   Islands out of Time: Towards a Critique of Island Archaeology. *Journal of Mediterranean Archaeology* 12(2): 216–234.

    2007   *The Archaeology of Islands.* Cambridge University Press, Cambridge.

Redman, Charles L.

    2005   Resilience Theory in Archaeology. *American Anthropologist* 107(1): 70–77.

Redman, Charles L., and Ann P. Kinzig

    2003   Resilience of Past Landscapes: Resilience Theory, Society, and the *Longue Durée. Conservation Ecology* 7(1): 14.

Swain, Simon, and Mark Edwards (editors)

    2004   *Approaching Late Antiquity: The Transformation from Early to Late Empire.* Oxford University Press, Oxford.

Terrell, John E.

    1977   Biology, Biogeography and Man. *World Archaeology* 8(3): 237–248.

    2008   Islands and the Average Joe. *The Journal of Island and Coastal Archaeology* 3(1): 77–82.

Theuws, Frans, and Janet Nelson (editors)

    2003   *Rituals of Power: From Late Antiquity to the Early Middle Ages.* Brill, Leiden-Boston-Köln.

Volpe, Giuliano, and Roberta Giuliani (editors)

    2011   *Paesaggi e insediamenti urbani in Italia meridionale fra tardoantico e altomedioevo. Atti del secondo seminario sul tardoantico e l'altomedioevo in Italia meridionale (Foggia – Monte Sant'Angelo 27–28 maggio 2006).* Insulae Diomedeae 14. Edipuglia, Bari.

Ward-Perkins, Bryan

    2006   *The Fall of Rome and the End of Civilization.* Oxford University Press, Oxford.

Wickham, Chris

    2005   *Framing the Early Middle Ages: Europe and the Mediterranean, 400–800*, Oxford University Press, New York.

The Occupation of Mallorca (Balearic Islands, Spain) in Late Antiquity: Tracing Change and Resilience

CATALINA MAS FLORIT AND MIGUEL ÁNGEL CAU ONTIVEROS

This chapter explores how the communities of the island of Mallorca adapted to a successive series of changes that occurred between the Roman period and the end of Antiquity. The available evidence shows a significant transformation in the cities and also in the countryside where the number of sites decreased in the third century A.D., and only a few large settlements remained occupied. This pattern changed abruptly at the end of the fifth or early sixth century with an increase in the number of rural settlements, including the reoccupation of old indigenous prehistoric sites and the construction of rural churches which are essential to understanding the process of Christianization of the countryside. Small villages or secondary agglomerations would also have played an important role in the configuration of the landscape.

The chapter briefly addresses the transformation of the city but is mainly focused on the transformation of the countryside. The phenomenon of the reoccupation of old indigenous sites, the fate of Roman rural sites, and the role of the early Christian churches are outlined to understand the transformation of this Mediterranean island between the fourth and the eighth centuries A.D.

Introduction

The Balearic Islands are the most remote archipelago of the Mediterranean sea. They lie off the coast of the Iberian Peninsula in a strategic position for navigation and trade routes in the western Mediterranean (Figure 1.1). Greek and Roman writers were fully aware of the archipelago and separated it into two groups of islands with substantial differences. On the one hand, Mallorca and Menorca formed the *Baliarides* (also called the *Gymnēsiai* by the Greeks), represented by the Talayotic culture. On the other hand, Ibiza

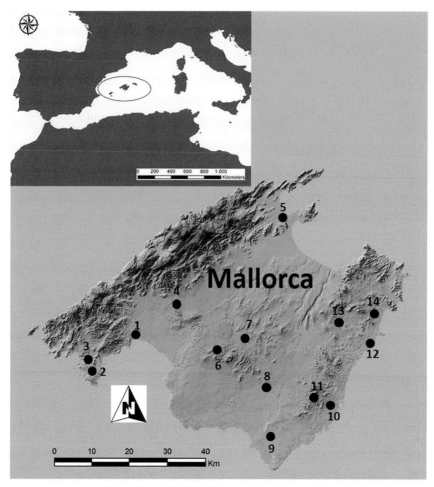

Figure 1.1. Location of the Balearic Islands in the western Mediterranean and map of Mallorca with the main sites cited in the text: 1. *Palma*; 2. Tumulus of Son Ferrer; 3. Rural Roman site of Sa Mesquida; 4. Basilica of Cas Frares; 5. *Pollentia*; 6. Puig de s'Escolà; 7. Talayotic village of Son Fornés; 8. Basilica of Son Fadrinet; 9. Es Fossar de Ses Salines; 10. Closos de Can Gaià; 11. Castell de Santueri; 12. Basilica of Sa Carrotja; 13. Basilica of Son Peretó; 14. Son Sard.

and Formentera were considered the *Pityussae*, with a strong Phoenician-Punic character.

The society of the *Baliarides* experienced significant impacts from the Roman conquest in 123 B.C. Despite their society's contacts with the Punic world and other influences, these islands were dominated by the Iron Age indigenous population at the time of the Roman military intervention. The Roman period brought with it the foundation of cities and the reorganization of the countryside. The islands were linked first to *Hispania Citerior* and later to *Tarraconensis*. The archipelago as a whole (i.e., the unified *Balearides* and *Pityussae*) did not become an independent province until the end of the fourth century. In A.D. 455, the Vandals conquered the islands and in A.D. 534 they fell into Byzantine hands. This latter dominance lasted, at least in theory, until the Islamic conquest of Isam-al-Jalawni in A.D. 902–903. The old Roman structures, transformed during Late Antiquity, probably vanished forever under the strong cultural influence of Islam.

Interest in the transformation of these islands in the period between the Roman military intervention and the Arab conquest of the tenth century is relatively recent. Written sources are in general very scarce, and much of the information has to come from archaeology. This chapter offers some insights into the occupation of Mallorca during Late Antiquity, trying to understand the changes witnessed and the strategies that the local population adopted in a period (or, better, subsequent periods) of crisis and upheaval.

The Transformation of the Cities

The Roman conquest in 123 B.C., led by Q. Cecilius Metellus, resulted in the foundation of two cities in Mallorca: *Palma* and *Pollentia* (Figure 1.1). Regarding the city of *Palma*, now under the current city of Palma, there are little data available to provide an outline of its transformation in Late Antiquity (Cau 2012). However, two ceramic deposits dated to the Vandal and the Byzantine periods show the occupation of the city (Cau et al. 2014). The evidence so far suggests that population at the time prior to the Muslim conquest of the city was both small and in decline (Gutiérrez 1987: 206). It seems that the Muslim city of *Madîna Mayûrqa* was placed over a former urban centre still in operation (Riera i Frau 1993: 27–29). Most of the available data for the study of the transformation of Mallorcan cities, therefore, comes from *Pollentia*.

Concerning *Pollentia*, archaeological data show continuous use of the urban space, albeit with various re-organizations, since the foundation levels dated around 70–60 B.C. The third century A.D. was a moment of serious disruption in the city. A major reorganization occurred either at the very end of the second century or the beginning of the third. The excavations in the forum have demonstrated a complete transformation of the so-called *Insula* I of *tabernae* to the West of the forum square. Many rooms were restructured, with walls rebuilt, changing the overall dimensions and building small buttresses in some of them. The streets were also profoundly modified, and many of the spaces between the columns of the porticoed streets were closed off (Cau 2012). At the end of the third century, a massive fire destroyed various parts of the city, as clearly attested in *Insula* I. This destruction has been dated with precision to around A.D. 270–280 (Arribas et al. 1973; Arribas and Tarradell 1987: 133; Equip d'Excavacions de Pollentia 1994: 142; Orfila 2000). The third century was, therefore, a time of strong disruption to the city. The construction of a wall in the so-called residential quarter of Sa Portella was probably done in the same century, as a response to this moment of upheaval (Figure 1.2) (Orfila et al. 2000; Riera i Rullan et al. 1999). Nevertheless, there is no doubt that inhabitation continued in the city after the third century. By the fourth and fifth centuries, there is apparently little building activity, but there exist some industrial structures in the forum of *Pollentia* built over the debris of the late third-century fire. Some of the *tabernae* seem to be re-occupied by squatters (Orfila et al. 1999: 112–113; Orfila 2000: 154). Public spaces were also occupied: in the fifth century, for example, a room was attached to the façade of the *Macellum*, invading the portico area on the east side of the forum. By this time the city was deeply transformed, and certain buildings, such as the *Macellum*, were now abandoned. Some *tabernae* and the forum square have provided materials that denote later reuse of these spaces.

The most significant structure in Late Antiquity, however, was the fortification located to the north of the forum area. Its construction involved the use of *spolia* from other buildings, with many elements being reused in the inner filling of the wall. This defensive structure closed off at least some of the old forum that was partially in ruins and occupied parts of public spaces,

Figure 1.2. View of the so-called residential quarter of Sa Portella in the Roman and Late Antique city of *Pollentia* (Alcúdia).

Figure 1.3. The Late Antique fortification of the forum of *Pollentia* occupying the porticoed street to the north of the forum with a wall dated to the end of the second century or beginning of the third century closing off the intercolumniation.

such as the north street (Figure 1.3). A dating in the Byzantine period has been suggested for this (Orfila et al. 1999: 113–116; 2000). The fortification indicates the enclosure of a protected perimeter, such as a citadel, in the very heart of the city, coinciding with the location of the forum and reusing the wall of the *Capitolium*, *Insula* I and the *Macellum*. Outside this citadel, there was continued inhabitation of the city, and Sa Portella shows clear signs of occupation dating to the Late Roman, Vandal, and Byzantine periods, with significant material culture (e.g., Arribas et al. 1973; Gumà et al. 1997).

The Christianization of the topography of the city is virtually unknown. Some early discoveries were claimed to be related to the presence of Christian buildings in the city. For instance, in a necropolis area within the suburbia known as Can Fanals, a large building in a very poor state of preservation was interpreted as a possible basilica (Llabrés and Isasi 1934). Moreover, further north, in the so-called area of Santa Anna de Can Costa, some graves and the early Christian inscription of *Arguta* were tentatively linked to the presence of another Christian building. These were already inside the urban layout, suggesting the transformation of the city.

Over the ruins of the old forum, a large necropolis has been radiocarbon-dated to the Muslim period. The most interesting aspect is that the inhumations were still in supine position and not in a lateral position, as would have been the norm for Islamic populations; this might be a sign of non-Muslim communities being buried between the tenth and the twelfth centuries on top of the ruins of the Roman city (Cau et al. 2017). The only structure respected by the graves we have excavated in the forum is the *Capitolium*, so it seems that this building was still partially standing or at least respected, although parts would surely have been dismantled by then. Some authors have proposed the possible transformation of the *Capitolium* as a place of Christian worship (e.g., Arribas and Tarradell 1987).

The Transformation of the Rural Areas

The initial interest in the Roman rural occupation provided the first systematic data to understand the transformation of rural landscapes in Mallorca (Orfila 1988). Recent fieldwalking surveys of several areas across the island have contributed to new information that allows a first interpretation of the changes that occurred in the countryside from the Early Roman period to the Early Middle Ages (Mas Florit and Cau 2013). The general pattern of settlement on the island seems to be defined by the continuity of prehistoric sites and the creation of newly-founded Roman settlements, apparently rather few in number (Cardell et al. 1990). Some of these possible *villae*, hamlets, farms or farmsteads have been located by fieldwalking, although excavation has occurred on very few of them. Therefore, the phenomenon of the implantation of the *villa* system and its evolution in the countryside, as well as the role of the indigenous settlements in this wider framework, is still not sufficiently studied. As we will see later, the few data available suggest that these *villae* were implanted around the Augustan era or slightly earlier (Mas Florit et al. 2015). The landscape was clearly divided and distributed, as traces of centuriation have been identified (e.g., Cardell and Orfila 1991–1992), something that indeed facilitated the administration of property and tax collection.

Studies undertaken on the eastern side of the island show the abandonment or decay of many medium- and small-size rural sites during the late second and the third century A.D. Only a few sites, always with large dimensions and located in areas of fertile plains, have been documented. This decrease in the number of sites, and the fact that only large settlements seem to survive, has been interpreted as a sign of the concentration of property (Mas Florit and Cau 2013). Such a development has also been observed in other areas of the western Mediterranean, where medium and small properties were concentrated to form large landholdings (e.g., Chavarría 2006; Sfameni 2004; Raynaud 2001).

The *villa* of Sa Mesquida, located in the western part of the island (Calvià), is one of the few sites that contribute to an understanding of the fate of rural Roman sites. It was occupied from the first century B.C., with a *floruit* in the first and second centuries A.D. At the very end of the second century or the beginning of the third, the settlement suffered a traumatic event, as witnessed by the evidence of fire. This fire caused the abandonment of the structures excavated so far. To date, archaeological excavations have uncovered a series of rooms ranged around a courtyard with a well, an industrial deposit, and a ceramic kiln for the production of common ware. This kiln was abandoned around the end of the second century and later reused as a dump at the end of the fourth or beginning of the fifth century A.D. (Mas Florit et al. 2015).

During the mid-fifth century, coinciding with the beginning of the Vandal period on the island, a new reorganization of the countryside took place, possibly marking the end of the large estates and the villa system (Mas Florit and Cau 2013). This does not necessarily mean that the Vandal conquest was the cause of the end of the villas, but it is interesting to note that the two phenomena are roughly contemporary. Both old indigenous sites and Early Roman sites, normally located in fertile plains or their foothills, were occupied once again. This new pattern shows a change in the system of exploitation of the countryside, with clear differences from the Late Roman model of exploitation. This reorganization intensified at the end of the fifth century and the beginning of the sixth, which coincided with the Byzantine domination. Apart from old prehistoric settlements in the plains, probably related to agricultural activities, some former prehistoric sites located in marginal areas and with no continuity into the Roman period, were also reoccupied. Some of these sites could have served as defensive places; others may have specialized in activities other than agriculture. Interestingly, in some cases, these enclaves were in proximity to areas potentially suitable for sheep- and goat-herding. In addition, some camps related to the exploitation of salt, in the southern part of the island in the area of Colònia de Sant Jordi (Guerrero 1987), and some caves near the sea on the eastern side of the island, probably linked to the exploitation of marine resources, were now occupied (Cau and Mas Florit 2013). Areas near the sea, although scarce, also show signs of occupation in Late Antiquity.

In the seventh century, a new decline in the number of sites is witnessed in the rural areas. There is evidence of the arrival of imported material until the end of this century. The eighth and ninth centuries remain a problem. The lack of knowledge of the material culture of these two centuries, with the absence of African Red Slip Ware as an index fossil, complicates the dating of rural settlements, particularly when excavation results are not available. In the last decade, however, evidence of late occupation has been found at several sites. Such is the case at the basilica of Son Peretó (Manacor) which remained occupied at least until the end of the seventh century or the beginning of the eighth, with sporadic inhumations dated even in the ninth century, or the basilica of Son Fadrinet (Campos), where two Byzantine gold solidi of around A.D. 737/38 or 739 have been found (Ulbert 2003). Likewise, in the prehistoric site of Closos de Can Gaià there is evidence of occupation in the eighth and ninth centuries (Servera et al. 2004).

Forms of Occupation in the Countryside

The disintegration of the large estates in the mid-fifth century in some ways saw a return to previous stages of organization of the countryside. Old prehistoric sites that were not occupied during the Roman period were now reoccupied. In the southern and eastern parts of the island, most prehistoric sites with evidence of Late Antique occupation are interpreted as farms. Their location is near cultivable areas, visually controlled from the sites themselves, and in locations with favorable exposure to the sun in both summer and winter. At some sites, mills have been found, indicating farming activities (Mas Florit and Cau 2011). This could be the case of the indigenous village of Son Fornés (Montuïri), with clear evidence of reoccupation of some buildings during Late Antiquity (Lull et al. 2001; Fayas 2005). Spatial analysis shows that, in the areas of Manacor and San Llorenç des Cardassar, some of these sites are found in locations that are topographically prominent but with relatively poor visibility, suggesting a defensive role in times of upheaval (Mas Florit and Cau 2011). Other examples could be linked to the reuse of sites for surveillance or control, as might be the case with the settlement of Puig de s'Escolà (Llucmajor), where a rock shelter was reoccupied from the mid- or late fifth century. This site's location is in a strategic spot that controls the only existing topographic passage through the immediate landscape. Also, at Closos of Can Gaià, one of the prehistoric buildings was reused, including a hearth dated by radiocarbon to the fifth or sixth centuries A.D.; this site also shows evidence of occupation between the eighth and the ninth centuries, as has already been mentioned (Servera et al. 2004).

New Late Antique foundations in pristine locations are in general very scarce across the island. These settlements appeared after the collapse of the villa system. In the eastern part of the island that has been studied in the most detail, only six of a total of 64 sites are thought to have been established in pristine locations. These new foundations are normally quite limited in extent (Mas Florit and Cau 2011), and some were placed in remote areas far from agricultural resources, which could be an indication of shepherding or defensive strategies (Mas Florit and Cau 2013). The presence of newly founded sites in pristine settings seems to be a marginal phenomenon in the context of the occupation of the Mallorcan Late Antique countryside.

From the available data, it is difficult to establish the role of the villas during these times. It seems clear that, after the collapse of the villa system, some parts of the *villae* were abandoned, but others remained occupied or were reused for other purposes. In the *villa* of Sa Mesquida, a pottery kiln and a cistern (Orfila and Cau 1994; Cau 2003) were reused as rubbish dumps in the fourth and fifth centuries respectively, and at least one of the productive areas was reused for graves during the sixth century. A Late Antique necropolis found in the village of Felanitx seems to be located over the ruins of an Early Roman ceramic workshop, possibly linked to a Roman *villa* or some form of rural settlement; the radiocarbon dates suggest a chronology between the sixth and the seventh century for these inhumations. Another case of reuse of Early Roman structures is the *balnea* recently discovered in Son Sard (Son Servera), associated with some form of rural settlement still to be determined. The structures were abandoned before A.D. 500 and re-used for productive purposes, with two different phases; one is of uncertain chronology, maybe Vandal or early Byzantine, and the second dates to the Byzantine period (Palomar et al. 2013).

Apart from the sites already mentioned, several defensives places in the mountains were clearly part of the Late Antique landscape of the island and probably fundamental for the last moments of Antiquity (Cau et al. 2005). Few Islamic written sources indicate that the population of the island prior to the Muslim conquest inhabited castles in naturally defended locations in the mountains (Kirchner 1998). The example of the castle of Santueri (Felanitx)

Figure 1.4. View of the Castell de Santueri, with the Serres de Llevant in the background.

(Figure 1.4), with numerous coins, lead seals (Illisch et al. 2005), and other remains of cultural material (e.g., Aguiló and Conde 2015; Gomila 2016), attributable to the Byzantine period, suggests the importance of the site and is reminiscent of the case of *Castrum Perti* in Liguria (e.g., Mannoni and Murialdo 2001). A relevant discovery comes from Menorca where a seal of an *archon* of Mallorca was found (Nicolás and Moll 2015). This suggest that Mallorca controlled Menorca and that the Balearics in the Byzantine period had a similar organization to that of neighboring Sardinia.

The Rural Basilicas and the Christianization of Rural Landscapes

The introduction and first implantation of Christianity probably came through ports, cities and their suburbia, and only later spread into rural areas. As already mentioned, there is insufficient knowledge of the Christianization of the topography of Mallorcan cities. For the neighboring island of Menorca, the Epistle of Bishop Severus, dated to A.D. 418, narrates the confrontation between Jews and Christians that ended with the massive conversion of the Jews in Magona (current Maò in the eastern part of the island) and the burning of the synagogue in the same city. This document depicts a well-organized Christian community and provides some insights into the organization and location of Christian worship (Amengual 1991–1992). In Mallorca, it is easy to suppose a similar organization, and the presence of churches in the cities of *Palma* and *Pollentia*, at the beginning of the fifth century.

The construction of rural churches seems, however, to be a later phenomenon, probably to be dated to the late fifth or the sixth century and probably linked to the reorganization observed in the countryside. Thus far, on the island of Mallorca, four basilicas of rural character have been excavated: Cas Frares (Santa Maria del Camí), Son Peretó (Manacor), Sa Carrotja (Porto Cristo, Manacor) and Son Fadrinet (Campos) (Figure 1.5). There has been a partial investigation into most of these churches, but many of the excavations had a primary interest in architecture and liturgy, rather than in understanding the buildings in the broader context of settlement patterns. As we have seen, at the end of the fifth century A.D., an increase in the number of settlements is again witnessed across the landscape. Probably, from this moment and during the sixth century, the construction of churches contributed to a further change in the configuration of the territory. The capability of some of these churches to provide burial and baptism, as well as to host a good number of believers, suggests that these basilicas were centers scattered throughout the diocesan territory to serve the faithful of a region. These acted as central elements in the landscape and could have had control over the agricultural activities in the area. They could also have served as poles of attraction for other settlements (Mas Florit and Cau 2011).

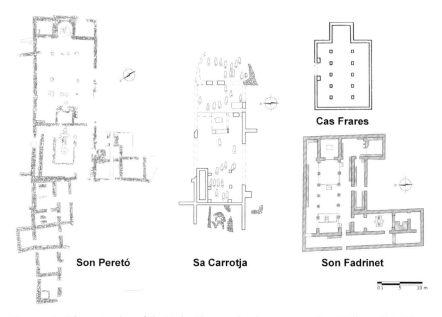

Figure 1.5. Schematic plan of the Early Christian basilicas excavated in Mallorca (Mas Florit and Cau 2013: figure 5).

Although these buildings have generally been considered in isolation, in recent years they have been explored within the wider perspective of settlement patterns in the countryside as a whole. It has been proposed that some were in fact built on a pre-existing nucleus, in *villae* or in secondary agglomerations—following the French nomenclature—which, in the majority of cases, were already occupied in Roman times. The construction of churches in these kinds of locations, often situated along important communication routes, would guarantee the success of such foundations, by providing services to the existing communities of the area (Mas Florit and Cau 2013). In the eastern side of the island, several sites of relatively large size, detected by fieldwalking, could well be secondary agglomerations. We know very little of these forms of settlement in Mallorca. One of the examples that has yielded the best evidence is the Early Christian complex of Son Peretó, with a church and a baptistery erected at some point after the end of the fifth century (Figure 1.6) (Cau et al. 2012). Some evidence suggests that Son Peretó had significant occupation from Early Roman times. The results of recent geophysical surveys, combining magnetometry and ground-penetrating radar, revealed some clear anomalies. Some, due to their orientation, could correspond to the continuation of the Early Christian complex. Additional graves surrounding the excavated area were also detected. More important

Figure 1.6. The Early Christian complex of Son Peretó (Manacor).

is the presence of the remains of a relatively large Roman villa not far from the church. The distance between some of these remains and their various orientations opens the possibility of significant complexity in surrounding areas. It seems that a Roman villa evolved into some kind of secondary agglomeration that was finally Christianized with the construction of the basilica. Another site that could be related to a secondary agglomeration is Son Fadrinet in the southern part of the island, near the village of Campos. The results of excavations undertaken at the end of the 1990s proved the existence of a basilica with a baptistery and associated cemetery built in the second half of the sixth century A.D. (Ulbert 2003). The discovery of a tomb located below the floor of the baptistery suggests the existence of a cemetery prior to the construction of the religious building; the presence of sites with Roman materials in the vicinity of the church, moreover, may indicate that it was built on a pre-existing settlement, or at least not far from some inhabited area (Mas Florit and Cau 2013). Geophysical surveys carried out recently have revealed the presence of other archaeologically relevant structures.

The construction of monasteries in coastal areas or on islets also seems to be witnessed in different areas of the Balearics, such as Menorca. Off the southern part of Mallorca, we know of the presence of a monastic community in the archipelago of Cabrera. The letter from Pope Gregory I to the defender Johannes in A.D. 603, ordering him to correct the licentious behavior of the monks of Cabrera, provides proof of the existence of these monks (Amengual 1991–1992), and recent archeological work has confirmed the intense occupation of the island in Late Antiquity (Riera i Rullan 2017). To date, there is no physical evidence of monasteries in Mallorca; but there can be no doubt about the existence of such complexes on the largest island of the Balearics, or at least on isolated islets close to the island, as exemplified by Cabrera. The presence of baptistries in all of the monasteries documented across the Balearics suggests that they contributed to the Christianization of the area, in addition to exploiting surrounding resources.

It should be assumed that in the Balearic Islands paganism would not disappear with the replacement of the pagan buildings by the basilicas. If we consider what councils reveal on the Iberian Peninsula, we know that fighting idolatry continued during Late Antiquity (Sotomayor 1982). According to some scholars, pagans were still present in the Balearic Islands for some centuries after Theodosius' law of A.D. 423 (Amengual and Orfila 2007). It is clear that the creation of basilicas in the countryside helped the penetration of Christianity in such areas, where the presence of paganism would have been stronger and offered more resistance to the new religion. In the context of ecclesiastical organization, the rural churches represent the most predominant presence of early Christianity in the Balearics. Clear archaeological evidence of pagan practices during Late Antiquity on the islands is lacking. However, the celebration of Christian rites in ancient pre-Roman buildings could indicate either the persistence of pagan elements within Christian practices, or the persistence, in the collective memory of the people, of important ancient sacred places. In Mallorca, there is evidence of Late Antique occupation at the Iron Age site of Son Ferrer (Calvià). It was originally a ceremonial center (in the Early Iron Age) that was later (in the Late Iron Age) used mainly as a necropolis. The presence of a few ceramic finds, such as Late Roman C and African Red Slip Ware, including one base with stamped decoration of a cross, documents its occupation in Late Antiquity. The scarcity of materials, the presence of tableware only, the forms (mainly large plates that could have a liturgical function), and the decoration, all suggest a very particular re-use of this prehistoric site (Albero et al. 2011: 383–384) that seems to point to possible Christian practices in the sixth century A.D. Could this have been a kind of syncretism between pagan and Christian practices?

Exploitation of Resources

Apart from the major contribution of ceramic studies in outlining the commercial dynamics of the islands during Late Antiquity (e.g., Orfila and Cau 1994; Reynolds 1995; 2010; Cau 2003; Cau et al. 2014), it has only been in recent years that faunal and botanical remains have yielded new information on the nature of resources and the development of economic activities.

At the end of the fourth century and during the first half of the fifth century, farming and animal husbandry were very important elements in the overall economic strategy. Archaeozoological studies at the *villa* of Sa Mesquida (Valenzuela 2015a) and at the site of es Fossar in Ses Salines[1] have shown that domestic species are the most important. Caprines predominate, cattle are modestly represented, and pigs, horse/donkey, dogs, and chicken are sporadically present. Nevertheless, the presence of wild species such as rabbits, fallow deer, and some red deer also suggests the importance of hunting practices. Fish bones have also been identified. Other activities such as the exploitation of salt or marine resources were also carried out on the island.

The case of the site of Sa Mesquida is particularly interesting, in light of its striking abundance of 'wild' livestock, emphasized by the notable presence of fallow deer. The samples studied suggest that fallow deer were kept to a very old age (generally, from nine to 15 years). This age-profile could be indicative of closely controlled husbandry on a "production site", with an over-representation of old breeding stock. In fact, the results obtained by the biometric sexing of some post-cranial bones suggest this interpretation (Valenzuela et al. 2016). All the measured bones correspond to female fallow deer. Taking into account the high frequency of deer bones and these ageing and sexing results, it seems likely that specialized farming of fallow deer was carried out at Sa Mesquida, probably through a constructed, fenced park (*vivarium*). Fallow deer were maintained within such parks and actively managed to provide venison for the urban table. While the pattern found in Sa Mesquida suggests a productive enclave, the archaeozoological data from *Pollentia* reveals that the city was a consumption center of fallow deer during the Late Roman period (Valenzuela et al. 2016). According to Valenzuela (2015a), the location of Sa Mesquida outside the area of influence of *Pollentia* reinforces the idea of the existence of Roman *villae* across the island serving venison to the different cities during the Late Roman period. The introduction and raising of hunting resources provided landowners not only with a way to display ostentation and social distinction, but also with a source of income (Valenzuela 2015a).

The production of purple dye was an important activity in the Balearics and it was controlled by a *procurator baphii insularum balearum,* mentioned in the *Notitia Dignitatum.* Archaeological evidence supports its production in the Balearics, with a main centre perhaps in Eivissa (Alfaro 2002; Alfaro and Costa 2006; Costa 2011), but with production also in Mallorca (e.g., Estarellas and Merino 2005; Valenzuela 2015b) and in Cabrera (Riera Frau and Riera Rullan 2005). Radiocarbon dating confirms a Late Antique chronology for some of these factories (Van Strydonck et al. 2012).

At the site of Puig de s'Escolà, dated from the mid- to late fifth century, wheat and barley have been identified through phytolith analysis. Domestic faunal remains are represented by ovicaprids, cattle, and pork, and hunting by the presence of fallow deer (Aramburu 2012). In Son Peretó, recent archaeological excavations have provided important information to understand the evolution of a series of rooms dated to the seventh century and attached to the baptistery. The presence of a deposit, silos, hand-mills, and other elements indicates that these rooms were used for domestic and productive purposes by people occupying and exploiting the territory. The analysis of organic residues, from a deposit found in one of the rooms of the so-called West Sector, revealed traces of wine and oil. This is very interesting as it suggests that both products were present in the same deposit. Phytolith analysis also revealed barley in the silos at the site. Another interesting feature of the study is the analysis of the faunal remains from the silos, which shows the exploitation of cattle, ovicaprids, and suids, together with some wild animals (Valenzuela and Ramis 2012). The presence of sheep is important, and the remains are typically in the juvenile age range, suggesting that the livestock were raised for meat. It is also noticeable that, while ovicaprids seem to have been butchered within the domestic space, cattle were butchered elsewhere. There is also some indication of the egalitarian distribution of the meat between the different rooms. Suids are represented by domestic varieties. Fish, poultry, and rabbit or hare are also present. In addition, a handle of a knife was carved from an antler of *Cervus elaphus* (red deer).

According to these archaeozoological studies, there occurred during Late Antiquity a considerable reduction in the consumption of pigs and cows (typical of the Early Roman period) and a return to higher percentages of caprines (Valenzuela 2015a). The faunal remains show the disintegration of the Roman economic system and the beginning of a model of subsistence economy in which caprines were essential. With the Roman conquest of the island, the intensification of agricultural practices was to the detriment of grazing lands. There was an increased specialization that benefited sheep flocks, above goat herds, with the intention of obtaining more meat and wool. The presence of pigs and cows in all the Late Antique sites that have been studied shows that husbandry practices did not return to those of the pre-Roman period, but they certainly shifted from the Roman production system. In an ever-changing and unpredictable insular environment, the versatility and adaptability of sheep and goat husbandry made it a very valuable asset (Valenzuela 2015a).

An economy based on agriculture and the shepherding of flocks and herds—with some contribution from domestic pigs and cattle, as well as hunting and fishing—seems to have been the subsistence basis during Late Antiquity. Wheat and barley were also important. Organic residue analyses have also proved the presence of oil and wine in the diet, usually including animal fats, vegetables, and in some cases fish (Pecci and Cau 2014).

Towards a Conclusion

The data available for Mallorca make it difficult to advance a synthesis of the change and resilience experienced in the island in the passage from the Roman to the Medieval period. We are certainly far from being able properly to apply some of the advances of Resilience Theory in this particular case. Production, expansion, collapse, and resilience are not well defined in this case for understanding the real framework. It is, however, interesting to explore how the communities of the island adapted to a successive series of changes, including Vandal and Byzantine domination, as well as the rise and consolidation of Christianity.

The third century was certainly a moment of change for the cities and the countryside. As we have seen in *Pollentia*, a major reorganization took place at the very end of the second century or the beginning of the third century, and serious destruction occurred at the end of that century. In the countryside, many sites were abandoned or underwent major disruptions, as for example at the Roman *villa* of Sa Mesquida. The initial Roman system probably turned into a major concentration of the property by this time. Some of these properties would have been devoted to farming fallow-deer through *vivaria* and provided venison to the cities.

By the fifth century, the cities were certainly deeply changed and transformed into a new concept. At *Pollentia*, some buildings were clearly abandoned in the fifth century, such as the *Macellum*. Only some *tabernae* and the forum square have provided materials that denote later reuse of these spaces. The construction of the fortification involved the use of *spolia* from other buildings, with many elements reused for the inner filling of the wall. This defensive structure closed off at least part of the old forum that was certainly partially in ruins and occupied part of the public spaces, such as the north street.

There is enough evidence to suggest the collapse of the *villa* system around the mid-fifth century, coinciding with the beginning of the Vandal period on Mallorca. After this period, the *villae* were transformed, and only some parts remained occupied, often reused for other purposes. By the second half of the fifth century and mainly the sixth century, there is again an explosion in the occupation of smaller locations, and the reoccupation of prehistoric and Roman sites that had been abandoned in the preceding centuries. Only a few new sites in fresh locations have been found. These were usually in marginal locations, probably linked to goat-herding activities or defensive purposes. This phenomenon can be connected to the study of faunal remains that have demonstrated that by this time there was a tendency towards a model of economic subsistence in which caprines were fundamental, abandoning the earlier Roman economic system. Regarding earlier prehistoric sites, we should ask ourselves to what extent their reoccupation had any symbolic meaning. This could be plausible in some cases, but for other settlements their re-occupation was perhaps due to their favorable locations and/or because of the presence of constructions attractive for re-use or to provide materials for new buildings which would require less physical and economic effort. In this regard, the lack of excavations does not help.

It is not unreasonable to relate the progressive transformation and dismantling of the urban life—from the fifth century and especially in the sixth century—to the increase of occupation of the countryside. There was even a tendency to occupy marginal areas and a growing move towards a self-sufficient economy.

The implantation of rural churches is connected to this process, at least as time progressed. It is, therefore, a relatively late phenomenon—related, on the one hand, to the Christianization of pre-existing communities, as shown clearly by the example of Son Peretó, and, on the other, to the possible presence of monastic communities. Christianity, which was probably relatively well-organized in the early fifth century in the cities, did not become consolidated in the rural areas until later, in some cases probably to evangelize areas that exhibited more pagan resistance. The churches themselves were transformed, and changes in their structures and decorative programs are evident. It is possible to suggest a phase of Byzantine embellishment with the use of mosaic pavements in different churches. The structures of the basilicas also changed, and, for some of them, it has been possible to trace their different construction phases. In the case of Son Peretó, it is interesting to observe how the church, built to provide service to a pre-existing population, probably gathered around a *villa* complex, and was later used as the center of habitation. There grew a nucleus attached to the western part of the ecclesiastical building, with rooms that developed mainly in the seventh century A.D., indicating domestic and productive activities. This part of the site was destroyed by a violent event at the end of the seventh or in the early eighth century (Cau et al. 2012).

Archaeological information from the seventh to the ninth centuries is scarce, both in the cities and the countryside. Part of the fortification of *Pollentia* was used as a rubbish dump around the seventh century, suggesting that it could have been at least partially dismantled. Over the ruins of the forum area, a large necropolis dated to the Muslim era, but where the inhumations were in supine and not in lateral position, suggests the presence of a non-Muslim community buried over the old forum, mainly between the tenth and the twelfth centuries. Who were these people? Could this be interpreted as a sign of the resilience of the local population? In the countryside, the settlement pattern changes again in the seventh century, with a drastic decrease of sites. It is unclear whether this is real or has to do with our inability at present to recognize the material culture of the eighth and ninth centuries. One of the latter forms of occupation were the rocky castles found in inaccessible mountains where resistance to the Muslim attack was organized at the beginning of the tenth century.

Despite its insular character, Mallorca was well connected to the mainstream of Mediterranean domination—first Vandal, and later Byzantine—and it was clearly linked to other neighboring territories, in particular to the island of Sardinia. But the island remained somehow isolated in the eighth and ninth centuries. In this sense, change did occur, but we are still far from understanding the role that elites played in the transition from a Roman to a peasant model.

Acknowledgments

The work of C. Mas Florit was possible thanks to a Beatriu de Pinós postdoctoral fellowship from the AGAUR, with the support from the Secretaria d'Universitats i Recerca of the Departament d'Economia i Coneixement of the Generalitat de Catalunya. This contribution is part of the research activities at the Equip de Recerca Arqueològica i Arqueomètrica de la Universitat de Barcelona (ERAAUB), Consolidated Group (2017 SGR 1043); thanks to the support of the Comissionat per a Universitats i Recerca del DIUE de la Generalitat de Catalunya. This work is part of the project *Archaeology, Remote Sensing, and Archaeometry: A multidisciplinary approach to landscape and ceramics from the Roman to the Medieval period in Mallorca (Balearic Islands) (ARCHEOREMOTELANDS)*, HAR2017–83335-P, funded by the *Ministerio de Ciencia, Innovación y Universidades*, with a contribution from the European Regional Development Fund from the European Commission.

Note

1. The data from es Fossar de Ses Salines, come from the poster presentation by Bartomeu Vallori Márquez, Catalina Mas Florit, Miguel Ángel Cau Ontiveros, and Damià Ramis Bernat, "Fifth century A.D. ceramic deposits from Ses Salines (Mallorca, Balearic Islands, Spain)", presented at the LRCW Sixth International Conference on Late Roman Coarse Wares, Cooking Wares and Amphorae in the Mediterranean: Archaeology and Archaeometry. Land and Sea: Pottery Routes, (Agrigento, 24th-28th May 2017).

References

Aguiló Fiol, Rosa Mª., and Elena Conde

2015   *Les sivelles del Castell de Santueri. De l'antiguitat tardana a l'edat mitjana.* Quaderns de Ca la Gran Cristiana 15. Museu de Mallorca/Amics del Museu de Mallorca, Palma.

Albero, Daniel, Maria Calderón, Manel Calvo, and Miquel Trías

2011   Patrimonio arqueológico de época romana y tardoantigua (123 A.C.–902 D.C.). In *Calvià: Patrimonio Cultural*, edited by Manel Calvo and Antoni Aguareles, pp. 373–386., Fundación Calvià, Palma.

Alfaro, Carmen

2002   Ebusus y la producción de púrpura en el Imperio romano. In *L'Africa Romana. Lo Spazio marittimo del Mediterraneo occidentale: geografia storica ed economia. Atti del XIV convegno di studio, 14, 7–10 dicembre 2000 Sassari*, edited by Moustapha Khanoussi, Paola Ruggeri, and Cinzia Vismara, pp. 681–696. Carocci editore, Roma.

Alfaro, Carmen, and Benjamí Costa

2006   Mobilité des gens et des techniques: la pourpre dans les provinces occidentales de l'Empire romain et le cas d'Ibiza. In *L'Africa Romana: Mobilità delle persone e dei popoli, dinamiche migratorie, emigrazione ed inmigrazioni nelle province occidentali dell'Impero romano. Atti del XVI convegno di studio. Rabat, 15–19 dicembre 2004*, edited by Aomar Akerraz, Paola Ruggeri, Ahmed Siraj, and Cinzia Vismara, pp. 2417–2432. Carocci, Roma.

Amengual, Josep

1991–1992 *Els orígens del Cristianisme a les Balears i el seu desenvolupament fins a l'època musulmana,* 2 vols. Editorial Moll, Mallorca.

Amengual, Josep, and Margarita Orfila

2007   Paganos, judíos y cristianos en las Baleares: documentos literarios y arqueológicos. *Ilu: Revista de Ciencia de las Religiones* 18: 197–246.

Aramburu-Zabala, Javier

2012   El Abrigo del Puig de S'Escolà (Llucmajor, Mallorca), Electronic document, http://www.arqueobalear.es, accessed January 12, 2013.

Arribas, Antonio, and Miguel Tarradell

    1987   El forum de *Pollentia*: Noticia de las primeras investigaciones. In *Los foros romanos de las provincias occidentales*, pp. 121–136. Ministerio de Cultura, Dirección General de Bellas Artes y Archivos, Madrid.

Arribas, Antonio, Miquel Tarradell, and Daniel E. Woods

    1973   *Pollentia I: Excavaciones en "Sa Portella", Alcudia (Mallorca).* Excavaciones Arqueológicas en España 75. Servicio de Publicaciones del Ministerio de Educación y Ciencia. Secretaría General Técnica, Madrid.

Cardell, Jaume, Miguel Ángel Cau, and Margarita Orfila

    1990   La continuidad de ocupación de los asentamientos indígenas de Mallorca en época romana. In *L'Africa Romana. Atti del VII convegno di studio*, edited by Atilio Mastino, pp. 703–725. Gallizzi, Sassari.

Cardell, Jaume, and Margarita Orfila

    1991–1992 Posible catastro romano en la isla de Mallorca: planteamiento metodológico. *Cuadernos de Prehistoria de Granada* 16–17: 415–423.

Cau Ontiveros, Miguel Ángel

    2003   *Cerámica tardorromana de cocina de las Islas Baleares: Estudio arqueométrico.* British Archaeological Reports International Series 1182. British Archaeological Reports, Oxford.

    2012   Urban Change on the Balearics in Late Antiquity. In *Vrbes Extinctae. Archaeologies of Abandoned Classical Towns*, edited by Neil Christie and Andrea Augenti, pp. 115–144. Routledge, Aldershot,

Cau Ontiveros, Miguel Ángel, and Catalina Mas Florit

    2013   Tracing Settlement Patterns in Late Antique Mallorca (Balearic Islands): A Field Survey in the Eastern Territories. *Hortus Artium Medievalium* 19: 209–227.

Cau Ontiveros, Miguel Ángel, Mateu Riera Rullan, and Magdalena Salas

    2012   The Early Christian Complex of Son Peretó (Mallorca, Balearic Islands): Excavations in the 'West Sector' (2005–2008). *Archeologia Medievale* 39: 231–243.

Cau Ontiveros, Miguel Ángel, Catalina Mas Florit, Paul Reynolds, and Jerónima Riutort

    2014   Two Late Antique Deposits from the City of Palma de Mallorca (Balearic Islands, Spain). In *LRCW 4 Late Roman Coarse Wares, Cooking Wares and Amphorae in the Mediterranean: Archaeology and Archaeometry. The Mediterranean: A Market without Frontiers,* edited by Natalia Poulou-Papadimitriou, Eleni Nodarou, and Vassilis Kilikoglou, pp. 1049–1060. British Archaeological Reports International Series 2616 (I). Archaeopress, Oxford.

Cau Ontiveros, Miguel Ángel, Catalina Mas Florit, and Juan Carlos Lladó Capó

    2005   Fortificaciones de la Antigüedad Tardía en Baleares. In *L'Antiguitat clàssica i la seva pervivència a les illes Balears. XXIII Jornades d'Estudis Històrics Locals, Palma, del 17 al 19 de novembre de 2004,* edited by María L. Sánchez and María Barceló, pp. 217–229. Institut d'Estudis Baleàrics, Palma.

Cau, Miguel Ángel, MarkVan Strydonck, Mathieu Boudin, Catalina Mas Florit, Joan S. Mestres, Francisca Cardona, Mª. Esther Chávez, and Margarita Orfila

    2017   Christians in a Muslim World? Radiocarbon Dating of the Cemetery over the Forum of *Pollentia* (Mallorca, Balearic Islands). *Archaeological and Anthropological Sciences* 9(7): 1529–1538.

Chavarría, Alexandra

2006   Villas en Hispania durante la Antigüedad Tardía. In *Villas tardoantiguas en el Mediterráneo Occidental*, edited by Alexandra Chavarría, Javier Arce, and Gian P. Brogiolo, pp. 17–35. Anejos de Archivo Español de Arqueología 39. Consejo Superior de investigaciones científicas, Madrid.

Costa Ribas, Benjamí

2011   Mapa de los yacimientos purpurígenos de las islas Pitiusas. Resultados de las prospecciones costeras realizadas en Ibiza y Formentera (2005–2007). In *Purpureae Vestes. III, Archéologie de l'artisanat Antique, 4. Textiles y tintes en la ciudad antigua,* edited by Carmen Alfaro, Pierre Brun, Philipe Bogard, and R. Pierobon Benoit, pp. 261–268. Universidad de Valencia, and Centre J. Bérard (CNRS-EFR), Naples.

Equip d'Excavacions de Pollentia

1994   Avanç dels resultats dels treballs d'excavació a l'àrea central de la ciutat romana de *Pollentia*. In *XIV Congrés internacional d'arqueologia clàssica, La ciutat en el món romà II. Tarragona, 5 al 11–9–1993: Actas,* edited by Xavier Dupré, pp. 140–142. Consejo Superior de investigaciones científicas, Barcelona.

Estarellas, Maria Magdalena, and Josep Merino

2005   Treballs arqueològics preliminars al Pedret de Bóquer. In *L'Antiguitat clàssica i la seva pervivència a les illes Balears. XXIII Jornades d'Estudis Històrics Locals, Palma, del 17 al 19 de novembre de 2004,* edited by María Luisa Sánchez y María Barceló, pp. 377–393. Institut d'Estudis Baleàrics, Palma de Mallorca.

Fayas, Blanca, Beatriz Palomar, Maria I. Piña, and Cristina Rihuete

2005   Son Fornés des de 1975 fins avui. In *Mirant el passat, Curs de prehistòria de Mallorca*, edited by Maria M. Sales, pp. 83–98. Papers de sa torre, Aplecs de Cultura i Ciències Socials, Manacor.

Gomila Gomila, Joana

2016   *Els anells del Castell de Santueri i un peu de canelobre bizantí.* Quaderns de Ca la Gran Cristiana 6. Museu de Mallorca/Amics del Museu de Mallorca, Palma.

Guerrero, Víctor

1987   *La Colònia de Sant Jordi (Mallorca): Estudis d'arqueologia i epigrafia*, Publicacions del Centre d'Estudis "Gabriel Alomar", Palma de Mallorca.

Gumà, Montserrat, Maria M. Riera, and Francesca Torres

1997   Contexts de ceràmica a Mallorca, segles IV-X. In *Contextos ceràmics d'època romana tardana i de l'Alta Edat Mitjana (segles IV-X),* edited by Montserrat Comas, Josep Mª. Gurt, Alberto López, Pepita Padrós, and Mercè Roca, pp. 249–256. Arqueo Mediterrània 2. Treballs de l'Àrea d'Arqueologia de la Universitat de Barcelona, Universitat de Barcelona, Barcelona.

Gutiérrez Lloret, Sonia

1996   Le città della Spagna tra romanità e islamismo. In *Early Medieval Towns in West Mediterranean*, edited by Gian Pietro Brogiolo, pp. 55–66. Documenti di archeologia 10. SAP Società Archeologica S.r.l., Mantova.

Ilish, Lutz, Michael Matzke, and Werner Seibt

2005   *Die mittelalterlichen Fundmünzen, Siegel und Gewichte von Santueri, Mallorca.* Arbeiten zur Islamischen Numismatik 1. Numismatischer Verlag der Münzgalerie München, Tübingen.

Kirchner, Helena

1998   Husun y alquerías campesinas en las islas Orientales del al-Andalus, In *L'incastellamento: confronto fra società feudale e non feudale nel Mediterraneo occidentale. Actes des rencontres de Gérone (26–27) novembre 1992) et Rome (5–7 mai 1994),* edited by Miquel Barceló and Pierre Toubert, pp. 249–269. Ecole française de Rome and Escuela Española de Historia y Arqueología en Roma, Rome.

Llabrés, Juan, and Rafael Isasi

1934   *Excavaciones en los terrenos donde estuvo enclavada la ciudad romana de Pollentia (Baleares, isla de Mallorca, término municipal de Alcudia).* Memoria 131 de la Junta Superior del Tesoro Artístico. Sección de Excavaciones, Madrid.

Llull, Vicente, Rafael Micó, Cristina Rihuete, and Roberto Risch

2001   *La Prehistòria de les Illes Balears i el jaciment arqueològic de Son Fornès (Montuïri, Mallorca).* Fundació Son Fornés, Montuiri.

Mannoni, Tiziano, and Giovanni Murialdo (editors)

2001   *S. Antonino: un insediamento fortificato nella Liguria bizantina.* Collezione di Monografie preistoriche ed archeologiche 12. All'Insegna del Giglio, Firenze.

Mas Florit, Catalina, and Miguel Ángel Cau

2011   From Roman to Byzantine: The Rural Occupation of Eastern Mallorca (Balearic Islands). *Journal of Mediterranean Archaeology* 24(2): 191–217.

2013   Christians, Peasants and Shepherds: The Transformation of the Countryside in Late Antique Mallorca (Balearic Islands, Spain). *Antiquité Tardive* 21: 27–42.

Mas Florit, Catalina, Bartomeu Vallori Márquez, Patricia Murrieta Flores, Ma José Rivas Antequera, and Miguel Ángel Cau Ontiveros

2015   The Roman Villa of Sa Mesquida: A Rural Settlement on the Island of Mallorca (Balearic Islands, Spain). In *SOMA 2011: Proceedings of the 15th Symposium on Mediterranean Archaeology, Held at the University of Catania 3–5 March 2011,* edited by Pietro Militello and Hakan Oniz, pp. 461–466. British Archaeological Reports International Series 2695. Archaeopress, Oxford.

Nicolás, Joan C. de, and Bernat Moll

2013   Sellos bizantinos de Menorca: un arconte mallorquín para las Baleares en el siglo VIII. *Tharros Felix* 5: 537–582.

Orfila, Margarita

1988   *La necrópolis de Sa Carrotja y la romanización del Sur de la isla de Mallorca.* British Archaeological Reports International Series 397. Archaeopress, Oxford.

2000   *El forum de Pollentia: Memòries de les campanyes d'excavacions realitzades entre els anys 1996 i 1999.* Ajuntament d'Alcúdia, Alcúdia.

Orfila, Margarita, Antonio Arribas, and Miguel Ángel Cau.

1999   La ciudad romana de *Pollentia*: el foro. *Archivo Español de Arqueología* 72: 99–118.

Orfila, Margarita, and Miguel Ángel Cau

1994   Las cerámicas finas procedentes de la cisterna de Sa Mesquida, Mallorca. In *III Reunió d'Arqueologia Cristiana Hispànica, Maó 1988,* pp. 257–288. Institut d'Estudis Catalans, Barcelona.

Orfila, Margarita, Mateu Riera Rullan, Miguel Ángel Cau, and Antonio Arribas

2000   Aproximación a la topografía urbana tardía de *Pollentia* (Mallorca): construcciones defensivas. In *V Reunió d'Arqueologia Cristiana Hispànica, Cartagena (1998)*, pp. 229–235. Institut d'Estudis Catalans and Universitat de Barcelona, Barcelona.

Palomar, Beatriz, Francisca Cardona, and Sebastià Munar

2013   La villa romana de Son Sard: dades preliminars de les intervencions arqueològiques subsidiàries de les obres de millora de les carreteres MA-4032 i MA-4034 de Son Servera-Mallorca. In *V Jornades d'arqueologia de les Illes Balears*, edited by Mateu Riera Rullan and Jaume Cardell Perelló, pp. 181–188. Documenta Balear, Palma.

Pecci, Alessandra, and Miguel Ángel Cau Ontiveros

2014   Residue Analysis of Late Roman Cooking Pots and Amphorae from Sa Mesquida (Mallorca, Balearic Islands). In *LRCW4. Late Roman Coarse Wares, Cooking Wares and Amphorae: Archaeology and Archaeometry. The Mediterranean: A Market without Frontiers*. British Archaeological Reports International Series 2616 (II), edited by Natalia Polou-Papadimitriou, Eleni Nodaru, and Vassilis Kilikoglou, pp. 833–842. Archaeopress, Oxford.

Raynaud, Claude

2001   Les campagnes languedociennes aux IVe et Ve siècles. In *Les campagnes de la Gaule à la fin de l'Antiquité: habitat et peuplement aux IVe et Ve siècles. Actes du IVe colloque de l'association Ager (Montpellier, 11–14 mars 1998)*, edited by Pierre Ouzoulias, Christophe Pellecuer, Claude Raynaud, P. van Ossel, and P. Garmy, pp. 247–274. Éditions APDCA, Antibes.

Reynolds, Paul

1995   *Trade in the Western Mediterranean, A.D. 400–700: The Ceramic Evidence*. British Archaeological Reports International Series 604. Tempus Reparatum, Oxford.

2010   *Hispania and the Roman Mediterranean, A.D. 100–700*. Duckworth, London.

Riera Frau, Magdalena

1993   *Evolució urbana i topografia de Madina Mayûrca*. Quaderns de la Gerència d'Urbanisme 1. Ajuntament de Palma, Palma.

Riera Frau, Magdalena, and Mateu Riera Rullan

2005   Un possible taller de producció de porpra de l'antiguitat tardana al Pla de ses Figueres (illa de Cabrera). *Bolletí de la Societat Arqueològica Lul·liana* 6: 377–390.

Riera Rullan, Mateu

2017   *El monacat insular de la Mediterrània occidental: El monestir de Cabrera (Balears, segles V-VIII)*. Col·lecció Studia Archaeologiae Christianae. Ateneu Universitari Sant Pacià (Facultat de Teologia de Catalunya i Facultat Antoni Gaudí), Bacelona.

Riera Rullan, Mateu, Margarita Orfila, and Miguel Ángel Cau

1999   Els últims segles de Pollentia. *Bolletí de la Societat Arqueològica Lul·liana* 55: 335–346.

Servera, Gabriel, Montserrat Vivó, David Javaloyas, and Llorenç Oliver
  2004   Les ocupacions històriques dels Closos de Can Gaià. In *II Jornades d'Estudis Locals de Felanitx*, pp. 187–200. Ajuntament de Felanitx, Felanitx.

Sfameni, Carla
  2004   Residential Villas in Late Antique Italy: Continuity and Change, In *Recent Research on the Late Antique Countryside*, edited by William Bowden, Luke Lavan, and Carlos Machado, pp. 335–375. Brill, Leiden-Boston.

Sotomayor, Manuel
  1982   La penetración de la Iglesia en los medios rurales de la España tardorromana y visigoda. In *Cristianizzazione ed organizzazione ecclesiastica delle campagne nell'Alto Medioevo: espansione e resistenze. XXVIII Settimana di Studi del Centro Italiano di Studi sull'Alto Medioevo II (Spoleto, 1982)*, pp. 630–670. Centro Italiano di Studi sull'Alto Medioevo, Spoleto.

Ulbert, Thilo
  2003   El yacimiento paleocristiano de Son Fadrinet (Campos, Mallorca). *Mayurqa* 29: 173–187.

Valenzuela, Alejandro
  2015a   *La gestió dels recursos animals en la integració de les Illes Balears al món romà.* Ph.D. dissertation, Universitat de Barcelona, http://hdl.handle.net/10803/395025.

  2015b   An Ancient Fishery of Banded Dye-Murex (*Hexaplex trunculus*): Zooarchaeological Evidence from the Roman City of Pollentia (Mallorca, Western Mediterranean). *Journal of Archaeological Science* 54: 1–7

Valenzuela Alejandro, Baker Karis, Ruth F. Carden, Jane Evans, Thomas Higham, A. Rus Hoelzel, Angela Lamb, Richard Madgwick, Holly Miller, Josep Antoni Alcover, Miguel Ángel Cau, and Naomi Sykes
  2016   Both Introduced and Extinct: The Fallow Deer of Roman Mallorca. *Journal of Archaeological Science: Reports* 9: 168–177.

Valenzuela, Alejandro, and Damià Ramis
  2012   Aproximació a la gestió dels recursos faunístics del Sector Oest de Son Peretó (Manacor) entre els segles VI i VIII dC, In *IV Jornades d'Arqueologia de les Illes Balears (Eivissa, 1 i 2 d'octubre, 2010)*, edited by Mateu Riera, pp. 159–168. Vessants, Arqueologia i Cultura, S.L, Palma.

Van Strydonck, Mark, Mathieu Boudin, and Damià Ramis
  2012   Direct ^{14}C-dating of Roman and Late Antique Purple Dye Sites by Murex Shells. *ArchaeoSciences: Revue d'archéométrie* 36: 15–22.

— 2 —

Between Change and Resilience: Urban and Rural Settlement Patterns in Late Antique Corsica

Gabriele Castiglia and Philippe Pergola

Corsica is one of the core areas for the understanding of Mediterranean history in the longue durée. *Literary sources are sporadic (besides nine letters by Gregory the Great) and must be integrated with an indispensable comparison with those relating to the other great islands (especially Sicily and Sardinia). Archaeological research, although very limited, has allowed considerable progress in knowledge of the territory and the dynamics of settlements.*

As far as urban areas are concerned, there are only two known civitates *in the island, Aleria and Mariana, while in the rural world, only the site of Castellu has benefited from long-term excavations. The rest of the data comes from the excavation of rural baptismal churches known since the 1980s, but these (except in the cases of* Adiacium *and* Saona*) unfortunately involve non-stratigraphic investigations.*

Both in the Vandal and Byzantine ages, as well as the initial Lombard period, Corsica seems to maintain a settlement dynamic that is entirely continuous from Roman times, as testified by finds that reveal Mediterranean exchanges ranging from the Iberian peninsula to Africa, Asia Minor, and the Syro-Palestinian area. In this chapter, we see how Corsica has been capable of progressive adaptation and morphogenesis over a long period of time which, however, counteracted the maintenance of typically "insular" peculiarities, rooted in historical memory, perfect exemplification of the concept of "resilience".

Corsica in Late Antiquity: An Introduction

Corsica is one of the most significant and peculiar contexts in the central Mediterranean in which to study the evolution of settlement, economy and religion during Late Antiquity and the Early Middle Ages.

The written sources are quite sporadic (leaving aside the high quality of the nine letters dedicated to the island by Pope Gregory the Great) and necessarily need to be integrated comparatively with those relevant to other islands, mainly Sicily and Sardinia, as well with those regarding the main political and economic powers active at the time. The archaeology, even though quite limited, has nonetheless allowed significant progress in our knowledge of territory and settlements.

As regards urbanism, the only two known *civitates* of the island were Aleria and Mariana, even though the latter alone has so far revealed a stratigraphic sequence that allows a diachronic approach to its evolution. In the rural areas, only the site of *Castellu* (in the municipality of Corte, in the center of Corsica) has produced broad-ranging data, albeit limited to the fifth to seventh centuries A.D. Other important information comes from the rural baptismal churches of Castellu di Rustinu and Linguizzetta (Diocese of Mariana), and also from the little funerary church of Propriano (Diocese of Ajaccio), all of them excavated between the early 1980s and the beginning of the twenty-first century, and still unpublished. Unfortunately, except for *Adiacium*-Ajaccio and *Saona*-Saona, some of them were not investigated stratigraphically, and in these cases we have no archaeological information relevant to their settlement contexts, although we can place them reliably in terms of chronology. These are the rural cathedrals of Ajaccio and Saona and the baptismal *ecclesiae* of Bravona (municipality of Linguizzetta, Diocese of Mariana) and Rescamone (Castellu di Rustinu, Diocese of Mariana).

Vandal, Byzantine and Lombard Corsica seem to demonstrate settlement patterns in direct continuity with the former Roman age: these aspects are well documented thanks to the massive presence of pottery coming from North Africa, the Iberian peninsula and the eastern Mediterranean (mainly Syria and Palestine), clear clues of long-distance trade.

Although the main chronological framework of this paper is Late Antiquity, we start with a brief overview of Corsica in the Classical centuries, even though the data relevant to this period are quite poor and muddled, as we will see. Nevertheless, this premise is fundamental, in order to better understand not only changes in the *longue durée*, but also (and mainly) to analyze the trends of "change" and "resilience" that are best appreciated by adopting an extensive and diachronic perspective.

The Written Sources and the Epistolary by Gregory the Great

Corsica (Figure 2.1), as is well known, is the fourth largest island of the Mediterranean (8,681 km²), and it is characterized by a landscape with few plains, something very important in the analysis of settlement processes and also, as discussed below, of Christianization. In the ancient sources, the island is referred to in Greek as *Kurnos* (literally "covered with forests") and, in Latin, always as *Corsica*. The island's inhabitation is very ancient, reaching

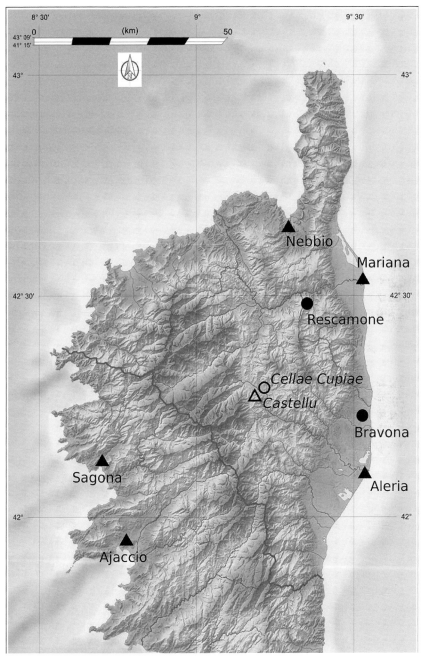

Figure 2.1. Corsica and its major Late Antique sites (G. Castiglia).

back nine millennia; but archaeological data relevant to the Republican and Imperial ages are very limited. Thanks to written sources, we know that the province *Sardinia et Corsica* was established in 227 B.C.; in the late third century A.D., subsequent to Diocletian's reforms, it came to be divided, although the two islands would somehow have remained linked, probably even more so than is sometimes supposed (Zucca 1996; Pergola 2018).

For the Roman centuries, a fundamental benchmark for the analysis of the settlement systems is provided by various geographic itineraries, such as Ptolemy's *Geography*, the *Itinerarium Antonini*, the *Cosmographia* by the Anonimo Ravennate, and the *Geographica* by Guidone. By interconnecting the different sources that we have at our disposal, we know that just two centers, Mariana and Aleria, had the status of *coloniae*, following the *deductiones* promoted by Marius and Sulla, respectively. Moreover, it is important to stress that—as we can see just by skimming the list of πόλεις mentioned by Ptolemy—the main settlements were concentrated mostly along the Tyrrhenian coastline. This is probably due both to the hydrological and geological suitability of this part of the littoral zone and to proximity to the Italian coast, chiefly that of present-day Tuscany. However, we have to highlight that, probably mainly during Late Antiquity, important settlements such as Saona and Agiation also developed in the western part of the island (Zucca 1996).

The approach to the study of Late Antique Corsica necessarily requires some preliminary considerations on the Vandal domination. Of course, this is not the time nor the place to go into a detailed analysis of the effects that the arrival of the Vandals had on the Mediterranean, even less of the catastrophic and negative interpretations that some historiography has promoted (often without considering the archaeological data *tout court*). Nevertheless, it is worth mentioning the fundamental reading of Christian Courtois who, in 1955, did not hesitate to talk about a "Vandal peace" and an "African prosperity", adopting a point of view that, at the time, was quite revolutionary and went against the flow (Courtois 1955). The archaeological information, in fact, even though quite fragmentary, reveals that precisely during the Vandal domination (between A.D. 455 and the Byzantine re-conquest in A.D. 532) Corsica went through one of its topographic and economic heydays; in this regard, the case of the heterogeneous material culture from *Castellu* is emblematic (see below; Istria and Pergola 2013b; for *Castellu*, Pergola and Vismara 1989). Moreover, the most ancient traces of Christianity in the island date back to this very period, since in Corsica we do not have monumental expressions of Christianity more ancient than the fifth century A.D. (Pergola 2018). The archaeology of churches is also very important, because in many cases it constituted the starting point for a better knowledge of Late Antique urban topographies, above all in the case of Mariana. The written sources relevant to Christianity, furthermore, are quite late, with the epistolary by Pope Gregory the Great as the main reference; it in any case denounces the presence of an episcopal organization that had to have been structured already before his pontificate (Pergola 1991). At the beginning of the sixth century, in fact, we know about the first bishops in Corsica, who had African origins and who had been exiled to Corsica after the stabilization of the Arian-Vandal Church in North Africa (Venturini 2007; Martorelli 2010). The cult of saints, moreover, was closely linked to the North African world: even Santa Giulia (the only one mentioned in the *Martyrologium Hieronymianum*) is probably to be considered as originating from Carthage, while the veneration of *Parthaeus* of Mariana, *Appianus* of Saona, *Euphrasius* of Ajaccio, *Restituta* of Calenzana and *Florentius* of Nebbiu are strictly dependent on the transfers of relics subsequent to the Vandal occupation (Zucca 2002; Pergola 2018; for the hagiography and the episcopal lists of Corsica, see also the fundamental work by Lanzoni 1927: 680–704).

It is now essential to return to the epistolary of Gregory the Great that, as we have already noted, stands out as the major written benchmark for the study of Late Antique Corsica, above all for the analysis of the dynamics of the diffusion of Christianity within the island (Pergola 1991; for the origins of Christianity, see also Istria and Pergola 2001). Nine letters dedicated to Corsica were written by the Pope (or, at least, nine have survived). They are rather few when compared to those he dedicated to other Mediterranean islands, such as Sardinia and Sicily (where, for example, we have an extraordinary apparatus of letters for Syracuse); but they nevertheless offer significant information, also relevant to the active role played by the *pontifex* in person. The letters are concentrated within just a few years, from A.D. 591 to A.D. 601, and it is worth recalling the contents of some of them. The first dates to June A.D. 591, when Gregory wrote to Symmachus, *defensor* of Corsica, after his request to the Pope to send some monks to the island, in order to settle them in a monastery built by the pious woman Labinia. In this letter, Gregory expresses his own disagreement about using this monastery, whose position he considered unsuitable, suggesting, instead, the erection of a new one. This new monastery *ut pro incertitudine temporis locus super mare requiri debeat, qui aut loci dispositione munitus exsistat* (hence it had to be fortified and on the seashore) (*Ep.* I, 50), and the Pope was open to contributing economically to it (*dignum parati sumus pretium dare*).

In August of the same year, Gregory wrote two other letters, first addressed to *Leoni episcopo in Corsica* (*Ep.* I, 76). There is no mention of his episcopal seat, even if it seems quite plausible that he may have been assigned to Mariana. In this letter, the Pope asks Leo to intervene in the critical situation of Saona, since *annos plurimos, obeunte eius pontefice, omnino destitutam agnovimus*, in order to ordain new presbyters and deacons to operate there. A fairly analogous situation is documented in the other letter of August 591, written to *Martino episcopo in Corsica*, of the church of Tadinas (*hostilitati feritate occupata atque diruta*, whose location remains unknown), ordaining him as titular bishop of Aleria, a seat that, evidently, had been vacant for many years.

On 1 June A.D. 595, Gregory wrote a fervent letter to the empress Constantina Augusta, wife of Flavius Mauritius Tiberius (*Ep.* V, 38), complaining about the strong and excessive fiscal pressure imposed on the people of Corsica by the Byzantine nobles. Because of this problem, in fact, *possessores eiusdem insulae ad nefandissimam Langobardorum gentem cogantur effugere*, a situation that probably persisted into the following year, as we read in a letter of October A.D. 596, addressed to *Gennadio patricio de Africa* (*Ep.* VII, 3).

In A.D. 596, Gregory wrote again to the diocese of Aleria, to the *episcopus* Peter, successor of Martinus, pushing him to spread Christianity also towards the rural areas, in particular asking him to erect a church with a baptistery (*ecclesia cum baptisterio*) *in loco Nigeuno*, within the area called *Cellas Cupias*, whose identification is still very problematic (*Ep.* VI, 22). The *Mons Nigeunus* is also mentioned in another letter—dated September A.D. 597, and once again addressed to the bishop of Aleria (*Ep.* VIII, 1)—where the above-mentioned *ecclesia cum baptisterio* already appears to have been built. In this letter it is of great interest that the Pope was concerned about the persistence of pagan rites in the rural areas, where people still adored *ligna et lapides* (even those who had been already baptized) and had gone back to the *cultum idolorum*; a similar phenomenon is also mentioned in Sardinia, in *Ep.* V, 38, of 1 June A.D. 595. In order to face this critical situation, Gregory solicited Peter to erect a new *episcopium*, close to the church in the *Mons Nigeunus*. This is evidently a command that revealed, if not the will to institute a new rural diocese, at least the intention of imposing a double episcopal seat for the bishop of Aleria.

The last letter that Gregory the Great addressed to Corsica, in August A.D. 601 (*Ep.* XI, 58), is full of bitterness and concern about a situation that appeared by then—if we want to trust the Pope's words—as a complete collapse. This letter was written to Bonifacius, *defensor*, who is blamed for the vacancy of the episcopal seats of Aleria and Ajaccio (*Experientia tua non sine colpa est*). The Pope, moreover, solicited Bonifacius to make the *clerum et populum* of both towns elect their own bishops and, if this did not happen, to refer directly to him in person, revealing Gregory's clear will to participate directly in solving this problem.

The overview that emerges from the epistolary of Gregory the Great, then, allows us to highlight some significant issues. A fairly recurrent topic is that of the precarious organization of ecclesiastical structures, as we can see from the Pope's constant concern over the continuous vacancies of many episcopal seats. The Christianizing of rural areas undoubtedly represents another major problem, as well as the monastic *quaestio*. As we have seen from the letter of A.D. 597, Gregory depicts a quite dramatic view of the countryside, where Christianity was struggling painfully to become stabilized. Analogously, the diffusion of monasticism, too, does not seem to be a widespread phenomenon, contrary to what happened, for example, in Sicily (Scalfati 1982; Istria and Pergola 2013e). Gregory the Great, moreover, shows an interest not only in pastoral matters, but also in administrative issues, as we can easily see in *Ep.* V, 38 and *Ep.* VII, 3, where a sincere worry emerges about what was defined as "Byzantine bad government" (Pergola 1981).

Mariana

After this brief and synthetic analysis of the epistolary by Gregory the Great, we need to deal with the archaeological data, in order to compare them, both in relation to the Vandal period and to the years following, at least until the beginning of the first part of the seventh century A.D. We start with the urban centers.

The town that is probably the better known from an archaeological point of view is Mariana, on the northeastern coast of the island at the mouth of the Golo valley (for Mariana, see, with related bibliographies: Pergola 2004; Corsi and Venditti 2010; Istria and Pergola 2014; Corsi and Vermeulen 2015; Istria and Dahy 2015a) (Figure 2.2). As Pliny says in his *Naturalis Historia*, it was founded in 90 B.C. by the will of Marius, who sent some veterans there (*Nat. Hist.* III, 6, 80). The urban organization is quite well known for the Imperial age, thanks both to stratigraphic excavations and to diagnostic surveys. Walls with a vaguely trapezoidal shape, which enclosed an area of about 30 ha, delimited the city. The *forum* was in its central part and there were at least four funerary areas, each one on the main suburban roads, in use since the Augustan age. From the third century onwards, the urbanism of Mariana went through significant re-configurations. In the southern part of the *colonia*, in fact, a market and some *tabernae* were built in front of a former wide, colonnaded space, while the so-called "*domus A*" (also in the southern part of Mariana) was completely destroyed by the end of the fourth century A.D.

It is the sixth century, however, that represents the moment of major changes within the town: it was at just this time (the first half of the sixth

Figure 2.2. Mariana: general plan of the town. The *ecclesia episcopalis* lies on the southwestern side of the map (after Corsi and Venditti 2010).

century), in fact, that the episcopal complex was built above the ruins of "*domus A*", annexing part of the former colonnade and, then, substantially altering the urban settings of the imperial age. The *ecclesia episcopalis* is mentioned in the written sources for the first time in A.D. 1115, dedicated to the Virgin Mary, and it was characterized, in its sixth-century phase, by a three-aisled space, divided by two rows of columns. A wide vestibule (a sort of esonarthex) preceded the entrance, while the semi-circular apse was provided with a southern and a northern access, both of them functioning to communicate with two side rooms. The baptistery, constructed mainly of brick, stood immediately to the south, with a cruciform plan and internal niches. The *fons baptismalis* underwent many structural changes: in its eastern part, it was delimited by a series of granite columns with marble bases— something that may suggest that this part of the baptistery could have been the place for an episcopal *cathedra*. The episcopal complex, besides its significant dimensions (the *basilica*, including the narthex, is about 30 m long), stands out also for its important decorative elements, mainly exemplified by the mosaic floors, belonging to the first phase. The geometric motives, in fact, are fully representative of the cultural and artistic trends of the late fifth to early sixth centuries A.D. One of the most important iconographic themes is inserted in the floor of the choir, depicting a scene that has been attributed to the book of Isaiah in the Bible. In this book, the prophet predicts the peace given by the Lord, exemplified here by a lion and an ox reunited; Pasquale Testini and Philippe Pergola have identified this as the allegory of the reconciliation between the persecutor and the persecuted (see Pergola 1984a for Testini's point of view; Pergola 1984b). More specifically, this scene may be an allusion to the concord reached by the African bishops, who had been exiled to the island. Important iconographic themes are also found in the baptistery, where, along with motives typical of the Hellenistic tradition (such as the personification of *Oceanus*), biblical references once again stand out. In particular, the image of a deer, seen in profile, side-by-side with a fountain, is undeniably a depiction of the celebrated words of Psalm XLI, 2: "*quemadmodum desiderat cervus ad fontes aquarum: ita desiderat anima mea ad te Deus*". This Psalm, as is well known, is one of the most oft-represented in Early Christian art, along with that of the heavenly rivers, placed in the quadrangular corners of the baptistery (Figure 2.3).

In very recent times, INRAP (*Institut national de recherches archéologiques préventives*) has made a sensational discovery, a few meters southeast of the *ecclesia episcopalis*, where a *mithraeum* was brought to light. The building

Figure 2.3. Mosaics from the baptistery of Mariana (photographs by Ph. Pergola).

comprises a main rectangular room (11×5 m), the location of the major rites, with a central corridor, flanked by two wide benches. Two niches have preserved intact oil lamps, while a fragmentary bas-relief with the god Mithras killing the bull comes from the terminal part of the main room. All this evidence makes clear and undeniable reference to a *mithraeum*, dated to the late third century A.D. This extraordinary discovery has led some scholars to hypothesize the presence, within Mariana, of two 'rival cults'—Mithraism and Christianity. This must be seen in the light of a very recent theory that proposes to push the chronology of the episcopal complex back to the fourth century A.D. (Istria 2015; Istria et al. 2018). While there is no doubt that the structures discovered by INRAP are relevant to a *mithraeum*, such an early date for the *ecclesia episcopalis* is, however, still not convincing. Equally unpersuasive is the idea of the intentional destruction of the *mithraeum* by Christians, as suggested in the INRAP report, both because we have no written evidence nor any direct archaeological traces to confirm it.

The making of the episcopal quarter also implies a topographic re-planning of the surrounding areas (Istria and Pergola 2013a). To the west of the *ecclesia episcopalis*, in fact, a great rectangular edifice made of pebbles and clay was constructed, divided into at least two main rooms. Their function is currently still difficult to interpret, but it is fair to think that, at least partially, it could have had a residential function; it is also noteworthy that in its interior there are significant traces of long use, testified by many post-holes relating to at least one (or two) huts of perishable materials, dated after the sixth century A.D. For the other, eastern side of the episcopal complex, we unfortunately do not have at our disposal the documentation of the excavations carried out there in 1960s. Nevertheless, some walls are still visible and it is possible to document how the colonnaded structure was partially reused, since later walls closed the spaces between the columns, in order to reorganize its function. In the late sixth to early seventh century A.D., in the southwestern *suburbium* of Mariana, was built the *extra moenia* funerary church dedicated to Saint Partheus, within the Augustan necropolis of *Palazzetto*. The church was completely rebuilt in the twelfth century (its dedication to Partheus is actually known to have been precisely in A.D. 1115), but the chronology of the first phase can be deduced thanks to studies of the more ancient tombs, where the amphorae used for the graves date back to the late sixth century A.D. (Istria and Dahy 2015b).

Rural Cathedrals: *Saona* and *Adiacium*

Turning now to the west coast, *Saona* is a site of importance, even if the archaeological data are somewhat patchy; it arose in the setting of a fluvial basin formed by the river *Sagone* (Istria and Pergola 2013d; 2014).

Information regarding the imperial period is scarce, but it is nonetheless possible to hypothesize an initial settlement that must have been fairly modest, organized around two distinct foci (*Sant'Appianu* and *A Sulana*) divided by a little stream. Diagnostic surveys and rescue archaeology have provided new data on the structure of the settlement during Late Antiquity: it consisted of four different residential centers (a sort of "sparse settlement" system), occupying an area of about 3.5 ha. The evidence coming from this research does not lead us to think of *Saona* as a proper town, but rather as a villa or a great *statio/mutatio*. On the promontory of *Sant'Appianu* there stands a large residential building with a wide apsidal hall, dating back to the fourth century A.D., where, from the fifth century onwards, a funerary area was established, probably at a time subsequent to the desertion of the former structures. On the promontory of *Sulana*, in contrast, lies another building of the late fourth to early fifth century A.D., whose typology seems typical of a rustic dwelling, probably a farm, with walls mainly made up of *spolia* and clay. Moreover, between the third and fifth century A.D., *Saona* also had an extensive necropolis located west of *A Sulana*, where different types of burials coexisted—simple graves, tombs "*alla cappuccina*" and interments in amphorae (*enchytrismòs*). *Saona*, then, is plausibly to be considered as a settlement structured around various nuclei, with a strong focus on agriculture, and that, at least from the sixth century A.D., was elevated to the status of an episcopal seat. As we have already seen in the epistolary of Gregory the Great, in fact, the Pope solicited the bishop Leo in A.D. 591 to reorganize the diocese of *Saona* which had been empty for many years (although the first bishop known from the written sources is *Montanus Sagonensi episcopus*, in A.D. 600).

The construction of the episcopal complex of *Saona* proves that an episcopal organization must already have been in place prior to this attempted re-launch promoted by Gregory the Great (Figure 2.4). At the end of the fifth to early sixth century A.D., the *ecclesia episcopalis* was built on the promontory of *Sant'Appianu*, exploiting a large part of the former apsidal building which by then was already deserted (see above). The church was about 20 m long and 8 m wide, with an apse that was internally semicircular and externally quadrangular. Close to its *presbyterium* there stood an elevated choir (with sides of about 5×4 m); Noël Duval (1995) thought that the *ecclesia* was also provided with a crypt, but it seems that this hypothesis should be now rejected, since the walls he attributed to the crypt are just substructures relevant to the support of the whole building. The baptistery stands about 10 m southwest of the church and it developed in different phases. The most ancient one had a circular plan (about 5 m in diameter), with the *fons baptismalis* resting on its central part, whose

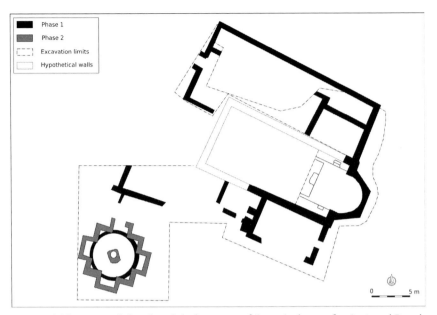

Figure 2.4. The episcopal church and the baptistery of *Saona* (redrawn after Istria and Pergola 2013d).

original configuration, however, is difficult to discern because of the many later phases. As suggested for Mariana, here too, probably, there was a space intended to accommodate a *cathedra* for the bishop, as a negative, semi-circular trace (associated with a niche) seems to demonstrate. The ceramics found here allow the baptistery to be dated to the beginning of the sixth century A.D., hence contemporaneous with the *ecclesia*. In fact the church has been dated thanks to an important inscription (+ *Sancti Apiani/+ iubante D(e)o Paulus fecit*), where the name of Apianus should refer, according to the hagiographic texts, to an African bishop of the late fifth century, exiled to Corsica by Hunneric. In a following phase (unfortunately not precisely datable), the baptistery was radically transformed by substituting for the former plan a more monumental and elaborate version, now cruciform (about 9 m long), with a replacement *fons*, internally octagonal and externally circular, and about 50 cm deep (Istria and Pergola 2014).

Saona, then, even though it never reached the rank of a proper town, was undoubtedly a very important center, at least in the first half of the sixth century A.D. Nevertheless, its life was evidently quite precarious and ephemeral, if—just a few decades later, in the late sixth century—Gregory the Great was moved to complain about its decadence and its episcopal vacancy.

Still in the western part of Corsica lies Ajaccio, another very important site for Late Antiquity, although here as well the data are rather disjointed (Istria and Pergola 2013d; 2014). Ajaccio too is mentioned in an *epistula* by Gregory the Great as *Aiacium* (*Ep.* XI, 58), and it shows an archaeological sequence very similar to that of *Saona*. Like *Saona*, in fact, knowledge of the Imperial Roman phase is basilar and ephemeral: only a few sporadic material traces make it possible to hypothesize a first phase running from the first century A.D. onwards. Moreover, there is no epigraphic or documentary evidence that allows us to attribute the status of *civitas* to Ajaccio (this description is given only in a letter of Gregory the Great, in A.D. 601, where the *pontifex* mentions *Aleria atque Aiuacium civitates Corsicae* – *Ep.* XI, 58). The archaeological data are not dispositive in this sense either, so that we can think of Ajaccio just as a settlement of limited dimensions, probably linked to a seaport.

The presence of many *spolia* in the walls of the *ecclesia episcopalis* may be an indicator of the existence of an important building within the former settlement, probably related to a storage room with *dolia*, something which is certainly plausible, if we consider the proximity to the seaport. *Aiacium*, moreover, had at least one necropolis on its periphery, once again with heterogeneous funerary practices, such as incineration, "*alla cappuccina*", *enchytrismòs* and, in two cases, burial in sarcophagi. The Christian origins of *Aiacium* are also rather confused, even if we can integrate them with the archaeological data. Of great importance is the letter already mentioned (*Ep.* XI, 58) that Gregory the Great addressed in A.D. 601 to the *defensor* Bonifatius, blaming him for the vacancies of the episcopal seats of *Aleria* and *Aiacium*, and urging him to make the *clerum et populum* of both centers elect their bishops. The first and only known *episcopus* is Benedictus, mentioned in A.D. 649 at the Lateran council (Mansi 1759–1798: coll. 865–866). Rescue archaeology in 2005 close to the medieval cathedral highlighted the traces of the first *ecclesia episcopalis*, whose level of preservation is very poor (Figure 2.5). The excavation led to the discovery of only the eastern part of the church, consisting of a wide apse (about 6 m deep) flanked by two side rooms (with funerary use); the rest of the *basilica* is unknown, since emergency excavations did not allow for investigation of its western part and how its aisles were arranged. A few meters southwest of the church stands the baptistery, about 3.5 m in diameter, inserted within a former semi-circular structure of unknown function). The *fons baptismalis* has an elongated shape, with little niches in its longer sides, and is 1.24 m deep; its typology readily recalls those known in North Africa and in the Balearic islands. The archaeological data from the episcopal complex, including the ceramics, allow it to be placed in the early sixth century A.D.—thus, in a

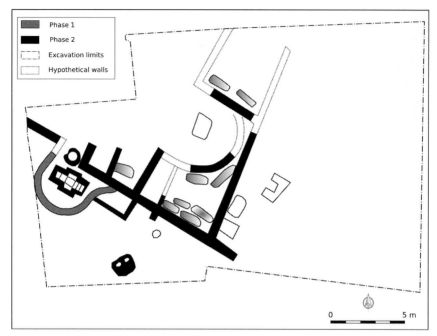

Figure 2.5. Ajaccio: the episcopal church and the baptistery (redrawn after Istria and Pergola 2013d).

phase considerably earlier than the first (and unique) attestation of a bishop in the episcopal list of *Aiacium* in A.D. 649, and than the letter by Gregory the Great of A.D. 601.

Castellu: A Rural Central Place?

If we look now at the rural areas, the general view we can deduce both from written sources and archaeological data is probably even more complex than for towns, albeit with some significant variations (Pergola 1999). Firstly, of fundamental importance is the invaluable stratigraphic sequence defined at the site of *Castellu*, which lies in the north-central area of Corsica (between the modern villages of Corte and Saint-Pierre de Venaco), in a semi-mountainous area, on the River Tavignano (Pergola and Vismara 1989). This site was the object of important archaeological excavations in the first half of the 1980s by Philippe Pergola and his team, who revealed a stratigraphic sequence that is fundamental to understanding some trends relevant to Late Antique Corsica and that is, still today, unique (Figure 2.6).

Castellu is a rural settlement—probably set within a wider system of other sparse villages—characterized by structures made up of mixed materials

Figure 2.6. Excavations in the rural site of *Castellu*, in 1984 (photograph by Ph. Pergola).

(mainly slabs of schist bonded with clay), often in association with simple planking levels in pressed earth. What makes the site exceptional, however, is the variety and richness of its material culture: its archaeological record, in fact, has a wide range of ceramics, animal bones and archaeobotanical finds, all of them revealing uninterrupted continuity of life at the site from the fifth century until at least the first decades of the seventh century A.D. Pottery from this period shows an heterogeneous assortment, presenting clues about long-range trade, as well demonstrated by the presence of *spathia* of North African production and by the many amphorae coming from Palestine, Turkey and the Iberian peninsula. The quantity of animal bones is also very large, with more than 25,000 studied items, valuable indicators of domestication, agricultural practices, and dietary habits in Late Antique Corsica. In the overall sample, just two percent of the bones are those of wild animals, indicating the very low significance of hunting activities for the domestic economy of the site, while certain peculiarities of the ovicaprid and bovid bones make them typologically distinct, when compared with those of the pre- and proto-historic ages. The archaeobotanical finds, too, are an expression of a diversified agricultural economy, where the exploitation of vines, olives, cereals and fruits coexisted.

The material culture found in *Castellu* is fundamental for reconsidering the interpretation of the transitional centuries between Late Antiquity and the Early Middle Ages as catastrophic. In the first place, the variety of pottery is testimony to the presence of long-distance trade, which was still active and diverse. Vandal government did not act as a brake on the island's economy but, on the contrary, still guaranteed lively commerce between the hinterland and the coastal areas, also thanks to the river Tavignano. The archaeozoological data, moreover, offer significant insights about the economy: the animal bones, in fact, signal processes of organizing the domestic animal economy whose roots go back at least to the era of Romanization (Pergola and Vismara 1989; Istria and Pergola 2013b).

Christian Topography of the Countryside: Rural and Baptismal Churches

The analysis of the diffusion of Christianity in the rural areas is, in many respects, not always very coherent, above all because there is so much archaeological potential that remains to be explored. In particular, many facets of the question still need in-depth research, such as the supposed presence of earlier Christian contexts beneath the medieval *plebes*, an hypothesis advanced by many scholars, but not always verified stratigraphically. As we have already highlighted, the main written source for Early Christianity in Corsica is the epistolary by Gregory the Great, which offers a desolate synopsis of the ecclesiastical network in towns and, especially, in the countryside. If we want to trust Pope Gregory's words, in the rural areas not only was the spread of the material and monumental expression of Christianity slowed down, but the more general process of evangelization, *stricto sensu*, seems ephemeral and not resilient. We have already seen that in *Ep.* VIII, 1 of September A.D. 597, addressed to the bishop of Aleria, Gregory was concerned about the fact that the inhabitants of the rural areas, even though already baptized, had gone back to the *cultum idolorum*, by adoring *ligna et lapides*, thus indicating the persistence of strong enclaves of resistance to the firm establishment of the new religion, in favor of devotion still strongly linked to pagan traditions. Yet we cannot exclude *a priori* that the dim outlook given by the Pope might have been excessively pessimistic, and the lack so far of any archaeological proof that reveals clear evidence of such a pagan revival calls for considerable caution. In any case, it is also true that, if this pagan revival were limited just to the adoration of *ligna et lapides*, the material evidence for it could well be ephemeral or altogether intangible.

The letter of A.D. 597, as we have noted, is directly linked to another one written by the *pontifex* just a year before, in A.D. 596, once again addressed to the bishop of Aleria. While the *Mons Nigeunus* is not yet identifiable, as it is not the toponym *Cellae Cupiae/Cellas Cupias*, the most important topic of this letter is the fact that, at the end of the sixth century A.D., the Pope commanded the building of a church with a baptistery (*ecclesia cum baptisterio*). Moreover, Gregory also ordered the building of an *episcopium*,

close to the former church, not far from the center of the diocese, which was
Aleria. We should not forget that the Pope also tried to spread Christianity
to minor islands as well, such as Gorgona and Montecristo—property of the
Church of Corsica—by constructing monasteries (*Ep*. I, 50). This choice
may indicate, on the one hand, the necessity of setting up a second residence
for the bishop besides his urban one, something that is clear evidence of
how the diffusion of Christianity in the countryside was struggling, even
requiring the physical presence of the *episcopus* himself. On the other hand,
it is probably more difficult, even though suggestive, to think in terms of
the institution of a proper rural diocese, since the letter by Gregory does not
seem to reveal the wish to appoint a new "autonomous" bishop, but rather,
somehow, to "split" the episcopal seat; from the letter, too, it seems beyond
doubt that the *Mons Nigeunus* was within the territorial jurisdiction of the
diocese of Aleria. Moreover, the construction of a baptismal church and of
an *episcopium* provides unavoidable evidence that the *pontifex* imposed the
baptismal rite to be administered directly by the bishop in the rural and
mountainous areas of the diocese as well.

About 10 km north of Aleria stands the rural site of Santa Maria di Bravona,
in the modern municipality of Linguizzeta, where archaeological data suggest
the presence of a baptismal church (Pergola 1999) (Figure 2.7). The site had

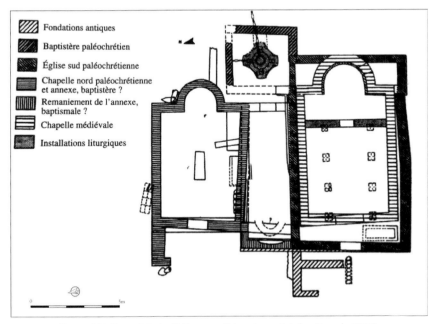

Figure 2.7. Santa Maria di Bravona (Linguizzetta) (after Pergola 1999).

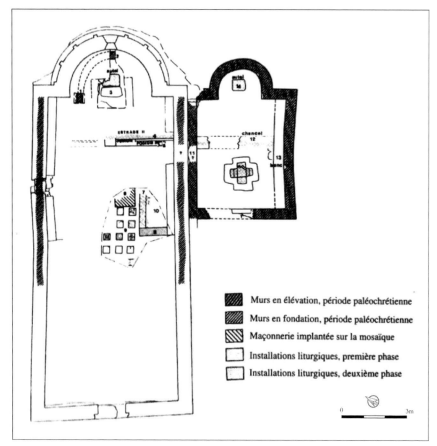

Figure 2.8. Santa Maria di Rescamone (after Pergola 1999).

been inhabited at least since the Imperial Roman age, a fact we may deduce from various sparse finds, mainly inscriptions, that suggest the presence of a funerary area, probably related to a rural settlement. The hagiotoponym is known only from the late Middle Ages and had to be relevant to the Romanesque *plebs*, while the first phase of the Christian complex (most likely dated to the sixth century A.D.) was probably characterized by the presence of two parallel apsed chapels, both of them with a single aisle, punctuated by a baptistery. Some graves, moreover, provide clear evidence of the use of the site for funerary purposes since its very first phase.

Farther north, in the hinterland of Mariana and not very far from the river Golo, the rural site of Santa Maria di Rescamone reveals a structural sequence similar to that of Bravona (Pergola 1999) (Figure 2.8). Here too the most recent evidence relates to a Romanesque *plebs* with, once again, a dedication that goes back to the late Middle Ages. Nevertheless, archaeological investigations have led to the discovery of an earlier Late Antique phase of the church, dated to the sixth century A.D.; the chronology is confirmed mainly by the typology of the mosaic floors. The church's plan comprises two parallel apsed halls of different dimensions. In the center of the smaller one there stands a cruciform *fons baptismalis*, faced by an altar whose base was inside the apse; the *fons* and the altar were divided by a chancel-screen, a probable sign of some sort of functional division required in performing an elaborate liturgy.

A very interesting rural site recently excavated by INRAP in Propriano in southern Corsica (probably in the territory of the diocese of Ajaccio) gives significant new insights on the diffusion of Christianity in the interior areas of the island (Figure 2.9). The development of this site began at least in the Roman period and, in its first phase, served as a villa: a series of walls and a circular structure (about 6.5 m in diameter) seem to be clearly parts of a residential-productive rural site. In the sixth century, when much of the villa was going through crisis (most of it was already deserted), a first church was erected. Its dimensions are quite important, being 16 m long and 8.5 m wide, and its inner space includes the base of an altar and a *cathedra* divided from the rest of the aisle by an enclosure that framed the *presbyterium*. The

Figure 2.9. The INRAP excavation at Quattrina-Propriano (after INRAP https://multimedia. inrap.fr/atlas/paleochretiens/sites/2468/Quattrina-les-egliees-oubliees-de-Propriano-#. XKRkn6ZS9E4, accessed April 4, 2019).

church also had external rooms, one of them provided with an apse, whose function however is still uncertain. Around the church there developed some small funerary areas, whose more ancient graves date back to the fourth century A.D., and thus are relevant to a phase prior to the Christian building. So we may suppose that the church was planned in close relation to a former necropolis, perhaps one with a venerated tomb (African relics or an exiled African bishop, who died in Corsica?)—although, of course, this is just a preliminary hypothesis still to be demonstrated. Later on, in a phase whose chronology is not clear, a new *ecclesia* (11×5.60 m) was built above the former one.

The structural typologies and the plans of the first phases of Santa Maria di Bravona and of Santa Maria di Rescamone suggest the need to widen the spectrum of possible comparisons towards the world outside Corsica, mainly looking at nearby Tuscany. Across the Tyrrhenian Sea, in fact, there are at least two sites that have architectural configurations very similar to those identified in Corsica: these are the rural churches of San Piero in Campo in Montecarlo (province of Lucca) and of the Pieve di Gropina (province of Arezzo). In both cases, their first phases were followed by later Romanesque churches—even if, of course, it is the Late Antique buildings that are more pertinent to our interests here. Two parallel apsed halls, in fact, characterize both San Piero in Campo and the Pieve di Gropina in their Late Antique phases. The most fitting comparison, without doubt, is that between San Piero in Campo (see Ciampoltrini 2008) and Santa Maria di Rescamone, since in both these cases there is a wider hall serving the role of *ecclesia*, and then a smaller one, as a baptistery (for the Tuscan sites, see Francovich et al. 2003; Castiglia 2017; 2018a; 2018b) (Figure 2.10). Of course, we may suppose that these analogies could be just accidental, but it is also true that, at least since the Lombard era, links between Corsica and Tuscany had been very strong (Istria and Pergola 2013c): for example, important indicators of this bond are the finds of Lombard pottery both in Mariana and Ajaccio, or the Lombard coins coming from Linguizzetta (Arslan 2011). Considering all these aspects, then, we should not exclude *a priori* that such ties had in fact already existed in Late Antiquity.

Final Remarks: Corsica between Change and Resilience

The topic of islands, *sensu lato*, represents one of the best ways to understand changes in the Mediterranean from a long and wide perspective, where the concepts of "persistence", "change", and "resilience" stand as a sort of *fil rouge*. If the definition of "change" does not need to be expanded, it is worth thinking briefly about how to interpret the notion of "resilience"

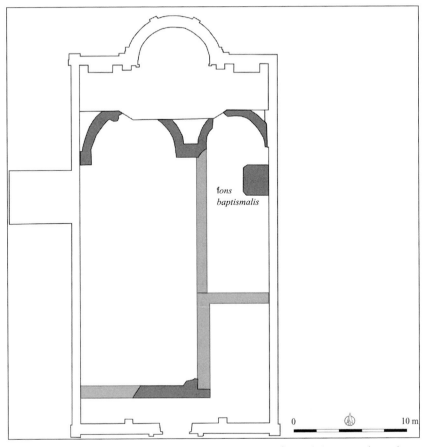

Figure 2.10. San Piero in Campo in Montecarlo (province of Lucca) (G. Castiglia, redrawn after Ciampoltrini 2008).

(for resilience theory in archaeology, see Redman 2005). This concept, in general, may be defined as the capacity to adapt to changes, and it has numerous applications in many disciplines, such as economy, psychology, computer science, etc., where it is always strictly bonded to the concept of "change". Resilience, then, can also be seen as the ability to adopt innovations (whatever they might be), without losing the main particularities of the original system. With this in mind, the site of *Castellu* is once again extraordinary, being a sort of magnifying glass on Late Antique Corsica. Against the background of Vandal domination, in fact, a relatively modest rural site reacted to political and institutional change with a wide-ranging and lively economy, where goods coming from all over the Mediterranean and diversified agricultural production are the main responses to the need for change. In all this, we can see full resilience: *Castellu* is just the tip of the iceberg, the terminal stage of an economy in significant re-launch in the fifth and sixth centuries A.D.

The coastal sites (above all, Mariana) become the exemplification of a trading potential still active both over very long distances (goods, as we have seen, coming from Africa, the Iberian peninsula and the Eastern Mediterranean) and over middle-range distances too (the geographical axis Mariana-*Castellu*), where the sea and rivers are the main facilitators of this process of resilience. Still in regard to *Castellu*, the data on the animal bones there exemplify the diffusion of livestock farming practices in which the peculiarities of the ovicaprids and bovids represent a sharp change in comparison to those of the pre-Roman centuries, emblematic of what we may call "resilience through novelty", already in effect before Late Antiquity.

Looking at the vectors of diffusion of Christianity, mainly in the countryside, it is possible to document a sort of "double soul" in Late Antique Corsica, in which adaptation to change—exemplified, in this specific case, by the Christian religion—is sometimes ambiguous. Generally, Christianity, both in towns and countryside, is a fairly late phenomenon, especially when compared to nearby continental areas (Istria and Pergola 2013b). Considering Tuscany once again, in its main towns bishops are attested sometimes already since the age of Constantine, with material traces of some of the *ecclesiae episcopales* dating back to the late fourth century A.D. (as in Lucca or Florence) (Castiglia 2017); in Corsica, by contrast, both written sources and archaeological data, as we have seen, are far later. If we trust the concerns expressed by Gregory the Great, moreover, the rural areas would seem less open to change, where the *cultum idolorum*, the failed establishment of monasticism, and the continuous episcopal vacancies may indicate a poor capacity (or lack of will) for resilience. What is evident, however, is that Late Antique Corsica was fully part of a wider network of commercial and cultural exchanges, well exemplified by the strong bond with North Africa (a true "supplier" of bishops and saints), by trade both with the East and the West, and by the close affinities with continental areas nearby, such as Tuscany. Corsica, then, is one of the central cores of the shimmering Mediterranean "corrupting sea", giving, on the one hand, a great impulse to resilience and adaptability and, on the other, preserving peculiarities that are, somehow, the mirror of a strong identity.

Notes

1. http://www.inrap.fr/un-sanctuaire-dedie-au-dieu-mithra-decouvert-en-corse-12313
2. A benchmark for the relations between a mithraeum and the building of a later Christian structure is, without doubt, the brilliant research conducted by Federico Guidobaldi in San Clemente in Rome (Guidobaldi 1992)

3. http://multimedia.inrap.fr/atlas/paleochretiens/sites/2468/Quattrina-les-eglises-oubliees-de-Propriano-#.WgiDBoZrxE7

References

Ep. = V. Recchia 1996–1999, *Opere di Gregorio Magno: Lettere*. Città Nuova, Roma.

Arslan, Ermanno
  2011   Moneta e forme di tesaurizzazione dei Longobardi e delle popolazioni romanze in Italia nel VI secolo. In *Archeologia e storia delle migrazioni: Europa, Italia, Mediterraneo fra tarda età romana e alto medioevo. Atti del Convegno internazionale di studi (Cimitile-Santa Maria Capua Vetere, 17–18 giugno 2010)*, edited by Carlo Ebanista and Marcello Rotili, pp. 309–337. Tavolario Edizioni, Cimitile.

Castiglia, Gabriele
  2017   La rete ecclesiastica in Toscana settentrionale (IV-X secolo): dati e riflessioni alla luce del progetto CARE. *Hortus Artium Medievalium* 23: 729–749.

  2018a   Topografia cristiana della *Tuscia Annonaria* e della *Tuscia Langobardorum* (IV–VIII sec. d.C.). *Papers of the British School at Rome* 86: 85–126.

  2018b   Rural Churches and Settlements in Late Antique and Early Medieval Tuscany. *Journal of Roman Archaeology* 31: 223–247.

Ciampoltrini, Giulio
  2008   Vie e pievi, pievi e castelli: Storie parallele di due plebes baptismales del territorio di Lucca. In *Chiese e insediamenti nei secoli di formazione dei paesaggi medievali della Toscana (V–X secolo). Atti del Seminario (10–11 novembre San Giovanni d'Asso)*, edited by Stefano Campana, Cristina Felici, Riccardo Francovich, and Fabio Gabbrielli, pp. 95–115. All'Insegna del Giglio, Firenze.

Corsi, Cristina, and Caterina Paola Venditti
  2010   The Role of Roman Towns in the Romanization Process in Corsica: The Case-Study of Mariana. In *Changing Landscapes: The Impact of Roman Towns in the Western Mediterranean. Proceedings of the International Colloquium, Castelo de Vide – Marvão fifthseventh May 2008*, edited by Cristina Corsi and Frank Vermeulen, pp. 69–84. Ante Quem, Bologna.

Corsi, Cristina, and Frank Vermeulen
  2015   La ville romaine de Mariana (Corse) et son urbanisme. *Mélanges de l'École française de Rome, Antiquité* 127–1 (https://mefra.revues.org/2758, accessed April 4, 2019)

Courtois, Christian
  1955   *Les Vandales et l'Afrique*. Arts et métiers graphiques, Paris.

Duval, Noël
  1995   *Les premiers monuments chrétiens de la France*, 1: *Sud-Est et Corse*. Picard, Paris.

Francovich, Riccardo, Cristina Felici, and Fabio Gabbrielli
  2003   La Toscana. In *Chiese e insediamenti nelle campagne tra V e VI secolo. IX seminario sul tardo Antico e l'Alto Medioevo (Garlate, 26–28 settembre 2002)*, edited by Gian Pietro Brogiolo, pp. 267–288. SAP, Mantova.

Guidobaldi, Federico
  1992   *San Clemente: Gli edifici romani, la basilica paleocristiana e le fasi altomedievali.*
            San Clemente, Roma.
Istria, Daniel
  2015   Mariana, de la colonie romaine au centre chrétien. *Les Dossiers d'archéologie* 370:
            56–57.
Istria, Daniel, and Isabelle Dahy,
  2015a   Mariana, cité romaine. *Congrès archéologique de France, 171e session, 2013, Corse*,
            pp. 267–272. Picard, Paris
  2015b   Mariana, l'église San Parteo. *Congrès archéologique de France, 171e session, 2013,
            Corse*, pp. 279–282. Picard, Paris
Istria, Daniel, Delfine Dixneuf, and Joël Françoise
  2018   Nouvelles données sur la chronologie du complexe paléochrétien de Mariana
            (Lucciana, Corse). *Études corses* 79 (2014): 88–99.
Istria, Daniel, and Philippe Pergola,
  2013a   La Corse byzantine (VIe-VIIe siècles). In *The Insular System of the Early Byzantine
            Mediterranean*, edited by Demetrios Michaelides, Philippe Pergola, and Enrico
            Zanini, pp. 77–85. *Limina/Limites: Archaeologie, storie, isole e frontiere (365–
            1556)*. British Archaeological Reports International Series 2523. Archaeopress,
            Oxford.
  2013b   La Corse, frontière septentrionale du royaume vandale d'Afrique. In *Histoire de
            la Corse.* Vol. 1*, Des origines à la veille des Révolutions: occupations et adaptations*,
            edited by Antoine-Marie Graziani, pp. 215–224. A. Piazzola, Ajaccio.
  2013c   La Corse lombarde et les temps incertains de la Corse pontificale. In *Histoire de
            la Corse.* Vol. 1*, Des origines à la veille des Révolutions: occupations et adaptations*,
            edited by Antoine-Marie Graziani, pp. 233–240. A. Piazzola, Ajaccio.
  2013d   Nouvelles données sur les groupes épiscopaux de Corse. In *Acta XV Congressvs
            Internationalis Archaeologiae Christianae (Toleti 8–12.9.2008): Episcopus, Civitas,
            Territorium*, pp. 515–526. Pontificio Istituto di Archeologia Cristiana, Città del
            Vaticano.
  2013e   Moines et monastères dans les îles des mers Ligure et Tyrrhénienne (Corse,
            Sardaigne, archipel toscan et archipel ligure). *Hortus Artium Medievalium* 19:
            73–78.
  2014   La Corse, Ajaccio, Aleria, Mariana, Sagone. In *Topographie chrétienne des cités de
            la Gaule,* vol. XVI, 1–2, pp. 329–345, 705–711, 712–778. De Boccard, Paris.
Istria, Daniel, and Philippe Pergola (editors)
  2001   *Corsica christiana: 2000 ans de christianisme.* Musée de la Corse, Corte.
Lanzoni, Francesco
  1927   *Le diocesi d'Italia, dalle origini al principio del secolo VII: studio critico.* F. Lega,
            Faenza.
Mansi, Johannes Dominicus
  1759–1798 [1960] *Sacrorum Conciliorum nova et amplissima collectio.* Firenze-Venezia.
Martorelli, Rossana
  2010   Vescovi esuli, santi esuli? La circolazione dei culti africani e delle reliquie nell'età
            di Fulgenzio. In *Lingua et ingenium: Studi su Fulgenzio di Ruspe e il suo contesto*,
            edited by Antonio Piras, pp. 385–442. Ortacesus, Cagliari.

Pergola, Philippe

1981   L'administration vandale; Grégoire le Grand et le malgoverno byzantin; les
           Lombards: un peuple majeur et organisé; la tentative manquée d'une hégémonie
           pontificale; la pieve. In *Le Mémorial des Corses*, vol. I: *Des origines à Sampiero,
           6500 av. J.C.–1570*, edited by Francis Pomponi and Michel-Claude Weiss, pp.
           226–255, 282–283. Gleizal, Ajaccio.

1984a   Observations sur la chronologie des mosaïques de la basilique et du baptistère de
           Mariana (Corsica). *III Colloquio Internazionale sul Mosaico Antico de l'A.I.E.M.A,
           Ravenne 1980*, pp. 401–404. Edizioni del Girasole, Ravenna.

1984b   Considérations nouvelles sur les mosaïques et les sculptures du complexe
           paléochrétien de Mariana (Corsica). *Actes du Xᵉ Congrès International
           d'Archéologie Chrétienne, Thessalonique, 28 septembre–4 octobre 1980*, pp.
           397–408. Pontifico Instituto di Archeologia Cristiana, Città del Vaticano.

1991   Gli interventi di Gregorio Magno in Corsica, aspetti religiosi, socio-economici e
           politici. In *Atti del Convegno Gregorio Magno e il suo tempo*, pp. 103–108. Studia
           Ephemeridis Augustinianum, Rome.

1999   La Corse. In *Alle origini della parrocchia rurale (IV-VIII sec.): atti della giornata
           tematica dei Seminari di archeologia cristiana, École Française de Rome, 19 marzo
           1998*, edited by Philippe Pergola and Palmira Maria Barbini, pp. 205–213.
           Pontificio Istituto di Archeologia Cristiana, Città del Vaticano.

2004   Mariana, capitale de la première Corse chrétienne. In *Paul-Albert Février de
           l'Antiquité au Moyen Âge: actes du colloque de Fréjus, 7 et 8 avril 2001*, edited by
           Michel Fixot, pp. 238–257. Université de Provence, Aix-en-Provence.

2019   Sardinia et Corsica. In *Reallexikon für Antike und Christentum: Sachwörterbuch
           zur Auseinandersetzung des Christentums mit der antiken Welt XXIX*, pp. 554–574.
           Hiersemann Verlag, Stuttgart.

Pergola, Philippe, and Cinzia Vismara (editors)

1989   *Castellu (Haute-Corse): Un établissement rural de l'antiquité tardive. Fouilles
           récentes (1981–1985).* Editions de la Maison des Sciences de l'Homme, Paris.

Redman, L. Charles

2005   Resilience Theory in Archaeology. *American Anthropologist* 107: 70–77.

Scalfati, Silio

1982   Il monachesimo in Corsica al tempo di Gregorio. In *Atti del VII Congresso
           Internazionale di Studi sull'Alto Medioevo: Norcia, Subiaco, Cassino, Montecassino,
           29 settembre–5 ottobre 1980*, pp. 761–772. Centro Italiano di Studi sull'Alto
           Medioevo, Spoleto.

Venturini, Alain

2007   Les évêques de Corse depuis les origines avérées à la réunion de l'évêché d'Accia
           à celui de Mariana (591–1563). *Etudes corses* 65: 1–40.

Zucca, Raimondo

1996   *La Corsica romana.* S'Alvure, Oristano.

2002   L'origine del cristianesimo in Corsica. In *Insulae Christi: il cristianesimo primitivo
           in Sardegna, Corsica e Baleari*, edited by Pier Giorgio Spanu, pp. 525–538.
           S'Alvure, Oristano.

Procopius' *Barbarikinoi* and Gregory the Great's *Barbaricini: Mauri* and Sardinians in the Sixth and Seventh Centuries A.D.

Pier Giorgio Spanu

Procopius and Gregory the Great both report the existence of the Barbarikinoi-Barbaricini *in Sardinia during the sixth and seventh centuries A.D., located in the central region known as* Barbaria. *These* Barbarikinoi-Barbaricini *should be identified with the African people known as the* Mauri, *who were deported to Sardinia while the island was part of the African* regnum Vandalorum. *Moving beyond past interpretations that localized this deported* Mauri *population in the* Sulcis *area of southwestern Sardinia and in the hinterland of Cagliari, today's understandings tend to connect the* Barbaricini *to the* civitate Barbaria, *delimited by the Romans since the third to second centuries B.C., which absorbed the three thousand* Mauri *brought to the island.*

The geography of Barbaria *has been shown to have been marked to the west and south by Roman military settlements that went on to maintain an urban dimension during the Vandal and Byzantine epochs. At the time of Mauritius Tiberius, the* Barbaricini *signed a peace treaty with the Roman Empire and were recognized as a dukedom held by the* dux Ospitone.

Research has confirmed the resilient and open cultural attitudes of the Sardinian population towards the Roman Empire. It was characterized by the prevailing palaeo-Sardinian onomastics that persisted into the Early Middle Ages of the Sardinian Judgeships.

Nuragic settlements continued to be exploited, but with new functions for their monumental buildings, such as the Nuraghi and Giant's Tombs which were often transformed into mausolea. Local, stamp-decorated, impasto pottery is found together with fine wares mainly imported from Africa.

Sardinia's Population between Late Antiquity and the Early Middle Ages: The Urban Settlements

In his *Cosmographia*, composed within the first half of the seventh century A.D., the *Anonimus Ravennate* reports that Sardinia was an island rich in cities. The geographer also provides a large list of urban centers. He seems to affirm that those which reached a certain standing at the threshold of the Early Middle Ages were even more numerous than those listed. Nonetheless, the work reflects the image of Sardinia in the midst of Imperial Rome and Late Antiquity: in fact, it uses pre-existing sources, such us the *itineraria*, certainly including the *Itinerarium Antonini*.[1] This was probably composed at the beginning of the third century A.D. under Caracalla's rule, and represents a multi-layered itinerary aimed at various purposes, among which was to function as reference for the *annona* (Rebuffat 1991).

In reality, the situation had to be quite different: along with several cities, most of which were founded in Phoenician and Punic times, the *Cosmographia* lists many other settlements that we should imagine as small *stationes, mansiones, mutationes*—that is, centers in the road network that had to be established in Roman times for it to function effectively. This network was characterized by at least four main routes. Therefore, the Ravennate's work may reflect a changed situation. It is also important to stress that, throughout its ancient history, Sardinia experienced only very limited urbanization, almost entirely concentrated in coastal areas. If we refer to the *formula provinciae* of the first century A.D.—handed down by Pliny (*Hist. Nat.* 3.7.85) but substantially of Augustan age—18 *oppida* (urban centers of various status, *coloniae, municipia, civitates stipendiariae*) were assigned to the island of Sardinia. Explicitly mentioned among these are *Carales, Nora, Sulci, Bithia, Neapolis*, and *Turris Libisonis*, all representing coastal centers, while *Valentia* (according to some scholars *Vselis*) is the only inland urban center. According to reconstructions of this list, almost all the other centers whose name is not mentioned are nonetheless coastal settlements. The only change in the administative subdivision of Sardinia during Imperial times, almost certainly during the Severan Age, was the achievement of *civitas* status for *Forum Traiani*. The center was already well-known for its thermal springs, the *Aquae Ypsitanae*, and for its location, 30 km inland from the west-central coast of the island (Zucca 2016a), in a border area between the flat regions with a prevalent agricultural economy and the mountain regions, characterized by a pastoral economy (Spanu 2006) (Figure 3.1).

The situation did not change in Late Antiquity or in the initial centuries of the Early Middle Ages. During these times, the population of Sardinia

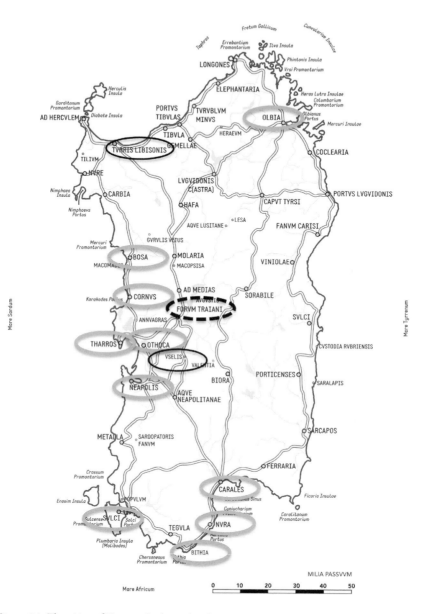

Figure 3.1. The cities of Roman Sardinia already existing in Punic times (gray), the coloniae (black) and the Forum Traiani (dashed).

continued to live mainly in rural centers or in scattered settlements, although the life of most of the cities continued into Late Antiquity and the Early Middle Ages, at least up until the seventh to early eighth centuries and beyond, at least in some cases (Spanu 1998: 129–143, 2002: 117–125, 2006). Among the rare exceptions we can mention *Bithia*, one of the first Phoenician colonies on the island, whose urban characteristics seem to decline around the fourth century A.D. (Bartoloni 1996: 31; Zucca 2004: 88–94).

Rural Settlements in the Plains and Hilly Areas with High Agricultural Potential

Concerning rural centers, the settlement typology differentiates clearly between areas in the mountains and the plains, in relation to available resources and the economic characteristics of specific territories. In fact, the economy of the mountainous zones was based primarily on sheep-farming and on locating supplementary resources in the wooded areas, while in the hills and plains the fertility of the soils and the abundance of water allowed intense agricultural exploitation, which characterized these regions since the Punic Age. As has repeatedly been pointed out, the Sardinian countryside was widely characterized by a *latifundus/*estate economy based mainly on cereal monoculture, one imposed in the Carthaginian Age and later favored by the economic system of Rome (Rowland 1994; Mastino 2005: 176–180). On the one hand, the capital of the Empire needed large quantities of grain to be allocated to the *annona*, while, on the other hand, the city initially set up a protectionist policy for the Italian production of oil and wine, thereafter exploiting the provinces for the supply of these goods.

The spread of villas in the rural areas of Sardinia was connected to this system of land management, based on large estates, that represents a legacy of Carthaginian rule (Colavitti 1996: 649–651; Nieddu and Cossu 1998a, 1998b; Nieddu in Mastino 2005: 180–183; Campus 2004: 158–161). Nonetheless, in the absence of specific archaeological surveys, it is important to stress the difficulty of attributing the numerous ruins identified in the countryside to a type of settlement that replicates the urban-rustic villa of Italian descent, which was divided into a *pars urbana* (the family residence of the *dominus*), and a *pars rustica* (where production activities were located). Beyond a generic attribution, the existence of different centers, both formally and functionally, seems more plausible. Coexisting with the infrastructural centers of the road network, the *villae*, villages, farms, and also the *vici* (see Trudu 2014) might have been connected in a hierarchical structure, according to the role that each type of settlement had in the overall territorial organization.

Obviously, it is not sure that a settlement always kept the same formal characteristics. A clear example is that of Santa Filitica di Sorso in northern Sardinia (Rovina 2007; Rovina et al. 2008, 2011; archaeological research at the site has recently been resumed under the direction of Elisabetta Garau). Here a stately residence close to the sea was probably able to fulfil the dual function of *villa maritima* and a center connected to agricultural exploitation of the fertile hinterland. The residential sector of the villa saw a change in use at the end of the fifth century A.D., during the Vandal period, when a series of bath-house rooms with mosaics were taken over for metallurgical and other activities. In the same period, a number of buildings, constructed about 100 m west of the baths, were used as service areas or as housing. The settlement was abandoned between the end of the sixth century and the beginning of the seventh. During the seventh century, on top of an alluvial layer, there is evidence of a small village inhabited by a community that was socially well-organized, as is clearly suggested by various aspects such as the regular arrangement of houses served by roads and the presence of communal areas. For the initial phase of the village, the material culture still indicates the frequency of trade, especially with Africa, but these contacts cease by the end of the seventh century and the pottery attested in the eighth and ninth centuries is of rough local production. The ninth century marks the abandonment of the settlement. This community was certainly dedicated to agriculture and stock-breeding, as evidenced by the faunal remains, and it also found alternative subsistence resources in hunting and fishing, in an economy that was probably dedicated to self-sufficiency. The site of Santa Filitica is certainly one good example, and the model can probably be adapted to other similar settlements of the Roman age that continued to exist, albeit with changed forms, up to the Early Middle Ages.

Landscape archaeology research carried out in different areas of Sardinia, at least, seems to confirm the hypothesis of settlements linked to each other in a strongly hierarchical organizational structure. For example, research conducted in the territory of *Nora* clearly draws attention to two aspects which characterize a particularly flourishing phase of the urban center during the end of the second and the beginning of the third centuries A.D., with the rise of an organized system of different *villae* and production centers, interconnected but closely dependent on the city—clearly highlighting a well-defined and osmotic relationship between the city and its countryside. Substantial continuity in this pre-existing articulation and hierarchy of settlements, with small farms or rural production centers dependent on large farms/rural villas, is recorded during the entire fourth century A.D., as well as in the fifth. The same situation recurs in the sixth and seventh centuries, although this period sees the passage from Vandal to Byzantine rule. Continuity is limited to certain parts of the territory, while the settlement dynamic appears more articulated in others, which are characterized both by abandoned settlements and others newly established, testifying to intensive exploitation of the territory. During this period, the central place is no longer located in *Nora*, which is now heading towards a profound phase of change and depopulation, but rather in the city of *Carales* (Garau and Rendeli 2006: 1252–1261, 1267–1274; Garau 2007: 59–69).

The *Nora* model can be applied to other territories—for example, that dependent on the city of *Tharros* in west-central Sardinia, which had been intensely cultivated since the Punic period and experienced particular vitality in Late Antiquity, perhaps as early as the third but certainly in the fourth century A.D. (Fois et al. 2013; Panico et al. 2015a, 2015b; Panico 2016; Panico and Spanu 2016: 42–45, 2018: 631–638). It is likely that alongside the estates, whether public or private, there were also other forms of territorial organization with broken-up landholdings, such as the *massae*, whose owners might be identified among the families of the senatorial class (Spanu 2018: 188; Panico and Spanu 2018: 632–634).

During the century when Sardinia was first annexed to the Vandal kingdom and then became a province of the Byzantine diocese of Africa (between the middle of the fifth and the end of the seventh centuries), its landscapes remained substantially unchanged. Considering the fact that the tax systems of the new rulers (Vandals and Byzantines) must substantially have inherited the Roman one (Spanu 1998: 129–131; Cosentino 2002: 5–6; Ibba 2010: 411–415; Mastino and Zucca 2007: 106–108; Simbula and Spanu 2012: 566), it can reasonably be assumed that the economic structures of Sardinia that were related to the tax system (including of course the settlements connected to these structures) must have remained unchanged, at least until the balance was disrupted by the raids of the Arabs in the Mediterranean.

In the almost total absence of epigraphic, literary, and legal sources for the Vandal and Byzantine periods, possibly indicating the existence of the imperial *latifundus* in Sardinia, we cannot ascertain for sure if and how a potential transfer of imperial properties from the state to the new rulers could have taken place. Likewise, between Late Antiquity and the first centuries of the Early Middle Ages, it is not possible to determine if these transformations involved the ownership and use of what were considered *fundi publici*. On the other hand, if there are real difficulties in defining the limits of imperial possessions on the island, it becomes even more problematic to offer any hypothesis about the *publica utilitas* of the land, both in the Late Imperial Age and during Vandal and proto-Byzantine times (Mastino and Zucca 2007: 107–108; Spanu and Zucca 2004: 105–108, n. 6, 2008: 170–172; Simbula and Spanu 2012: 366–367).

All things considered, the agricultural areas of Sardinia in general witnessed continuity rather than resilience, despite the political and military events that, in the space of a few centuries, led to the frequent alternation of hegemonic powers on the island. The transformations mostly concerned cities, where defensive requirements, the growth of Christian communities, along with various other factors in individual cases, led to profound changes in urban structure and sometimes to changes in the functions and hierarchical relationships that these centers had had in ancient times (Spanu 2006).

The Mountainous Areas and the Pastoral Economy

What forms did settlement take in the mountainous territories, where geographical factors did not allow extensive cultivation and where stock-breeding was most widespread?

Sardinia, at the time of the Roman conquest in 238/37 B.C., had vast areas inhabited by native populations, in particular the *Ilienses, Balari,* and *Corsi* (Raimondo Zucca, in Mastino 2005: 306–315). These peoples experienced harsh encounters with Rome, and by the first century B.C. they had been relegated to the inland regions of the island, an area contemptuously defined by the Romans as *Barbaria*, a place inhabited by Barbarians (Farre 2016a). As we will see, these territories were divided into *civitates*; they made an act of submission to Rome and could certainly develop trade with the cities and other centres of the coast and plains. Yet the people who lived in the inland regions must have represented a constant danger to the hegemonic power not only of Rome, but also in Vandal and Byzantine times. Perhaps the *Barbaricini* and their territorial organization represent a real phenomenon of resilience, recognizable in the *longue durée*. We want to dwell on this here, analyzing different types of sources.

But first, another consideration is necessary. The ancient sources have helped to foster the image of a divided ancient Sardinia, defined by a sharp contrast between flat areas and mountainous territories, the latter inhabited exclusively by shepherds involved in nomadic pastoralism and in constant conflict with agricultural farmers working on the plains (Spanu 2015: 29–31, 37–39). Nowadays this vision seems outdated, in part thanks to archaeological research. This contrast, reflecting different ethnic and political positions, appears problematic, since it should be contextualized and not generalized, given the broad chronological span involved. Space does not allow us to explore the problem in greater depth, so we simply refer to the most recent discussions that have tended to critique this traditional vision of a 'bipartite' Sardinia (Guido 2006; Trudu 2012a; Ibba 2015: 11, 51–52; Stiglitz 2015; Farre 2016a; 2016b: 7).

But let us come to the core of the matter.

Vandals and Byzantines in Sardinia

The establishment of the Vandal kingdom of Africa, sanctioned by a peace treaty signed by the Emperor Valentinian III and the Vandal Genseric in A.D. 442, did not exhaust the expansionist aims of the Germanic population, which had initially been pushed from southeastern Europe as far as the Iberian peninsula and then to coastal areas in North Africa. Unable to go southwards, given the hostility of indigenous peoples (although in reality they were not very interested in the unproductive desert regions), the Vandals began to move by sea: after the seizure of important ports in Sicily in 440, and the sack of Rome in 455, the interests of Genserico turned to other islands of the western Mediterranean (Aiello 2014: 117–126). Although the written sources are not explicit in this regard, Sardinia, together with Corsica, probably endured for some time as still subject to the payment of heavy taxes to Rome. In any case, the conquest of these two islands, given their position, was fully part of the expansionist interests of Genserico—like the Balearic Islands, which fell into the hands of the Vandals in those same years. Sardinia and Corsica could on the one hand guarantee control of the traffic taking place in the western Mediterranean basin, in particular the goods destined for the *annona*; but the system of islands could also guarantee the Vandal state a first position for the defense of Africa, the location of its central government. On the basis of some less than explicit indications in the sources, the conquest probably took place between 460 and 467. The fact that these sources do not refer to any warlike action suggests that the Vandals did not encounter much resistance, perhaps thanks to the support of prominent individuals and *possessores*, crushed by the increasing pressure of the tax authorities (Spanu, in Mastino 2005: 499–500; Spanu and Zucca 2014: 39–42; Ibba 2010: 397–400).

More information is available on the collapse of the Vandal kingdom in Africa and on the Byzantines' conquest of Sardinia, between 533 and 534. These happened to be fundamental events for the politics of Justinian, whose main policy objective was the *restauratio* of the Empire (Spanu 1998: 14–16; Spanu, in Mastino 2005: 504–507). It should be noted that the sources allow us to define a picture of the political and institutional aspects of this period that saw Rome, the Vandals, and Byzantium in possession of Sardinia. On some aspects, however, we still know very little: little thought has been given to the relationships between the hegemonic powers and indigenous peoples, nor to the identification of signs of major transformations and elements of continuity and resilience. Nonetheless, we can deduce from the sources that no great changes occurred in the Vandal age. The foreign presence was in fact limited to (i) the ruling classes (the Godas gothus governing the island at the end of the Vandal kingdom is an example: see Ibba 2010: 402–404; 2017);

(ii) the military elements; (iii) members of the African Church, including prominent figures exiled by the Arian Vandals because they were faithful to Catholic orthodoxy (Artizzu 1996; Pani Ermini 1988: 299–301; Turtas 1999: 85–98; Martorelli 2010: 453–457, 470–484); and, perhaps, (iv) recipients of *sortes* (i.e., fiscal lands; Ibba 2010: 409–411), among whom family groups of rebellious *Mauri* exiled by the Vandals could also be included.

The same must have happened following the Byzantine conquest, when the need for military control certainly led to a stronger presence of soldiers of different origins. One type of evidence for this can be seen in the data provided by the military equipment frequently found on the island (e.g., those of San Giorgio of Sinis, now in the process of being published: Spanu and Zucca 2004: 79–86; Panico 2012–2013). Also from outside the island were probably the officials who, with different assignments, represented the power of Byzantium (such as the *Nikitas mizoteros* of the lead seal found in Siurgus-Cagliari: Spanu and Zucca 2008: 148–154).

Mauri and *Barbarikinoi* as Cited in Procopius and Gregory the Great

The events relating to the *Barbarikinoi* mentioned by Procopius and later by Gregory the Great are interesting for an understanding of the problematic relationships between indigenous and foreign peoples, in order to identify elements of resilience in Sardinia during these centuries.

Procopius, in *De Bello Vandalico*, informs us that the Vandals from Africa had transported for exile in Sardinia some groups of the *Mauri* barbarians, along with their wives. These groups would have reached *ta ore… Karanaleos eggys*, which is generally understood by most scholars as 'the mountains near Carales' (Procopius, *Vand.* II.13.44) (Figure 3.2). No fewer than 3,000 of these *Mauri*, as Procopius states, were the instigators of raids in the surrounding areas, and for this reason they were named *Barbarikinoi* by the same people who lived in the neighbouring territories—that is, the Sardinians of inner Barbaria. During the winter of 537, in order to limit these incursions and to repel the *Barbarikinoi* within the territories from which they had moved, the Prefect of the Pretorio Solomon organized a military expedition against them (Procopius, *Vand.* II.13.45).

The identification of the location of the territories where these *Mauri* (defined as *Barbaricini* by the historian officer of the Emperor Justinian) settled poses many problems (Ibba 2010: 405–409). On the other hand, the imperial *constitutio* of Justinian himself (A.D. 534), in which the Byzantine emperor established the seat of the highest military charge on the island (the *dux*), is clearer in this regard: *iuxta montes ubi Barbaricini*

Figure 3.2. According to Procopius' *De bello vandalico*, the Vandals exiled rebel *Mauri* groups (later termed *Barbarikinoi*) to Sardinia and perhaps settled in the mountains near Karales (black triangles); Justinian's *Constitutio* of A.D. 534 settled the seat of the *dux* at Forum Traiani, near the mountains inhabited by the *Barbaricini* (white triangles).

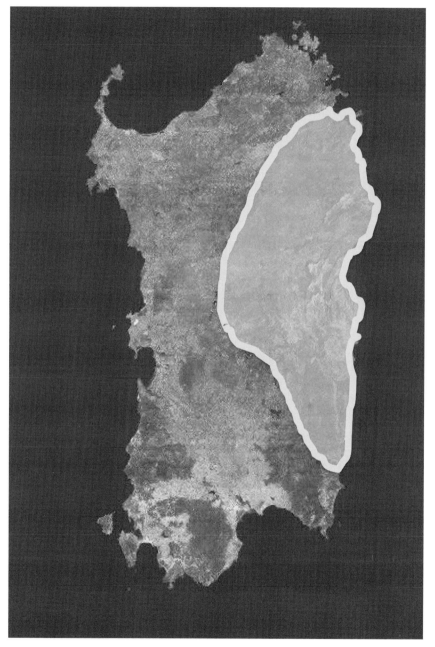

Figure 3.3. Hypothetical extension of the *Barbariae* in east-central Sardinia.

videntur sedere (Codex Justinianus, *De officio* I, 27, 2, 3) (Figure 3.2); many scholars concur in locating these mountains at *Forum Traiani*, in an area on the border between the fertile plains of west-central Sardinia and the mountainous inland territories of the island. Yet Procopius himself in *De Aedificiis*, after mentioning the fortifications ordered by Justinian at *Forum Traiani*, adds that despite these defensive preparations, the *Mauri*, whom they call *Barbaricini*, managed to seize the city whenever they wanted (Procopius, *De Aedificiis* VI.7. 12–13).[2] It is clear that the *Barbaricini* are located in the mountains that dominate *Forum Traiani* (*contra* this interpretation, see Serra 2006b: 306–308), so if we do not suppose a corruption of Procopius' excerpt in which there is a reference to the *Mauri* rebel population, called *Barbaricini*, who lived in the mountains near *Carales* (Procop. *Vand.* II, 13, 44), we must admit a transfer or movement of the *Mauri* – *Barbarikinoi* in the neighbouring areas of *Forum Traiani*, taking place prior to A.D. 534 (Spanu 1998: 174). We should not, however, overestimate the numerical and cultural importance of Procopius' *Mauri*, disdainfully assimilated by the court historian of Constantinople to the Barbarians/*Barbaricini* of Sardinia.

In any case, in subsequent sources we do not hear of the *Mauri* – *Barbarikinoi* of Sardinia, but only of the *Barbaricini*. From comparative examination of linguistics, toponymy, onomastics, and archaeological documentation, it is evident that they derived from the protohistoric world of Sardinia, in conflict first with the Carthaginians, then with the Romans, with the Byzantines, and on through the rebelliousness documented in the Middle Ages. In fact, it should not be excluded that the *Barbaricini* could extend over a much wider area, corresponding to a circumscribed territory, endowed with a certain autonomy and which, as we will see, could include wide areas of east-central Sardinia (Spanu 2000: 501, 511–516, 2008a: 360–361, n. 38; Farre 2016a: 91–92; *contra* Guido 2006: 1–3, 50–53) (Figure 3.3).

Another reference to the animosity of the *Barbaricini* is offered by the letters of Gregory the Great, where reference is made to the peace stipulated between the Byzantines and the *dux* of the *Barbaricini*, Ospitone (*Ep.* IV, 25). The terms of the treaty brokered between the Byzantine *dux* Zabarda and Ospitone are not known, but it seems clear that the presence of a diplomatic agreement itself indicates the official recognition by the representatives of the imperial power of a well-defined political and military entity; to this recognition is added that of the highest religious authority of Christianity. At the time of Mauritius Tiberius (A.D. 594), the literary source seems to indicate the existence of a sort of autonomous kingdom where the populations inhabiting the centre of Sardinia and organized into tribes gathered together (Spanu 2000). As the archaeological sources show, the people of the *Barbariae* carried out raids and looting, of which traces exist—for example, in the shrine of the martyr Luxurius at *Forum Traiani* (Spanu 1998: 72).

The Location of the Sardinian *Barbariae*

Further references to the *Barbaricini* are found in the hagiographic sources, relevant among which is the Life of Saint Senzio of Blera and his associate Mamiliano, like Senzio also a priest, written around the eighth century by a monk of the islands of the Tuscan archipelago.[3] The story narrates the escape from Arian Africa of the two presbyters, Senzius and Mamilianus, accompanied by three monks, Covuldus, Istochius, and Infans. The various references to Sardinia demonstrate direct knowledge by the author of the topography of the island: of particular importance is the episode in which the characters, after being abandoned on a small island located near the east coast of Sardinia, are saved by a *parva navicula* (small vessel), coming *ex partibus Barbariae, quae subiacet in potestate Sardiniae*. From this excerpt, it is clear that the mountainous territories of *Barbariae* had an outlet to the sea, probably the coastal regions neighbouring the Gulf of Orosei (Spanu 2008a: 360–361, n. 38).

Late Antique and Early Medieval sources therefore confirm that the Sardinian Barbariae[4] came to gravitate around *Forum Traiani*, from which comes an inscription (Figure 3.4), found in the Roman baths, dedicated by the *civitates Barbariae* to the emperor Tiberius (Sotgiu 1961: 126–127, n. 188):

> [—Caesa]ri Aug(usto) p[ont(ifici) max(imo)—]
> [—civ]itates Barb[ariae —]
> [—prae]f(ecto) provincia[e Sard(iniae)—][5]

Reference to such *civitates* can be found in a previous inscription (*CIL* XIV: 314, n. 2954) from Praeneste in Latium that mentions a figure of equestrian rank, Sextus Iulius Rufus, son of Sextus, inscribed in the Pollia tribe, who under Augustus had simultaneously to manage the command of the *cohors prima Corsorum* and the prefecture of the *civitates* of *Barbaria* in Sardinia:

> Sex(tus) Iulius S(purii) f(ilius) Pol(lia tribu) Rufus
> evocatus Divi Augusti
> praefectus I cohortis
> Corsorum et civitatum
> Barbariae in Sardinia[6]

The simultaneous management of these prefectures seems to be linked to the fact that, in order to exercise the prefecture on the Barbariae *civitates*, it

Figure 3.4. Forum Traiani (Fordongianus, Oristano): inscription found in the Roman baths, dedicated by the civitates *Barbariae* to the emperor Tiberius. (After Zucca 2016b.)

was necessary to have a military force that acted as a deterrent against the always resurgent rebellious population of the Barbariae (Zucca 2016a: 213).

These *civitates*, known in the Early Imperial age, could correspond to "cantons" without cities—i.e., territorial districts inhabited by non-urbanized populations who lived in small settlements, but who nonetheless had developed some degree of organization. In this regard, it is appropriate to recall other areas, such as Germany and Gaul, in which *pagi* and *vici* lacked a corresponding *urbs*, even though acting as political and administrative units (Simbula and Spanu 2012: 572–576; Spanu 2012: 152–155).

This is not to say that these local forms of organization were indications of limited Roman penetration of the interior areas of the island, or of a lack of Roman control in these mountainous territories; rather, we should consider the level of Romanization and to what extent it might have affected indigenous populations (Spanu 2012: 161, n. 50). The presence of Rome in these areas is in fact attested at various archaeological sites and by the existence of the *via per mediterranea* that crossed them in a north–south direction (Mastino 2005). The *via* and its infrastructure survived until at least the Early Byzantine period (Spanu 2002: 115–117). Among the more interesting locations is Sant'Efis of Orune, where archaeological investigations have brought to light a settlement, possibly abandoned by the end of the fifth century A.D., which played an important role as a redistribution center for the territory, as evidenced by many imported artefacts, some of high value; unfortunately, however, it is not possible to specify the legal-administrative status of this center. Fabrizio Delussu has compared it in general terms to the so-called "small-towns" in Britain, or rather to the *agglomérations secondaires* (Delussu 2008; 2009). It is likely that this center owed its fortune to the proximity of the road axis (Spanu 2012: 155; Delussu 2012: 57; on these types of settlements, see also Trudu 2014).

In the case of Sardinia, and not only for the *Barbaria* territories (which only partially corresponded to modern-day "Barbagie"), it seems plausible that these territorial structures—the *civitates*—were the continuation of organizational forms that had already existed in the Nuragic age, in the second and first millennia B.C. These had forms of population and territorial organization of the "cantonal" type, in which there existed a hierarchical organization of settlement agglomerations, variable in number, such as simple and complex Nuraghi, villages, cemeteries, places of worship, trade, and production, all functionally interdependent (Usai 2003; 2006; Depalmas 2006). These forms of organization and management of the territory must have survived through the Carthaginian and Roman ages.

It can therefore be hypothesized that even in several *populi* known from numerous Roman sources, and widely located in various parts of Sardinia, including those of the *Barbariae civitates*, similar social and territorial structures were in place. These were probably still in existence during the Justinianic age among the *Barbarikinoi* cited by Procopius, in the area upstream of *Forum Traiani*, where the seat of the Byzantine *dux* in Sardinia was established. Still in the Byzantine age, these territories were controlled by a series of small *castra* presumably guarded by soldier-colonists who settled there with their families, often making use of existing structures (Spanu 1998: 173–190).

The Onomastics of Inland Sardinia between Antiquity and the Middle Ages

The ethnonyms, passed down in the literary and epigraphic sources that concern the Sardinian people, indicate a clear paleosardinian matrix (e.g., *Nurritani, Ilienses, Balari, Celsitani, Cunusitani*). Zucca (2016b: 407) asserts that these ethnic names are in reality heteronyms; in other words, they represent names that Greeks and Romans attributed to the Sardinian *ethne*, perhaps deriving from an actual paleosard root, and that did not necessarily correspond to the name the individual *ethne* used to define themselves. This is also reflected in the anthroponomastics documented in the Latin epigraphic texts of Barbaria, as noted long ago by Theodor Mommsen (*CIL* X: 816), later by Gasperini (1992a; 1992b), Mastino (1993: 57–58), and Zucca (1990b; 1999: 58–75, 2002: 118–119), and, more recently, by Ibba (2006) and Farre (2016b: 12–13). The continuation of this onomastic system into the Early Middle Ages is confirmed by its attestation in the first sphragistic, epigraphic, and paper or parchment documents of the Judgeship of Sardinia, beginning in the eleventh century.

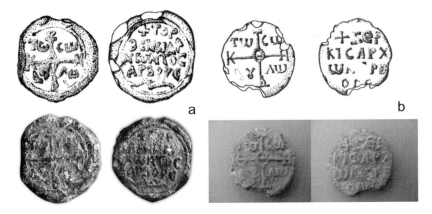

Figure 3.5. Cabras, San Giorgio: a) Seal of the *archon* Torbennios (eleventh to twelfth centuries A.D.); b) seal of the *archon* Zerchis (eleventh century A.D.)

Contrary to common opinion, derived from Serra's seminal research (1949: 225–230) on personal names of Greek-Byzantine origin among members of the Judgeship or noble families of the Sardinian Middle Ages, the most recent studies by Paulis (1983: 182–198) and Bortolami (2000: 194–195) have shown that the attribution of such names to Byzantine influence must be entirely reconsidered. Furthermore, for the dynastic names of Torchitorio and Salusio, and for the names of various judges, such as *Orthoccor, Ithoccor,* or *Zerchis* (Figure 3.5a), such influence should be excluded and these names instead attributed (with greater or lesser certainty) to their paleosardinian linguistic context.

The earliest mention of an *Orthoccor*—problematic to identify, but probably a member of the judicial family—can be found in the Greek inscription on the shelf-lintel of a *ciborium*, from a now-destroyed church located between Villasor and Decimoputzu, near Cagliari (Figure 3.6a). The inscription should be dated to the middle of the tenth century (Coroneo 2000: 217–218, cat. 4.2; for the medieval Byzantine dedicatory inscriptions of southern Sardinia, see Coroneo 1995: 103–112). One of the two *Orzokor archons,* known from the Judgement of Arborea between the end of the eleventh and the beginning of the twelfth century, can be recognized on a lead seal in Greek characters, perhaps coming from San Giorgio of Sinis, near *Tharros* (Spanu and Zucca 2004: 146–147, n. 78).

Numerous characters named *Ithoccor* belonged to different families of judges and other noble families (Brook et al. 1984), while among those who bear the name *Zerchis* must certainly be the *archon* of Arborea, recognizable on another lead seal written in Greek characters found in the area of San

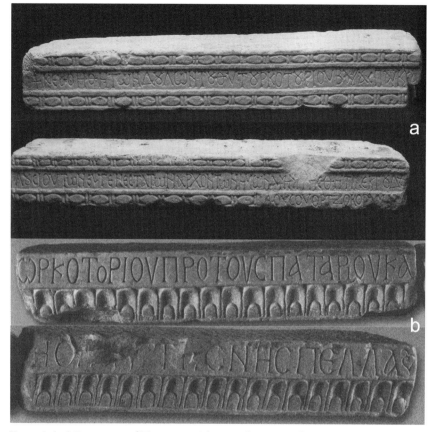

Figure 3.6. a) Inscription of Torcotorio, Salusio and Orztocor from Santa Sofia of Villasor (Cagliari), currently in the museum of Cagliari (tenth century A.D.); b) Inscription of Torcotorio, Salusio and Nispella in the catacombs of Sant'Antioco (tenth century A.D.). (After Coroneo 2000.)

Giorgio of Sinis (Spanu andv Zucca 2004: 145–146, n. 77). This is perhaps the same individual who lived in the middle of the eleventh century and was mentioned in a *charta* of the Condaghe of Santa Maria of Bonarcado; a reference to the donation of land properties located in an inland area of Sardinia, close to the Barbagie, occurs in a document transcribed within the Condaghe (Virdis 2002: 53–54, n. 66). At least so far as *Orthoccor* and *Ithoccor* are concerned, Bortolami (2000: 184, 195) believes that these names belong to a paleosardinian linguistic stratum, and he also suggests that the name *Zerchi(s)* is a Byzantine form derived from *Sergius*.

On the basis of Latin epigraphic documents from the middle valley of the Tirso (in western *Barbaria*), however, we can prove that a series of anthroponyms of judges are already attested in the first to second centuries A.D. in inland areas of the island and these should refer back to a paleosardinian stratum.

In fact, we have *Torbenius/Torvenius*, the same name as the *iudex arborensis Torbenius* de Lacon (Brook et al. 1984: 163; I, 15), documented in the form *Torbennios archon* on a Greek seal (Spanu et al. 2013: 529–531) (Figure 3.5b), and in a document of the Judgeship of Arborea dated to A.D. 1102 (Tola 1861: 165–166, sec. XI, doc. XXII, best dated in later editions such as Blasco Ferrer 2003: I, 99–103). It occurs twice in Busachi:

> *D(is) M(anibus) /*
> *Torbenius /*
> *Kariti (filius) vixit /*
> *an(n)is LXX. Fili(i) patri bene meranti*
>> (Farre 2016b: 65–66, BUS006; first decades of the second century A.D.)

> *D(is) M(anibus) /*
> *[T]uri Torveni (filius) /*
> *[v]i(xit) an(nis) LXII. F(ecit) Tu /*
> *marg coiu /*
> *gi. Fruniti /*
> *an(norum) XXXXVIIII f(ecit) b(ene) m(erenti)*
>> (Farre 2016b: 74–75, BUS013; end of the first and the first decades of second century A.D.)

It also occurs once in Ula Tirso:

> *D(is) M(anibus) /*
> *L(ucius) Valerius Torbe /*
> *nius Iunior vixit an /*
> *norum XXVII. Pla /*
> *utia Acutia mater /*
> *fecit*
>> (Farre 2016b: 162–164, ULA008; second half of second century A.D.)

Iettocor is documented in Busachi:

> *Ietoccor Torc /*
> *eri filius vix /*
> *it annis XXXII. /*
> *Fecit pater filio suo*
>> (Farre 2016b: 76–78, BUS015; second half of the first century A.D.)

Nispelli is known in Ula Tirso:

> *D(is) M(anibus) /*
> *Nispelli Pipedionis f(ilius) vix /*
> *it annis LXXVI s(emis) I*
>> (Farre 2016b: 159–160, ULA003; end of the first and the first decades of the second century A.D.).

This last anthroponym, moreover, reappears in the Middle Ages among the members of the judicial families. In fact, a *Nispella* is remembered, together with her husband *Torcotorio* and *Salusio*, in the Greek inscription from the Sant'Antioco catacombs (Coroneo 2000: 240–241, cat. 13.8), and in two more epigraphs, also in Greek, from the San Giovanni Battista church in Assemini (CA), all dated between the end of the tenth and the beginning of the eleventh century A.D. (Coroneo 2000: 208–209, cat. 1.2 e 1.4) (Figure 3.6b).

It is also important to note that *Hospito*, the *dux Barbaricinorum* known from the correspondence of Pope Gregory the Great (*Ep.* IV, 25), bears an anthroponym characterized by the paleosardinian root *OSP- (Bortolami 2000: 181). In fact, Paulis (1987: 443) has included the following place names in his paleosardinian series: *Osp-ai* (Nuoro; Olzai, Nulvi), *Osp-e* (Oliena), *Osp-è* (Pattada), *Osp-ene* (Oliena, Dorgali), *Osp-idd-ai* (Oliena), *Osp-ola* (Posada, San Teodoro), *Osp-olo* (Siniscola), *Osp-olocos* (Urzulei), *Osp-oro* (Cargeghe, Siniscola), *Osp-orr-ai* (Orgosolo, Oliena), and *Osp-os-idda* (Orgosolo).

Settlement Models and Economic Structures of Rural Communities in Late Antique and Early Medieval Sardinia

There are no certainties about the settlement patterns and economic structures that characterized such rural communities during these centuries. There do exist sufficient data, however, to identify elements of resilience in the frequent reoccupation of protohistoric settlements already as early as Roman times, but particularly in the period between Late Antiquity and the Early Middle Ages.

The percentage of Nuragic settlements at which reoccupation in the Roman era is attested is very high—as much as 85% according to an estimate made in the early 1990s (Webster and Teglund 1992: 466). But it should be remembered that in this and other cases the chronological definitions are rather broad and may include Nuraghi and Nuragic contexts with Late Antique and/or Early Middle Age occupation. The intensification of field research and, above all, the refinement of archaeological methods of survey and excavation now allow us to read the data in broader context, even if the number of systematic investigations is still limited. Among many contributions to these questions, those of Lilliu (1990), Pala (1990), and Rowland (2001: 123–124, 138–139) still remain valid, and it is also worth mentioning the 2012 Congress held in Cagliari, entitled *Daedaleia: Le torri nuragiche oltre l'età del Bronzo*, whose proceedings include various contributions on both individual sites and wider territorial analysis. Among relevant case studies (not limited to the areas discussed here), for example, are those in the territory of *Forum Traiani* (Dyson and Rowland 1989), in the *ager Bosanus* (Biagini 1998: 688–693), in Montiferru and northern Campidano (Maisola 2011–2012; 2015a; 2015b), in the *ager Tharrensis* (Panico 2015–2016; 2016; Panico and Spanu 2016; 2018), in the territory of Dorgali (Delussu 2016), in Trexenta and Gerrei (Serra 2016), and in Marmilla and Sarcidano (Trudu 2016; Muresu 2016).

Despite the large number of examples, there are still few contexts where systematic investigations and stratigraphic excavations have taken place. Nonetheless, a few significant instances show that, centuries or even millennia later, settlement choices were being made that were similar to those of Nuragic people. That is, small rural communities, mostly reliant on subsistence self-sufficiency, existed in a poor economy that forced them to exploit the pre-existing resources found on the site as much as possible, including structures—evidently ruined, but with substantial parts still standing—now reused for different types of functions: as places of residence, for production or storage, and sometimes as "elite" funerary structures. Nuraghe San Pietro of Torpé (NU), probably used as a granary between the fifth and sixth centuries, is a good example (D'Oriano 1985; Spanu 1998: 125).

The members of such communities were able to produce the items necessary for their needs, including ceramic containers for cooking and storing food, even if these products, because they were technologically and formally impoverished, had a very modest distribution. These poor communities (even single-family ones) likewise consumed imported products, albeit to a limited extent. Characterized by a mixed economy and the variable exploitation of resources, scattered settlement is attested in these centuries in northeastern Sardinia as well (Campus 2004: 161–165). It is conceivable that settlements of this kind may sometimes be recognized in those rural villages where the villas and farms are found, inhabited by peasants who worked in the agricultural structures connected to the production centers (Spanu 2012: 153–154; Simbula and Spanu 2012: 574–575).

An example can be seen at Nuraghe Nuracale in the territory of Scano Montiferro, in west-central Sardinia, located in a central area of the Montiferru mountain range. Different parts of the megalithic structure, in particular the upper compartment of the circular central tower and the adjacent courtyard, were reoccupied between the fifth and sixth centuries A.D. Materials found in the occupation layers included containers for the preservation of foodstuffs and, above all, ceramics shaped by hand on the slow wheel, probably locally produced, in standardized forms that are attested with increasing frequency on Sardinia at this time (generically defined as *céramique modelée*). In addition to the reoccupation of the tower and courtyard, in the same centuries other facilities were built from re-used materials, some of which overlap or lean against the Nuragic structures (Usai et al. 2009; 2011) (Figure 3.7). Considering its position and the nature of the archaeological finds there, Nuraghe Nuracale could well have been inhabited by a small rural community that survived thanks to the diverse resources of its territory, in an economy of self-sufficiency, but one also open to a wider

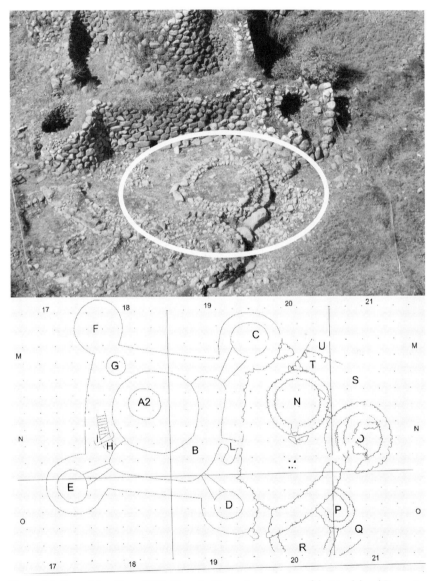

Figure 3.7. Scano Montiferro (OR), Nuraghe Nuracale: structures of the Vandal and Byzantine periods.

Figure 3.8. Milis (OR), Nuraghe Cobulas: the protohistoric monument and (outlined) Late Antique structures (fourth to seventh centuries A.D.) (after Usai et al. 2009).

range of traffic, as some of the artefacts indeed indicate (Usai et al. 2011: 793–795).

Among the Nuragic monuments that may have been connected to productive settlements, we may recall the case of Su Nuraxi of Sisini, in the province of Cagliari; rectangular structures were built next to this Nuraghe, probably in the sixth century A.D. to judge from the associated material culture (Soddu 2005). It is interesting to note that the territory in which the Nuraghe is located had had a high level of agricultural production since ancient times. Economic and fiscal organization that was certainly based on the Roman imperial heritage passed to the Constantinopolitan *patrimonium*, as is testified by the discovery of a seal of *Nikitas mizoteros*—in other words, an official responsible for the control of production on the imperial properties of Byzantium, active in an area close to Su Nuraxi of Sisini (Spanu and Zucca 2008: 148–160).

Similarly, investigations have very recently been carried out in the Cobulas Nuraghe of Milis. These document reoccupation of the site between the fourth and seventh centuries A.D., with the construction of houses and other structures dedicated to production leaning up against the Nuraghe,

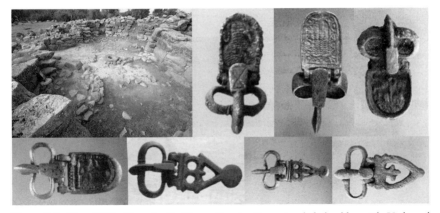

Figure 3.9. Uras (OR), Nuraghe Sa Domu Beccia: Byzantine belt buckles with U-shaped plaque and of Corinth- and Balgota-types, found in tower A and in the courtyard (after Serra 2002b).

and these appear to confirm a connection between the small settlement and the intensive agrarian exploitation of its territory, on the border of the fertile plains of the northern Campidano (Santoni et al. 1991; Serra 1995: 188–193, tables 10–16) (Figure 3.8). These new excavations at Cobulas Nuraghe have been directed by the present author in collaboration with Giuseppe Maisola, and the results are in process of publication. Other significant examples of the reuse of Nuraghi in Late Antiquity and Early Medieval times have been discussed by Serra (2008).

The reuse of Sardinian megalithic towers of the Middle and Recent Bronze Age (16th–13th centuries B.C.) as mausolea is documented in various parts of the island and becomes particularly important during the Byzantine period (Spanu 1998: 125–128). Aside from cases of reappropriation of these same towers for Byzantine troops—as is clearly visible at Sa Domu Beccia in Uras (OR) (Serra 2002b, 2008: 734–737) (Figure 3.9) and Su Nuraxi, adjacent to the St Teodoro church in Siurgus (CA) (Ugas and Serra 1990) (Figure 3.10), just two of many examples—there is evidence of Sardinian people from the *Barbaria* reusing Nuraghi and Giants' Tombs for their burials (Farre 2017: 47–50).

The framework we have outlined here seems to indicate a socio-political organization in inland Barbaria that, in the *longue durée*, shows some constant elements. We can identify the establishment of new cultural traditions, alongside more long-established ones. There is, for example, the persistence of well-established forms of structures and settlements, in conjunction with innovations in technology, such as the import of ceramics and metal artefacts. The neo-Latin Sardinian language, influenced by Byzantine lexemes, existed

Figure 3.10. Siurgus (Ca), Nuraghe Su Nuraxi, photo, plan, and section; in level 2B there were mounds with Byzantine funerary remains (after Ugas and Serra 1990).

alongside a palaeosard toponymy which even today comprises more than half of the local toponyms in the interior of Barbagia (Paulis 1987: XI–XXIV, 423–456; Wolf 1998: 19–89). And, finally, the Christian religion was practiced alongside widespread forms of popular medical and magical traditions that were part of the established framework of protohistoric religion (Spanu 2008b: 1057–1067, 1076–1077).

Acknowledgements

It is my duty to thank my friends and colleagues Catalina Mas Florit, Miguel Ángel Cau Ontiveros and Peter van Dommelen for their invitation and excellent hospitality, and Raimondo Zucca for discussing with me some of the issues presented in this paper.

Notes

1. See Ravennatis *Anonymi Cosmographia et Guidonis Geographica,* ed. M. Pinder and G. Partney, Berolini 1860, V, 26: 411–413; *Itinerarium Antonini* (*Itin. Anton. Aug.*), ed. P. Wesseling, Amsterdam 1735: 82–84).
2. The first link to be made between this excerpt from *De aedificiis* and the *Barbarikinoi* problem can be found in Zucca 1990a: 182–183, from which later contributions derive: Spanu 1998: 173–175; Turtas 1999: 100–101, n. 7; Vacca 2002: 189–192, 198; see also Guido 2006: 338, n. 131, and above all the broad analysis in Serra 2006a: 1293–1300; 2006b.
3. *Vita ss. Senzii et Mamiliani* (*BHL* 7581, 7582, 7582b); *Acta Sanctorum de Sancto Senzio presbitero, Blerae in Hetruria. Commentarius praevius*, in *Acta Sanctorum, Maii,*

tomus VI, Antuerpiae 1687: 70–73. The contribution of this source to the history of Early Medieval Sardinia has already been analysed in Spanu 2000: 505–508, and 2008a: 360–362, to which reference should be made for analysis of the Sardinian episode of the hagiographic account and for the dating issues.

4. On the problem of the *civitates Barbariae* see in particular Zucca 1988; Spanu 2000; Zucca, in Mastino 2005: 306–311; Guido 2006; Serra 2006a; 2006b; Mayer 2009; Simbula and Spanu 2012: 572, n. 30; Spanu 2012: 161, n. 35; Trudu 2012a; 2012b; 2014: 111–113; Farre 2016a; Zucca 2016a: 213–215.

5. On this inscription see Zucca 1988: 349; Mastino 2005: 126, 309–310, 394; Ibba 2006: 14–15; Mayer 2009: 45–46; Faoro 2011: 60–64; Zucca 2016a: 214; Farre 2016b: 106–108.

6. See Zucca 1988: 349; Mastino 2005: 309, 395; Ibba 2006: 15; Mayer 2009: 46–49; Faoro 2011: 49–55, 95; Farre 2016a: 91. Guido (2006: 50–51) is the only scholar to report the hypothesis, one that is difficult to accept, that in the inscription a reference is made to a department composed of *Corsi* and elements of the now-pacified *civitates*.

References

Ep. = V. Recchia 1996–1999, *Opere di Gregorio Magno: Lettere*. Città Nuova, Roma.

Aiello, Vincenzo
    2014   I Vandali nel Wentisleo. In *Guerrieri, mercanti e profughi nel mare dei Vandali. Atti del Convegno Internazionale (Messina, 7–8 ottobre 2009)*, edited by Vincenzo Aiello, pp. 111–126. Pelorias 22. DICAM, Messina.

Artizzu, Giovanna
    1996   La Sardegna e la politica religiosa dei re vandali. *Studi Sardi* 30 (1992–1993): 497–512.

Bartoloni, Piero
    1996   *La necropoli di Bitia I*. Consiglio Nazionale delle Ricerche, Roma.

Biagini, Marco
    1998   Archeologia del territorio nell'Ager Bosanus: ricognizioni di superficie nel comune di Magomadas (Nuoro). In *L'Africa romana. Atti del XII convegno di studio (Olbia, 13–15 dicembre 1996)*, edited by Paola Ruggeri and Cinzia Vismara, pp. 667–693. Editrice Democratica Sarda, Sassari.

Blasco Ferrer, Eduardo
    2002   *Crestomazia sarda dei primi secoli*. Ilisso, Nuoro.

Bortolami, Sante
    2000   Antroponimia e società nella Sardegna medioevale: caratteri ed evoluzione di un 'sistema' regionale. In *Giudicato d'Arborea e Marchesato d'Oristano: proiezioni mediterranee e aspetti di storia locale. Atti del Convegno internazionale di studi (Oristano, 5–8 dicembre 1997)*, I, edited by Giampaolo Mele, pp. 175–252. ISTAR, Oristano.

Brook, Lindsay Leonard, Francesco Cesare Casula, María Mercedes Costa, Anna Maria Oliva, Romeo Pavoni, and Marco Tangheroni (editors)
    1984   *Genealogie medioevali di Sardegna*. Due D editrice mediterranea, Cagliari-Sassari.

Campus, Franco G.R.

2004   L'insediamento umano: processi formativi e dinamiche di trasformazione nel medioevo (secc. VI-XIV). In *Oschiri, Castro e il Logudoro Orientale*, edited by Giuseppe Meloni and Pier Giorgio Spanu, pp. 151–188. Carlo Delfino Editore, Sassari.

CIL X

1883   *Corpus Inscriptionum Latinarum. X. Pars posterior, Inscriptiones Siciliae et Sardiniae*, edidit Theodorus Mommsen. Berolini apud Georgium Reimerium.

CIL XIV

1887   *Corpus Inscriptionum Latinarum. XIV. Inscriptiones Latii Veteris latinae*, edidit Hermannus Dessau. Berolini apud Georgium Reimerium.

Colavitti, Anna Maria

1996   Per una storia dell'economia della Sardegna romana: grano ed organizzazione del territorio. Spunti per una ricerca. In *L'Africa romana. Atti dell'XI Convegno di studio (Sassari, 15–18 dicembre 1994)*, edited by Attilio Mastino, pp. 643–652. Editrice Il Torchietto, Ozieri.

Coroneo, Roberto

1995   Marmi epigrafici mediobizantini e identità culturale greco-latina a Cagliari nel secolo X. *Archivio Storico Sardo* 38: 103–121.

2000   *Scultura mediobizantina in Sardegna*. Poliedro, Nuoro.

Cosentino, Salvatore

2002   Potere e istituzioni nella Sardegna bizantina. In *Ai confini dell'Impero: storia, arte e archeologia della Sardegna bizantina*, edited by Paola Corrias and Salvatore Cosentino, pp. 1–13. M & T, Cagliari.

Delussu, Fabrizio

2008   L'insediamento romano di Sant'Efis (Orune, Nuoro): scavi 2004–06. Nota preliminare. In *Le ricchezze dell'Africa. Risorse, produzioni, scambi. Atti del XVII convegno di studio su L'Africa romana (Sevilla, 14–17 dicembre 2006)*, edited by Julián González, Paola Ruggeri, Cinzia Vismara, and Raimondo Zucca, pp. 2657–2671. Carocci, Roma.

2009   La Barbagia in età romana: gli scavi 2004–2008 nell'insediamento di Sant'Efis (Orune, Nuoro). *FOLD&R. The Journal of Fasti Online*: 1–8.

2012   Note sulla romanizzazione del territorio di Orune. In *Historica et philologica: studi in onore di Raimondo Turtas*, edited by Mauro G. Sanna, pp. 48–68. Collezione Agorà 54. AM & D Edizioni, Cagliari.

2016   Il riutilizzo dei nuraghi in età romana nel territorio di Dorgali. In *Daedaleia: le torri nuragiche oltre l'età del Bronzo. Atti del Convegno di Studi (Cagliari, 19–21 aprile 2012)*, edited by Enrico Trudu, Giacomo Paglietti, and Marco Muresu. *Layers. Archeologia, Territorio, Contesti* 1: 128–144.

Depalmas, Anna

2006   Guerra e pace nell'interpretazione dell'architettura nuragica. In *Studi di protostoria in onore di Renato Peroni*, pp. 567–572. All'Insegna del Giglio, Firenze.

D'Oriano, Rubens
    1985   Torpé (Nuoro). Notiziario. *Nuovo Bullettino Archeologico Sardo* 1 (1984): 381.
Dyson Stephen L., and Robert J. Rowland Jr
    1989   The University of Maryland-Wesleyan University Survey in Sardinia – 1988. *Quaderni della Soprintendenza Archeologica per le province di Cagliari e Oristano* 6: 157–185.
Faoro, Davide
    2011   *Praefectus, procurator, praeses: genesi delle cariche presidiali equestri nell'Alto Impero Romano*. Le Monnier, Milano.
Farre, Claudio
    2016a   Alcune considerazioni sulla Barbaria: definizione, percezione e dinamiche di romanizzazione della Sardegna interna. In *Il processo di romanizzazione della provincia Sardinia et Corsica. Atti del Convegno Internazionale di Studi (Cuglieri-OR, 26–28 marzo 2015)*, edited by Salvatore De Vincenzo and Chiara Blasetti Fantauzzi, pp. 89–105. Quasar, Roma.
    2016b   *Geografia epigrafica delle aree interne della Provincia Sardinia*. Sandhi Edizioni, Ortacesus.
    2017   Il riutilizzo delle tombe di giganti in età romana: osservazioni preliminari su alcuni contesti della Sardegna centro-orientale. *Studi Ogliastrini* 13: 31–50.
Fois, Piero, Pier Giorgio Spanu, and Raimondo Zucca,
    2013   Gli insediamenti rurali della Sardegna tra Tarda Antichità e Alto Medioevo (V-IX secolo). In *Settecento-Millecento. Storia, Archeologia e Arte nei "secoli bui" del Mediterraneo. Dalle fonti scritte, archeologiche ed artistiche alla ricostruzione della vicenda storica: la Sardegna laboratorio di esperienze culturali. Atti del Convegno di Studi (Cagliari, 17–19 ottobre 2012)*, vol. II, edited by Rossana Martorelli, with Silvia Marini, pp. 533–551. Scuola Sarda Editrice, Cagliari.
Garau, Elisabetta
    2007   *Disegnare paesaggi della Sardegna*. Nuove Grafiche Puddu, Ortacesus.
Garau, Elisabetta, and Marco Rendeli
    2006   Tra Africa e Sardinia: mobilità di merci e mobilità di genti (?) a Nora nella tarda antichità. In *Mobilità delle persone e dei popoli, dinamiche migratorie, emigrazioni ed immigrazioni nelle province occidentali dell'Impero romano. Atti del XVI convegno di studio su L'Africa romana (Rabat, 15–19 dicembre 2004)*, edited by Aomar Akerraz, Paola Ruggeri, Ahmed Siraj, and Cinzia Vismara, pp. 1247–1278. Carocci, Roma.
Gasperini. Lidio
    1992a   Ricerche epigrafiche in Sardegna (I). *In Sardinia Antiqua: studi in onore di Piero Meloni in occasione del suo settantesimo compleanno*, edited by Piero Meloni, Enrico Atzeni, and Marcella Bonello Lai, pp. 287–323. Edizioni della Torre, Cagliari.
    1992b   Ricerche epigrafiche in Sardegna (II). In *L'Africa romana. Atti del IX convegno di studio (Nuoro, 13–15 dicembre 1991)*, edited by Attilio Mastino, pp. 571–593. Gallizzi, Sassari.
    1996   Olbiensia epigraphica. In *Da* Olbìa *ad Olbia: 2500 anni di storia di una città mediterranea. Atti del Convegno internazionale di Studi (Olbia, 12–14 maggio 1994), I: Olbia in età antica*, edited by Attilio Mastino and Paola Ruggeri, pp. 305–316. Editrice Democratica Sarda, Sassari.

Guido, Luca

2006   *Romania vs Barbaria: Aspekte der Romanisierung Sardiniens*. Shaker Verlag,
            Aachen.

Ibba, Antonio

2006   Integrazione e resistenza nella provincia Sardinia: Forum Traiani e il territorio
            circostante. In *Scholia epigraphica: saggi di storia, epigrafia e archeologia Romana*,
            edited by Antonio Ibba, pp. 11–37. Studi di Storia antica e di Archeologia 2,
            Nuove Grafiche Puddu, Ortacesus.

2010   I Vandali in Sardegna. In *Lingua et ingenium: studi su Fulgenzio di Ruspe e il
            suo contesto*, edited by Antonio Piras, pp. 385–426. Sandhi Editore, Ortacesus-
            Cagliari.

2015   Processi di "romanizzazione" nella Sardinia repubblicana e alto-imperiale (III
            A.C.–II D.C.). In *Colonisation and Romanisation in Moesia Inferior. Premises
            of a Contrastive Approach*, edited by Lucretiu Mihailescu-Bîrliba, pp. 11–76.
            Parthenon Verlag, Kaiserslautern und Mehlingen.

2017   Fra Cartagine e Bisanzio: Godas, i Vandali, i Mauri e i Sardi in Sardegna. In
            *Tradimento e traditori nella Tarda Antichità. Atti del II Convegno internazionale
            (Roma, 18–19 marzo 2015)*, edited by Luca Montecchio, pp. 115–131. Graphe.it
            Edizioni, Perugia.

Lilliu, Giovanni

1990   Sopravvivenze nuragiche in età romana. In *L'Africa romana. Atti del VII convegno
            di studio (Sassari, 15–17 dicembre 1989)*, edited by Attilio Mastino, pp. 415–446.
            Gallizzi, Sassari.

Maisola, Giuseppe

2011–2012   Ricerche di Archeologia dei Paesaggi nell'alto Oristanese. Unpublished Ph.D.
            dissertation. Facoltà di Lettere e Filosofia, Università degli Studi di Sassari,
            Scuola di Dottorato di Ricerca in Storia, Letterature e Culture del Mediterraneo,
            XXIV ciclo.

2015a   Paesaggi del Montiferru meridionale e del Campidano di Milis: continuità e
            trasformazioni tra I e VII secolo. In *Momenti di continuità e rottura: bilancio di
            trent'anni di convegni L'Africa romana. Atti del XX convegno di studio su L'Africa
            romana (Alghero-Porto Conte, 26–29 settembre 2013)*, edited by Paola Ruggeri,
            pp. 2021–2031. Carocci, Roma.

2015b   Paesaggi medievali della Sardegna centro – occidentale: dinamiche insediative
            e organizzazione del territorio nel Montiferru meridionale e nel Campidano di
            Milis. In *Archeologi in progress: il cantiere dell'archeologia di domani. Atti del V
            Convegno nazionale dei giovani archeologi (Catania, 23–26 maggio 2013)*, edited
            by Rodolfo Brancato, Gesualdo Busacca, and Martina Massimini, pp. 494–508.
            BraDypUS Editore, Bologna.

Martorelli, Rossana

2010   Vescovi esuli, santi esuli? La circolazione dei culti africani e delle reliquie nell'età
            di Fulgenzio. In *Lingua et ingenium: studi su Fulgenzio di Ruspe e il suo contesto*,
            edited by Antonio Piras, pp. 453–510. Sandhi Editore, Ortacesus-Cagliari.

Mastino, Attilio

1993   Analfabetismo e resistenza: geografia epigrafica della Sardegna. In *L'epigrafia del
            villaggio (Atti del Colloquio Borghesi)*, edited by Alda Calbi, Angela Donati, and

Gabriella Poma, pp. 457–536. Epigrafia e Antichità 12. Stabilimento Grafico Lega, Faenza.

2005   *Storia della Sardegna antica.* Il Maestrale, Nuoro.

Mastino, Attilio, and Raimondo Zucca

2007   Le proprietà imperiali della Sardinia. In *Le proprietà imperiali nell'Italia romana: economia, produzione, amministrazione. Atti del Convegno (Ferrara-Voghiera, 3–4 giugno 2005),* edited by Daniela Pupillo, pp. 93–124. Quaderni degli Annali dell'Università di Ferrara, Sezione Storia 6. Le Lettere, Firenze.

Mayer, Marc

2009   Las civitates Barbariae: una prueba de la realidad de la organización territorial de Sardinia bajo Tiberio. In *Naves plenis velis euntes,* edited by Attilio Mastino, Pier Giorgio Spanu, and Raimondo Zucca, pp. 43–51. Tharros Felix 3. Carocci, Roma.

Muresu, Marco

2016   Dati statistici sulla pubblicazione dei reperti postclassici nella edizione delle indagini archeologiche sulla civiltà nuragica. In *Daedaleia: le torri nuragiche oltre l'età del Bronzo. Atti del Convegno di Studi (Cagliari, 19–21 aprile 2012),* edited by Enrico Trudu, Giacomo Paglietti, and Marco Muresu. *Layers. Archeologia, Territorio, Contesti* 1: 382–405.

Nieddu, Giuseppe, and Consuelo Cossu

1998a   Ville e terme nel contesto rurale della Sardegna romana. In *L'Africa romana. Atti del XII convegno di studio (Olbia, 13–15 dicembre 1996),* edited by Paola Ruggeri and Cinzia Vismara, pp. 611–656. Editrice Democratica Sarda, Sassari.

1998b   *Terme e ville extraurbane della Sardegna romana.* S'Alvure, Oristano.

Pala, Paola

1990   Osservazioni preliminari per uno studio della riutilizzazione dei nuraghi in epoca romana. In *L'Africa romana. Atti del VII convegno di studio (Sassari, 15–17 dicembre 1989),* edited by Attilio Mastino, pp. 549–555. Gallizzi, Sassari.

Pani Ermini, Letizia

1988   La Sardegna nel periodo vandalico. In *Storia dei Sardi e della Sardegna* 1, edited by Massimo Guidetti: 297–327. Jaka Book, Milano.

Panico, Barbara

2012–2013 PARA THN LIMHN. L'insediamento di San Giorgio di Sinis: la memoria dei metalli. Unpublished dissertation. Dipartimento di Storia, Scienze dell'Uomo e della Formazione, Università degli Studi di Sassari, Scuola di Specializzazione in Beni Archeologici.

2015–2016 Paesaggi del Sinis: fonti per paesaggi dell'archeologia rurale. Unpublished Ph.D. dissertation. Dipartimento di Storia, Scienze dell'Uomo e della Formazione, Università degli Studi di Sassari, Corso di Dottorato di Ricerca in Archeologia, Storia e Scienze dell'uomo, XXIX ciclo.

2016   Archeologia di Paesaggi del Sinis intorno a Mont'e Prama: scenari tardoantichi nell'ager tarrense. In *La ricerca archeologica di Forum Traiani, Othoca e Mont'e Prama: Progetto Archeo,* edited by Rita Fanari and Raimondo Zucca, pp. 209–215. Nuove Grafiche Puddu, Ortacesus.

Panico, Barbara, and Pier Giorgio Spanu

2016   Archeologia dei paesaggi di Mont'e Prama. In *I riti della morte e del culto di Monte Prama – Cabras. Atti del Convegno presso l'Accademia dei Lincei (Roma, 21 gennaio 2015)*, pp. 31–47. Atti dei Convegni Lincei 303. Bardi Edizioni, Roma.

2018   Archeologia globale dei paesaggi fluviali e costieri della Sardegna: la foce del Tirso e le aree umide del golfo di Oristano. In *Storia e archeologia globale dei paesaggi rurali in Italia fra Tardoantico e Medioevo*, edited by Giuliano Volpe, pp. 623–248. Insulae Diomedae 34. Edipuglia, Bari.

Panico, Barbara, Pier Giorgio Spanu, and Raimondo Zucca

2015a   Civitates Sancti Marci, Sancti Avgvstini, Sancti Salvatoris et Oppida Domu de Cubas, Sancti Satvrnini, Sancti Georgii in saltibus de Sinnis. In *Itinerando, senza confini dalla preistoria ad oggi: studi in ricordo di Roberto Coroneo*, edited by Rossana Martorelli, pp. 441–464. Morlacchi Editore, Perugia.

2015b   Ricerche archeologiche nell'ager Tharrensis: gli insediamenti tardoantichi. In *Isole e terraferma nel primo cristianesimo: identità locale ed interscambi culturali, religiosi e produttivi. Atti dell'XI Congresso Nazionale di Archeologia Cristiana (Cagliari-Sant'Antioco, 23–27 settembre 2014)*, edited by Rossana Martorelli, Antonio Piras, and Pier Giorgio Spanu, pp. 457–464. PFTS University Press, Cagliari.

Paulis, Giulio

1983   *Lingua e cultura nella Sardegna bizantina. Testimonianze linguistiche dell'influsso greco.* L'Asfodelo Editore, Sassari.

1987   *I nomi di luogo della Sardegna* I. Carlo Delfino Editore, Sassari.

Rebuffat, René

1991   Un document sur l'économie sarde. In *L'Africa romana. Atti dell'VIII Convegno di studio (Sassari 14–16 dicembre 1990)*, edited by Attilio Mastino, pp. 719–734. Edizioni Gallizzi, Sassari.

Rovina, Daniela

2007   L'insediamento costiero di Santa Filitica a Sorso tra età romana e Alto Medioevo. In *Castelsardo: novecento anni di storia*, edited by Antonello Mattone and Alessandro Soddu, pp. 110–123. Carocci, Roma.

Rovina, Daniela, Elisabetta Garau, and Paola Mameli

2008   Attività metallurgiche presso l'insediamento tardo antico di Santa Filitica a Sorso: dati preliminari archeologici e archeometrici. In *Le ricchezze dell'Africa: risorse, produzioni, scambi. Atti del XVII convegno di studio su L'Africa romana (Sevilla, 14–17 dicembre 2006)*, edited by Julian Gonzales, Paola Ruggeri, Cinzia Vismara, and Raimondo Zucca, pp. 2673–2696. Carocci, Roma.

Rovina, Daniela, Elisabetta Garau, Paola Mameli, and Barbara Wilkens

2011   Attività produttive nell'insediamento romano e altomedievale di Santa Filitica (Sorso-SS). *Erentzias* 1: 245–268.

Rowland Jr., Robert J.

1994   Sardinia Provincia frumentaria. In *Le ravitaillement en blé de Rome et des centres urbains des débuts de la République jusqu'au Haut-Empire. Actes du colloque international de Naples (14–16 Février 1991)*, pp. 255–260. Publications de l'École Française de Rome 196. École Française de Rome, Rome.

2001   *The Periphery in the Center: Sardinia in the Ancient and Medieval Worlds*. British Archaeological Reports International Series 970. Archaeopress, Oxford.

Santoni, Vincenzo, Paolo Benito Serra, Francesco Guido, and Ornella Fonzo

1991   Il nuraghe Cobulas di Milis-Oristano: preesistenze e riuso. In *L'Africa romana. Atti dell'VIII Convegno di studio (Sassari 14–16 dicembre 1990)*, edited by Attilio Mastino, pp. 941–989. Edizioni Gallizzi, Sassari.

Serra, Giandomenico

1949   Nomi personali d'origine greco-bizantina fra i membri delle famiglie giudicali sarde. *Byzantion* 19: 223–246.

Serra, Maily

2016   Attestazioni di età medievale e postmedievale in alcuni siti nuragici di Trexenta e Gerrei. In *Daedaleia: le torri nuragiche oltre l'età del Bronzo. Atti del Convegno di Studi (Cagliari, 19–21 aprile 2012)*, edited by Enrico Trudu, Giacomo Paglietti, and Marco Muresu. *Layers. Archeologia, Territorio, Contesti* 1: 346–370.

Serra, Paolo Benito

1995   Campidano Maggiore di Oristano: ceramiche di produzione locale e d'importazione e altri materiali d'uso nel periodo tardoromano e altomedievale. In *La ceramica racconta la Storia. Atti del Convegno "La ceramica artistica, d'uso e da costruzione nell'Oristanese dal neolitico ai giorni nostri" (Oristano 1994)*, pp. 177–220. S'Alvure, Oristano.

2002a   L'armamento. In *Ai confini dell'Impero: storia, arte e archeologia della Sardegna bizantina*, edited by Paola Corrias and Salvatore Cosentino, pp. 149–157. M & T Sardegna, Cagliari.

2002b   Uras: materiali dell'equipaggiamento dei guerrieri e dell'ornamento femminile dal nuraghe Domu Beccia. In *Ai confini dell'Impero: storia, arte e archeologia della Sardegna bizantina*, edited by Paola Corrias and Salvatore Cosentino, pp. 211–212. M & T Sardegna, Cagliari.

2006a   *Popolazioni rurali di ambito tardoromano e altomedievale in Sardegna*, In *Mobilità delle persone e dei popoli, dinamiche migratorie, emigrazioni ed immigrazioni nelle province occidentali dell'Impero romano. Atti del XVI convegno di studio su l'Africa romana (Rabat, 15–19 dicembre 2004)*, edited by Aomar Akerraz, Paola Ruggeri, Ahmed Siraj, and Cinzia Vismara, pp. 1279–1306. Carocci, Roma.

2006b   I Barbaricini di Gregorio Magno, in *Per longa maris intervalla: Gregorio Magno e l'Occidente mediterraneo fra tardoantico e altomedioevo*, edited by Lucio Casula, Giampaolo Mele, and Antonio Piras, pp. 289–361. Pontificia Facoltà Teologica della Sardegna, Cagliari.

2008   Su un ponte nuragico a Desulo e sugli insediamenti tardoromani e altomedievali in ambito rurale nell'isola. In *La civiltà nuragica: nuove acquisizioni. Atti del Convegno (Senorbì, 14–16 dicembre 2000)* II, pp. 729–746. Soprintendenza per i Beni Archeologici della Sardegna, Cagliari.

Simbula, Pinuccia F., and Pier Giorgio Spanu

2012   Paesaggi rurali della Sardegna tra Tardo Antico ed età giudicale. In *Paesaggi, comunità, villaggi medievali. Atti del Convegno Internazionale di Studio (Bologna, 14–16 gennaio 2010)*, edited by Paola Galetti, pp. 567–597. Fondazione CISAM, Spoleto.

Soddu, Ottaviana

2005   Un inedito insediamento tardo romano-altomedievale a "Su Nuraxi" di Sisini (Senorbì-Cagliari): nota preliminare. In *La civiltà nuragica: nuove acquisizioni. Atti del Congresso (Senorbì, 14–16 dicembre 2000)* I, pp. 301–319. Quaderni della Soprintendenza Archeologica per le province di Cagliari e Oristano. Atti e Monografie 1.

Sotgiu, Giovanna

1961   *Iscrizioni latine della Sardegna* 1. Cedam, Padova.

Spanu, Pier Giorgio

1998   *La Sardegna bizantina tra VI e VII secolo*. Mediterraneo tardoantico e medievale: scavi e ricerche 12. S'Alvure, Oristano.

2000   Le Barbariae sarde nell'alto medioevo: sulla possibile esistenza di un "ducato" dei Barbaricini. In *ALETHS: Miscellanea per i 70 anni di Roberto Caprara*, edited by Andrea Caprara, Francesca Galli, and Marcello Scalzo, pp. 402–419. Archeogruppo, Massafra.

2002   La viabilità e gli insediamenti rurali. In *Ai confini dell'Impero: storia, arte e archeologia della Sardegna bizantina*, edited by Paola Corrias and Salvatore Cosentino, pp. 115–125. M & T Sardegna, Cagliari.

2006   «Insula quae dicitur Sardinia, in qua plurima fuisse civitates legimus» (Ravennatis Anonymi Cosmographia V, 26): note sulle città sarde tra la tarda antichità e l'alto medioevo. In *Le città italiane tra la tarda antichità e l'alto medioevo. Atti del Convegno di Studi (Ravenna, 26–29 febbraio 2004)*, edited by Andrea Augenti, pp. 589–612. All'Insegna del Giglio, Firenze.

2008a   Dalla Sardegna bizantina alla Sardegna giudicale. In *Orientis radiata fulgore: la Sardegna nel contesto storico e culturale bizantino. Atti del Convegno Internazionale (Cagliari, 30 novembre–1 dicembre 2007)*, edited by Lucio Casula, Antonio M. Corda, and Antonio Piras, pp. 353–387. Nuove Grafiche Puddu, Ortacesus-Cagliari.

2008b   Fons Vivus: culti delle acque e santuari cristiani tra tarda antichità e alto medioevo. In *L'acqua nei secoli altomedievali. Atti della LV Settimana internazionale di studio del Centro Italiano di Studi sull'Alto Medioevo (Spoleto, 12–17 aprile 2007)*, pp. 1029–1077. Fondazione CISAM, Spoleto.

2012   La Sardegna rurale tra l'età tardoantica e l'alto medioevo. In *Historica et philologica: studi in onore di Raimondo Turtas*, edited by Mauro G. Sanna, pp. 147–164. Collezione Agorà 54. AM & D Edizioni, Cagliari.

2015   Dall'età fenicio-punica all'Alto Medioevo. In *Formaggio e pastoralismo in Sardegna: storia, cultura, tradizione e innovazione*, edited by Anna Saderi, pp. 29–39. Ilisso Edizioni, Nuoro.

2018   I clarissimi Probus e Venusta in un nuovo laterizio dall'ager tharrensis. In *Studi in memoria di Fabiola Ardizzone* 1: *Epigrafia e Storia*, edited by Rosa Maria Carra Bonacasa and Emma Vitale, pp. 179–195. Antipodes, Palermo.

Spanu, Pier Giorgio, and Raimondo Zucca

2004   *I sigilli bizantini della Sardenía*. Carocci, Roma.

2008   Nuovi documenti epigrafici della Sardegna bizantina. In *Epigrafia romana in Sardegna. Atti del I Convegno di studio (Sant'Antioco, 14–15 luglio 2007)*, edited by Francesca Cenerini and Paola Ruggeri, pp. 147–172. Carocci, Roma.

2014   Sardinia, Corsica et Baliares regni Vandalorum. In *Guerrieri, mercanti e profughi nel mare dei Vandali. Atti del Convegno Internazionale (Messina, 7–8 settembre 2009)*, edited by Vincenzo Aiello, pp. 35–69. Pelorias 22. DICAM, Messina.

Spanu, Pier Giorgio, Piero Fois, Renato Zanella, and Raimondo Zucca

2013   L'arcontato d'Arborea tra Islam ed eredità bizantina. In *Tharros Felix* 5, edited by Attilio Mastino, Pier Giorgio Spanu, and Raimondo Zucca, pp. 515–536. Carocci, Roma.

Stiglitz, Alfonso

2015   L'invenzione del "sardo pellita": biografia di una ricerca. In *Momenti di continuità e rottura: bilancio di trent'anni di convegni L'Africa romana. Atti del XX convegno di studio su L'Africa romana (Alghero-Porto Conte, 26–29 settembre 2013),* edited by Paola Ruggeri, pp. 2123–2132. Carocci, Roma.

Tola, Pasquale

1861   *Codex Diplomaticus Sardiniae* I, edited by Pasquale Tola. Tipografia Regia, Torino.

Trudu, Enrico

2012a   Civitates, latrunculi mastrucati? Alcune note sulla romanizzazione della Barbaria. In *Trasformazione dei paesaggi del potere nell'Africa romana settentrionale fino alla fine del mondo antico. Atti del XIX convegno di studi su L'Africa romana (Sassari, 16–19 dicembre 2010)*, edited by Maria Bastiana Cocco, Alberto Gavini, and Antonio Ibba, pp. 2445–2659. Carocci, Roma.

2012b   Sacrum Barbariae: attestazioni cultuali nelle aree interne della Sardegna in epoca romana. In *Meixis: dinamiche di stratificazione culturale nella periferia greca e romana. Atti del Convegno Internazionale di Studi "Il sacro e il profano" (Cagliari, 5–7 maggio 2011)*, edited by Simonetta Angiolillo, Marco Giuman, and Chiara Pilo, pp. 217–236. Giorgio Bretschneider Editore, Roma.

2014   Vici, pagi, agglomérations secondaires: insediamenti e abitati di epoca romana nella Sardegna centro-orientale. *ArcheoArte: Rivista elettronica di Archeologia e Arte* 3: 105–125.

2016   Il riutilizzo dei nuraghi tra Marmilla e Sarcidano in epoca romana. In *Daedaleia: le torri nuragiche oltre l'età del Bronzo. Atti del Convegno di Studi (Cagliari, 19–21 aprile 2012)*, edited by Enrico Trudu, Giacomo Paglietti, and Marco Muresu. *Layers. Archeologia, Territorio, Contesti* 1: 326–345.

Turtas, Raimondo

1999   *Storia della Chiesa in Sardegna dalle origini al 2000*. Città Nuova, Roma.

Ugas, Giovanni, and Paolo Benito Serra

1990   Complesso sepolcrale bizantino nel mastio del nuraghe su Nuraxi di Siurgus Donigala – Cagliari. In *Le sepolture in Sardegna dal IV al VII secolo. Atti del IV Convegno sull'archeologia tardoromana e medievale in Sardegna (Cagliari-Cuglieri, 27–28 giugno 1987),* pp. 107–131. Mediterraneo tardoantico e medievale: scavi e ricerche 8. S'Alvure, Oristano.

Usai, Alessandro

2003   Sistemi insediativi e organizzazione delle comunità nuragiche nella Sardegna centro-occidentale. In *Le comunità della preistoria italiana: studi e ricerche sul neolitico e le età dei metalli. Atti della XXXV Riunione Scientifica dell'Istituto*

Italiano di Preistoria e Protostoria (Lipari, 2–7 giugno 2000), pp. 215–224. Istituto italiano di preistoria e protostoria, Firenze.

2006   Osservazioni sul popolamento e sulle forme di organizzazione comunitaria nella Sardegna nuragica. In *Studi di protostoria in onore di Renato Peroni,* pp. 557–566. All'Insegna del Giglio, Firenze.

Usai, Alessandro, Tatiana Cossu, and Federica Dettori

2009   Primi dati di scavo sul nuraghe Nuracale di Scano Montiferro. In *Archeologia tra Planargia e Montiferru*, by Pietro Pes, edited by Alessandro Usai and Tatiana Cossu, pp. 297–313. Edizioni AV, Cagliari.

2011   Primi dati sul contesto tardo romano e altomedievale dal nuraghe Nuracale di Scano Montiferro. In *Oristano e il suo territorio* 1: *dalla preistoria all'alto Medioevo*, edited by Pier Giorgio Spanu and Raimondo Zucca, pp. 777–796. Carocci, Roma.

Vacca, Antonio

2002   Forum Traiani: Pólis teikéres. In *Città, territorio, produzione e commerci: studi in onore di Letizia Pani Ermini,* edited by Rossana Martorelli, pp. 187–206. AM & D Edizioni, Cagliari.

Virdis, Maurizio

2002   *Il Condaghe di Santa Maria di Bonarcado*, edited by Maurizio Virdis. Cuec, Cagliari.

Webster, Gary S., and Maud Teglund

1992   Toward the Study of Colonial-Native Relations in Sardinia from 1000 B.C.–A.D. 456. In *Sardinia in the Mediterranean: A Footprint in the Sea*, edited by Robert H. Tykot and Tamsey K. Andrews, pp. 317–346. Monographs in Mediterranean Archaeology 3, Sheffield Academic Press, Sheffield.

Wolf, Heinz Jürgen

1998   *Toponomastica barbaricina*. Insula, Nuoro.

Zucca, Raimondo

1988   Le Civitates Barbariae e l'occupazione militare della Sardegna: aspetti e confronti con l'Africa. In *L'Africa romana. Atti del V convegno di studio (Sassari, 11–13 dicembre 1987)*, edited by Attilio Mastino, pp. 349–373. Dipartimento di Storia, Sassari.

1990a   Ricerche storiche e topografiche su Forum Traiani. *Nuovo Bullettino Archeologico Sardo* 3 (1986): 167–187.

1990b   Le persistenze preromane nei paleonimi e negli antroponimi della Sardinia. In *L'Africa romana. Atti del VII convegno di studio (Sassari, 15–17 dicembre 1989)*, edited by Attilio Mastino, pp. 655–667. Gallizzi, Sassari.

1999   *Ula Tirso: un centro della Barbaria Sarda*. Grafica del Parteolla, Dolianova.

2002   Il castello di Laconi e le origini del Giudicato d'Arborea. In *La civiltà giudicale in Sardegna nei secoli XI-XII: fonti e documenti scritti. Atti del Convegno Nazionale (Sassari-Usini, 16–18 marzo 2001),* pp. 115–126. Associazione 'Condaghe S. Pietro di Silki, Sassari.

2004   Sufetes Africae et Sardiniae. *Studi storici e geografici sul Mediterraneo antico*. Carocci, Roma.

2016a   Le Aquae Ypsitanae tra la tarda Repubblica e il primo Impero. In *Il processo di romanizzazione della provincia Sardinia et Corsica. Atti del Convegno Internazionale di Studi (Cuglieri-OR, 26–28 marzo 2015)*, edited by Salvatore De Vincenzo and Chiara Blasetti Fantauzzi, pp. 213–231. Quasar, Roma.

2016b   Sardi Ilienses (Livio, XLI, 12, 4). In *Daedaleia: le torri nuragiche oltre l'età del Bronzo. Atti del Convegno di Studi (Cagliari, 19–21 aprile 2012)*, edited by Enrico Trudu, Giacomo Paglietti, and Marco Muresu. *Layers. Archeologia, Territorio, Contesti* 1: 406–423.

Sicily from Late Antiquity to the Early Middle Ages: Resilience and Disruption

Alessandra Molinari

Over the last decade, Sicily in its Late Antique, Byzantine, and Islamic periods has been at the center of renewed interest from both historians and archaeologists. This paper considers the links that could be established between observed socio-political structures and the transformation or persistence of exchange networks, settlements, and agricultural and ecological systems. Sicily seems to have had a very long "Late Antiquity" lasting until the seventh century, as indicated by its close connections with the remaining international networks of exchange, a high level of coin use, and thriving countrysides (where villages were gaining importance, at the expense of the villae*). During the eighth century, we can see that many things changed markedly, before Sicily was conquered by Muslim invaders. The networks linking Rome, North Africa and Sicily, if they existed, are nevertheless archaeologically invisible. In the western part of Sicily rural settlement are almost undetectable, while in the east a number of very small sites indicate the weakening of the central places; in some parts of the island, at least, the cultivation of plants, especially cereals, collapsed, and a period of increased dryness started as well. After many centuries, Sicily for the first time had to feed only its own population! Amidst all this disruption, what can be shown to have had significant resilience were the very large villages, the so-called agro-towns (Sofiana and Casale San Pietro). They were sometimes able to last at least until the twelfth century, ending only during the Norman age.*

Introduction

Over the last decade, Sicily in its Late Antique, Byzantine, and Islamic periods has been at the center of renewed interest from both historians and archaeologists. New data and new interpretations have emerged, calling for reconsideration of the identification and explanation of rupture on the one hand, or resilience on the other.[1] In particular, I would like to consider the links that could be established between observed socio-political structures and the transformation or persistence of exchange networks, settlements, and agricultural and ecological systems.

Among recent research (Figure 4.1) are elements that prompt serious reflection: the volumes edited by Malfitana and Bonifay (2016) on African ceramics imported into Roman and Late Roman Sicily; recent excavations and new analysis of previously known structures at the Villa del Casale near Piazza Armerina (Pensabene and Sfamemi 2014; Pensabene 2016) and the nearby *vicus* of Sofiana (Vaccaro 2017), and the new data that are emerging from towns.[2] Extensive surveys—for example, in the territory of Iato (Alfano 2015) and Entella (Corretti et al. 2014)—are providing precious information on changing settlement systems in the *longue durée*. Studies of mints, the circulation of coins, and lead seals in Byzantine Sicily continue to provide important elements of analysis (Prigent 2012; 2013). Of great interest is also the combined study of the pollen sequence and the stable isotopes of oxygen and carbon in the Pergusa Lake (near Enna), with crucial information on climatic and vegetation sequences in the last two millennia (Sadori et al. 2016). Much new data is also being assembled by the "Sicily in Transition" project which addresses some 20 sites in Sicily, including intensive research in the area of Castronovo di Sicilia.[3]

It is now increasingly possible to consider whether or not observed changes in society are coeval with documented moments of major discontinuity in the history of Sicily and the Mediterranean: for example, the fifth-century Vandal conquest of Africa and collapse of the population of Rome, or the Byzantine (A.D. 535) and Islamic (starting in A.D. 827) conquests. We can already take as a premise that, not surprisingly, transformations in economy, social structures or ecology do not slavishly follow a change in regime.

In the following pages I first describe some of the phenomena that are being read with increasing clarity in the fields of exchange networks, settlement systems, and partly also in climatic variations and agricultural practices. I then focus on the research in progress at Castronovo di Sicilia and, finally, bring these new observations together.

Networks of Exchange

The extensive census undertaken by Malfitana and Bonifay (2016) of all kinds of African ceramics imported into Sicily between the first and seventh century, accompanied by more than 500 petrographic thin-section analyses, has provided new insights into the exchange mechanisms that allowed Sicily to receive large quantities of pottery and food products from different areas of North Africa, from Mauretania to Cyrenaica.[4]

In particular, within Sicily, three main areas have been identified (albeit with different sub-areas of overlap) that are clearly characterized by different modes of supply. In southern Sicily, the direct supply of African products was a consequence of *cabotage* connecting these two coasts of the Mediterranean. It is probable that the south coast of Sicily exported sulfur (extracted in the area of Agrigento) to North Africa, at least until the end of the seventh century. Conversely, northern Sicily was likely to have received North African ceramics via redistribution through the port of Rome, given the close similarity of ceramic types with what has been found in that city and beyond. A third area, that of southeastern Sicily, benefitted from both types of supply, thanks to routes passing through the Strait of Messina. Sicily would have been incorporated into the very close trade relationship that bound North Africa to Rome, after Egyptian grain was diverted to Constantinople in the fourth century. The demand for food in the megalopolis, in the view of many scholars, would have been the main engine underlying these networks.

Following the central decades of the fifth century, in Malfitana's and Bonifay's opinion, the conquest of North Africa by the Vandals, on the one hand, and the gradual collapse of the population of Rome, on the other, would completely disarticulate the system we have just described. For this reason, in the sixth and seventh centuries, after the Byzantine reconquest of North Africa, African ceramic arrivals in Sicily should have been largely dependent on *cabotage*. As we will see later, however, it is really difficult to discount Rome's role in the economic and social life of the island during these centuries, as well as in wider Mediterranean affairs. Although it is true that the overall structure of imports was altered in the fifth century (for example, with a major increase in imports from southern Italy), African ceramics nevertheless continued to arrive in Rome in large numbers (Panella et al. 2010; Casalini 2015). African pottery was still reaching deposits at *Crypta Balbi* in the second half of the seventh century. The distribution of both ceramics and coins (the latter in particular from the mints of Syracuse and Carthage) demonstrate that Sicily and parts of North Africa were crucial for the sustenance of both Rome and Constantinople during the seventh century (Prigent 2006; Morrisson 2015).

Imports from North Africa to Sicily in the seventh century, generally speaking, are quantitatively smaller than in previous centuries. But in some contexts—and not only on the southern coast, such as at Cignana near Agrigento (Rizzo and Zambito 2016), but also in the northwest, including Segesta and its territory (Faccella and Gagliardi 2016)—African imports still constitute the most prevalent pottery and local products are represented only by cooking pots. The same is true for the island of Marettimo, near the northwest coast (Ardizzone and Pisciotta 2016). Furthermore, we have

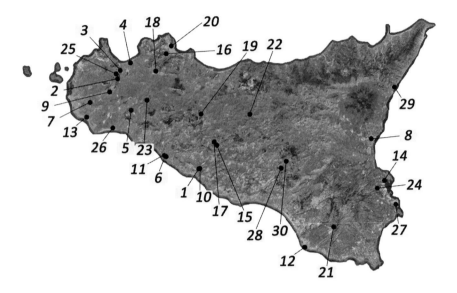

Figure 4.1. Map of Sicily with main medieval archaeological sites: 1. *Agrigento*; 2. *Calatafimi*; 3. *Calathamet*; 4. Calatubo; 5. Calliata; 6. Campanaio; 7. Casale Nuovo; 8. Catania; 9. Contrada Miceli; 10. Contrada Saraceno; 11. Eraclea Minoa; 12. Kaukana/Punta Secca; 13. Mazara del Vallo; 14. Megara; 15. Milena; 16 Monreale; 17. Monte Conca; 18. Monte Jato; 19. Castronovo di Sicilia; 20. Palermo; 21. Ragusa; 22. Resuttano; 23. Rocca di Entella; 24. Santa Caterina/Melilli; 25. Segesta/Caltabarbaro; 26. Selinunte; 27. Siracusa; 28. Sofiana; 29. Taormina; 30. Villa del Casale/Piazza Armerina (after Google maps, by F. Giovannini).

to remember that Sicily was also producing wine in its own right. The information we have on the amphorae, such as those of the type *Crypta Balbi* 2, tell us that they continue to be produced in eastern Sicily and exported to Rome throughout the seventh century (Capelli and Franco 2014).

The eighth century, however, is very different, and not just because we are less able to recognize the local pottery typical of this period and even less so any imports from North Africa. Actually, in the few published contexts we notice a drastic fall in imports, now represented mainly by the so-called globular amphorae, emanating perhaps from the area of Naples, but especially from the Eastern Mediterranean (Ardizzone 2010; Arcifa 2010). In the ninth century, Syracuse had rather significant ceramic assemblages, but supposed mainly to consist of local products (Cacciaguerra 2015). The challenge now is to discover whether these local amphorae, which have many analogues with those of the eastern Mediterranean, are containers that traveled both inside and outside the island. In sum, much or all seems to have changed in Sicily in the eighth century concerning exchange networks.

If we analyze the circulation and minting of coins, the phenomena are quite complex (Morrisson 1998; Prigent 2012; 2013). During the seventh century there was a significant circulation of gold and bronze coins in Sicily, including those minted on the island, in comparison with other areas of Italy or the Byzantine Empire (with the exception of Constantinople). However, from the second half of the seventh century coins circulating in Sicily are mainly issues of local mints. During the eighth century there are major changes: the supply of bronze coinage contracts from the beginning of the century (Prigent 2012) and the circulation of gold coins diminishes, especially in its second half. A consistent recovery occurred in the first decades of the ninth century, most probably due to needs linked to the costs of military activities for the defense against the Islamic invasion. The gold monetary types coined later by the Muslim mints were influenced by the latest issues of the preceding Byzantine era.

Settlement Systems

In various parts of the island during the fifth century,[5] we can see growth in the number of settlements, and in many cases a substantial expansion of rural sites like villages or so-called agro-towns. This latter term has generally been used with reference to modern and contemporary times (e.g., in the south of Italy) and normally refers to rather extensive settlements, mainly occupied by peasants, with low levels of craftsmanship and generally without any precise administrative role (e.g., see Curtis 2014). Probably no new grand villas such as those at Piazza Armerina, Tellaro or Patti Marina were built. However, in the case of at least the first of these, it has been ascertained that, as late as the fifth century, they sought to maintain the quality and function of the structures through restoration (although in a rougher way), for example, of the floor mosaics.[6] In several cases in the fifth century, even after abandonment phases, rural settlements, some classifiable as villages, are implanted on *villae* sites, as is the case at Cignana (AG) (Rizzo and Zambito 2010).

Villages and agro-towns endured during the sixth and seventh centuries, although in many areas there was a substantial decline in the overall number of sites (for Sofiana's territory, for example, see Bowes et al. 2011). In some cases, different sites in new locations also emerged. If several *villae* were abandoned, others, such as the Villa del Casale at Piazza Armerina, were clearly restored in more rustic forms, hosting workshops and burials where once there were rooms with mosaics; one of the *triclinia* seems to have been transformed into a chapel (Pensabene 2016).

We do not have a very clear idea of what was going on during the eighth century. It has only been a few years since we began to recognize objects useful for dating sites and contexts (Arcifa 2010; Ardizzone 2010). In any case, data from systematic excavations can be counted on the fingers of one hand; this makes the dating of sites identified only by field surveys very critical. In cases where particular attention has been paid to the early Middle Ages, it seems that a further reduction in the number of sites can be identified, not compensated for by the foundation of new settlements (for example, on hilltops), as in the case of the territory of Segesta (Molinari and Neri 2004). In other territories, such as those of Agrigento (Rizzo et al. 2014) or Entella (Corretti et al. 2014; Corretti, personal communication), the increase in the number of sites corresponds to the emergence of very small settlements, identifiable by just a few ceramic sherds, which seems to be evidence of a disarticulation of the previous settlement system rather than clear growth. In addition, these very small sites seem to be of ephemeral duration. However, some of the major agro-towns seem to continue and remain prosperous—as in the case of Sofiana, which still extended for ca. 10 ha, and where several ceramic kilns dating to this period (i.e., the eighth century) were found (Vaccaro 2017; Vaccaro et al. 2015). Although it is unclear how the structures of the old *villae* were being used, some of those that had been transformed in the previous two centuries have continued traces of occupation (e.g., pottery and coins) in the eighth and ninth centuries, and often later still. In general, eastern Sicily seems to have shown a much greater resilience in its settlement system (Cacciaguerra 2009).

In the tenth century, when the Islamic State had fully consolidated its control, almost everywhere, but especially throughout western Sicily, the growth in the number, type and size of sites and of the quantity of movable finds can be easily seen. If agro-towns continue to play an important role, competition with the hilltop sites becomes progressively more visible, insofar as the latter show the tendency of becoming the new central places.

Pollen and Climatic Sequences

Research recently carried out by Laura Sadori along with other specialists (Sadori et al. 2016), using joint analyses of pollen sequences and stable isotopes of carbon and oxygen in the Pergusa Lake deposits (near Enna), offer some remarkable data for reflection and discussion. The combined analyses of climate and pollen trends, coupled with tighter dating, allowed them to establish more complex relationships between climate dynamics, vegetation history, anthropogenic interventions, and precise historical phases for the last 2,000 years. The pollen and isotopic sequences of Lake Pergusa have helped identify two periods of greater humidity and intensification of agricultural activities: A.D. 450–720 and A.D. 1400–1800. Between the eighth and the fourteenth centuries there would have been a more arid period. According to these scholars, agricultural recovery was evident, despite the increased dryness, from the twelfth century. This set of results, which seems to be confirmed above all by the pollen series in the Gorgo Basso Lake in southwestern Sicily (but not only there), allows many observations, although it naturally implies the need for the future extension of research of this type in other parts of the island as well. We can focus here especially on the data concerning Late Antiquity and the Early Middle Ages. The period from 450 to 720, besides being more humid, is characterized by significant quantities of the pollen of synanthropic taxa and in particular of cultivated plants, with strong representation of different types of cereals (barley, wheat, and rye). The real collapse of cultivated species by ca. A.D. 750 would also coincide with the increased dryness. These last phenomena were also associated with a possible sharp decline in population. It is known that a further pestilence had touched Sicily right in the middle of the eighth century (Little 2007). According to Pergusa's research team, this climatic and demographic crisis would have weakened the island to such a degree that efforts to resist the Islamic invasion were lacking. This peak of agricultural activities between the fifth and eighth centuries and their collapse after the second quarter of the eighth century are worthy of further reflection (see below).

Investigations at Castronovo di Sicilia

Many of these themes are being further pursued by the project "Sicily in Transition" (Carver and Molinari 2016; Carver et al. 2017).[7] The aim of this project is to investigate how changes during the period between the sixth and thirteenth centuries (i.e., the Byzantine, then Islamic, and finally Norman-Swabian regimes) have influenced (or not) the standards and ways of living, the composition of the subject populations, and more generally the economic structures, settlements and ecological systems in Sicily. In addition to analyzing samples from more than 20 different Sicilian sites, the team has since 2014 been pursuing intensive research in the territory of Castronovo di Sicilia (Figure 4.2). The purpose of this work at Castronovo is not only to collect first-hand data from controlled sequences, but also to examine how a territory in a markedly interior part of the island has reacted to socio-political changes. The present and earlier investigations at Castronovo have allowed a preliminary knowledge of the main archaeological sites from the Roman to the Medieval period (Maurici 2000; Vassallo 2007; 2009; 2010; Castrorao Barba 2015).

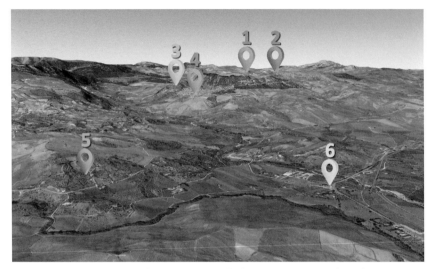

Figure 4.2. The territory of Castronovo with the sites investigated in the SicTransit project: 1. Mount Kassar; 2 San Luca Roman Villa; 3 San Vitale Hill; 4 Castronovo Town; 5 Ministalla; 6 Casale San Pietro (by G. Ciccone—SicTransit Project).

In our research strategy we have planned to conduct intensive investigations at those sites that seem to have been central places between the sixth and the thirteenth century, to perform extensive new surveys, to explore with new methods the origin of some agricultural systems that can be identified in the territory, and to use different approaches to analyze the botanical and animal finds, above all applying the new techniques of molecular bioarchaeology.[8] Many of our research topics are only just beginning and so we cannot yet comment on their results, but the evaluation and excavation activities of the main sites are already yielding appreciable, though preliminary, results. In the Castronovo area, the settlements under investigation are (see Figure 4.2): an extensive agro-town at Casale San Pietro, with phases at least from Roman to Norman times; the Byzantine fortress of Mount Kassar, with its main occupation between the end of the seventh and the ninth centuries; and Colle San Vitale, perhaps inhabited from the late tenth to the eighteenth centuries.

The site of Casale San Pietro occupies a basically flat area at the confluence of the Saraceno and Platani rivers and should probably be identified as one of the *stationes* along the *via publica*, which served the route from Palermo to Agrigento at least from Roman times. Earlier work suggested that the site here extends at least over four ha (this estimate is provisional). Current investigations are examining several aspects of the history of this site, which, although exposed to the floods of the nearby rivers, has undoubtedly had remarkable continuity of occupation. Fieldwork at Casale San Pietro up to now has included the systematic survey of the area with the largest variety of ceramics, with the collection of all visible artefacts using a grid of 10 m squares; we have investigated about 7000 sq. m in this way. In this same field, magnetometer survey has revealed a large number of anomalies, including one or two probable kilns. In four different places, we have opened three small test-trenches and a larger area of ca. 15×16 m (Figure 4.3). This has begun to outline a complex story of the site, which still needs much clarification. Finds collected in the surveys and the test trenches suggest an extensive occupation between the fifth and the seventh centuries.[9] Surface surveys have also turned up some fragments provisionally dated to the eighth to ninth centuries.[10] Casale S. Pietro seems to have been very lively in the Islamic age, still occupying a fairly extensive area. Finally, it had a much more sporadic occupation after the twelfth century: buildings that are still standing on the site may be attributed, at least in part, to the later Middle ages and have undergone modifications, even until quite recently.

The larger area (Figure 4.3, intervention 5) has rewarded us with a rich and coherent sequence of stratified assemblages, layers, and structures (Figures 4.3 and 4.4), and at least eight distinct phases of occupation have been identified. The earliest structures are constructed of ashlar bonded with good lime mortar and probably date from the third to sixth centuries. One

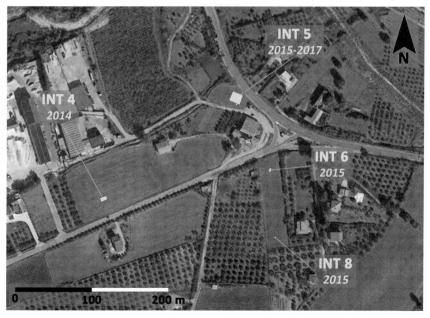

Figure 4.3. The area of Casale San Pietro.

Figure 4.4. One of the trenches (int. 5) at Casale San Pietro (Byzantine to Norman Phase) (Photograph: G. Ciccone/A. Meo—SicTransit Project) (September 2018).

of these structures was reused and extended probably in the Late Byzantine age and in any case before the tenth century. During the Islamic age (ninth to eleventh centuries), the pre-existing buildings were not demolished, but rebuilt several times, using walls made with clay-bonded, rough-cut stones. This stage is rich in finds of all kinds, including glazed ceramics and red-painted amphorae from Palermo, the Islamic capital of the island. The last construction phase dates to the Norman age. In the thirteenth and fourteenth centuries the area was no longer inhabited and was perhaps dedicated only to agricultural activities.

Less than 10 km west of Casale San Pietro stands the imposing massif of Mount Kassar (Figure 4.5), which reaches 1030 m above sea level. Previous research, especially that by the Soprintendenza of Palermo, mapped and examined the fortification wall, explored a gateway, and located a central military building and a possible church.[11] The main phase of occupation is represented by an imposing fortification about 2 km long, with walls over 3 m wide with walkways, 11 towers, and two doors. The area enclosed by the wall on one side and the steep drops on the others was calculated as ca. 90 ha. It contains several water sources, and good arable and grazing land,

Figure 4.5. Mount Kassar with the Byzantine fortifications.

but as far as we can see at present human occupation seems to have been quite sporadic. On the highest peak in the northwest, pottery dating from the eighth to the fifth century B.C. indicates the existence of an Archaic village, while a small scatter of ceramics from the fifth to sixth centuries A.D. has also been located. In all likelihood, the imposing Byzantine fortress was built between the end of the seventh and the beginning of the eighth century[12]— coinciding, significantly, with the establishment of the Sicilian *thema*.

As part of our programme, we have conducted magnetometric surveys and opened areas for excavation in five different places (Figure 4.5). Judging by the results obtained so far, the building of the fortification did not in any way lead to the foundation of a town. The enclosed area seems to have been occupied only in some places, linked to control of the fortification and the surrounding countryside. The military building (about 30 m overall), sited on a hill that controls the east gate, proved to have been built in two phases, with a small tower at one corner (Figure 4.6). In 2014–15 we excavated small houses built against the internal face of the defensive wall, which seem to have collapsed in the eighth century or later (Figure 4.7). Over the interior as a whole, however, the small quantities and undiagnostic character of the finds indicate that the fortress, probably built to defend this part of Sicily from Islamic invasions, did not survive beyond the middle of the ninth century.

Figure 4.6. Mount Kassar: the military "headquarter" (intervention 7).

At present, no coin dating to the main period of occupation has been found on Mount Kassar. However, some valuable items have been discovered in the excavation of the dwelling area on the top of the mountain: a Hippo type buckle, glass goblets, and necklace beads.

After many centuries of total abandonment, a small church was built during the twelfth century (probably over the ruins of an earlier Byzantine building), on a promontory overlooking the so-called S. Calogero spring. The area to the north of the church was explored in a limited area, revealing paved structures adjoining it (Figure 4.5, intervention 11). These structures, possibly part of a small rural monastery, were completely abandoned towards the end of the thirteenth or the beginning of the fourteenth century. After this short and limited episode of reoccupation, the mountain seems to have been largely abandoned until very recent times.

To conclude this brief presentation of the intensively investigated sites, mention can be made of Colle San Vitale (Figure 4.2), a narrow rocky spur (about 3.5 ha) that rises above the current town of Castronovo di Sicilia. In this "citadel", defensive and religious structures still stand. Archaeological excavations were carried out in the 1990s and the early 2000s (Canzonieri 2007). In 2015–16 we carried out a stratigraphic analysis of the walls and in 2017 dug a small test trench to ascertain the stratigraphic sequence. We are now able to say that substantial construction activity dates back to the thirteenth century, but is preceded by at least two other building phases, which could date to the Norman age. A hypothesis that is gaining increasing strength is that the part of the current old town of Castronovo that is called Rabato could date back to the late Islamic era, perhaps around the second

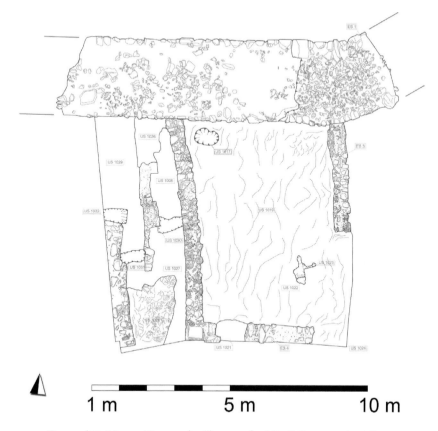

Figure 4.7. Mount Kassar: the "house of soldier" (intervention 6).

half of the tenth century. It is here, however, that the Normans arrived in 1077 and it is Castronovo, with its citadel, that has prospered to this day. Linked to these settlements is a water supply originating on the hills above that feeds a series of irrigated terraces and fountains in the town, before descending to the River Platani, driving several watermills along the way. A new program of investigations is planned to describe and date the origin of this water-management system.

We can summarize the data from current and previous research at Castronovo in the following way. In Roman times, the main settlements of this territory would seem to be located especially in its northernmost part, where a peristyle villa (Villa di San Luca) flourished between the first century BC and second century A.D. (Vassallo and Zirone 2009; Castrorao Barba 2015). A similar settlement can be inferred in the area of Casale San Pietro.

While the third- to fourth-century phases are not clear, a new investment in settlement is evident in the fifth century: the San Luca Villa is reoccupied with the construction of a building with an apse (a church?), and the agro-town of Casale San Pietro is bigger and more prosperous. Several small sites surround the hilltop of Ministalla, a few miles south of Casale. A small farm is perhaps established on a knoll on Mount Kassar. This territorial layout seems to last until the seventh century. In a still viable, but city-free territory, well-positioned in relation to the north-south and east-west road axes and the Platani River Valley, the Byzantine state decided to build the great fortification of Mount Kassar, coinciding with the reorganization of the island as a *thema* and the recurrence of Saracen raids. The fortress of Kassar seems to have had a mainly military character and did not prompt any extensive and lasting settlement within its enclosure. The defensive structure would require the presence of a garrison, but it could also accommodate the surrounding population in the event of danger. Meanwhile, the peasant population probably continued to live mainly at Casale San Pietro. After the Islamic conquest, Kassar was abandoned, while the agro-town continued to be settled, still occupying a large area. The inhabited nucleus around the citadel of Colle San Vitale (perhaps the new central place) could have developed particularly between the tenth and eleventh century, in connection with a system of irrigated terraces. Casale San Pietro would seem to have been reduced to a sparsely settled agricultural area following the Swabian age. It is therefore only the village of Castronovo–San Vitale that continued to thrive in the following centuries.

Concluding Remarks

It is not easy to speak unambiguously of resilience or continuity in periods of change, nor to identify precise hiatus in the settlements, ecosystems and exchange networks, given the present state of research in Sicily. The structures that probably show the most resilience are the ones we have been calling agro-towns (i.e., extensive settlements inhabited mainly by peasants). However, it seems that the term can also be used for some of the main rural settlements of Late Roman Sicily. There are not many systematic excavations of this kind of site, although we have cited the cases of Sofiana (near Piazza Armerina) and Casale San Pietro (near Castronovo); but it would seem that almost every area that has been subjected to surface survey had such sites (Molinari 2013; 2016a; 2016b). They usually extend over several hectares, are located in areas of the plain or on low hills along the main road and were also connected to trans-regional exchange networks. In the case of Sofiana we know that they could have churches, baths, and workshops. In Sicily, this type of site sees significant expansion between the fourth and fifth centuries, but it also often endured for many centuries and persisted even into Islamic times; it is only during the Norman age that the crisis for this kind of settlement could lead to their complete abandonment. Their main expansion would coincide with the increasing frequency of extensive *latifundia*, the *massae fundorum*, linked to owners rarely residing locally and relying on the work of *coloni* (Vera 1997–1998; 1999; 2012; Wickham 2005).

The first question that needs to be discussed is their connection with the *villae*, which are considered to be the directional centers from which the estates were directed. In the case of Sofiana, it has long been believed that it should be the *vicus*, the settlement where peasants dependent on the luxurious Villa del Casale (near Piazza Armerina) lived. Recent research that identified the nearly 23 ha extent of Sofiana in the fifth century suggests that this supposed relationship is over-simplified, because in the fifth century Villa del Casale was "surviving", while Sofiana thrived (Bowes et al. 2011). Even in the case of Castronovo's territory, the Villa di San Luca in the fifth century would seem to be much less prosperous than the Casale San Pietro site. In this regard, however, it should be remembered that between the fifth and sixth centuries there is an important transfer of the great Sicilian estates from the hands of the lay aristocracy to religious institutions (e.g., the churches of Rome, Ravenna, and Milan) or to the imperial domain (Prigent 2017; Vera 2006). This change seems to have determined the loss of importance of the *villae*, which, where they survive, do not seem to maintain the same architectural organization and value. Gregory the Great's *Registrum Epistularum*, according to the reading recently given by Prigent (2017), would point out that the center of management of the estates, by now owned by the Church, would no longer be the *villae*, but the *condumae*. These would be substantially identifiable with villages in which lived the peasants and also the *conductores* (supposed to represent a kind of peasant elite). All this would also explain the dynamics between Villa del Casale and Sofiana. But why would the *condumae*/agro-towns be able to withstand the changes of regime and social structures between the Byzantine and Islamic ages? We must probably imagine that there was strong social cohesion within the peasant communities that lived there, so as to allow for "resilience".[13] The crisis and the abandonment of many of these settlements in the Norman and Swabian age could therefore be linked to the agency of new elite and social groups that broke the system of solidarity within local communities (Molinari 2010).

Regarding the persistence and transformation of internal and interregional exchange networks, we can see, on the one hand, the lengthy persistence of ties (especially with North Africa and with Rome) and, on the other, what appears to be a rather neat break—but only in the eighth century. The fifth century does not seem to see the disruption of the distribution and redistribution of African goods, in which the supply of food to the ancient capital was one of the main engines. Not only would Rome still look like a very big city in the fifth century,[14] but we can also see that goods did not cease to arrive there from North Africa as well. The role of Sicily as one of the main suppliers of wheat to Rome has an interesting effect not only in the vitality of agricultural settlements, in particular during the fifth century, but also in the pollen diagrams of Lake Pergusa, which mark the decisive increase of all kind of cereal cultivation right from this period.

The Byzantine conquest of North Africa and Sicily allows for the continuity of these exchange relations, basically until the seventh century. Recent studies are also trying to show how North African and Sicilian economies would not be stagnant or collapsing during the whole of the seventh century.[15] In Sicily, monetary circulation, the arrival of African goods even in inland locations, and again the pollen data would all seem to agree with this picture. Apparently in the seventh century the island was crucial to the supply of food to both Rome and Constantinople (Prigent 2006; 2010). We may also add that in Proto-Byzantine Sicily there was immense pressure on its resources, when imperial taxation, great properties of non-local churches, and the imperial domain drained resources that were not consumed locally. Along with the *cabotage* between the south coast of the island and the north coast of North Africa, there was still the possibility that African goods were redistributed through Rome as well. In the same period, the routes to Constantinople from eastern Sicily were certainly improved.

Concerning this trade system, closely linked to social and political dynamics, the eighth century appears to mark a turning point. The fracture between the papacy of Rome and the Byzantine empire that was apparently accomplished within the first half of the eighth century, as well as the ultimate conquest of North Africa by Islamic armies, would seem to be clearly tangible, even in the archaeological record. To understand how important the break between the papacy and its Sicilian possessions may have been (Prigent 2004; 2010), we can remember that not only did the church possess a very large portion of the island's cultivable land, but it also played a prominent role in local social life in a truly pervasive way, as evidenced again by Gregory the Great's letters. The Church of Rome was responsible for the management of its own estates, the levying of taxes or loans to its peasants, and the choice of the *conductores* for its estates, but it also played a big part in the election of the bishops in the towns, the protection of the property of aristocratic orphans, ending with its role in the election of the *Praetor Siciliae*—just to cite a few examples. As is well-known, some scholars believe that the loss of Sicilian properties was the basis for a complete switch of Rome's economy during the eighth century to the exploitation of exclusively local resources. The result of the loss of control by the Church of Rome, for at least part of Sicily, must have been a decisive loss of social complexity and the impoverishment of peasant elites as well. It may also be added that Sicily was still important for Byzantium in the eighth century, but somewhat less crucial to its supply. The collapse of A.D. 750 indicated by the pollen sequence in Lake Pergusa does not seem so much the result of climate change, but perhaps of the fact that for the first time in many centuries Sicily had only (or mainly) to feed its own inhabitants.

The persistence of the issue of coins (mainly gold ones) during the eighth and ninth centuries would seem to be linked more to the continuity of the Byzantine state system and its taxation, especially sensitive to the needs of military defense financing (Prigent 2012), than a reflection of a commercialized economy. Exchange networks therefore persisted until the end of the seventh century, but they seemed to have been disrupted during the eighth century. Only ties with the eastern Mediterranean seem to continue, as well as greater vitality in the towns (particularly Catania and Syracuse) and the countryside of the eastern part of the island.

One of the tasks of archaeological research over the next few years is to understand whether the low numbers of sites in the eighth and ninth centuries is due to their poor recognition in the archaeological record, or to a dramatic decline in population. As Wickham (2005: 535–550) has repeatedly argued, the impoverishment of aristocracies can indeed result in a sharp simplification in the quality of material culture. Finally, we can also remember how new phases of marked change (e.g., agricultural transformations and new trade networks) occurred during the Fatimid period (Molinari 2016b); brutal breaks also happened in the late Norman–Swabian period (Molinari 2010).

Sicily seems to have had a very long "Late Antiquity" lasting until the seventh century, as indicated by its close connections with the remaining international networks of exchange, a high level of coin use, and thriving countrysides (where villages were gaining importance, at the expense of the *villae*). During the eighth century, we can see that many things changed markedly, before Sicily was conquered by Muslim invaders. The networks linking Rome, North Africa, and Sicily, if they existed, are nevertheless archaeologically invisible. In the western part of Sicily rural settlements are almost undetectable, while in the east a number of very small sites are a sign of the weakening of the central places; in some parts of the island, at least, the cultivation of plants, especially cereals, collapsed, and a period of increased dryness started as well. The overall context is that in which Carthage was definitively conquered, and the Popes had lost their huge properties in Sicily and were finding new alliance with the Carolingians. On the other hand, Sicily was still important to Byzantium, but not as crucial as it had been in the seventh century. It bears repeating that, after many centuries, Sicily for the first time had to feed only its own population.

Amidst all this disruption, what can be shown to have had significant resilience were the very large villages, the so called agro-towns (Sofiana and Casale San Pietro). They were sometimes able to last at least until the twelfth century, ending only during the Norman age. The strong resilience of the Late Medieval and modern agro-town in the south of Italy has been explained by the socially cohesive bonds of the peasant communities living in them. Similar communities in Sicily were apparently able to resist the changes of Byzantine and Islamic times, but were probably broken by the new Norman social system.

Notes

1. The new data have led me to expand, refine and better articulate the reflections already proposed in Molinari 2013.
2. In particular from Agrigento (Parrello and Rizzo 2016), but also from Palermo (Nef 2013). For a general overview, see Arcifa 2016.
3. *Sicily in Transition* is an ERC project of the Universities of York, Rome and Lecce, co-directed by the author and Martin O.H. Carver.
4. The editors of these volumes in particular are keen to point out that this region is very large and therefore it is immensely reductive and basically wrong to use the general term "African pottery".
5. See for instance Molinari 2013, 2016a; Cacciaguerra et al. 2015, with references.
6. For recent papers on the transformations of the *villae* in Sicily, see Pensabene and Sfamemi 2014; Castrorao Barba 2016.
7. See www.sicilyintransition.org
8. Understanding of changes in the population, its diet and origins are being sought through the analysis of DNA, stable isotopes of plants, animal and human bones, and organic residues in transport and cooking pottery, undertaken in the laboratories at the University of York (BioArch).
9. African Red Slip Ware forms Hayes 61A, 102A, 104B, 105B and African amphorae type Keay LXI-LXII can be cited from previous survey (e.g., Castrorao Barba 2015) and also new ones (unpublished materials, studied by C. F. Mangiaracina). A probable decanum of Constans II was also found.
10. For example, casseroles with inturned rims and amphorae with handles with deep median incision (unpublished data provided by C. F. Mangiaracina)
11. The wider report on the characteristics of the walls is in Vassallo 2009; 2010.
12. A house dated to the beginning of the eighth century was built against the fortress wall. The defensive wall shows a masonry style mainly consisting of limestone elements and different kind of tiles datable between the fifth and eighth centuries bonded with lime mortar (cf. Vassallo 2009; 2010; Carver and Molinari 2016).
13. On this same topic, but for different times and places (the south of Italy in the late Middle Ages and modern times), see Curtis 2014.
14. Although the demographic decline was very substantial compared to the fourth century and the estimates are not concordant, it would seem that it was only at the end of the

fifth or beginning of the sixth century that a vertiginous collapse of the population was recorded. The estimate of 60,000 inhabitants for the Byzantine age still makes Rome a very big city by the standards of the period, and in the meantime the areas of possible food supply had been greatly reduced (Meneghini and Santangeli Valenzani 2004).

15. E.g., Morrisson 2015; Reynolds 2015; Fenwick 2013 for North Africa; Prigent 2013 for Sicily.

References

Alfano, Antonio

2015   I paesaggi medievali in Sicilia. Uno studio di archeologia comparativa: le valli dello Jato e del Belìce Destro (PA), la Villa del Casale (EN) e Valcorrente (CT). *Archeologia medievale* 42: 329–352

Arcifa, Lucia

2010   Nuove ipotesi a partire dalla rilettura dei dati archeologici: la Sicilia orientale. In *La Sicile de Byzance à l'Islam*, edited by Annliese Nef and Vivien Prigent, pp. 15–49. De Boccard, Paris.

2016   Trasformazioni urbane nell'altomedioevo siciliano: uno *status quaestionis*. In *Paesaggi urbani tardoantichi*, edited by Maria Concetta Parello and Maria Serena Rizzo, pp. 31–40. Edipuglia, Bari.

Ardizzone, Fabiola

2010   Nuove ipotesi a partire dalla rilettura dei dati archeologici: la Sicilia occidentale. In *La Sicile de Byzance à l'Islam*, edited by Annliese Nef and Vivien Prigent, pp. 50–76. De Boccard, Paris.

Ardizzone, Fabiola, and Filippo Pisciotta

2016   Marettimo (TP) (sito 84), In *La ceramica africana nella Sicilia romana,* edited by Daniele Malfitana and Michel Bonifay. Monografie dell'Istituto per i Beni Archeologici e Monumentali, CNR, 12, pp. 213–219. CNR IBAM, Istituto per i Beni Archeologici e Monumentali, Catania.

Bowes, Kim, Mariaelena Ghisleni, Gioacchino Francesco La Torre, and Emanuele Vaccaro

2011   Preliminary Report on Sofiana/Mansio Philosophiana in the Hinterland of Piazza Armerina. *Journal of Roman Archaeology* 24: 423–449.

Cacciaguerra, Giuseppe

2009   Dinamiche insediative in Sicilia tra V e X secolo: tre contesti a confronto nell'area megarese. In *V Congresso Nazionale di Archeologia Medievale*, edited by Giuliano Volpe and Favia Pasquale, pp. 296–301. All'Insegna del Giglio, Firenze.

2015   Cultura materiale e commerci in Sicilia fra bizantini e arabi (VIII–metà X secolo): nuovi dati sulle ceramiche fini e le anfore dai contesti altomedievali di Siracusa. In *Congresso Nazionale di Archeologia Medievale 7*, vol. 2, edited by Paul Arthur and Marco Leo Imperiale, pp. 367–372. All'Insegna del Giglio, Firenze.

Cacciaguerra, Giuseppe, Antonino Facella, and Luca Zambito,

2015   Continuity and Discontinuity in Seventh-Century Sicily: Rural Settlement and Economy. In *The Long Seventh Century: Continuity and Discontinuity*, edited by Alessandro Gnasso, Emanuele Ettore Intagliata, Thomas J. MacMaster, and Bethan N. Morris, pp. 199–234. Peter Lang, Oxford.

Canzonieri, Emanuele

2007   Il castello di S. Vitale. In *Archeologia nelle vallate del Fiume Torto e del San Leonardo,* edited by Stefano Vassallo, pp. 50–56. Comune di Roccapalumba, Roccapalumba.

Capelli, Claudio, and Carmela Franco

2014   New Archaeological and Archaeometric Data on Sicilian Wine Production in the Roman Period (First to Sixth Century A.D.): Typology, Origin and Distribution in Selected Western Mediterranean Contexts. *Rei Cretariae Romanae Fautorum Acta* 43: 547–556.

Carver, Martin O.H., and Alessandra Molinari

2016   Sicily in Transition Research Project: Investigation at Castronovo. Results and Prospects. www.fastionline.org/docs/FOLDER-it-2016-352.pdf.

Carver, Martin O.H, Alessandra Molinari, Veronica Aniceti, Francesca Colangeli, Nicoletta Giannini, Fabio Giovannini, Madeleine Hummler, Claudio Filippo Mangiaracina, Antonino Meo, and Paola Orecchioni

2017   Ricerche 2016 a Castronovo di Sicilia: Sicily in Transition (Progetto ERC Advanced Grant 2016–693600). *Notiziario Archeologico Soprintendenza Palermo* 23/2017.

Casalini, Marta

2015   Roma e il Mediterraneo dal IV al VI secolo. In *Le forme della crisi: produzioni ceramiche e commerci nell'Italia centrale,* edited by Enrico Cirelli, Francesca Diosono, and Helen Patterson, pp. 535–546. Ante Quem, Bologna.

Castrorao Barba, Angelo

2015   Entroterra tra due mari: il territorio di Castronovo di Sicilia (Palermo) tra età romana e periodo bizantino. In *Storia e archeologia globale 2. I pascoli, i campi, il mare. Paesaggi d'altura e di pianura in Italia dall'Età del Bronzo al Medioevo,* edited by Franco Cambi, Giovanni De Venuto, and Roberto Goffredo, pp. 253–267. Edipuglia, Bari.

2016   Sicily before the Muslims: The Transformation of the Roman Villas between Late Antiquity and the Early Middle Ages, Fourth to Eighth Centuries CE. *Journal of Transcultural Medieval Studies* 3: 145–190.

Corretti, Alessandro, Antonino Facella, and Claudio Filippo Mangiaracina

2014   Contessa Entellina (PA): forme di insediamento tra tarda antichità e età islamica. In *Les dynamiques de l'islamisation en Méditerranée centrale et en Sicile: nouvelles propositions et découvertes récentes,* edited by Annliese Nef and Fabiola Ardizzone, pp. 341–348. Collection de l'École française de Rome 487. Edipuglia, Bari.

Curtis, Daniel R.

2014   *Coping with Crisis: The Resilience and Vulnerability of Pre-industrial Settlements.* Routledge, New York.

Facella, Antonino, and Vanessa Gagliardi

2016   Segesta (TP) (Sito 79). In *La ceramica africana nella Sicilia romana,* edited by Daniele Malfitana and Michel Bonifay. Monografie dell'Istituto per i Beni Archeologici e Monumentali, CNR, 12, pp. 204–212. CNR IBAM, Istituto per i Beni Archeologici e Monumentali, Catania.

Fenwick, Corisande

2013   From Africa to Ifriqiya: Settlement and Society in Early Medieval North Africa (650–800). *Al-Masaq* 25: 9–33.

Little, Lester Knox (editor)

2007   *Plague and the End of Antiquity: The Pandemic of 541–750.* Cambridge University Press, Cambridge.

Malfitana, Daniele, and Michel Bonifay (editors)

2016   *La ceramica africana nella Sicilia romana,* 2 vols. Monografie dell'Istituto per i Beni Archeologici e Monumentali, CNR, 12. CNR IBAM, Istituto per i Beni Archeologici e Monumentali, Catania.

Maurici, Ferdinando

2000   Problemi di storia, archeologia e topografia medievale nel territorio di Castronuovo di Sicilia in provincia di Palermo-I. In *Atti II giornate internazionali di studio sull'area Elima,* pp. 755–776. Scuola normale superiore di Pisa, Pisa – Gibellina.

Meneghini, Roberto, and Riccardo Santangeli Valenzani

2004   *Roma nell'Altomedioevo: topografia e urbanistica della città dal V al X secolo.* Libreria dello Stato, Roma.

Molinari, Alessandra

2010   Paesaggi rurali e formazioni sociali nella Sicilia islamica, normanna e sveva (secoli X–XIII). *Archeologia Medievale* 37: 229–246.

2013   Sicily between the Fifth and the Tenth Century: Villae, Villages, Towns and Beyond. Stability, Expansion or Recession? In *The Insular System of the Early Byzantine Mediterranean: Archaeology and History. Atti del seminario internazionale di studi Nicosia (Cipro), 24–26 ottobre 2007,* edited by Demetrios Michaelides, Philippe Pergola, and Enrico Zanini, pp. 97–114. British Archaeological Reports International Series 2523. Archaeopress, Oxford.

2016a   Fortified and Unfortified Settlements in Byzantine and Islamic Sicily: Sixth to Eleventh Centuries. In *Fortified Settlements in Early Medieval Europe: Defended Communities of the 8th to 10th Centuries,* edited by Neil J. Christie and Hajnalka Herold, pp. 320–332. Oxbow, Oxford.

2016b   'Islamisation' and the Rural World: Sicily and al-Andalus. What Kind of Archaeology? In *New Directions in Early Medieval European Archaeology: Spain and Italy Compared. Essays for Riccardo Francovich,* edited by Sauro Gelichi and Richard Hodges, pp. 187–220. Brepols, Turnhout.

Molinari, Alessandra, and Ilaria Neri

2004   Dall'età tardo-imperiale al XII secolo: i risultati della ricognizione eseguita nel territorio di Calatafimi. *Mélanges de l'Ecole française de Rome: Moyen Âge* 116(1): 109–127.

Morrisson, Cécile

1998   La Sicile byzantine: une lueur dans les siècles obscurs. *Numismatica e antichità classica* 27: 307–334.

2015   *Regio dives in omnibus bonis ornata*: The African Economy from the Vandals to the Arab Conquest in the Light of Coin Evidence. In *North Africa under Byzantium and Early Islam,* edited by Jonathan P. Conant and Susan T. Stevens, pp. 173–199. Dumbarton Oaks Research Library and Collection, Washington, DC.

Nef, Annliese (editor)

2013   *A Companion to Medieval Palermo: The History of a Mediterranean City from 600 to 1500.* Brill, Leiden.

Panella, Clementina, Lucia Saguì, Fulvio Coletti, and Marta Casalini

2010   Contesti tardoantichi di Roma: una rilettura alla luce di nuovi dati. In *LRCW 3, Late Roman Coarse Wares, Cooking Wares and Amphorae in the Mediterranean: Archaeology and Archaeometry. Comparison between Western and Eastern Mediterranean*, edited by Gabriella Guiducci, Marinella Pasquinucci, and Simonetta Menchelli, pp. 57–78. Archaeopress, Oxford.

Parello, Maria Concetta, and Maria Serena Rizzo (editors)

2016   *Paesaggi urbani tardoantichi: casi a confronto. Atti delle Giornate gregoriane, VIII edizione (29–30 novembre 2014).* Edipuglia, Bari.

Pensabene, Patrizio

2016   Il contributo degli scavi 2004–2014 alla storia della Villa del Casale di Piazza Armerina tra IV e XII secolo. In *Silenziose rivoluzioni: la Sicilia dalla tarda antichità al primo medioevo. Atti dell'Incontro di studio, Catania-Piazza Armerina, 21–23 maggio 2015*, edited by Claudia Giuffrida and Margherita Cassia, pp. 223–271. Edizioni del Prisma, Catania.

Pensabene, Patrizio, and Carla Sfamemi (editors)

2014   *La villa restaurata e i nuovi studi sull'edilizia residenziale tardoantica. Atti del convegno internazionale del Centro interuniversitario di studi sull'edilizia abitativa tardoantica nel Mediterraneo (CISEM) (Piazza Armerina 7–10 novembre 2012).* Edipuglia, Bari.

Prigent, Vivien

2004   Les empereurs isauriens et la confiscation des patrimoines pontificaux d'Italie du Sud. *Mélanges de l'Ecole française de Rome: Moyen Âge* 116: 557–594.

2006   Le rôle des provinces d'Occident dans l'approvisionnement de Constantinople (618–717): témoignages numismatique et sigillographique. *Mélanges de l'Ecole française de Rome: Moyen Âge* 118: 269–300.

2010   La Sicile byzantine, entre papes et empereurs (6ème – 8ème siècle). In *Zwischen Ideal und Wirklichkeit: Herrschaft auf Sizilien von der Antike bis zum Spätmittelalter*, edited by David Engels, pp. 201–230. Franz Steiner, Stuttgart.

2012   Monnaie et circulation monétaire en Sicile du début du VIIIᵉ siècle à l'avènement de la domination musulman. In *L'héritage byzantin en Italie (VIIIᵉ – XIIᵉ siècle)*, II: *Les cadres juridiques et sociaux et les institutions publiques,* edited by Jean-Marie Martin, Annick Peters-Custot, and Vivien Prigent, pp. 455–482. Ecole Française de Rome, Rome.

2013   La circulation monétaire en Sicile (VIᵉ–VIIᵉ siècle). In *The Insular System of Early Byzantine Mediterranean: Archaeology and History. Atti del seminario internazionale di studi Nicosia (Cipro), 24–26 ottobre 2007*, edited by Demetrios Michaelides, Philippe Pergola, and Enrico Zanini, pp. 139–160. British Archaeological Reports International Series 2523. Archaeopress, Oxford.

2017   Le grand domaine sicilien à l'aube du Moyen Âge. In *L'héritage byzantin en Italie (VIIIᵉ-XIIᵉ siècle)*, IV: *Habitat et structure agraire,* edited by Jean-Marie Martin,

Annick Peters-Custot, and Vivien Prigent, pp. 207–236. Collection de l'Ecole Française de Rome 531. Ecole Française de Rome, Rome.

Reynolds, Paul

2015   From Vandal Africa to Arab Ifrïqiya: Tracing Ceramic and Economic Trends through the Fifth to the Eleventh Centuries. In *North Africa under Byzantium and early Islam,* edited by Jonathan P. Conant and Susan T. Stevens, pp. 129–172. Dumbarton Oaks Research Library and Collection, Washington, DC.

Rizzo, Maria Serena, and Luca Zambito

2010   Ceramiche comuni ed anfore dal villaggio tardoantico di Cignana (Naro-Agrigento, Sicilia, Italia. *In LRCW 3, Late Roman Coarse Wares, Cooking Wares and Amphorae in the Mediterranean: Archaeology and Archaeometry. Comparison between Western and Eastern Mediterranean,* edited by Simonetta Menchelli, Sara Santoro, Marinella Pasquinucci, and Gabriella Guiducci, pp. 293–300. Archaeopress, Oxford.

2016   Naro (AG). Cignana (sito 67). In *La ceramica africana nella Sicilia romana,* edited by Daniele Malfitana and Michel Bonifay. Monografie dell'Istituto per i Beni Archeologici e Monumentali, CNR, 12, pp. 167–175. CNR IBAM, Istituto per i Beni Archeologici e Monumentali, Catania.

Rizzo, Maria Serena, Laura Danile, and Luca Zambito

2014   L'insediamento rurale nel territorio di Agrigento: nuovi dati da prospezioni e scavi. In *Les dynamiques de l'islamisation en Méditerranée centrale et en Sicile: nouvelles propositions et découvertes récentes* edited by Annliese Nef and Fabiola Ardizzone, pp. 351–364. Edipuglia, Bari-Roma.

Sadori, Laura, Carlo Giraudi, Alessia Masi, Magny Michel, Elena Ortu, Giovanni Zanchetta, and Adam Izdebski

2016   Climate, Environment and Society in Southern Italy during the Last 2000 Years: A Review of the Environmental, Historical and Archaeological Evidence. *Quaternary Science Reviews* 136: 173–188.

Vaccaro, Emanuele

2017   Philosophiana in Central Sicily in the Late Roman and Byzantine Periods: Settlement and Economy. In *Encounters, Excavations and Argosies: Essays for Richard Hodges*, edited by John Moreland, John Mitchell, and Bea Leal, pp. 300–314. Archaeopress, Oxford.

Vaccaro, Emanuele, Gioacchino La Torre, Claudio Capelli, Mariaelena Ghisleni, Giulia Lazzeri, Michael MacKinnon, Anna Maria Mercuri, Alessandra Pecci, Eleonora Rattighieri, Stefano Ricchi, Elisa Rizzo, and Marco Sfacteria

2015   La produzione di ceramica a Philosophiana (Sicilia centrale) nella media età bizantina: metodi di indagine ed implicazioni economiche. *Archeologia Medievale* 42: 53–91.

Vassallo, Stefano

2009   Le fortificazioni bizantine del Kassar di Castronovo di Sicilia: indagini preliminari. In *Immagine e immagini della Sicilia e di altre isole del Mediterraneo antico. Atti delle seste giornate internazionali di studi sull'area elima e la Sicilia occidentale nel contesto mediterraneo, Erice, 12–16 ottobre 2006,* vol. II, edited by Carmine Ampolo, pp. 679–696. Edizione della Normale, Pisa.

2010   Il territorio di Castronovo di Sicilia in età bizantina e le fortificazioni del Kassar. In *La Sicilia bizantina: storia, città e territorio. Atti del VI convegno di studi*, edited by Marina Congiu, Simona Modeo, and Massimo Arnone, pp. 259–276. Sciascia, Caltanissetta.

Vassallo, Stefano (editor)

2007   *Archeologia nelle vallate del Fiume Torto e del San Leonardo*. Comune di Roccapalumba, Roccapalumba.

Vassallo, Stefano, and Davide Zirone

2009   La villa rustica di Contrada San Luca (Castronovo di Sicilia, Palermo). In *Immagine e immagini della Sicilia e di altre isole del Mediterraneo antico. Atti delle seste giornate internazionali di studi sull'area elima e la Sicilia occidentale nel contesto mediterraneo, Erice, 12–16 ottobre 2006*, vol. II, edited by Carmine Ampolo, pp. 671–678. Edizione della Normale, Pisa.

Vera, Domenico

1997–1998 Fra Egitto ed Africa, fra Roma e Costantinopoli, fra annona e commercio: la Sicilia nel Mediterraneo tardoantico. *Kokalos* 43/44: 33–74.

1999   *Massa fundorum*. Forme della grande proprietà e poteri della città in Italia fra Costantino e Gregorio Magno. *Mélanges de l'Ecole française de Rome: Antiquité* 111: 991–1026.

2006   L'altra faccia della luna: la società contadina nella Sicilia di Gregorio Magno. *Studi storici* 47: 437–462.

2012   Questioni di storia agraria tardoromana: schiavi, coloni, villae. *Antiquité tardive* 20: 115–122.

Wickham, Chris

2005   *Framing the Early Middle Ages: Europe and the Mediterranean, 400–800*. Oxford University Press, Oxford.

The Transformation of the Adriatic Islands from Antiquity to the Early Middle Ages

Miljenko Jurković

The communities living on Adriatic islands needed to adapt to processes that had an impact on settlement patterns during the long time span from Antiquity to the Early Middle Ages: the Romanization of Dalmatia, from the first century A.D.; the great migrations in the fifth; the Gothic wars in the first half of the sixth; the incursion of Avars and Slavs at the beginning of the seventh; and finally the clash of two superpowers—Byzantium and the Carolingian empire at the end of the eighth century.

In Late Antiquity some of the Roman towns became bishoprics, and most of the villae *continued to be inhabited and had churches built within them. During the Gothic wars some of the* villae *were fortified; the towns rebuilt their defensive walls. A huge number of* castra *was built, protecting the maritime routes. After the Avar and Slav incursions the islands on the northern Adriatic were not much affected, but on the islands of Central Dalmatia the decline of towns is visible, as well as ruralization, and the abandonment of settlements.*

The last impact resulted from the Carolingian expansion towards southeastern Europe. The end of Late Antiquity and the beginning of the Early Middle Ages were marked by forming new frontiers between the empires, involving the islands.

The Adriatic: A Highway between a Thousand Islands

The Adriatic Sea, seen as just a large gulf of the Mediterranean, with its 1185 islands, offers huge possibilities in tracking the changes that occurred over the long time-span between imperial Roman times and the Early Middle Ages (Figure 5.1). Unfortunately, even with almost a hundred populated islands, the problem of very scarce data on settlement patterns is one that needs to be dealt with. In fact, until recently, Croatian archaeology has never dealt with rural or secondary settlements from Late Antiquity and the Early Middle Ages. This is probably to be expected, given that much better choices existed. For example, in Istria (part of the Roman *Regio X—Venetia et Histria*) and in the Roman province of Dalmatia there are more than 30 Roman towns, many of which still survive today with only slightly changed layouts: thus developed urban archaeology and *poleogenesis*. On the other hand, in the same territory there are hundreds of Late Antique and Early Medieval churches in different stages of preservation, so the archaeology of their walls developed long before it became fashionable. Finally, we come to an absurdity: hundreds of cemeteries have been excavated, but very little is known about where those people lived.

With new technologies (e.g., remote sensing) it has become possible to gain information more quickly and easily, reducing the burden of laborious fieldwork by traditional techniques that sometimes produces only meagre results. The question of the occupation of islands in Late Antiquity, at least, can now be approached from different points of view, depending on the kind of material one is dealing with. In the region considered here, towns, *castra*, churches, and monasteries provide substantial information, while Late Roman public or funerary sculpture, and cemeteries around suburban churches complete the picture. Rural settlements offering only limited information are not the primary target, especially given that neither the domestic ceramic wares nor poorly constructed walls offer very precise dating tools. Patterns of transformation in the *longue durée*, as well as the use of landscape in micro- and macro-situations, need to be processed so as to understand all aspects of the historical landscape.

Since periodizations are not the same in different parts of the ancient world, due to different historical situations, here, for the sake of clarity, I use more general terminology: Late Roman or Late Imperial ends with Diocletian; Late Antiquity starts with the Tetrarchy; and the Early Middle Ages begin with the Carolingian expansion in the last decades of the eighth century. The beginning of Late Antiquity is marked by an outstanding monument—the palace that Diocletian built to retire to after resigning the imperial throne.

During the chronological span considered here, a few political moments had a huge impact on settlement patterns: the great migration of the fifth century pushing people to more secure places, and possibly the islands; the Gothic wars in the first third of the sixth century; and the incursion of Avars and Slavs in the Roman province of Dalmatia at the beginning of the seventh. But were the islands affected? The next and final episode of turbulence is marked by the Carolingian conquest at the end of the eighth century. After the peace treaty of Aachen in A.D. 812, the coastal towns and islands returned to the hands of Byzantium (Krk, Osor, Rab, Zadar, Trogir, Split, Dubrovnik, and Kotor), while all the rest entered the newly formed principality of Croatia, under Carolingian supremacy.

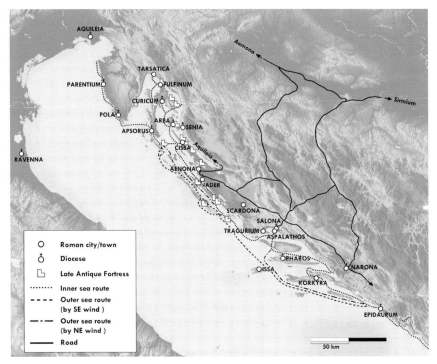

Figure 5.1. The eastern Adriatic coast in Late Antiquity (M. Jurković).

So there was, in general, a smooth passage from the Imperial period to Late Antiquity. Most of the towns continued to exist, the only change being the shift of their focal point from the Imperial forum to the Christian cathedral complex. What happened to the rural settlements is as yet difficult to tell. The villas mostly lived on, many with a new church. Commerce, using maritime routes, also persisted. The change to Late Antiquity is marked by Christianization taking place, as far as we can tell, already at the end of the fourth century A.D. in the most important centers, in the fifth for other towns, and in the sixth for the *pagus*. But was there uninterrupted continuity in the life of villas or other rural settlements on the islands? And what was the impact of wars? We will try to examine these questions by analyzing a few case-studies, tracking change through to the end of the eighth century. These case studies have been chosen purposefully. On the one hand, the islands of central Dalmatia have shown evidence of ruptures in continuity after the Avar and Slav expansion in the early seventh century; on the other hand, the Quarnero islands (*Sinus Flanaticus*) had a much smoother transition and are also, perhaps, better researched. I start, therefore, with the small island of Rab and then compare the general conclusions there with the other, much

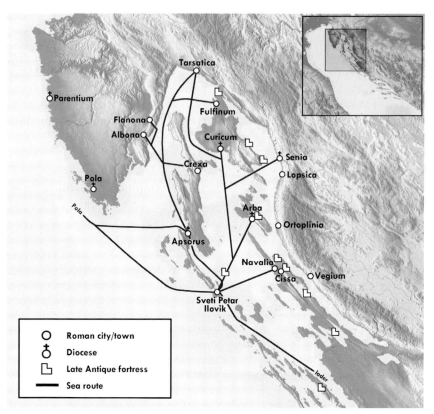

Figure 5.2. The Quarnero Gulf in Late Antiquity (M. Jurković).

bigger islands of the Quarnero Gulf. I will refer to the general situation in the rest of the Adriatic in the conclusions.

A Case Study: The Island of Rab

Rab (*Arba*) is a relatively small island (93.6 km²) situated in the southern part of the Quarnero Gulf (Figure 5.2). The east-northeast and northwest zones are karstic, the northeast with numerous *doline*, but the south-southwest part is a fertile zone. A noticeable presence of flysch fields and a system of streams made it suitable for settlement and exploitation. In pre-Roman times the Illyrian tribe of the *Liburni* lived in hill forts (*casteglieri*). After the Roman conquest the most prominent of those settlements, *Arba*, gained the rank of *municipium* (Suić 1976: 188).

The island, because of its territorial organization, seemed very promising for tracking changes in settlement patterns in the urban and rural landscape: it had only one Roman town, maritime *villae* (one possibly fortified in Late

Antiquity), a Justinianic *castrum*, and rural settlements (some of prehistoric origin), and churches and settlements along the Roman road. This diversity of settlements and their functions attracted our attention more than 10 years ago. A research program was established by the International Research Centre for Late Antiquity and the Middle Ages at Zagreb University (Croatia) and the University of Padova (Italy). The lack of previous excavations on the island made us first consider excavating some of the most important sites, while at the same time surveying the whole territory.

Tracking Changes in the Town of Rab

In general, the town of Rab (Figure 5.3) shows continuity of settlement. In pre-Roman times it was a typical Liburnian settlement on a peninsula flanked on both sides by harbors. The walls of the Roman town were erected in the time of the Emperor Augustus (*CIL* III, 3117), but very little is known about them: only sporadic finds and *spolia* in Medieval houses show the quality of long-vanished architecture. There is also evidence of a number of now-disappeared imperial statues from the second and third centuries, the time when the town reached its peak, with a new water supply and new buildings (Nedved 1989). Thus the reconstruction of the Roman town was based only on the shape of the street grid (Suić 1976: 168), and there has been a long-lasting debate, still largely unresolved, as to the extent of the town both to the west and to the north (Budak 2006: 125). Recently, however, we were able to map the first two locations to yield Roman architecture. The excavation in 2016, aiming to find the bishop's palace in the garden of the Benedictine nunnery, revealed, beneath Medieval walls, a small portion of a luxurious early Imperial *domus* with floor mosaics. Without jumping to premature conclusions, we can state that this position, overlooking the southern cliff-edge of the town

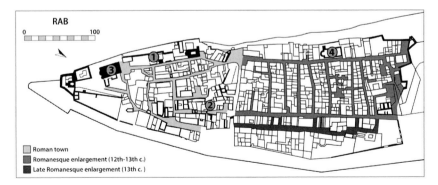

Figure 5.3. Rab, plan: 1. the Roman *domus;* 2. the Roman mausoleum; 3. the cathedral; 4. the Late Antique church of St John (M. Jurković).

and near the forum, is a privileged one, being used in Late Antiquity for the bishop's palace. Another excavation revealed the location of a house in the northern part of the town. In the garden of a restaurant in Srednja ulica (Middle Street), we had the opportunity to excavate a portion of the town wall (see below). In the Imperial Roman stratigraphic layer, we found a huge doorstep of what seems to be a mausoleum in a cemetery zone, with four sarcophagi. Thus, according to the present state of research, Rab was a fairly small town occupying the eastern part of the peninsula.

Huge changes occurred in Late Antiquity. At the eastern end of Gornja ulica (Upper street) the cathedral complex was built, comprising the cathedral, with an atrium on the west side, and a baptistery on the north, linked to the cathedral through a passage (Domijan 2007: 89–92). Farther west, the bishop's palace occupied the place of the former Roman *domus*. The complex may be supposed to have been built (as in Zadar, for example) on or near the Roman forum, of which there is still no knowledge. Along the same street towards the west, later documents mention the parish church of St Thomas, no longer extant, but of probable Late Antique origin (Domijan 2007: 47). Farther west again was built the three-nave basilica of St John, with floor mosaics (Jurković 1990); it was a suburban, possibly funerary church.

For the purpose of the present topic, however, the most instructive evidence comes from the excavation of a small section of the town walls in Srednja ulica (Middle Street). This portion of the walls clearly cut the afore-mentioned possible mausoleum. The construction is clumsy, using *spolia* (mostly the sarcophagi), and it was undoubtedly carried out in an unplanned manner, using whatever material was to hand. The overlapping of the former structure tells us that the Late Antique town shrank in comparison with the Imperial one. Contextualizing that fact, the only moment when the town might have been threatened is the Gothic war in the first half of the sixth century. As for the space behind the new wall, it was later used for a blacksmith's workshop.

There are no other data for the town in Late Antiquity. Further changes occurred in the Early Middle Ages, when the cathedral received new liturgical furnishings. This fact is of utmost importance, because it can be contextualized within a much larger picture, that of the political and diplomatic activities of the two superpowers—Byzantium and the Carolingian realm—before their clash in the first decade of the ninth century. The altar screen was sculpted by the "Quarnero workshop" in the last decades of the eighth century (Jurković 2016). The *ciborium* was made by the "Master of Zadar ambos", a workshop linked with Cividale, and thus only possible in the first decade of the ninth century, when the Carolingians entered Dalmatia and before the peace treaty of Aachen in A.D. 812, when Rab returned under the supremacy of Byzantium (Jurković 2015).

The Transformation of the Rural Landscape

In order to establish the changes that occurred in rural settlement patterns, we undertook an extensive survey of different parts of the island, accompanied by strategic excavations of the most promising archaeological sites, covering different micro-regions. I attempt to depict them here following a geographical order, starting from the town of Rab and moving first toward the southeast and then to the northwest (Figure 5.4).

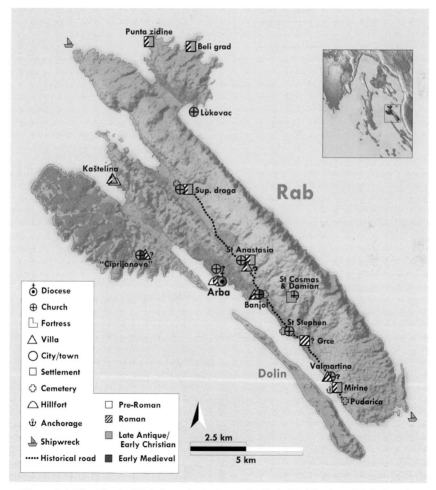

Figure 5.4. The island of Rab from Antiquity to the Early Middle Ages (M. Jurković).

The Banjol Zone. During survey of the southeast part of the island (the zone of Banjol), we recognized the potential of the site of St Lawrence, located 3.5 km south of the town of Rab, in a large agricultural area covering most of the central strip of the island (Brogiolo et al. 2017).

The church, given its size, is too important to have stood in isolation in the landscape, and its liturgical furnishings speak of huge wealth on the part of the individual who commissioned it (Figure 5.5). Thus it had to belong to a settlement, probably a residential villa. Its position, some 50 m from the shore, along the only road from the town towards Barbat, and fertile fields to the north, suggest a villa. The whole of the Banjol zone is densely urbanized today, having destroyed most of the remnants of earlier buildings, but there are enough elements to deduce the history of the site. The very name Banjol (Lat. *balneolum*) already suggests baths of some sort and there are four springs in the vicinity. The descendants of people who built their homes in this zone tell of finding vaulted rooms, mosaic floors, and walls everywhere. Every house in the neighbourhood keeps fragments of

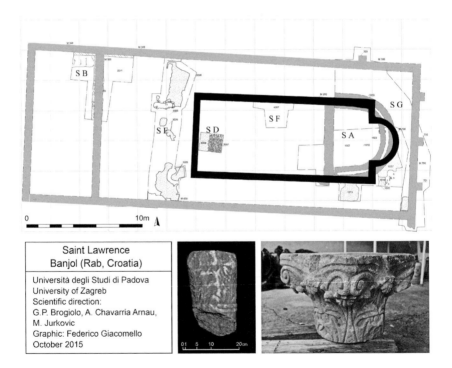

Figure 5.5. (Above) Island of Rab, Banjol, church of S. Lawrence, plan: grey, the Late Antique church; black, the Early Medieval church (after Brogiolo et al. 2017). (Below) capital, sixth century; marble altar screen capital, sixth century (photos by I. Kranjec).

sculpture from the Roman, Late Antique, and Medieval periods, which they always say were found in their gardens; finds of ceramics are ubiquitous. This is enough to hypothesize a Roman settlement, probably a villa of some important person, who in Late Antiquity commissioned the building of the church and furnished it with marble sculpture imported probably from Constantinopolitan workshops. We cannot of course know if the settlement was in continuous use from Roman times to Late Antiquity, but the supposition is of continuity. On the other hand, the abandonment is clearly shown by the church itself. Its liturgical furnishings date to the mid-sixth century, probably immediately after the Gothic wars. We can presume it functioned at least for some time. The discovery of an *ossuarium* (probably created in its last two centuries), with finds such as belt buckles of the Corinth type, dated to the second half of the seventh century (Brogiolo et al. 2017: 672), speaks of a cemetery around the church still active at least during the seventh century. The buckles are often associated with military or administrative dignitaries, again shedding light on the importance of the site.

The church eventually fell into ruin. Inside its presbytery a smaller church, single nave with a semicircular apse has been constructed. There is as yet no evidence of the time of destruction and new construction; similar cases throughout the Adriatic give a span from Early Middle Ages to the eleventh century, but not later.

The Barbat Zone. Following the Roman road towards the southeast, a few other Roman and Late Antique sites have been reported. In Barbat, a zone of dense construction, the monastery of St Stephen was founded in the eleventh century, probably on the site of an older church. Under the modern church, two early Christian sarcophagi were excavated, dated to the sixth century (Brusić 1926: 59–61). An exceptional find, a gold *encolpion,* dated again to the seventh century, has been connected to those sarcophagi (Basić 2012). Walls that can be seen around the modern cemetery argue in favour of a settlement with a church.

Above Barbat on the mountain ridge, a *castrum* with the church of St Cosmas and St Damian (Figure 5.6) was built during the Gothic war (Jurković and Turković 2012). Analysis of its structures has revealed constant changes during the Middle Ages. It can be concluded that, after having lost its primary function as a military outpost, it served as a *refugium* for people living in the zone in times of danger.

Around Grce, again along the historic road, the walls of multiple habitations, mosaic *tesserae*, and an inscription had been documented already in the first half of the twentieth century (Brusić 1926: 58). Further southeast along the Roman road, two more sites were spotted, both Late Antique. Valmartina was interpreted either as a huge early Christian church (Čaušević-Bully et al. 2012) or as a settlement (Lipovac and Konestra 2015: 129). Five hundred meters further south Late Antique building remains can be seen, near underwater harbor structures in the Barbat Channel in front of the site of Mirine (Lipovac et al. 2016: 205). To complete the landscape, graves were recently found at Pudarica, dated to the fifth century (Konestra et al. 2017).

From Banjol to Mundanije to Supetarska draga. Returning towards the northwest, on the border between Mundanije and Banjol is the locality called Kaplak—from *caput* (head) and *lacus* (lake), referring to wells and springs—with the church of St Anastasia. A Roman *stela* (funerary monument) was also found on the site. At the locality za Markovićem, survey and excavations have defined a rural complex (Lipovac and Konestra 2015: 129) in use from the third to the sixth century.

In Supetarska draga, in the vicinity of the eleventh-century abbey of St Peter, a few Early Christian fragments of liturgical furnishings have been found; and, as the founding document says that a church already existed here, it is logical to locate it under the Medieval one. For that reason, we have undertaken intensive survey in the surrounding arable fields and conducted an excavation in front of the abbey church. The results show long-term

Figure 5.6. Island of Rab, Barbat, fortress St Cosmas and St Damian: view towards Barbat and the town of Rab, with apse of the sixth-century church in the foreground (photo from 1930).

continuity. A few hundred metres to the east, traces of a settlement can be seen, maybe those of a villa. In front of the medieval church was a graveyard. Under the eleventh–twelfth century layer, and below a destruction horizon, a dry-stone wall perpendicular to the façade of the church has been excavated, and this already existed in Late Antiquity. In the cemetery, large quantities of Late Antique ceramics have been found, along with *amphorae* from the sixth century and a huge quantity of *luminae*, glass oil lamps that belonged to the Early Christian church. As there exist a few fragments of an Early Medieval altar screen, continuity of this church is attested from Late Antiquity to the middle Medieval period.

The Zone of Kampor. We started with what was believed to be a late antique *castrum* on the peninsula of Kaštelina in Kampor (Tomičić 1990). The excavations we undertook from 2005 to 2008 showed, on the contrary, that the site is a Roman villa, probably of the maritime type (Jurković et al. 2008), from the Imperial period. At some point during the third century, the villa was partially demolished and then reconstructed, subsequently being abandoned sometime in Late Antiquity. Structures raised above the abandonment layer are for the moment not datable, as there is still no evidence of fortifying the villa in the sixth century.

The Zone of Kalifront. The survey of the peninsula of Kalifront, today under dense forest, gave different results. There was no evidence of any Roman, Late Antique or Early Medieval settlement, except for the apse of a Late Antique church (Jurković and Tenšek 1990). For better understanding of the transformations of the historical landscape, we decided to start from that point and excavate the church, before proceeding to intensive survey of the zone. The first campaign in 2017, not yet published, gave some expected, but also totally unexpected results. The church is located in the southeast of Kalifront, on a slight slope in dense forest, 600 m from the cove of Gožinka, on a location called Ciprijanovo. The land has been in the possession of the nunnery of St Andrew in Rab since the Middle Ages, and served for agriculture. As the nunnery, founded in the eleventh century, is for members of wealthy families, it can be supposed the land was donated by one of the prominent members of the *patriciate* of Rab.

The first campaign revealed the partial layout of a Late Antique church with an apse, polygonal on the exterior and semi-circular internally, typical of the fifth and sixth centuries. Its length could not be measured because of a modern road that destroyed the façade, but it must have been around 20 m; whether it was single- or three-aisled could not be established at this point. The church, being too big for a votive church out in the countryside, had to be connected to some sort of settlement—and, indeed, survey of the immediate vicinity north of the church revealed a rectangular structure of some 400 m², together with another nearby wall. Near this structure, a huge partially-worked block was found, probably the base of a Roman semi-column. Small finds were scarce, but three fragments of marble slabs speak of the rich liturgical furnishings, while two bronze coins found outside the church are preliminarily dated to the late fourth or fifth century. The church is obviously connected with the structures to the north, which, judging from the quality of furnishings and the length of the church, should be some kind of villa. Whether it was of Roman origin or newly built in Late Antiquity is too early to tell.

The most fascinating finds belong to the transformation of the church, shedding totally new light on the understanding of political changes in the Early Middle Ages on the island. Within the still-standing apse, a new one was incorporated, divided by a wall, creating a new double-apsed space, with an altar in each one; a third altar was constructed in front of this dividing wall. The former nave was used as it is, showing that the first church was neither destroyed nor abandoned. It was now divided into three naves by pilasters and was shortened. A few fragments of liturgical furnishings were found, decorated with interlace patterns, thus belonging to the pre-Romanesque era of the eighth–ninth centuries. But the interesting liturgical organization of the presbytery gives a very precise date of construction. The Late Antique liturgy does not use three altars in a presbytery. Rab is supposed to be under Byzantine sovereignty, where that installation is also liturgically not possible. It thus has to be concluded that that kind of arrangement is imported from the West, namely from the Carolingian empire. The only moment for this is the very first decade of the ninth century, when the Carolingians entered Dalmatia, and before the peace treaty of Aachen in A.D. 812, when the island returned under Byzantine sovereignty. As for the nearby structures, even before excavations, it could be concluded that in Late Antiquity they were part of an estate of some wealthy member of society. Apparently it was neither abandoned nor destroyed, but further occupied by a member of the Carolingian elite. As for the abandonment of that second phase, we do not yet know. But the almost total lack of material—in both phases of the church only small fragments of sculpture and very few ceramic sherds have been found around both structures—could mean that the population simply left precipitately, at a moment still unknown. Are we in the presence of a site where political circumstances (the peace treaty of A.D. 812) obliged the owner of the estate simply to leave it?

The Zone of Lopar. The territory of the peninsula of Lopar in the northwest of the island gives a slightly different picture than elsewhere, as a result of its geomorphological characteristics. The survey conducted by the Institute for Archaeology in Zagreb has produced some interesting results. The peninsula was inhabited from the Palaeolithic, due to its good position. The survey established a network of sites. In Roman times, a few settlements of rural type were founded, the largest one being Punta Zidine on the northeast part of the peninsula, comprising Cape Zidine, the Bay of Sića, and Cape Dedan (Skelac and Radić Rossi 2006: 272). Georadar investigation and test trenches showed walls and other structures in an area of 600 m², lying parallel (east–west) to the terraces on the slopes descending to, and into, the sea. Ceramics found around the settlement date from the first to the fourth–fifth centuries; it is thus a rural settlement active until Late Antiquity. Another rural site has been located in the location called Beli grad, connected to a pottery kiln in Podšilo Bay, active in the second half of the third century (Lipovac and Šiljeg 2010). Walls were spotted north of the kiln, suggesting a huge complex (Lipovac and Šiljeg 2012: 28). Another site with at least two kilns is located in Mahućina cove (Lipovac et al. 2014: 206; 2015: 80). It has been suggested that this huge pottery production centre is linked to commerce with the neighbouring towns of Rab and *Senia* (Senj) on the mainland which underwent major reconstruction in the second and third centuries. At this time, as has been pointed out, imports from Italian and other regional workshops had ceased, thus the necessity of providing local products for those renovations. Aside from the largest agricultural fields, some more small Roman rural sites have been noted on the peninsula.

There are far fewer data for Late Antiquity. Some have suggested that the Roman settlement in Punta Zidine continues, and maybe also Beli grad. There is no evidence for the Early Middle Ages.

The small island of Lukovac in front of Lopar is all built. A church dated to the sixth century stands right in the middle of the island and is flanked by a huge cistern. The function of the other structures has not yet been determined, but Čaušević-Bully and Bully (2015: 20–25) have suggested that they represent either a fortification or a monastic compound. The position of this islet in front of Lopar Bay and its settlements, the possibility of control, its inaccessibility, and the huge water tanks and storage spaces, in my opinion, might also suggest some administrative defensive function within its immediate surroundings.

Preliminary Conclusions

The island of Rab is indeed a good case study for understanding changes in settlement patterns. It is of course still a work in progress, but we can already offer some conclusions. In the early Imperial period, already in the first century, the most prominent of the pre-Roman settlements was walled by the Emperor Augustus, gaining the rank of municipium. It remained the only town until the end of the twentieth century, as the administrative center of the island.

Of the 25 pre-Roman sites, there is no systematic evidence yet for their use in later periods, except for the town of Rab itself and the maritime villa at Kaštelina. It should therefore be concluded that the pre-Roman settlements were in general abandoned and the indigenous population descended to the flatlands.

In the Roman period, the town of Rab developed, reaching its peak in the second half of the second and the third centuries A.D. As for the rural landscape, we have strong evidence only for the maritime villa on Kaštelina in Kampor, with a first phase dated to the first to second centuries, major transformations in the third to fourth, and abandonment in Late Antiquity, not later than the sixth century (the chronology is still to be refined more closely). We can presume a residential villa in Banjol too, judging by the quality of findings.

In the other part of the island, on the Lopar peninsula, several rural settlements came into existence (such as Punta Zidine, Beli grad, and a few smaller ones), all of them dated to the first to fourth centuries. Aside from these, two other sites with pottery kilns were discovered, active in the second half of the third century. In this somewhat isolated part of the island, the economy obviously relied on pottery production and trade with the mainland town of *Senia*/Senj (see Figure 5.2). This part of Rab has produced no evidence of settlements after Late Antiquity and it seems that the whole peninsula was abandoned for a substantial period, the rural landscape starting to revive only in the Late Middle Ages. The same goes for the peninsula of Kalifront in the west-southwest, where the only find so far is the Late Antique church from the fifth century, connected to an unexplored settlement in Gožinka Bay that may be a villa of either Roman or Late Antique origin. This site was in continuous use until the Early Middle Ages, when the church was reconstructed (very probably in the first decade of the ninth century) and connected by liturgical function to Carolingian rule. The lack of small finds suggests a momentary abandonment that can be connected to a political event. The whole of the peninsula thereafter remained depopulated for a long time: there is evidence only of isolated churches in some of the coves, dated to the Middle and Late Middle Ages, from the twelfth century on.

Thus, population on the island was concentrated in the fertile zone, and numerous surveys of the territory have revealed a possible settlement pattern. In the extensive agricultural area from Supetarska draga to Barbat, a number of rural settlements have been documented along the Roman road; they are dated by ceramics finds, all of them covering the span from the third to the sixth century. There is no doubt that the third century was a century of affluence, but were all these settlements really founded only then? Excavations alone can provide the answer. And did they all cease to exist after the sixth century? That is hardly credible. I believe, rather, that dating ceramics is not so easy, especially domestic wares in rural settings. The only site—Banjol—whose chronology depends not on ceramics, but on metalwork, existed during the seventh century as well, after which it was abandoned for a short period.

Certainly, Late Antiquity brought about transformations in the landscape, first with the spread of Christianity, and then as a result of political changes. Some of the settlements received churches, as in the cases of Banjol, Barbat, the *castrum* of St Cosmas and St Damian, St Anastasia, Supetarska draga, and Gožinka. The ecclesiastical network must have been larger, Rab being a bishopric. On the other hand, a military *castrum* was built in Barbat, and the structures on the islet of Lukovac might have had a defensive function. But if there was any impact of the Gothic war in the sixth century, it may have been only on the Lopar peninsula, where life in most of the settlements is dated by ceramics until the fourth to fifth centuries, but not later. At any rate, the sixth century shows a strong presence of the eastern Roman Empire (not to call it Byzantium yet), with the *castrum* in Barbat, and the large church in Banjol with Constantinopolitan sculptures, and the refurbishing of the cathedral, expressing the wealth of the local elites.

The Early Middle Ages was definitely shaped by political and diplomatic activities. After the incursion of Avars and Slavs at the beginning of the seventh century, the whole landscape of the Roman province of Dalmatia changed. The question is: did it affect the islands immediately or only somewhat later? Did the islands serve as places of refuge, with a consequent substantial augmentation of population? There is unfortunately still no trace of such a process, but, there again, practically all the known settlements seem to have been abandoned after the sixth or seventh centuries. A new impulse seen at the end of the eighth century is certainly to be connected to political and diplomatic events. While formally under Byzantine sovereignty, the bishopric of Rab was nonetheless dependent on Rome; but it seems that in the dark centuries after the Avar incursions, not only Rab, but other bishoprics as well, lost connections with their ecclesiastical centre and were practically left alone. This is the only way to understand the diplomatic activities of both major powers—Byzantium on one side and the Carolingians with the Papacy on the other.

In fact, Rab, as no other island, has provided enough data for understanding these processes. The renewal of the cathedral, with new liturgical furnishings executed by the "Quarnero workshop", and the rebuilding of the church in Gožinka Bay show them clearly. Exactly the same thing happened in the neighbouring bishopric of Osor (see below), where the self-same workshop produced the altar screen. Similarly, in Istria, in Novigrad (a Roman workshop), in Zadar (the workshop of the Zadar cathedral slabs), in Split (the Split workshop), and in Kotor (the workshop of the time of Bishop John), all these workshops used the same compositional patterns and motifs, originating in Rome (Jurković 2016). This fact is of great importance for understanding political events: they are the reaction of Rome to the attempt by Byzantium to bribe Dalmatian bishops. In A.D. 787, four of those bishops (from Rab, Osor, Split, and Kotor) were summoned to the Council of Nicea in an attempt to turn them to the Byzantine side. Rome reacted by sending sculptors and probably financed the embellishment of all those cathedrals, returning those bishoprics to Rome.

Subsequently, when the Carolingians entered the province of Dalmatia in the first decade of the ninth century, the political infrastructure was already in place. On the island of Rab two cases show it. The *ciborium* in the cathedral was executed by the Master of the Zadar ambos, active in the first decade of the ninth century, and probably coming from Cividale, the political centre of the Carolingian realm in southeastern Europe. The liturgical installations in the church in Gožinka Bay clearly follow Carolingian models.

Immediately after the peace treaty of Aachen in A.D. 812, Rab returned to Byzantine supremacy, the church in Gožinka being abandoned. The long-lasting Late Antique period came to its end.

The Quarnero Gulf Islands: A Comparative Approach

The Apsyrtides Archipelago

On the archipelago of *Apsyrtides*—the islands of Cres (404 km^2) and Lošinj (75 km^2), and a dozen smaller islands—the situation is quite the opposite of that on Rab, attesting continuity from the pre-Roman to Early Medieval periods (Figures 5.7 and 5.8). It has to be said, however, that data gathered here come from old field surveys, with the exception of some new excavations of late antique churches connected to habitats of various kinds and importance.

There is evidence of a total of 43 pre-Roman hilltop settlements on the archipelago: 19 on Cres, 18 on Lošinj, two on Unije, and one each on Veli Osir, Vele Srakane, Sveti Petar, and Ilovik (Ćus-Rukonić 1982: 10–11). A considerable number of them continued to be inhabited in the Roman period, in Late Antiquity and in the Early Middle Ages, the rest being

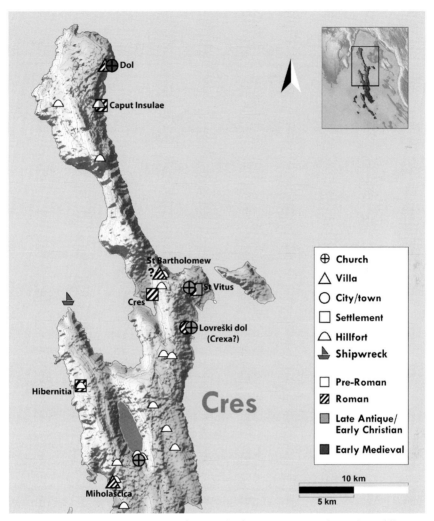

Figure 5.7. Islands of the archipelago of Apsyrtides from Antiquity to the Early Middle Ages, northern part (M. Jurković).

abandoned. Even two of the four caves from the pre-Roman period, at Jami na Sredi on the island of Cres, were occasionally inhabited from the Mesolithic until the Early Middle Ages (Mirosavljević 1959).

The types of transformations are different in scale. Four of the 19 pre-Roman settlements on the island Cres became Roman, Osor (*Apsorus*) being the most important town, while Beli (*Caput insulae*), Lubenice (*Hibernitia*) and Ustrine are smaller in scale. The reasons are obvious: all are in good

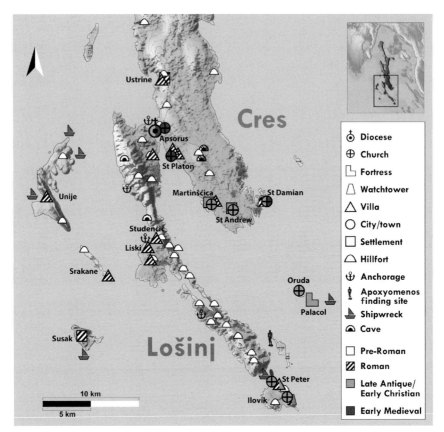

Figure 5.8. Islands of the archipelago of Apsyrtides from Antiquity to the Early Middle Ages, southern part (M. Jurković).

strategic positions. Osor is on the most important maritime route from the inner to the outer sea, on a kind of shortcut, controlling the channel between two islands (see Figure 5.2). This channel between Cres and Lošinj is artificial, created in protohistory. The port north of the town is well protected, and there is also evidence of the manual transportation of boats on that northern side from one bay to the other. Osor became a major commercial *emporium* in imperial times and remained so in subsequent periods.

Beli controls the maritime route between the islands of Cres and Krk, Lubenice the west coast maritime route, while Ustrine, above Osor, seems to have provided some sort of control of the road approaching Osor from the north. It is worth noting that Ustrine has a cemetery far too big for the small settlement, and it has been suggested that it served the people from Osor too (Imamović 1975: 220). Those four towns have uninterrupted continuity until the present day.

There is written evidence of another Roman town on the island—*Crexa*—but it has not yet been identified. Occasional archaeological excavations in the town of Cres have not afforded enough material (just a few graves and some walls) to ascertain its position, although the bay in which it lies is a spectacular one. The common opinion is that it has to be identified with the pre-Roman hillfort of St Bartholomew that overlooks the bay, with a view to both sides of the island; here Roman ceramics in large quantity, as well as some walls, certainly indicate a settlement. Others think that *Crexa* should be identified with the Roman settlement at Lovreški on the opposite side of the island.

The other pattern that can be observed on the island of Cres is the relocation of the population from a hillfort to the sea shore, as for example at Miholašćica or again at Ustrine, a pattern that can be observed for all the cases on the island of Lošinj.

Osor became a bishopric in Late Antiquity, creating a network of churches on all of the islands. On Cres those churches are either within a former Roman settlement, as at Lovreški, Beli, Saint Vitus, Saint Damian, and Martinšćica, or possibly new settlements such as St Andrew in Punta Križa.

On the island of Lošinj, four Roman settlements have been noted. All of them are near the shore, below pre-Roman hilltop settlements. The villa in Studenčić Bay definitely continued into Late Antiquity, when a church was built; the others were abandoned at some as yet undefined point. The fate of the island's settlements is peculiar. All of them disappeared, and the whole island was never repopulated until the Late Middle Ages, the only exception being a few places of eremitic habitation on the slopes of Osorčica connected to churches built in the eleventh century. The same happened to the small islands west of Lošinj (Unije, Srakane), where Roman settlements were abandoned in Late Antiquity.

On the other hand, all of the small islands south and east of Lošinj had a different fate. The anchorage between the islands of St Peter and Ilovik must have been an important one on the maritime route. On St Peter, a Roman villa occupied half of the island, and a huge church was built near it in Late Antiquity (Bully and Čaušević-Bully 2012). On Ilovik, the church of St Andrew was built near a Late Antique watch-tower in the sixth century (Starac 2011). At the same time a fortress was built on the islet of Palacol (Badurina 1982) and, in the immediate vicinity on the island Oruda, the Late Antique church of St John was constructed (Čaušević-Bully and Bully 2014); those living on these two islands could communicate on foot at low tide. There is not much evidence for the function of this isolated church, but some later documents indicate that it could had been used by a community of eastern Basilian monks.

It seems that all these small islands were deserted in the Early Middle Ages. The period is documented only in the southern part of Cres, near the bishop's see in Osor, and exclusively by churches: St Damian, St Plato, Osorski dolac, St Vitus in Srem, and naturally in Osor itself. As in the case of Rab, the cathedral received new liturgical furnishings, executed by the same Quarnero workshop, at the same time. It can therefore be contextualized in the same way as described above for Rab—Rome regaining control over bishoprics that had been bribed by the Byzantines in A.D. 787.

Even if the available evidence does come mostly from old field surveys, some general conclusions can nonetheless be put forward. Many of the pre-Roman hill forts were abandoned, people descending to the shores or to the flatlands, but few were transformed into Roman towns, especially those on strategic points. In general, the Romans preferred the west coast of the two bigger islands and the small western islands, looking at the outer sea.

All four of the Roman towns continued through Late Antiquity and into the Early Middle Ages, but most of the secondary settlements were abandoned at some point in Late Antiquity. It is worth mentioning that the island of Lošinj, and the small islands of Unije and Srakane were totally abandoned. The settlements that remained were all on the eastern shores and eastern small islands of the archipelago. This clearly points to the importance of the inner maritime route, with security provided by fortresses and watchtowers built by Justinian during the Gothic wars. All those Late Antique settlements had a church, being part of the church network of the bishopric of Osor, or in some cases monastic churches (Čaušević-Bully and Bully 2015). Another pattern seems to be obvious in the Early Middle Ages: most of the settlements on the small islands of the archipelago were abandoned, life concentrating exclusively on the largest island of Cres, around the bishopric of Osor. Whether these developments were the result of earlier changes on the mainland is a matter still to be investigated.

The Island of Krk

The island of Krk (404 km2) is the nearest to the mainland (Figure 5.9). Two Roman towns developed on opposite sides of the island: Krk (*Curicum*) on the south side and Omišalj (*Fulfinum*) on the north. Their fates were totally different: while Krk became a bishopric in Late Antiquity, *Fulfinum* started to decline and was eventually abandoned (Čaušević-Bully and Valent 2015). Other Roman settlements, almost all on the coast, are *villae* or other smaller habitations: Njivice, Soline, Ogrul, Korintija, St George at Mala Krasa, Košljun, Punat, St Fosca, St Chrisogonus at Glavotok, and Voz; only one villa has been noted in the central part of the island, at Cickini (Starac

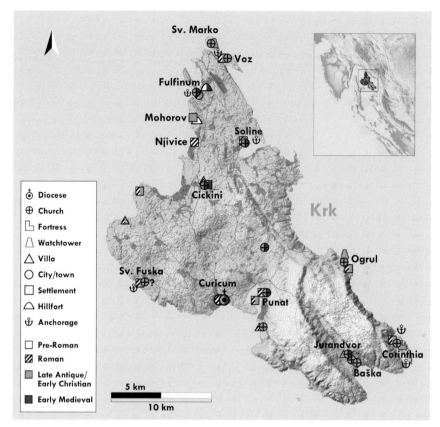

Figure 5.9. Island of Krk from Antiquity to the Early Middle Ages (M. Jurković).

2014). They all show continuity into the Late Antique period. As far as we know, only a few new settlements were formed in Late Antiquity: Mohorov, Jurandvor, and Baška.

Being the nearest to the mainland, the island developed a defensive system in the sixth century corresponding to the same system on the mainland itself: *castra* or simple watchtowers. Three were built on the northeast coast of the island, all with churches: St Marc, Ogrul, and Korintija (Brusić 1989). It seems that the sixth century, as on all of the islands, was a time of wealth. In the southeastern part of the island at Jurandvor, protected by a mountain range, a Late Antique villa was built, with a small church. In the vicinity, the large basilica of St Nicholas with floor mosaics (Starac 1996) and a huge basilica at Baška reflect the wealth of the elites. The fragments of liturgical furnishings can, once again, be connected to Constantinopolitan workshops.

The state of research does not allow firm conclusions about settlement patterns on the island, but some of the evidence is clear enough to state that Krk had a different fate than the rest of the Quarnero Gulf islands. Due to its position near the mainland, it was much more vulnerable, and obviously dependent on political events to a greater extent. Taking into consideration just a few fairly well-established facts leads to some general inferences. The Roman *municipium Fulfinum*, the town nearest the mainland, is the only Roman town within a much larger area, including all the Quarnero islands, to have been abandoned at some point in Late Antiquity. The exact time is hard to tell, but the most recent research gives evidence of material dating to the seventh, or maybe even the eighth, century (Čaušević-Bully and Valent 2015). The inhabitants moved back up to the pre-Roman settlement on the nearby hill of Omišalj, where there is good evidence of church architecture and sculpture already in the early ninth century. On the other hand, the large church in Mirine, in the former suburbs of *Fulfinum*, seems to function throughout, a small Early Medieval church being built in its vicinity. This model of spatial reorganization is very similar to what happened on the islands of central Dalmatia.

The abandonment of different kinds of habitation can be documented mostly on the northern shores of the island. There is practically no evidence of continuity in the two *castra* from the time of Justinian (Corinthia and St Marc), only Ogrul showing signs of later use, still without any sure evidence of continuity or rupture. The residential complex with a large church in Cickini, along the road from *Fulfinum* to *Curicum*, suggests probable reasons for the transformation of the historical landscape. It was built very near an Early Imperial Roman villa, no earlier than the mid-sixth century, and probably only after Justinian's reign (Starac 2014). The church with its baptistery, as well as the residential complex, were subsequently modified several times, always resulting in the contraction of various spaces, and terminating with a burnt layer. As most of the material finds fall within the time-span from the mid-sixth to the ninth centuries, this, as well as the cases mentioned above, has to be the last echo of the Avar-Slav incursions in Dalmatia during the first half of the seventh century, or even a connection to the Carolingian spread at the beginning of the ninth century.

As a matter of fact, the Late Antique villa at Kanajt might provide some good answers for better understanding of the astonishing liturgical installations in Gožinka on the island of Rab. The church within the villa was rebuilt in the Early Middle Ages (Starac 2004); within the apse were inserted two apses and the church was shortened (Figure 5.10). Since finds were scarce during excavation and there were no clues about the liturgical installations, the church was dated within the broad time-span of the ninth and tenth

Figure 5.10. Island of Krk, Kanajt, church of St Peter, plan (R. Starac).

centuries. But now, after the first excavation campaign at Gožinka on the island of Rab (discussed above), the architectural type can be recognized and connected to liturgical functions typical of the Carolingians. The same pattern is visible: in both cases the Late Antique church within a villa was remodelled in a very specific way, gaining two apses within the former one. Even with no material evidence for St Peter in Kanajt, we can confidently assume that there was a third altar in front of the two apses. And in that case, it can only be the result of the Carolingian expansion on the island before A.D. 812. This conclusion, as totally unexpected as that on Rab, changes our perception of historical changes at the beginning of the Early Middle Ages on the eastern Adriatic coast.

Political Impacts on Settlement Patterns in the Adriatic Islands: Some Conclusions

Depicting the settlement patterns over a long time-span and on such a huge number of islands in the Adriatic is an impossible task within limited space. As the general picture is known for the islands of central Dalmatia, I have tried here to incorporate new results, collected mostly on the islands of the northern Adriatic. It is now time to see if they correlate during any of their chronological phases.

The eastern Adriatic was systematically Romanised, as were all its islands as well. The only difference is in the number of urban centers. While the northern Adriatic islands were fairly densely urbanized, central and southern Dalmatian islands mostly depended on urban centers on the mainland, not counting a few towns of Greek origin (e.g. Issa, Pharos, or Korkyra). The same happened with Christianization: each of the northern Adriatic islands got a bishopric—Osor, Krk, Rab—while the other Dalmatian islands none (except Pharos, that would anyway soon be extinguished). That surely affected the creation of independent ecclesiastical networks on the north Adriatic islands, while the ones in central and southern Dalmatia depended on their bishoprics on the mainland. In fact, on the bigger islands of central Dalmatia the towns did not play a role either in further urbanisation or in Christianization. On the contrary, the towns at Issa, Pharos, and Korkyra, on their respective islands, were slowly ruralized, while the island of Brač did not even have a town, being totally dependent on its centre on the mainland, Salona and afterwards Split.

The next moment that had an impact on the islands were the Gothic wars of the first half of the sixth century. A number of fortresses were built by Justinian's administration to protect the maritime routes of the eastern Adriatic. Yet, again, it seems that the northern Adriatic and northern Dalmatia (around Zadar) were more privileged than central and southern Dalmatia (see Figure 5.1). This is obviously due to geopolitical reasons. Even if we can see some clumsiness in protecting and reconstructing town walls (as in Rab, but everywhere else too), at the same time hundreds of churches were built on the islands, reflecting a new level of welfare. After the Gothic war, prosperity is apparent on all the Adriatic islands, seen in commerce, building that often reflected the tastes of the eastern empire, imports of sculpture, and so on.

The seventh century brought dramatic changes in the historical landscape of the islands, not reflected everywhere at the same level. After the Avar-Slav incursion and the fall of Salona, as well as some other important towns on the mainland such as Narona, the islands were cut off from the mainland. We can see rapid ruralization of the few island towns, and the affluence of a new population fleeing the danger on central Dalmatian islands (Brač, for example). On the other hand, the islands of the northern Adriatic were not so much affected. There is no evidence of new population for at least another century. Certainly, the abandonment of secondary settlements has been noted (e.g., on Rab, Cres, and Krk), but the concentration of the population in towns or other larger settlements might also be interpreted in terms of economy, not only by political events. The only island in the northern Adriatic that was directly affected by changes on the mainland is Krk, where one of the two towns was eventually abandoned.

The century and a half of general crisis is visible on all the Adriatic islands in different ways, some of them depicted here. Things were to change again in the last quarter of the eighth century when the Adriatic became the stage for the clash of two superpowers—Byzantium and the Carolingians helped by the Papacy. Once again, the northern Adriatic islands played a much more important role, changing their historical landscape at the twilight of Late Antiquity.

Acknowledgments

This work has been supported in part by the Croatian Science Foundation under the project 6095 "Croatian Medieval Heritage in European Context: Mobility of Artists and Transfer of Forms, Functions and Ideas" (CROMART). All the maps and other drawings were created with the technical assistance of Ivor Kranjec.

References

Badurina, Anđelko
　1982　　Bizantska utvrda na otočiću Palacol. *Izdanja Hrvatskog arheološkog društva* 7: 171–178.

Basić, Ivan
　2012　　Prilog datiranju zlatnog enkolpija iz Barbata na Rabu. In *Rapski zbornik* II, edited by Josip Andrić and Robert Lončarić, pp. 427–442. Ogranak Matice hrvatske u Rabu, Rab.

Brogiolo, Gian Pietro, Alejandra Chavarria Arnau, Federico Giacomello, Miljenko Jurković, and Goran Bilogrivić
　2017　　The Late Antique Church of Saint Lawrence, Banjol (Island of Rab, Croatia): Results of the First Two Archaeological Campaigns (2015–2016). *Hortus Artium Medievalium* 23: 666–673.

Brusić, Vladislav
　1926　　*Otok Rab*. Franjevački samostan sv. Eufemije, Rab.

Brusić, Zdenko
　1989　　Kasnoantička utvrđenja na otocima Rabu i Krku. *Izdanja Hrvatskog arheološkog društva* 13: 111–120.

Budak, Neven
　2006　　Urban Development of Rab: A Hypothesis. *Hortus Artium Medievalium* 12: 123–135.

Bully, Sébastien, and Morana Čaušević-Bully
　2012　　Saint-Pierre d'Ilovik: une station maritime majeure du nord de l'Adriatique, de l'antiquité au moyen-age. *Histria Antiqua* 21: 413–426.

CIL
　1873　　*Corpus Inscriptionum Latinarum*, Vol. III, edited by Theodor Mommsen. Berlin.

Čaušević-Bully, Morana, and Sébastien Bully
　2014　　Oruda – sveti Ivan – sveti Pantaleon. *Hrvatski arheološki godišnjak* 10: 415–418.

2015 Archipel du Kvarner (Croatie). Prospection-inventaire des sites ecclésiaux et monastiques: campagne 2014. *Chronique des activités archéologiques de l'Ecole française de Rome [en ligne], Balkans* 2015: 1–27.

Čaušević-Bully, Morana, Sébastien Bully, and Mia Rizner

2012 Sveti Martin na Rabu (Valmartina, Valmartin). *Hrvatski arheološki godišnjak* 9: 529–530.

Čaušević-Bully, Morana, and Ivan Valent

2015 Municipium Flavium Fulfinum: Dijakronijska studija gradske strukture s posebnim osvrtom na forumski prostor. *Prilozi instituta za arheologiju u Zagrebu* 32: 111–146.

Ćus Rukonić, Jasminka

1982 Arheološka topografija otoka Cresa I Lošinja. *Izdanja Hrvatskog arheološkog društva* 7: 9–17.

Domijan, Miljenko

2007 *Rab: Città d'Arte*. Barbat, Zagreb.

Imamović, Enver

1975 Antička naselja na otočnoj skupini Cres – Lošinj. *Otočki ljetopis Cres – Lošinj* 2: 212–229.

Jurković, Miljenko

1990 Oratorij-relikvijarij i deambulatorij crkve sv. Ivana u Rabu. *Radovi instituta za povijest umjetnosti* 14: 81–91.

2015 Un raro motivo iconografico sulla scultura altomedievale: i *senmurv* di Arbe e Nevidane. In *Scripta in honorem Igor Fisković*, edited by Miljenko Jurković and Predrag Marković, pp. 43–51. Dissertationes et Monographiae 7. International Research Center for Late Antiquity and the Middle Ages (IRCLAMA), Zagreb.

2016 Quando il monumento diventa documento: una bottega lapicida del Quarnero. In *Alla ricerca di un passato complesso: Contributi in onore di Gian Pietro Brogiolo per il suo settentesimo compleanno*, edited by Alejandra Chavarria Arnau and Miljenko Jurković, pp. 231–242. Dissertationes et Monographiae 8. International Research Center for Late Antiquity and the Middle Ages (IRCLAMA), Zagreb.

Jurković, Miljenko, Gian Pietro Brogiolo, Javier Arce, Iva Marić, and Alejandra Chavarria Arnau

2008 La villa romana di Kaštelina (isola di Rab): indagini archeologiche 2005–2007. In *Eredità culturali dell'Adriatico: Archeologia, storia, lingua e letteratura* I, edited by Silvana Collodo and Giovanni Luigi Fontana, pp. 91–109. Collana Interadria. Culture dell'Adriatico, Rome.

Jurković, Miljenko, and Ivan Tenšek

1990 Novootkrivena ranokršćanska crkva na otoku Rabu. *Obavijesti Hrvatskog arheološkog društva* 1: 38–40.

Jurković, Miljenko, and Tin Turković

2012 Utvrda sv. Kuzme i Damjana u Barbatu na otoku Rabu. In *Rapski zbornik* II, edited by Josip Andrić and Robert Lončarić pp.15–36. Ogranak Matice hrvatske u Rabu, Rab.

Konestra, Ana, Nera Šegvić, Paula Androić Gračanin, and Ranko Starac

2017 Arheološka topografija otoka Raba: geofizička, sondažna i topografska istraživanja u 2016. godini *Annales Instituti Archaeologici* 13: 103–110.

Lipovac Vrkljan, Goranka, and Ana Konestra

2015   Projekt Arheološka topografija otoka Raba – rezultati terenskog pregleda na
            području grada Raba u 2014. godini i izložba Arheološka topografija: putovanje
            kroz prošlost Lopara. *Annales Instituti Archaeologici* 11: 128–132.

Lipovac Vrkljan, Goranka, Ana Konestra, and Irena Radić Rossi

2016   Rezultati aktivnosti projekta "Arheološka topografija otoka Raba" u 2015 godini:
            terenski pregledi, obrada arheološke građe, popularizacija znanosti, *Annales
            Instituti Archaeologici* 12: 201–205.

Lipovac Vrkljan, Goranka, Branko Mušič, Bartul Šiljeg, and Ana Konestra

2015   Geofizička istraživanja antičkih struktura u uvali Mahućina na otoku Rabu
            (općina Lopar) 2014. Godine (projekt RED, Hrvatska zaklada za znanost).
            Annales Instituti Archaeologici 11: 80–82.

Lipovac Vrkljan, Goranka, and Bartul Šiljeg

2010   Lopar-Podšilo: zaštitno arheološko istraživanje rimske keramičarske peći 2009.
            Godišnjak Instituta za Arheologiju 6: 64–69.

2012   Prilog antičkoj topografiji otoka Raba – rimska keramičarska peć na Loparu.
            Senjski zbornik 39: 5–34.

Lipovac Vrkljan, Goranka, Bartul Šiljeg, Ivana Ožanić Roguljić, Ana Konestra, Iva Kostešić,
and Nera Šegvić

2014   Projekt Arheološka topografija otoka Raba: rezultati terenskog pregleda
            poluotoka Lopara u 2013. godini. *Annales Instituti Archaeologici* 10: 202–208.

Mirosavljević, Vladimir

1959   Jamina Sredi, prilog prethistorijskoj kulturi na otoku Cresu. *Arheološki radovi i
            rasprave* 1: 131–174.

Nedved, Branka

1989   Felix Arba. *Izdanja Hrvatskog arheološkog društva* 13: 29–44.

Skelac, Goran, and Irena Radić Rossi

2006   Zaštitno iskopavanje na lokalitetu Punta Zidine u Loparu. *Hrvatski arheološki
            godišnjak* 2: 272–274.

Starac, Ranko

1996   Sulla scoperta di un'altra chiesa paleocristiana nell'isola di Krk (Veglia). *Hortus
            Artium Medievalium* 2: 137–141.

2004   Two Examples of Rural Ecclesiastical Architectural Continuity on the Island of
            Krk. *Hortus Artium Medievalium* 10: 231–236.

2011   Ilovik – Sićadrija (crkva sv. Andrije). *Hrvatski arheološki godišnjak* 7: 466–467.

2014   Cickini. *Hrvatski arheološki godišnjak* 10: 392–394.

Suić, Mate

1976   *Antički grad na Jadranu.* Sveučilišna naklada Liber, Zagreb.

Tomičić, Željko

1990   Arheološka svjedočanstva o ranobizantskom vojnom graditeljstvu na
            sjevernojadranskim otocima. *Prilozi Instituta za povijesne znanosti u Zagrebu*
            5/6: 29–53.

Macro-economy, Micro-ecology, and the Fate of Urbanized Landscape in Late Antique and Early Byzantine Crete

Enrico Zanini

In the case of the Cretan Late Antique/Early Byzantine landscape, the dichotomy between change and resilience could be easily defined in terms of changing relationships between long-term local micro-ecology and medium-term Mediterranean macro-economy. The former is to be understood as a long-lasting relationship between a single city and its surrounding territory (i.e., a factor of resilience); the latter as the sum of the changing relationships between the same city and the wide variety of economic, political, administrative, and military systems that connected cities, provinces, and regions across the Mediterranean.

The specific case of Crete is of great interest in this respect, because a major event in local history—the huge earthquake of A.D. 365—chronologically coincides with the shifting of many macro-economies from a Rome-centered system to a Constantinople-centered system. The "rebirth" of Cretan cities after the devastating earthquake—mainly the provincial capital, Gortyn, but also in other case studies—appears to be directly related to the role that the Byzantine imperial administration assigned to Crete as a substantial component of the 'island backbone' of the Mediterranean. This new, and closer, macro-economic relationship between Crete and the Early Byzantine empire made the island and its cities very sensitive to the changes in the political and economic scenario. The vain economic effort made by the Empire to regain the West, and the shifting of the imperial center of gravity toward the East after the Arab conquests, created the conditions for a deep change in the local micro-ecology, determining the decline of cities and the creation of a new "city-less" Cretan landscape.

Foreword 1: A Critical Assumption

I would like to ground my discussion of the transformation of the human settlement patterns in Crete during Late Antiquity and the Early Byzantine period (roughly between the fourth and the eighth centuries A.D.) on a critical assumption, that is, on a general view that human settlement in the Late Antique Mediterranean was governed by the interaction of two distinct but complementary elements. On the one hand, there is the local ecology (the natural and anthropogenic landscape of Crete in a *longue durée* perspective), tending by its nature to be "stable" and thus a factor of resilience; on the other hand, there is the Mediterranean macro-economy (or macro-economies), represented by the political and administrative choices made by the imperial administration at different times, which constitute factors of change. In general, I would encompass within the word "micro-ecology" all the practices of daily life, such as food production and consumption, organization of housing, and basic infrastructures indispensable to everyday life. Under the category of macro-economies, however, fall all the elements related to the life of a complex society at a Mediterranean-wide scale, with a higher level of social/political/economic differentiation, such as the distribution of goods at a supra-regional scale, the public administration, and defense strategies.

Following the approach proposed by Horden and Purcell (2000: 96–101) in their seminal and widely-discussed book on the Mediterranean, this distinction between micro-ecologies and macro-economies can be extended to all forms of human settlement within a natural landscape. In this view, cities and countryside are not seen as two different forms of population, but as a *continuum*, where the cities are just nuclei of "intensification," both in quantitative and qualitative terms.

Most interestingly, cities are clearly situated at the contact point between local micro-ecologies and Mediterranean macro-economies. They are strictly connected with local micro-ecology, because they largely depend on their surrounding territory (the *chora*) for their daily life (food, natural resources, etc.). At the same time, they are the touch-points of the macro-economies within the same territory, being the "terminals" of imperial administration (Figure 6.1). This approach proves to be particularly interesting when dealing with the cities of a large island like Crete, which is—to use Horden and Purcell's terms—the embodiment of both insularity and connectivity. Crete is insulated by definition, as it is perhaps the most "invisible" island in the Mediterranean, being the sole large island that cannot be seen from the surrounding Mediterranean coast. At the same time, it possesses a fundamental element of connectivity, being a landmark along the large insular backbone that runs from east to west, representing the major axis of commerce, population mobility, and defense (Zanini 2013a). In other words, in dealing with Cretan towns it is quite easy to distinguish between micro-ecological and macro-economic factors, between "local" and "external" factors, and (following the perspective adopted in the present volume) between *resilience* and *change*.

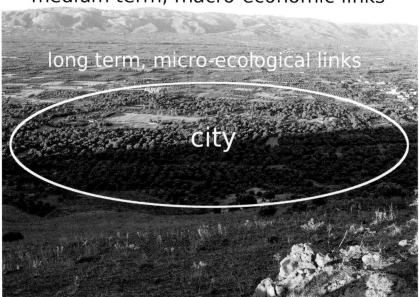

Figure 6.1. City, micro-ecology, and macro-economy.

Moreover, Crete itself occupies a very special place in the Late Antique and Early Byzantine Mediterranean, since it is placed exactly at the intersection point of the Roman and Byzantine large Mediterranean macro-economic systems. This is true in both spatial and chronological terms. Late Antiquity in Crete has a very recognizable starting point in the huge earthquake/tsunami of 21 July A.D. 365 (Stiros 2001), which coincides with the first large change in the macro-economic system in the Mediterranean, due to the affirmation of Constantinople as the place of a second Mediterranean polarity. Furthermore, it is interesting to note that the fault line between the western and eastern Empires passed exactly through Crete, as, in those same years, did the fault line between the two different areas of influence of the Roman and Byzantine Churches (Stiernon and Stiernon 1986).

In short, Crete being a very remote island in the very center of Mediterranean (Arnaud 2005: 30–31), its cities were nuclei of intensification of a human landscape that responded to the "rules" of local micro-ecology. At the same time, on a larger scale, they were contact points between this "stable" local situation and the much more "unstable" Late Antique/Early Byzantine macro-economic system, where resilience and change coexist and can be investigated, starting from the principle of asynchrony: changes occur in different places and in different ways (Bowersock et al. 1999). Our capability to detect them is dependent upon the specific marker which we decide to take into account.

Foreword 2: What Do We Really Know About the Subject?

This complexity, so worthy of archaeological investigation, is confronted by a substantial lack of knowledge. Only in relatively recent years have the most important archaeological sites of Crete been investigated with a specific interest in the Late Antique and Early Byzantine periods, and it is only recently that focus has been placed on the questions concerning models of settlement change. This is quite evident if one examines the indices of the first four volumes of the *Ergon Kriti* (the large international conference at which the most up-to-date results of ongoing archaeological projects are presented), where the Late Antique and Early Byzantine evidence is scarcely presented and discussed, compared to the attention devoted to the Minoan, Greek, and Roman periods.

The second limiting condition derives from the fact that our knowledge is essentially based on excavations and research focused on cities (Sanders 1982; Francis and Kouremenos 2016). This is mainly because Late Antique and Early Byzantine levels were accidentally encountered—and often rudely removed—in the process of excavating the monumental fabric of ancient Cretan cities. Consequently, our sample is particularly weak from a statistical point of view: if the image we have is mostly one of deep "transformation" or even of "decadence", this is largely due to the fact we have excavated ancient monuments which were quite obviously abandoned and/or transformed when they became obsolete in the new "ideal" conception of urban life in Early Byzantine times. On the other hand, there have been few urban excavations undertaken with the specific goal of investigating the non-monumental parts of an ancient city, the most extensive examples being Eleutherna and Gortyn. So, if we want to distinguish between the "cities of monuments" and the "cities of people", we would imagine the Late Antique or Early Byzantine cities as "cities of monuments," based mainly on churches and, to a decidedly lesser extent, on civil and defensive architecture. We know much less about the ways in which the men, women, and children lived in and interacted with those spaces between the fifth and eighth centuries.

The picture becomes much more complicated if we try to move towards a landscape perspective, because this is still a largely unexplored research field in Late Antique/Early Byzantine Crete (Figure 6.2). This situation is obviously very common all around the Mediterranean basin, but in the Cretan case it is especially problematic, as it is a potentially extremely rich

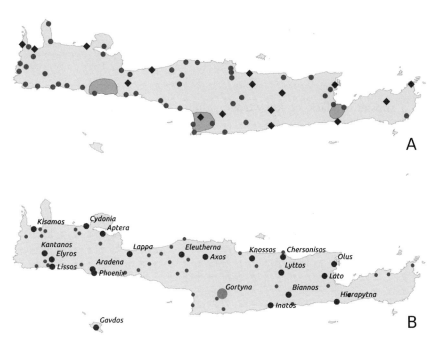

Figure 6.2. The basis of knowledge about the settlement pattern in Late Antique/Early Byzantine Crete: A) cities of Classical tradition (diamonds = Greek cities; dots = Roman cities; shaded areas = published or ongoing survey projects); B) Late Antique/Early Byzantine cities and large villages (small dots = Early Christian basilicas; large dots = cities reported in Hierokles' *Synekdemos*).

territory. Crete is often called the "island of one hundred cities" in the literary sources, and this image is confirmed by the famous distribution map of Late Antique cities in the Mediterranean basin prepared by A.H.M. Jones in 1937 on the basis of Hierokles' *Synekdemos*, on which Crete appears to have one of the highest densities of cities. The same image appears to be corroborated by the distribution of Christian basilicas in Crete between the fifth and the sixth centuries (Volanakis 1990). We have to acknowledge that, for most of these basilicas, we know little more than the location and the dedication, but even the very fact of their uniform distribution throughout the island suggests a dense urban and rural settlement system.

A comparable picture comes from the three major territorial surveys that have been conducted and (more or less extensively) published on Crete: one in the western Messara (Watrous et al. 1993), one in the Sphakia area along the southwest coast (Nixon et al. 2009), and one in the Vrokastro area in the eastern part of the island (Hayden 1990). Here again, we have to be aware of the diversity of approaches and operational practices that make an overall synthesis of data difficult. But "new generation" projects—such as the one centered on the settlement of Priniatikos Pyrgos (Molloy and Duckworth 2014)—have been conceived to integrate the *longue durée* dimension of the single site with an overall view at the regional scale, with the goal of understanding the changing relationships between the central site and its surrounding landscape.

The development during over the last decade of an intensive program of preventive rescue archaeology connected with small private and large public works, such as the one necessitated by the new highway that will connect Heraklion with the southern part of the Messara plain, is very promising. During these years, despite the great economic crisis, Greek archaeologists have been digging extensively in Crete, and one would predict that—if these excavations are published within a reasonable time frame—we will have a new and extremely interesting dataset about the shape of the Cretan landscape in Late Antiquity and the Early Byzantine era. This would offer an even more interesting picture, since it is based on a random statistical sample (i.e., independent from of the different interests of individual research groups) and this should provide us with fresh and relatively "unbiased" data.

Last but not least, I will mention the very valuable research carried out in recent years by the University of Rethymno, jointly with the IMS—FORTH, with a focus on the fortification systems of Early Byzantine Crete (Tsigonaki and Sarris 2016). It is, to my mind, an exceptionally important piece of work that, despite the difficulty in obtaining a precise and reliable date for every single site, will certainly put new arguments on the table and perhaps produce new critical approaches to changes in settlement models for the Early Byzantine Mediterranean islands.

A Starting Point

As already noted, a point that makes Crete a unique case in the context of the Late Antique and Early Byzantine Mediterranean insular system is represented by the great earthquake (and associated tidal wave) of 21 July A.D. 365. There is ongoing discussion of the real destructive power of that single event and the size of the area affected by the earthquake, and others possibly linked to a "seismic swarm" that may have afflicted Crete for many decades (Di Vita 1979); but it is not particularly relevant to our discussion here.

An earthquake is a specific event, but its archaeological visibility is clearly related to what happens before (i.e., the general conditions of the affected areas before the event) and to what happens afterwards (i.e., the response of the affected society). The destructive power of the A.D. 365 earthquake is evident in the archaeological record from several Cretan sites. In Gortyn,

Figure 6.3. The collapsed *scaenae frons* in the Pythion theater at Gortyn, after the A.D. 365 earthquake.

the *scaenae frons* of the Roman theatre connected with the temple of Pythian Apollo collapsed (Bonetto et al. 2009) (Figure 6.3), and the same occurred to many houses at Eleutherna, where some people were also buried by roof collapses (Themelis 2005). But, beyond simply recording the event, it is more interesting to reflect on the image of the urban landscape in both these cities just a minute before the earthquake itself. In Gortyn, for example, both the temple of Apollo and its related theatre appear to have been in deep crisis: the scene-building had already been converted into a stable where horses and mules were housed, while the *cavea* itself was re-used as a workshop for cutting up marbles (mainly large statues) to convert them into slabs. The same image derives from a small circular building excavated in front of the entrance to Apollo's shrine: this small but elegant monument had been transformed into a small stable, perhaps to house sheep (Zanini et al. 2009).

It goes without saying that the circumstances of the abandonment of the Pythion theatre prior to the earthquake cannot be automatically extended to the whole city: we know that the celebration of Apollo's cult was probably halted in Gortyn, as in other Greek cities, some decades before the mid-fourth century, and was not necessarily directly linked to the affirmation of Christianity (Tzouvara-Souli 2001). The same image of abandonment arises in the excavation of the *stadium* at Gortyn, some hundred metres away from the theater, and that may originally have been connected with the temple and theater of Apollo as different parts of a single, large sanctuary complex (Lippolis 2005). It is very difficult to say whether the semblance of relative crisis evident from Gortyn's public monuments must be connected with a specific situation (all the cited monuments were more or less related to a pagan cult, already abandoned and rejected by rising Christianity), or if it could be extended to the rest of the city.

At Eleutherna, the excavated fourth-century contexts are related to a couple of large urban *domus* that do not seem to present any symptoms of crisis before the earthquake, since their inhabitants were caught out by the seismic event during their daily activities (Themelis 2009). At present, it is hard to know whether this "double" image of Crete on the eve of the A.D. 365 earthquake (continuity of private life, some difficulty in maintaining public monuments or, at least, some of them) may be linked in some way to another well-known, apparently "inexplicable" archaeological indicator: the drastic decline in the presence of Cretan amphorae in the markets of the western Mediterranean, and primarily in Rome, between the second half of the third and the beginning of the fourth centuries (Marangou 1999).

In this case, the image of Crete in those years would not be that of a province that had fallen into a deep economic crisis, but perhaps rather that of an island more "insulated" than before; more "marginalized" within the overall context of the Roman Mediterranean. This was a new situation to be read, possibly, as a form of a new "remoteness" for an island situated exactly on the new inner border between the two parts of the Empire. At present, this could be just a matter of speculation, but it seems to me to be a working hypothesis worthy of discussion within the framework of a *longue durée* perspective (as proposed by the general theme of the present volume).

In fact, the image of a "weak" city is replicated—at least in the case of Gortyn—in the years immediately following the great earthquake, when urban reconstruction ensued. The rebuilding of the monumental fabric of the city is certain, witnessed by a large number of inscriptions, mainly concentrated—at least among the areas that have actually been excavated—in the *praetorium* (Gasperini 2004). But even in that area, so evidently central to the image of the capital city of the province of Crete, the reconstruction was not as rapid as one might imagine: the main building (the *praetorium* itself) was finished around A.D. 382/383 (Di Vita 2000), more than 15 years after the disaster. This is nothing, for example, like the very quick rebuilding of Antioch after the Persian attack and strong earthquake in the time of Justinian. This slow, rather unimpressive reconstruction of the administrative core of a province's capital city poses a question about the scarce capacity—

Figure 6.4. General view of Late Antique Eleutherna: in the foreground, a large peristyle *domus*; in the background, the Christian basilica.

or perhaps the scarce determination—of the late Roman macro-economic system to convey money and resources towards a place that was probably perceived as increasingly distant from the interests of the Roman ruling class.

The same image, moreover, comes from both the excavated parts of Eleutherna and from the countryside. At Eleutherna, the real reorganization of the urban fabric, with the building up of the new Christian basilica, must be dated to the fifth century (Themelis 2004)—incidentally, perhaps, the same date as the new and very large episcopal basilica in Gortyn. The same goes for the large majority of the urban and rural basilicas in other centers of the island (Figure 6.4).

To return to our initial distinction between local micro-ecology/economy and general/Mediterranean macro-economy, the image could be one of a prevailing local dimension for the fourth century and one of a progressive upswing of the Mediterranean dimension in the fifth, when the central administration adopted a massive programme of building churches, as a strategy to reorganize the network of one of the most important macro-economic systems in the new form of Empire.

A New Macro-economic Centrality

This new Mediterranean perspective seems to be radically reinforced in the sixth century, when the appearance of Cretan cities appears to be more in line with those of the eastern Mediterranean cities than with the (more or less accentuated) crisis evinced by the cities of the Late Antique West.

In Gortyn, the signals are numerous and unequivocal: the renewal of the monumental landscape of the city is marked by the construction or substantial renovation of churches, by the reorganization of urban infrastructures (roads and water networks), and by the presence of private houses of good quality. The same picture emerges from the register of extra-archaeological sources: Gortyn is one of the very few cities of the Empire in which a hippodrome is stated as operating in the mid-sixth century, where the Green and Blue factions are attested (Spyridakis 1992). Urban elites are still well-structured, as evidenced by the role of archbishops and curials: some decades later, once again from Gortyn, we have the very last attestation of a "curial" that was well aware of his role in power management (Brandes 1999: 30). The landscape looks more or less analogous to Eleutherna, although the forms in which this positive phase of urban life is manifested may be different.

As always, we are more poorly informed about what the Cretan countryside looked like in the sixth century. The network of urban and rural basilicas should have continued to thrive and grow, simply because there is no reason why this should not happen, but we do not yet have a sufficiently reliable statistical basis for judgement. Systematic archaeological surveys are more difficult to read, on the one hand because, from a few potsherds picked up on the ground, it is difficult to get dates precise enough to allow us to distinguish timespans of a century or less; on the other hand because all these projects are, by their nature, more oriented towards the long-term relationship between people and the environment than the definition of specific chronological phases (the centuries that we are dealing with now, for example, are included variously under the "Roman and Late Roman" or "Byzantine and Turkish" labels).

Among the signals I have indicated, it is particularly interesting, for a number of reasons, to focus on the rebuilding of Gortyn's urban water system. First, control and management of water resources is a central theme, very frequently discussed in all the Early Byzantine literary sources, especially in the sixth century, when the imperial administration decided to place this important item mainly under the control of bishops. Second, archaeology testifies to the fact that even in Crete this was a "hot topic," as we have significant waterworks in Eleutherna and in other centers distributed across the island (Kelly 2006). Third, the renewal of the water distribution system at Gortyn has been the focus of an extensive study (Giorgi 2016). We now have excellent knowledge of the material structures and a refined functional analysis of the whole system, and this allows us to use water as an excellent archaeological indicator to study, in Gortyn, the "city of people" as distinct from (and somehow opposed to) the "city of monuments" (Zanini in press b).

The urban water distribution system at Gortyn in the Early Byzantine period is based on a pre-existing Roman aqueduct, but significant transformations were made to it. The original Roman aqueduct was probably built in the second century A.D., to bring to Gortyn—which at that stage was finally taking on the monumental features of a "standard" Roman provincial capital—a large quantity of water, captured at the foot of the Ida mountain massif, which constitutes the only important aquifer basin in Crete. The Roman aqueduct of Gortyn is important, first, for its dimensions (ca. 15 km long, almost entirely made with underground tunnels, following the natural slope of the terrain); second, for its flow rate (an average of 7,000 m^3 per day); and finally, due to the extraordinary availability of water that provided for a city of between 15,000 and 25,000 inhabitants, guaranteeing the daily needs of the population and in addition supplying several *thermae* and *nimphaea*, in accordance with the typical Roman approach to the use (and abuse) of water (Giorgi 2007).

Yet what is most interesting about the Roman aqueduct of Gortyn is its ecological impact. To create this urban water system, the hydraulic engineers of the Severan Age had to intervene dramatically in the whole ecosystem of the Messara, re-routing virtually all the water that had previously flowed to the western part of the plain (through a valley near the ancient city of Festos) to the provincial capital at Gortyn instead. The result was that the western part of the Messara, which until then had been particularly rich in water resources (even resulting in large semi-marshy areas), radically changed its water regime. Conversely, the eastern portion of the same plain came to enjoy a generous and reliable irrigation regime, in lieu of the highly seasonal nature of water availability that had until then been afforded only by the courses of the two main rivers (the Ieropotamos, which cuts longitudinally across the plain from east to west, and the Mitropolianos, its main tributary, and along the course of which the city of Gortyn is located). In this way, the new aqueduct became a sort of artificial river with a constant flow that was substantially similar to that which had previously irrigated, and perhaps flooded, the Festos plain. In addition, a second branch of the aqueduct was designed to capture the waters of the Gergeri springs, which were also at the foot of the Ida massif, likewise contributing to this important reorganization of the ecosystem of the central part of the Messara.

The immediate effect of this intervention—which one can certainly read in terms of a "macro-economic" decision, i.e., a deliberate choice by the imperial administration—was to make a decisive impact on the local micro-ecology, by shifting the main fundamental resource (providing drinking water and irrigation) in a semi-permanent way, since the functionality of the Gortyn water system continued throughout the Early Byzantine period.

In the late Justinianic age—this dating, suggested by a series of convergent clues, is now, after much discussion, generally agreed—the Gortyn water system was restored, probably after a long period of difficulty following the fourth-century earthquake, and it was integrated by a new capillary distribution system, based on a network of reservoir-fountains distributed throughout the city. In this new system, two items are particularly worthy of attention for our reasoning: the functional restoration of the entire water-capture and water-supply system to the city; and the distribution system organized by means of large reservoir-fountains (Figure 6.5).

Functional restoration necessarily involved the continuity of the huge ecological impact determined four centuries before. All the water springing from the Ida massif was again captured and diverted to Gortyn, renewing the earlier image of an artificial river with a considerable and constant flow rate, fueling urban consumption. This supports the idea of Gortyn's continuity, both in the number of inhabitants and in the "quality" of water use (i.e., continuity of baths and *nymphaea*). Moreover, this amount of water also seems to be intended to support a large cultivated area around the city, thus renewing the basic site-catchment area for city consumption and commerce.

In other words, the restoration of the aqueduct in the sixth century actually renewed the local, productive micro-ecological system that had been artificially built in the Severan age. It is not difficult to see that both the Cretan capital city supply and, very probably, the wealth of Gortyn's urban élites (through the enhancement of agricultural production), was based on this basic resource in Early Byzantine times,

The new element of Gortyn's urban water system in the age of Justinian is represented, as noted above, by a network of over 50 reservoir-fountains, irregularly but logically dispersed in clusters throughout the urban fabric, and tied into the urban branches of the aqueduct that were either restored or newly built *ex-novo*. Starting from the obvious assumption that the aqueduct branches and the fountains connected to them were designed to reach the areas where the water was needed—that is, where the main population nuclei were located in the sixth-century town—we may draw an unexpected picture of the "city of people" that overlaps only partially with the "city of monuments", at least what little we know of it today (Giorgi 2016: 91–118) (Figure 6.6).

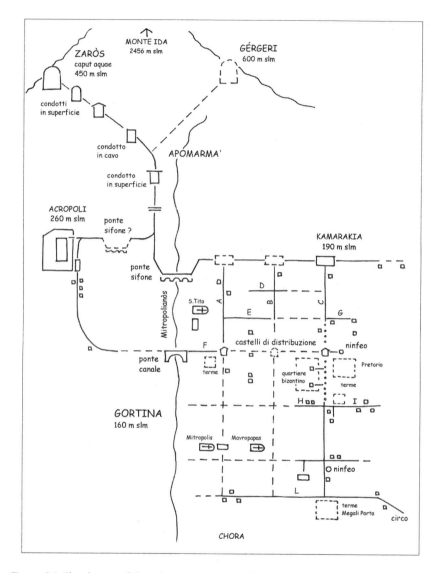

Figure 6.5. Sketch map of the urban water system of Gortyn in Early Byzantine times (after Giorgi 2016: figure 39).

Considering all these archaeological indicators, we have quite a "positive" image for Cretan economic and social life. It is an image that, on the one hand, relies on the quality of local micro-ecology, in terms of continued availability of important natural resources. On the other hand,

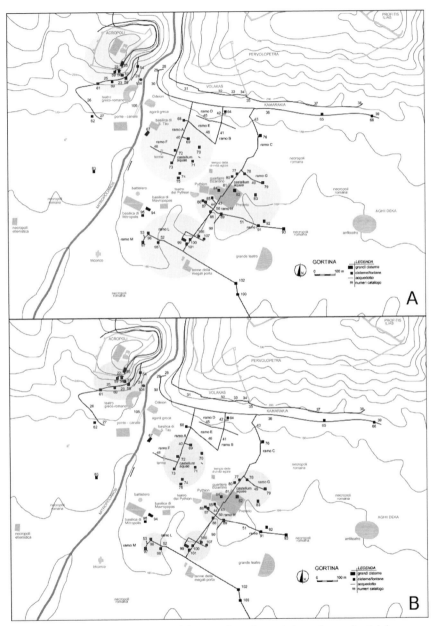

Figure 6.6. The city of monuments and the city of peoples in sixth- and seventh–eighth-century Gortyn (redrawn after Giorgi 2016: figure 62).

this same positive image rests on the renewed centrality of the role of Crete in the political-administrative, economic, and strategic scenario of the Early Byzantine Mediterranean. Clues in this direction are certainly not lacking. The main one, in my opinion, is the prestige enjoyed by Gortyn's archbishopric seat, whose holders subscribed to the Church councils of the sixth century in an absolutely privileged position, being positioned immediately after the archbishops of the most important cities of the Early Byzantine empire. Gortyn and Crete, therefore, occupy a very important place in the Mediterranean world of the Early Byzantine emperors and this macro-economic element can well explain the very positive phase that this island, so central but also so isolated, experienced in these decades.

A Mediterranean-sized Macro-economic Crisis?

The close link between Crete and the macro-economics of the Early Byzantine Mediterranean is further underlined, I believe, by the abrupt change of image we have by the last third of the sixth century. The phenomenon is particularly evident in Gortyn, largely because the recent excavations on this site have dealt extensively with urban contexts dating to this period.

The archaeological remains indicate a sharp change in quality of urban life: fragmentation of buildings to create smaller housing units; coexistence of residential and craft areas; encroachment of streets; and the infilling of spaces and partially abandoned public buildings. In short, the whole repertoire is typical of the transformation of urban spaces in most Mediterranean cities around this time (Zanini 2013b; 2015).

In Gortyn, once again, we have been able to match the information that comes from the tightly-controlled stratigraphic sequences of a small urban district with the transformation of the water distribution system into the city. What seems to be the case is that—together with an objective fall in the quality of the buildings, and with an equally objective change in the urban social fabric—there is also the gradual concentration of settlement around the nuclei of the reservoir-fountains. If the reservoir-fountains system, only a few decades before, seemed to have been designed to reach the large areas where people were living, quite the opposite phenomenon is now the case: the reservoir-fountains became so many *foci* surrounded by smaller and poorer districts (Giorgi 2016: 111–117). The picture is one of an urban settlement with many nuclei (the so called "islands-shaped" urban settlement): that is, a new type of urban landscape, in which no new public buildings were erected, while the old ones were restored with poorer materials (e.g., a limestone slab pavement covered the mosaics in the old episcopal basilica in the district of Mitropolis; the "new" *Praetorium* was made with re-used stones).

Now this new situation has been documented, the real question is: what made this change so rapid and evident? In the case of Crete, it seems impossible to take into account the two elements that are usually believed to be responsible for any abrupt changes in the pace of a city's life: war and natural disasters (particularly earthquakes).

So far as war is concerned, Crete in this era was firmly in the hands of the Byzantine administration and well-protected from external invasions by its very isolation in the middle of the Mediterranean. In the literary sources, we have no trace of substantial attacks on Crete until the Arab conquest of the first half of the ninth century, and I would argue that this element may be safely discarded. With natural disasters, the situation is more complicated, because Crete certainly was—and still is today—a land of great seismic risk. The role of earthquakes has, in the past, been emphasized by such experts in Gortyn's archaeology as Antonino Di Vita, who saw a sequence of devastating earthquakes as the main cause of the decline of the city (Di Vita 1996). More recently, however, the review of stratigraphic sequences has seriously questioned this oversimplified explanation of a phenomenon that, today, appears to be extremely complex. In the case of Gortyn, we could examine this change in urban fabric from at least three different scales: the individual areas already investigated; the city seen as a whole; and the city in its wider Mediterranean context.

At for the smallest scale (that of the single area investigated), I can only refer to the context I have been excavating for over 15 years—the so-called Early Byzantine district next to the Pythion shrine—which has allowed us to observe an interesting phenomenon. The excavated contexts tell of a seemingly bizarre asynchrony, with a very narrow spatial co-existence between areas where we have important traces of this "involution" of urban life, and areas where, simultaneously, we have equally important traces of construction of a large, high-quality building, probably a residential one (Zanini et al. 2009). It seems to be a great manor house (or a somewhat similar building, perhaps a monastery), which is surrounded by very poor houses, workshops, stables, and even some burials: in other words, a "rich" building and some "poor" buildings appear to have a direct spatial and functional relationship to each other, opening the door to the hypothesis that this may be one nucleus within a new type of city (Figure 6.7). It goes without saying that it is problematic to extend the image derived from this one small district to the whole city; but the physical and functional relationship with the two main urban infrastructures (the street grid and the network of reservoir-fountains) could be used to project this image onto other parts of an urban fabric whose spatial coordinates escape our comprehension.

Figure 6.7. General view of the seventh-century A.D. large *domus*(?) in the Early Byzantine district of Gortyn.

At the intermediate scale (the whole city), the other elements we can take into account are the modest restoration of some monumental buildings, as we have already mentioned, and some other excavations currently conducted by other Italian teams. These have so far been published only in the form of preliminary reports, but, on the whole, they seem to suggest a similar picture to that just outlined (Lippolis et al. 2010). More complicated are the problems associated with the city's only major structural element that, according to orthodox opinion, has to be attributed to a large urban reorganization of the seventh century A.D.: the walls that enclose the acropolis of the city, which represent the only surviving element of Gortyn's urban fortification system dating later than the early urban phase of the seventh to sixth centuries B.C. (Perna 2012). The dating of these walls is doubly important: first, because they could be connected to a major change in the spatial organization of the city and, second, because it could provide a solid basis for an absolute chronology of several other fortified enclosures that are now under investigation on various hilltops elsewhere in Crete (see Tsigonaki, Ch. 7 in this volume). If the acropolis walls really should be dated to the seventh century A.D., we would have an extremely interesting point to consider, since we would have two contemporary and perhaps complementary phenomena: the formation of an "island city" on the plain with many small nuclei centered around reservoir-fountains and, in parallel, the repositioning of the main civil and military functions onto the acropolis hill. Unfortunately, at present, we are still far from having a secure date for the construction of the Gortyn acropolis, because the available evidence is the result of poor excavations, and so of dubious quality and even mutually contradictory.

Still at the intermediate "urban" scale, a third aspect has to be considered: the "Mediterranean" dimension of the transformation of urban fabric. The same image of rapid change in urban landscapes occurs simultaneously in many areas of the Early Byzantine Mediterranean, often very distant from one another in terms of geography and diverse local ecological and micro-economic situations. The hypothesis—at present it is not much more than this—around which I am working is that this brutal change in the appearance of many different cities of the Early Byzantine Mediterranean between the last decades of the sixth and the first decades of the seventh century originates not in changes to the different local ecology (or micro-economies), but in a large-scale change, a decisively macro-economic one.

If the same phenomenon occurs in the context of the capital city of one of the largest and most isolated islands of the Early Byzantine Mediterranean, in a city of extraordinary symbolic importance such as, for example, Prima Iustiniana (Zanini in press a), and in dozens of large and small cities distributed across different regions, it is quite plausible that the fundamental cause (or at least one of them) could be a failure by the Byzantine administration in managing the empire's macro-economic forces—in other words, the incapacity to properly manage an empire that was economically exhausted by the tremendous military expenditures of the great Justinianic conquests and debilitated, in terms of manpower and the ability to produce primary resources, by the great plague of the sixth century. It was an empire that may no longer have been able to handle the great macro-economic practices (essentially the collection and management of taxes) on which the basic structural systems of the empire depended: the defensive system, which we see in severe crisis on many fronts during these decades, and the administrative system, based on the dichotomy of provinces and cities.

A Return to Micro-ecologies?

The trend inversion we have outlined in Cretan cities by the last third of the sixth century seems to continue in the subsequent 100 to 150 years. A deep change in urban settlements becomes more and more evident in the archaeological stratigraphy: transformation of buildings and spaces, always involving their diminution; impoverishment of construction techniques; and reduction of imported goods, which are generally replaced by local productions. At the urban scale—especially at Gortyn, but also at Eleftherna—it seems possible to see a sort of selection of spaces and monuments to be maintained (for example, the main paved streets running across the city center), as opposed to an urban fabric that appears increasingly impoverished and scattered (Baldini et al. 2012).

An emblematic image of this latter phase of urban life emerges, for example, from the stratigraphy investigated in our excavation area in Gortyn, the Early Byzantine district next to the Pythion shrine, where we have been able to excavate an entire ensemble of collapsed roofs, probably due to an earthquake to be dated to the middle or second half of the eighth century. This simultaneous collapse of roofs sealed a complex situation. To the south of the street that, since the fifth century, had divided the district in two, and later (very probably in the seventh century) was converted into a sort of elongated private courtyard, the situation underneath the collapsed roof is one of a very poor human landscape: a small stable; very small houses with a single room probably shared by people and animals; and impoverished artisanal activities.

Yet just on the other side of the courtyard, the picture is completely different: a large building, which we were able to excavate only in part (perhaps its service area), which has yielded strong evidence of a higher

Figure 6.8. Eighth-century A.D. assemblage found under the collapsed roof of the large *domus*(?) in the Early Byzantine district of Gortyn.

economic and social status. (Figure 6.8). Among the ruins was a marble slab with a monogram, perhaps gilded, that we are not yet able to resolve properly, but that surely refers to a high-ranking person and/or office. In the cellar of the same building, we found many amphorae, still intact at the time of roof collapse; while in the internal courtyard we found a marble *sigma*-shaped *mensa*, and a largely preserved *saltsario* produced in Constantinople at the beginning of the eighth century, together with some bronze belt buckles and other objects of personal ornament (Zanini et al. 2009; Zanini 2013b).

The overall picture is, therefore, that of an individual (or a group of individuals) that had a recognized social status: he/they lived, worked, or acted in a large building still characterized by large spaces; he/they had the right to a precise and recognized definition of his name and/or function (the monogram); he/they still had contact with the Mediterranean exchange of precious goods (the *saltsario*); he/they based his/their status on an economic well-being that was probably derived from land possessions in the surrounding territory (local amphorae in the cellar). This high social and economic status is reshaped and mitigated by other pieces of evidence: in the courtyard of the building, at the time of the collapse, some sheep were being housed, and the luxurious floor paved with limestone slabs appears very worn, probably because of the frequent passage of heavy animals.

In short, the evidence suggests a complex and multifaceted scenario, where some form of recognized power still survives. This same power, however, is based more on a local ecological and micro-economic dimension than on a macro-economic dimension at the Mediterranean scale, as it was only a few decades before. From this point of view, the macro-phenomenon of the decay and then disappearance of the long-standing hegemonic centers of Early Byzantine Crete could perhaps also be seen in terms of transition from a Mediterranean macro-economic dimension to a local micro-ecological dimension, because the Cretan cities progressively lost their fundamental role as centers for the different élites connected with central administration (civil, religious, and military) and the wider economy.

It is difficult to evaluate the fate of the great Cretan cities after the early or mid-eighth century. Based on the excavations in Gortyn—which comprised only a small portion of the settlement in the plain (less than 0.05% of the total urban area)—it appears that there was an abandonment, one that took place well before the arrival of the Arabs around A.D. 825. If this interpretation proves correct, the arrival of the Arabs would have been not the cause, but rather the effect of a deep transformation in the role of Crete in the strategic and economic geography of the Byzantine Empire. It goes without saying that this interpretation could be largely overturned by the excavations on the Gortyn acropolis, for example, and what currently appears to have been an irreversible crisis for the whole city could alternatively be read as the effect of a socio-economic élite moving to new, better-defended positions.

This is, again, a broader possibility that also finds some analogies with roughly parallel phenomena present in other areas of the Byzantine world (Saradi 2006). At the moment, however, we can only imagine a generalized crisis of the traditionally-based, long-standing urban settlement in Crete during the eighth century, most likely due to a total loss of interest in the island, and in particular its southern portion, by the Byzantine administration. We may also interpret the choice made by the imperial administration at the time of the reconquest of Crete in the mid-tenth century in this context. After A.D. 961, Nikephoros Phokas decided not to return the dignity of a provincial capital to Gortyn: the focus of imperial attention moved to the port cities of the northern coast, perceived as being much more conducive to the new image of the Middle Byzantine Empire, shifting from a fully Mediterranean entity to a rather more Aegean-Anatolian one. According to a recent re-interpretation of some problematic literary sources, this change of attitude by the imperial administration towards Crete would have occurred well before the Arab attacks, and the moving of administrative centres to the northern coast would have been a strategic choice dating back to the second half of the seventh century (Baldini et al. 2012: 246).

This is a very interesting hypothesis, which, if validated, would go in the direction I have discussed in this chapter. The great phenomenon of the end of the long-lasting Cretan cities and the overall change in the settlement model on the island would be the product of two concomitant phenomena: first, the progressive dominance of a local ecological/economic dimension on the macro-economic Mediterranean scale, which had instead sustained the Roman and Late Antique urban system until the generalized crisis of the Byzantine imperial system unfolded following the "golden" age of Justinian the Great; and second, the emergence of a new, purely Byzantine, macro-economy, geographically based in the Aegean and primarily focused on defence.

References

Arnaud, Pascal
   2005   *Les routes de la navigation antique: itinéraires en Méditerranée.* Éditions Errance, Paris.
Baldini, Isabella, Salvatore Cosentino, Enzo Lippolis, Enrica Sgarzi, and Giulia Marsili
   2012   Gortina, Mitropolis e il suo episcopato nel VII e nell'VIII secolo: ricerche preliminari. *Annuario della Scuola Archeologica di Atene e delle Missioni Italiane in Oriente* 90: 239–310.

Bonetto, Jacopo, Francesca Ghedini, Marina Bressan, Denis Francisci, Giovanna Falezza, Stefania Mazzocchin, and Eleni Schindler Kaudelka

    2009   Gortyna di Creta, Teatro del Pythion: ricerche e scavi 2007–2010. *Annuario della Scuola Archeologica di Atene e delle Missioni Italiane in Oriente* 87 (2): 1087–1098.

Bowersock, Glenn W., Oleg Grabar, and Peter Brown

    1999   Introduction. In *Late Antiquity. A Guide to the Postclassical World*, edited by Glenn W. Bowersock, Oleg Grabar, and Peter Brown, pp. vii–xii, Harvard University Press, Cambridge, MA and London.

Brandes, Wolfram

    1999   Byzantine Cities in the Seventh and Eighth Centuries: Different Sources, Different Histories? In *The Idea and Ideal of the Town between Late Antiquity and the Early Middle Ages*, edited by Gian Pietro Brogiolo and Brian Ward Perkins, pp. 25–57. Brill, Leiden-Boston-Köln.

Di Vita, Antonino

    1979   I terremoti a Gortina in età romana e proto-bizantina: una nota. *Annuario della Scuola Archeologica di Atene e delle Missioni Italiane in Oriente* 57–58: 435–440.

    1996   Earthquakes and Civil Life at Gortyn (Crete) in the Period between Justinian and Constant II (6th–7th Century A.D.). In *Archaeoseismology*, edited by Stathis C. Stiros and Robert E. Jones, pp. 45–54. Fitch Laboratory Occasional Paper 7. British School at Athens, Athens.

    2000   Il Pretorio fra il I secolo a. C. e l'VIII d.C. In *Gortina* V, edited by Antonino Di Vita, pp. 35–74. Bottega d'Erasmo, Padova.

Gasperini, Lidio

    2004   Le iscrizioni gortinie di età tardoantica e protobizantina. In *Creta romana e protobizantina*, vol. 1. *Atti del congresso internazionale, Iraklion, 23–30 settembre 2000*, pp. 157–162. Bottega d'Erasmo, Padova.

Giorgi, Elisabetta

    2007   L'approvvigionamento idrico di Gortina di Creta in età romana. *Annali della Facoltà di Lettere e Filosofia dell'Università di Siena* 28: 1–28.

    2016   *Archeologia dell'acqua a Gortina di Creta in età protobizantina*. Archaeopress, Oxford.

Hayden, Barbara J.

    1990   The Vrokastro Survey Project. *Expedition Magazine* 32 (3): 42–53.

Horden, Peregrine, and Nicholas Purcell

    2000   *The Corrupting Sea: A Study of Mediterranean History*. Blackwell Books, Oxford.

Kelly, Amanda

    2006   The Impact of Aqueduct Construction on the Demographic Patterns in Crete. In *Cura Aquarum in Ephesus. Proceedings of the Twelfth International Congress on the History of Water Management and Hydraulic Engineering in the Mediterranean Region, Ephesus/Selçuk, October 2–10, 2004*, vol. 2, edited by Gilbert C. Wiplinger, pp. 303–310. Peeters, Leuven-Paris-Dudley (MA.).

Francis, Jane E., and Anna Kouremenos (editors)

    2016   *Roman Crete: New Perspectives*. Oxbow Books, Oxford and Philadelphia.

Lippolis, Enzo

2005   Il tempio del Caput Aquae e il tessuto urbano circostante: campagna di scavo 2005. *Annuario della Scuola Archeologica di Atene e delle Missioni Italiane in Oriente* 83 (2): 625–648.

Lippolis, Enzo, Monica Livadiotti, Giorgio Rocco, Isabella Baldini Lippolis, and Giorgio Vallarino

2010   Gortyna. Il tempio del Caput Aquae e il tessuto urbano circostante: campagna di scavo 2007. *Annuario della Scuola Archeologica di Atene e delle Missioni Italiane in Oriente* 88: 511–537.

Marangou, Antigone

1999   Wine in the Cretan Economy. In *From Minoan Farmers to Roman Traders: Sidelights on the Economy of Ancient Crete*, edited by Ángelos Chaniótis, pp. 269–278. Franz Steiner Verlag, Stuttgart.

Molloy, Barry P. C., and Chloë N. Duckworth (eds.)

2014   *A Cretan Landscape through Time: Priniatikos Pyrgos and Environs.* British Archaeological Reports International Series 2634. Archaeopress, Oxford.

Nixon, Lucia, Simon Price, Oliver Rackham, and Jennifer Moody

2009   Settlement Patterns in Mediaeval and Post-Mediaeval Sphakia: Issues from the Environmental, Archaeological, and Historical Evidence. In *Medieval and Post-Medieval Greece: The Corfu Papers*, edited by John L. Bintliff and Hanna Stöger, pp. 43–54. British Archaeological Reports International Series 2023. Archaeopress, Oxford.

Perna, Roberto

2012   *L'acropoli di Gortina: la Tavola «A» della carta archeologica della città di Gortina.* Edizioni Simple, Macerata.

Sanders, Ian

1982   *Roman Crete.* Aris and Phillips, Warminster.

Saradi, Helen G.

2006   *The Byzantine City in the Sixth Century: Literary Images and Historical Reality.* Society of Messenian Archaeological Studies, Athens.

Spyridakis, Stylianos V.

1992   Macedonian Settlers in Sixth-Century Crete? In *Cretica: Studies on Ancient Crete*, by Stylianos V. Spyridakis, pp. 141–148. Caratzas, New Rochelle, NY.

Stiernon, Daniel, and Lucien Stiernon

1986   s.v. Gortyna. In *Dictionnaire d'histoirorie et de géographie ecclésiastique*, vol. 21, pp. 766–781. Letouzey et Ané, Paris.

Stiros, Stathis C.

2001   The A.D. 365 Crete Earthquake and Possible Seismic Clustering during the Fourth to Sixth Centuries A.D. in the Eastern Mediterranean: A Review of the Historical and Archaeological Data. *Journal of Structural Geology* 23: 545–562.

Themelis, Petros G. (editor)

2004   *Protobyzantini Eleutherna* I. Panepistimio Kretes, Rethymno.

2005   Eleutherna: The Protobyzantine City. In *Mélanges Jean-Pierre Sodini*, Travaux et Mémoires de l'Association des amis du Centre d'histoire et civilisation de Byzance 15, pp. 343–356. Association des amis du Centre d'histoire et civilisation de Byzance, Paris.

2009   *Ancient Eleutherna Sector I*. University of Crete, Athens.

Tsigonaki, Christina, and Apostolos Sarris

2016   Recapturing the Dynamics of the Early Byzantine Settlements in Crete: Old Problems | New Interpretations through an Interdisciplinary Approach. In *Proceedings of the 3rd International Landscape Archaeology Conference, 2014*.

Tzouvara-Souli, Chryseis

2001   The Cults of Apollo in Northwestern Greece. In *Foundation and Destruction. Nikopolis and Northwestern Greece: The Archaeological Evidence for City Destructions, the Foundation of Nikopolis and the Synoecism*, edited by J. Isager, pp. 233–255. Aarhus University Press, Aarhus.

Watrous, Vance L., Despoina Xatzi-Vallianou, Kevin Pope, Nikos Mourtzas, Jennifer Shay, C. Thomas Shay, John Bennet, Dimitris Tsoungarakis, Eleni Angelomati-Tsoungarakis, Christophoros Vallianos, and Harriet Blitzer

1993   A Survey of the Western Messara Plain in Crete: Preliminary Report of the 1984, 1986, and 1987 Field Seasons. *Hesperia* 62 (2): 191–248.

Volanakis, Johannes

1990   s.v. Kreta: Kreta von der frühchristl. Epoche bis zur Zeit der Araberherrschaft. In *Reallexikon zur Byzantinischen Kunst*, edited by Marcell Restle, vol. 4, coll. 814–905. Hiersemann, Stuttgart.

Zanini, Enrico

2013a   Creta in età protobizantina: un quadro di sintesi regionale. In *The Insular System in the Early Byzantine Mediterranean: Archaeology and History*, edited by Demetrios Michaelides, Philippe Pergola, and Enrico Zanini, pp. 173–190. Archaeopress, Oxford.

2013b   L'VIII secolo a Gortina di Creta e qualche idea sulla fine della città antica nel Mediterraneo. In *Settecento-Millecento Storia, Archeologia e Arte nei "secoli bui" del Mediterraneo*, edited by Rossana Martorelli, pp. 177–206. Scuola Sarda, Cagliari.

2015   Il dissolversi della figura: la fine della città antica in una prospettiva mediterranea di lungo periodo. In *Medioevo: natura e figura*, edited by Arturo C. Quintavalle, pp. 113–128. Electa, Milano.

In press a   Caričin Grad, Gortys in Crete, the End of the Ancient City and the Contemporary Idea of the Early Byzantine City. In *Early Byzantine City and Society*, edited by Vujadin Ivaniševic and Ivan Bugarski. Ecole Française de Rome, Rome.

In press b   The "Byzantine District" of Gortyn (Crete) and the End of a/the Mediterranean City. In *Byzantine Greece: Microcosm of Empire?*, edited by Archibald Dunn. Routledge, London.

Zanini, Enrico, Stefano Costa, Elisabetta Giorgi, and Elisa Triolo

2009   Indagini archeologiche nell'area del quartiere bizantino del Pythion di Gortyna: quinta relazione preliminare (campagne 2007–2010). *Annuario della Scuola Archeologica di Atene e delle Missioni Italiane in Oriente* 87 (2): 1099–1129.

Crete, A Border at the Sea: Defensive Works and Landscape–Mindscape Changes, Seventh–Eighth Centuries A.D.

Christina Tsigonaki

This chapter presents new archaeological data concerning defensive works in the cities and major settlements of Crete, probably dated to the seventh century. From the mid-seventh century, the rapid spread of the Arabs shattered Byzantine sovereignty within the Mediterranean Sea, and a period of prolonged insecurity began for the inhabitants of Crete. The formerly central island became a border region of the empire within the vastness of the Mediterranean; it was eventually conquered by the Arabs in ca. A.D. 827–828. Radical spatial transformations occurred in Cretan settlements, primarily as a response to the need for security. Fortification walls were erected and became the physical and structural limits which redefined the relationship between cities or settlements and the outside world, as revealed by three important case-studies: (1) the fortifications at Gortyn, the capital and metropolitan seat in the center of the Messara plain; (2) Eleutherna, a small, semi-mountainous city, the last in the hierarchy of Cretan bishoprics; and (3) Polyrrhenia, a settlement with no particular status. Fortifications also defined new spatial relations for civic populations, by delimiting distinct districts for the authorities. The militarization of the island was imposed by the central government through the implementation of a dual mechanism of "framing" landscape and mindscape. Church authorities as agents of divine intervention (such as Andrew, the Metropolitan of Crete) were responsible for the latter.

Crete and the Arabs (Seventh–Eighth Centuries)

"In this year Abdelas, the son of Kais, and Phadalas wintered in Crete." With this simple phrase, Theophanes the Confessor describes one of the Arab attacks against Crete in their early efforts to dominate the Mediterranean, under the first Umayyad caliph Muʻāwiya. The event mentioned by the Byzantine chronicler takes place at A.D. 674 (Chronicle of Theophanes:

542.11–12). ʿAbdallah b. Qays al-Ashʿarī, was nominated admiral of the fleet by Muʿāwiya, when he got permission from Caliph Uthman to conduct the first naval warfare against the Byzantines (year 28/648–649). Al-Ṭabarī presents ʿAbdallah b. Qays as a legend of the seas who "conducted fifty campaigns on the sea, in both winter and summer, and not one man was drowned or injured" (al-Ṭabarī, vol. 15: 29). Phadalas is probably to be identified with Fadala b. ʿUbayd al-Ansari, a companion of the Prophet, who participated in the occupation of Egypt. He then settled in Syria, from where he also launched naval raids against Byzantine territories. Khalīfa b. Khayyāṭ reports that in the year 51/671–672, Fadala conducted a winter naval campaign in the land of the Byzantines. He died the year 59/678–679 (Khalīfa b. Khayyāṭ: 74 and 87).

The Arab invasion of A.D. 674 against Crete was probably not the first and certainly not the last. Michael the Syrian reports that in the Syrian year 965 (653/654) Abu'l-Aʿwar and his army, after a raid against the island of Cos, crossed to Crete and pillaged it. Then, they went to Rhodes, destroyed it, and took down the Colossus (Michael the Syrian, Vol. 2: 442). Abu'l-Aʿwar, admiral of the Syrian fleet, confronted the fleet of Emperor Constans in the naval battle known as the Battle of Phoenix or the Battle of the Masts, which took place just off the Lycian coast. In this crucial stand-off, the Byzantine fleet was decisively defeated by the Arabs.

According to al-Ḥimyarī, Crete was invaded by the governor of Egypt ʿAbdallah b. Saʿd b. Abi Sarh, accompanied by his wife Qayla bint ʿUmar (Lévi-Provençal 1956: 55). Marius Canard has questioned the credibility of this testimony (Canard 1971: 1082), while Vassilios Christides (1984: 88) considers al-Ḥimyarī a reliable source and places the incident ca. 656, a few years after the successful expedition of ʿAbdallah b. Saʿd against Carthage in the year 27/647–648.

Junādah ibn Abī Umayyah al-Azdī was another naval commander under the Caliph Muʿāwiya, who developed significant actions against the Aegean islands. Both al-Balādhurī and al-Ṭabarī report that Junādah captured Rhodes in the year 52/672–673 or 53/673–674. Muslim colonisers were settled on the island for seven years, but they were recalled by order of Muʿāwiya's successor, the second Umayyad caliph Yazīd (al-Ṭabarī, vol. 18: 166; al-Balādhurī: 375–376). According to al-Balādhurī "Junādah led a razzia against Crete, a part of which he conquered at the time of al-Walīd" (al-Balādhurī: 376). However, the historian in his narrative about the capture of Rhodes mentions that Junādah died in the year 80/699–700, during the reign of ʿAbd al-Malik—in other words five years before al-Walīd became Caliph (reg. years 86–96/705–715).[1] Khalīfa also mentions the same year of death (Khalīfa b. Khayyāṭ: 142). The attack on Crete by Junādah should be dated around the time of the Arab occupation of Rhodes. The Egyptian encyclopedist al-Nuwayri (d. 1332), came to the same conclusion. He mentions that "the Muslims who came to Rhodes under the leadership of Junādah, also came to Crete, but they were unable to conquer it". Al-Nuwayri places the assault on Crete during the reign of al-Walīd: the Berber commander Tarik b. Ziyād, after the conquest of Andalusia in 92/710, also conquered the Mediterranean islands and "then he also sent an army against the island of Crete and was able to subdue certain parts of it" (Stavrinidis 1961–1962: 80; Christides 1984: 90). Even if this reference seems unrealistic, it reveals the Arab stranglehold on the Mediterranean islands, since the Arabs finally had the ability to attack from the east and south, but also from the west.

The attacks of the Arabs against Crete and the naval battles in the first decades of the eighth century are confirmed through the writings of Andrew of Crete, the head of the Church of Crete during the crucial period of the transition from the seventh to the eighth centuries. Andrew, a Greek-speaking Syrian monk, was appointed Metropolitan of Crete in Constantinople in approximately 710; he died in 740 (Auzépy 1995). The two *enkômia* that Andrew of Crete wrote in honor of Saint Titus (*BHG* 1852) and the Saint Ten (Laourdas 1949) were composed and delivered at Gortyn in the early eighth century. According to Vassilios Laourdas, both works would have been written during the co-regency of Leo III and his son Constantine V (720–726). Siméon Vailhé (1902: 386) has more accurately dated the *enkômion* of the Saint Ten to 724–725. Although lacking the specific information that is of use to a historian, the two *enkômia* convey the atmosphere of war on the island in general, and Gortyn in particular. Moreover, valuable information about the Arab invasions and the attack on Gortyn with siege engines are contained in the Life of Saint Andrew by *patrikios* and *kyestor* Niketas (*BHG* 113), which probably dates to the second half of the eighth century—thus very close to the events it relates (*Vita Andreae Cretensis:* 177.3–16; Detorakis 1969: 122–124; see below).

According to al-Ṭabarī, at the time of the caliphate of Hārūn al-Rashīd, ʿAbd al-Raḥmān b. ʿAbd al-Malik b. Ṣāliḥ in the year 175/791–792 carried out the summer expedition and reached Crete (al-Ṭabarī, vol.30: 114). One more campaign against Crete during the caliphate of al-Rashīd was conducted under the command of Maʿyūf al-Hamdānī, "who conquered part of the island" (al-Balādhurī: 376). Eventually, Crete was captured by Abū Ḥafṣ ʿUmar ibn ʿĪsa al-Andalusī, also known as al-Iqrīṭishī (the Cretan) during the caliphate of al-Maʾmūn (reg. years 198–218/813–833). The exact chronology of the conquest is difficult to ascertain, but the majority of scholars agree that it took place in the years A.D. 827–828 (Tsougarakis 1988: 30–41; cf. Christides 1984: 85–91). According to Genesios, Abū Ḥafṣ

(Apochaps) founded the town of Chandax. From there, the Arabs then captured 29 Cretan *poleis* (Genesios: 33.11–21). The same information is given in Theophanes Continuatus, most likely having been copied from the same source (Theophanes Continuatus: 114.6–14). According to the Arab sources, part of the island probably had already been conquered slightly earlier. The uncertainty of the sequence of events which characterizes both Byzantine and Arab written sources most likely reflects the fact that the island was conquered in stages (Panayotakis 1961–1962: 9–28). Although the Byzantine state made persistent efforts to recapture Crete, it regained control of the island only in 961, due to the victorious campaign of the domesticus Nikephoros Phokas.

Why Study the Fortifications?

The seventh and eighth centuries, the period that marks the definitive division into the Christian and Muslim worlds of the formerly unified Roman Mediterranean, marks a turning point for the history of Crete. The island that was once central, after the definitive conquest of Alexandria in 646, became a border region of the empire, a border within the vastness of the Mediterranean. As Piero Fois (2014) has recently argued, the Arab raids on the Mediterranean islands during the great Arab conquests aimed to deprive their enemies of the possibility of using the islands as naval bases; as such, they prevented Byzantine counter-attacks in the newly occupied territories of North Africa. The Arab attacks on the islands appear to have been one part of a carefully planned strategy and did not constitute a form of raiding or looting simply to obtain spoils.

Modern scholars underestimate the strategic importance of Crete for the Byzantine response during the Arab expansion of the seventh and eighth centuries. It was common in scholarly bibliography to assert that the urban population had abandoned the island's cities already in the second half of the seventh century, so that Crete fell defenseless into the hands of the Arabs (Tsougarakis 1991: 596–598; Baldini et al. 2012: 247–248). This assumption, however, constitutes a historiographical paradox. It is doubtful that the Byzantine central administration left Crete unprotected during this period of crisis.

Recent studies that have identified Early Byzantine fortifications at Kydonia (Andrianakis 2012), Eleutherna (Tsigonaki 2007: 272–276, 2015: 402–404), Lyttos (Gigourtakis 2011–2013), and Heraklion (Sythiakaki et al. 2015), as well as the publication of the Acropolis of Gortyn (Perna 2012: 145–167), have served to re-open this scholarly debate. Michalis Andrianakis has assumed that, although coastal settlements were abandoned during the seventh century, the Byzantines decided to fortify Kydonia and Heraklion

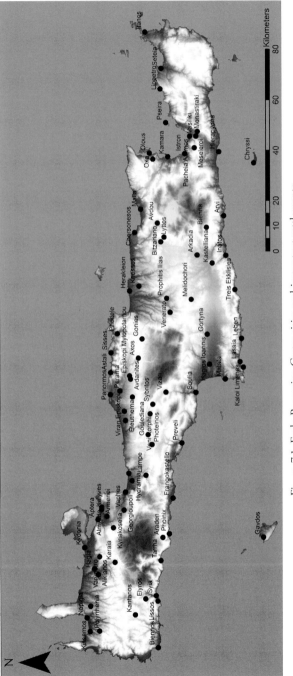

Figure 7.1. Early Byzantine Crete: cities and important settlements.

due to their important role in the defense of the island's north shores. I have argued that cities that enjoyed the status of official *polis* and were seats of bishoprics must have been fortified during the seventh century. Important evidence, derived from a recent research project, sheds light on the dense network of the Early Byzantine cities and settlements in Crete (Figure 7.1), illustrating a more complex situation.[2] Regardless of their political or ecclesiastical status, settlements with strategic importance, both along the shores and in the interior of the island, were endowed with fortifications (Tsigonaki and Sarris 2016).

This paper focuses on three case-studies: (1) the fortifications at Gortyn in the center of the Messara plain, capital and metropolitan seat; (2) Eleutherna, a small, semi-mountainous city, the last in the hierarchy of Cretan bishoprics; and (3) Polyrrhenia, a settlement with no particular status. They share a common characteristic in that they were all diachronically inhabited and therefore present a complex archaeological signature.

Fortifications, as physical and structural limits, are the primary indication for the spatial re-organization of cities and settlements, assuring their survival during a period of insecurity. Their study involves broader historical issues, such as the involvement of the central government—especially with regard to the militarization of the island—and its collaboration with local authorities, the isolation of certain districts within the cities, and the ensuing redefinition of social relations. At the same time, fortifications control the movement of people and redefined the relationship between cities or settlements and the countryside. Combining a reading of historical and archaeological evidence, I attempt to identify the changes in both landscape and mindscape in the period preceding the Arab conquest of Crete.

Gortyn

Gortyn occupies the northeast part of the Messara plain, the largest plain on the island. Low hills delimit the city to the north. The Mitropolianos River runs in between the two westernmost hills, Agios Ioannis and Pervolopetra; it continues toward the south, crosses the plain and acts as the western limit of the city (Di Vita 2010: 3–5, plate I). At its acme, in the second to third centuries A.D., Gortyn occupied a vast area of approximately 400 ha.

Early Byzantine Gortyn presents all the features of a grand capital and metropolis, except a major one: a fortification wall around the city's lower districts in the plain. This absence is inexplicable, given the city's official status. One might ask if this is not an oversight of modern scholarship. It should be noted that no traces of the city's Hellenistic period fortification walls in the plain have been found either. The hypothetical reconstruction proposed for the Hellenistic wall of the *asty* has been accepted with slight

Figure 7.2. Gortyn: Agios Ioannis hill.

differentiations concerning the exact course of the fortification circuit (Allegro and Ricciardi 1999: figure 264; Di Vita 2010: 75–76).

Important defensive structures dated to the Early Byzantine period are still visible on the Agios Ioannis hill, the ancient acropolis of Gortyn (Figure 7.2). The fortified enclosure has an irregular polygonal shape. It is enlarged on the higher part of the hill (altitude 240–250 m ASL) enclosing an area of 2.74 ha. Roberto Perna has described in detail all of the surviving constructions that relate to the fortification, as well as the intra- and extramural structures (Perna 2012: 145–190).

The wall remains show solid construction of ashlar masonry with mortared rubble cores whose width ranges from 2.5 to 3.1 m. The foundations are situated directly on the bedrock. Externally, on both faces, the wall consists of well-hewn blocks of varying dimensions, many of them in secondary use; they were arranged in courses of stretchers, but in a few places as headers. The mortared rubble can be seen in places where the stretchers have been removed. Brick and stone chips with mortar have been used in the joints (Perna 2012: 159–165). In the west section of the enclosure—which is the most exposed to an enemy attack—four towers are attached externally. Three are square, while one is polygonal and prow-shaped (Figure 7.3); the latter is the largest and best-preserved structure of the entire fortification (Perna 2012: 153–158, 161–163). A gate probably existed between the southern tower and the pentagonal tower.

Figure 7.3. Gortyn: Early Byzantine pentagonal tower.

Excavations on the acropolis were undertaken in the 1960s and focused on the Archaic phase (Rizza and Santa Maria Scrinari 1968). Unfortunately, the finds from the Early Byzantine period were never published systematically. On the interior of the fortification there are still remains of a large-scale public building (75.10 × 38.25 m), the so called *Kastron*, that has been dated to the late third century A.D. Small rooms were added onto its western and southern faces at a later phase; these additions have been dated to the Early Byzantine period on account of the masonry that resembles that of the fortification itself. Since archaeological excavations have not been undertaken in the interior of the building, its use cannot be defined. Many scholars have interpreted the complex as a military quarter for soldiers, a suggestion that Di Vita also supported at least for the last phase of the building's use (Di Vita 2010: 337–339). Perna, however, does not distinguish two construction phases, and concludes that the building functioned as a cistern (Perna 2012: 91–99, figure 54).

To the west of the so-called *Kastron*, excavations have revealed two churches, one on top of the other, in the area previously occupied by an Archaic temple (Rizza and Santa Maria Scrinari 1968: 68–96). According to Di Vita (2010: 334–337), the two churches date to the sixth and seventh century, respectively. A small cemetery was organized inside and around them. Some scattered buildings appear to be the remains of the acropolis district during the Early Byzantine period. Structures have also been identified outside of the fortification on the southeastern slopes of the hill. Cisterns and water channels secured the water supply. Perna thinks it probable that the organization of the neighborhood on the foothills of the acropolis was contemporary with the construction of the fortification. He concludes that the fort—actually a *Fortezza*—housed the administrative center of Gortyn, and consequently of the entire island (Perna 2012: 192).

For the chronology of the fortification on the acropolis there is no agreement among scholars. A. di Vita has dated it to the seventh century (Di Vita 2010: 340–342). The pentagonal towers in the fortifications of Ankara, Ephesus (Ayasoluk), Pliska, and Caričin Grad that present morphological similarities to the one at Gortyn led Perna to date it between the second half of the seventh and the early eighth century (Perna 2012: 161–163). However, it is difficult to determine a strict typological development without first identifying the particular geomorphological characteristics of each fortified location.

Most of the proposed dates for Gortyn's fortifications are based on historical arguments that have a common denominator: they suppose that the inhabitants of Gortyn moved to the fortified acropolis only after the urban fabric of the once-famous capital had dissolved. One especially important reference concerning the fortification of Gortyn is contained in the Life of Saint Andrew. According to this Life, during an Arab raid, the metropolitan and the people of Gortyn sought refuge "as they usually did, within the fort called *Tou Drimeos*" (*Vita Andreae Cretensis*: 177.4–16). This passage in the text indicates the first decades of the eighth century as a *terminus ante quem* for its construction. *Ochyroma* is the Greek word used in the text. Gilbert Dagron, and more recently Adam Izdebski, argued that the word *ochyroma* provides a general notion of a defensible site and characterizes every naturally defensible location on mountains, where the inhabitants of a region could find refuge (*Skirmishing* 1986: 219, 225–231; Izdebski 2013: 80–83). A careful reading of the *Strategikon* of Maurice does not leave any doubt that the term refers to a built construction (*Strategikon*: 336–348). As I have proposed in the past, the fort *Tou Drimeos* should be identified with the fortification on the Agios Ioannis hill (Tsigonaki 2012: 87). The passage from Saint Andrew's Life indirectly confirms that the city was not confined to the fortified acropolis. The finds of recent excavations in the district of the Praetorium and the so-called "Byzantine Quarter" near the Pythion, as well as those in the area of the monumental cathedral, confirm that urban life continued in the *asty* on the plain (Baldini et al. 2012; Perna 2017; Zanini 2017).[3]

Eleutherna

Eleutherna is located on a naturally fortified site in the northwest foothills of Mount Ida in central Crete. Its position is privileged: it is sheltered by mountains to the south, has unrestricted access to the sea to the north, and controls major roads towards the island's north and west. At times, the city may have occupied an area of 100–200 ha; we are, however, still unable to accurately determine the city's residential organization and urban development through time. The full extent and limits of the Roman city are unknown, as are those of Early Byzantine Eleutherna. The acropolis, which constitutes the core of the settlement diachronically, is identified with Prines hill, the so-called Pyrgi (altitude: 370–380 m ASL). The base of this elongated (ca. 800 m) and, at places, extremely steep rise is flanked by two small rivers (Figure 7.4). On its western slope, two large, rock-hewn, Roman

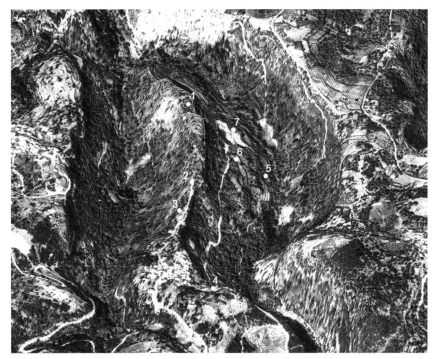

Figure 7.4. Eleutherna: the acropolis and lower city viewed from the south. 1. Central Plateau; 2. Cisterns; 3. Tower; 4. Church of Christ the Saviour; 5. Basilica; 6. Basilica, 7. Basilica of the Archangel Michael.

cisterns constitute an infrastructure vital for city life. From the south, the hilltop was accessible only through a very narrow passage controlled by a tower—hence the hill's name Pyrgi (Kalpaxis 2004).

Much of the Roman and Early Byzantine habitation spread out on the narrow, elongated terraces along the hill's eastern base. The concentration of four churches here indicates the general location of the Early Byzantine city's neighborhoods. A three-aisled basilica was excavated by Petros Themelis, who dated its foundation to the middle of the fifth century. The building was refurbished in the seventh century. A small bath, identified to the basilica's northwest, was also certainly functioning throughout the seventh century (Themelis 2009: 80–92). Ceramic evidence from the church area suggests that, even though the church had shrunk, it was in use until the eighth century (Yangaki 2005: 310–313). The finds include bronze belt buckles dating from the mid-seventh to the eighth centuries (Poulou-Papadimitriou 2005). In Eleutherna, as in the case of Gortyn, no fortification has been identified so far that encloses the lower districts of the city.

The defensive upgrade of the acropolis in the Early Byzantine period was probably the most radical change in the city-scape of Eleutherna, which for centuries after the Roman conquest did not offer a wall. The sections of the wall that have been mapped so far indicate that the defensive perimeter enclosed the entire hilltop. If this is true, the estimated enclosed area is 47,671 m^2 (Tsigonaki 2007: figure 4). The only tower that has been identified is the square one that controls the north passage to the acropolis; it had a compact core formed of rubble, bricks, and mortar, while the outer faces were lined with well-hewn blocks with broken tiles and mortar between the joints (Figure 7.5).

The wall runs in a straight line and is interrupted at intervals by projections at right angles. These ensured both the stability and defensive quality of the fortification, since they functioned as defensive towers. Recent excavations on the Central Plateau of the Acropolis have revealed new sections of the circuit on the eastern and the western slopes of the hill (Tsigonaki 2015). The eastern part is the best preserved: the facing is in ashlar masonry, composed of blocks laid in parallel courses as stretchers, while in a few places they are arranged as headers (Figure 7.6, left). A large portion of the construction material is reused. Broken tiles and small stones are used in the joints, and mortar is used for binding. In the parts where the lining is missing, the interior wall construction appears built in horizontal zones, though less carefully. Smaller partially worked stones or rubble, reused materials such as fragments of column shafts, and abundant mortar have been used here. The foundations of the wall rest directly on the natural bedrock.

Figure 7.5. Eleutherna, Pyrgi: square tower.

Figure 7.6. Eleutherna, Pyrgi: (left) detail of the enclosure's eastern section (Early Byzantine masonry); (right) detail of the enclosure's western section (Hellenistic masonry).

At least two construction phases can be discerned on the part of the wall uncovered on the west slope. The southern end of the section discovered so far was constructed in finely dressed stones with dry binding (Figure 7.6, right). The rectangular pseudo-isodomic wall construction is attested in similar structures of the Hellenistic period (mid-4th century B.C.). The foundations lay in a trench carved out of the natural rock. The situation on the north end of the section is very different. An ashlar wall with rubble core construction survives there only to a very short height. Until now it was known that the Early Byzantine fortifications followed the course of the earlier Hellenistic walls. In the case of Eleutherna it becomes clear that sections of the wall date to different periods resulting in a single fortified enclosure, but eventually many centuries have elapsed between the construction of the different parts of the wall.

The wall of Eleutherna is an integral part of the district that it protected. Archaeological evidence from the Central Plateau indicates that a monumental church, the buildings around it, and the wall belong to the same building program, which can be dated to the seventh century. This is documented by the pottery and coins discovered so far (Yangaki 2005: 88–100; Tsigonaki 2007). The district's water supply was ensured by the two large rock-hewn Roman cisterns, which were still in use and included within the walled area (Tsigonaki and Yangaki 2015). The church's large size and the discovery of artifacts relating to administrative functions, such as lead seals and bronze weights, suggest that the city's religious and administrative center moved to the Central Plateau of the fortified acropolis. However, the archaeological finds from the Central Plateau do not give a clear picture of the function of the buildings discovered around the church. The discovery of a Syracuse-type belt buckle, together with an arrowhead, in a stratigraphic horizon belonging to the second half of the seventh century may indicate the presence of soldiers.

Polyrrhenia

Polyrrhenia was one of the most powerful cities of west Crete in the Hellenistic and Roman periods. Located inland, approximately seven km south-southwest of the important city-harbor of Kissamos, it occupies a naturally fortified hill (highest altitude ca. 410 m ASL). The ancient city developed along the steep terraces of the hill sloping toward the south. An element vital for urban life was the sophisticated public aqueduct that still functions today even without maintenance (Christodoulakos 2015: 152–153; Markoulaki and Christodoulakos 2018: 96–104). In modern times, the village of Ano Palaiokastro occupied the lower part of the ancient city.

Figure 7.7. Polyrrhenia: topographical plan (after Savignoni and de Sanctis 1901).

Early Byzantine written sources do not mention the settlement. Scant archaeological finds—graves and inscriptions (Theophanidis 1942–1944: 30)—indicate that the settlement continued to be inhabited in the Early Byzantine period, most likely dependent on Kissamos, a "recently made *polis*" and already a bishop's seat in the fourth century A.D. (Tsougarakis 1988: 228, 388, plate 6). A lead seal of the church of Kissamos (*Ekklisia Kisamou*) that can be dated to the beginning of the eighth century shows that the bishopric was active until such a late date (Tsigonaki 2007: 285).

Ancient Polyrrhenia was surrounded by a fortification. The total fortified area appears to be quite large. The perimeter of the wall is about 1,855 m and encloses around 16.5 ha. In the Byzantine period, the upper part of the hill, the acropolis, was isolated with a strong fortification. In addition, north of the acropolis, a long and narrow area was fortified (6,091 m^2), with a series of terraces laid out sloping toward the north, and thus creating a secondary fortified district (Christodoulakos 2015: 148–149, map 2). Toward the west is preserved a circular tower, from which one could visually control the surrounding area.

Figure 7.8. Polyrrhenia: Middle Byzantine circuit on the acropolis.

Polyrrhenia's fortification has been known since the nineteenth century (Pashley 1837, vol. 2: 47–48; Spratt 1865, vol. II: 212–214). Luigi Savignoni provided its first detailed description. He published a topographical plan, which was reprinted in later publications (Figure 7.7), as well as many photographs of sections of the wall and the towers that are not preserved in the same condition today (Savignoni and de Sanctis 1901: 314–328). From the description of the different types of masonry, it becomes clear that the initial circuit wall and the towers have undergone extensive reconstructions at different periods. Giuseppe Gerola reached the same conclusion and dated the reconstructions to the Byzantine period (Gerola 1905: 72–80).

For most scholars, the initial phase of the fortification belongs to the Hellenistic period (Coutsinas 2013: 249–250, 444–445). In the publication of the results of a recent excavation around the semi-circular tower on the southwest flank of the circuit, Stavroula Markoulaki and Dimitra Goula argued that the fortification of Polyrrhenia is Hellenistic, with Roman restorations. They dated only the two fortified districts on the hill's edge to the Byzantine period. The inherent question is why a fortification would be built during a period of peace, as was the time of Roman rule on Crete. The authors argue that this was done for reasons of prestige and consolidation of the new authority. They dismiss the possibility that the restorations belong to the Early Byzantine period, based on the different composition of the binding mortar

Figure 7.9. Polyrrhenia: view of the fortification's north section.

on the semi-circular tower at the southwest of the lower circuit and on the Byzantine fortification of the acropolis (Markoulaki and Goula 2015: 142–143).

The dating of the Hellenistic fortification's reconstruction to the Roman period cannot be accepted for several reasons. There is nothing in the history of Poryrrhenia that would justify this local particularity, making Poryrrhenia unique in Crete—the only Cretan city to have been fortified in the Roman period purely for reasons of ostentatious display and prestige. The various repairs, reconstructions, and additions to Poryrrhenia's fortifications most likely belong to different phases of the Byzantine period. Nikos Gigourtakis (2011) dates the fortification of the two upper districts to the Middle Byzantine period. The masonry of these wall sections and of the only semi-circular tower that survives there consists of small stones and an abundance of whitish mortar (Figure 7.8).

An impressive section of the fortification wall is preserved on the north slope (Figure 7.9). This section is founded directly on the rocky crags, filling the gaps between them. The fortification of this particularly steep terrain required considerable effort and skill. Nothing betrays a desire to impress. On the contrary, the sturdy construction appears to have been dictated by the fear of enemy attacks and a concern for the protection of the population. The masonry presents all of the characteristics of an ashlar wall with mortared rubble core of the seventh or eighth century. The two faces consist of rectangular blocks of various sizes; flat stones, broken bricks, and mortar in the joints fill the gaps left by the different sized ashlar blocks; *spolia* from ancient buildings, such as marble column shafts, are attested in the base of a wall section in the north (Markoulaki 1987: 563 and 566, figure 6, plate 332a). The two towers, which projected to the north side of the circuit, present masonry with similar characteristics (Markoulaki and Christodoulakos 2018: figures 13 and 14b).

The semi-circular tower to the southwest belongs to the same building phase. In the photograph published by Savignoni, the tower was preserved to a height of approximately 12 m. The same type of masonry described above is evident, with incorporated spoils from ancient monuments (Savignoni and de Sanctis 1901: 324–325, figure 21). The tower was built in front of a rock-cut cistern. At its base is a built opening, 0.50 m wide and 1.4 m high, which constitutes the mouth of the conduit that passes under the tower and connects with the aqueduct (Christodoulakos 2015: 152; Markoulaki and Christodoulakos 2018: figures 42a, 45a, 45b, and dessin 7).

An arched postern at the site of Poros Peristeras, on the fortification's southeast section, features the same characteristic masonry. Repairs with smaller stones and part of the wall-walk are preserved in the postern's upper part (Markoulaki and Christodoulakos 2018: figure 17 and dessin 3).

Archeological evidence for the use of the space within the fortification wall is scant. Vaulted cisterns that should possibly be dated to the Early Byzantine period rather than to the Roman period (cf. Markoulaki and Christodoulakos 2018: 98, figure 32) have been identified in the two upper fortified districts. The remains of an Early Byzantine (?) church are located in the northernmost of them.

The archaeological evidence indicates that the fortification wall of Poryrrhenia was rebuilt in the Early Byzantine period, following the line of the ancient ruined circuit and using building materials both from it and from other ruined monuments. The date of the fortification wall cannot be determined with certainty, since one can only argue based on the type of masonry, which is not a reliable chronological tool. The similarities, however, with the fortifications of Gortyn and Eleutherna are obvious.

Fortifications and Landscape–Mindscape Changes

The study of the fortifications places the issue of the abandonment of Cretan cities on a new footing. The widely accepted assumption that Cretan cities were abandoned before the Arab conquest no longer appears valid. Instead, there appears to have been a strengthening of Crete's defenses through the construction of powerful fortifications in cities and important settlements throughout the island. These fortifications drastically changed Crete's urban landscape. They also changed the physiognomy of the Cretan countryside.

Archaeological evidence confirms the Arab written sources, which speak of fortresses. Balādhurī mentions that Abū Ḥafṣ "first reduced one fort (ḥiṣn) and occupied it. Then he kept on reducing one part after another until none of the Greeks were left. He also dismantled their forts" (al-Balādhurī: 376).

The fortification does not signal the shrinking of the city and subsequent decline of the urban space, but rather the demarcation of controlled areas within the city. The establishment and separation of districts appears to follow the principles of urban design that had appeared in the Balkans in the sixth century. Excavations at *Justiniana Prima*, the most representative example of a newly founded city, shed light on the new urban design principles that were dictated by the need for security (Ivanišević 2017). The fortification of the acropolis was intended to isolate the district where the authorities lived and exercised their power from other inhabited neighborhoods, by controlling access to it. The towers of these fortified districts look out not towards an outside enemy, but towards the inhabitants of the neighborhoods of the city itself. This may reflect the administration's response to the constant social upheaval mentioned in seventh-century historical sources. According to Georges Kiourtzian (2013), a civilian riot, not an Arab raid, is implied in a seventh-century inscription from Heraklion.

Written sources reveal the role of *ochyromata* in the protection of civilians. In case of enemy attack, the inhabitants of the *asty* sought refuge there. In the Life of Saint Andrew, the metropolitan is praised for his role in the rescue of the citizens of Gortyn, who took refuge with him in the *ochyroma Tou Drimeos*. As mentioned in the collection of miracles of Saint Theodore the Recruit (*BHG* 1764), during a wintering Arab raid, which must be dated in the 660s, the citizens of Euchaïta who lived in the *asty* sought refuge in the *ochyromata* (*Miracula S. Theodori Tironis*: 197.25–27, 198.28–31, 199.23–26; Haldon 2016: 51–53 and 108–110). Modern archaeological research confirms the identification of Euchaïta with the village of Beyözü in the Mecitözü Valley. Scant traces remain of the fortification wall, built by Emperor Anastasius in response to a Hun raid in 515. The acropolis was located on the Kale Tepe hill, where the remains of a rampart are preserved. Kale Tepe was probably fortified during the reign of Constans II: it provided a refuge for the citizens of the lower parts of the city and probably also a base for the military authorities (Haldon 2016: 13–15; Haldon et al. 2017). It becomes apparent from the above that the *ochyromata* of the Byzantine written sources also should be sought in the cities' ancient acropoleis.

Byzantine texts abound with references to civilians, who seek refuge in fortified cities and *kastra*, without, however, clear differentiation between the urban and rural population. In the anonymous Byzantine treatise *On Strategy* (1985), which a recent study attributes to Syrianus Magister, "the security of the forward walls (*proteichisma*) is also to be considered. They are used to receive our own people when they come in from the country to seek refuge behind the walls. This relieves congestion in the city, and the refugees can also stand there and fight against the enemy" (*On Strategy* 1985: 34.31–36, 35). A well-known passage from the Life of George of Amastris (*BHG* 668), a text composed in the ninth century, refers to an event that took place at the end of the eighth century. During an Arab raid, both the urban population and the population of neighboring villages took refuge inside the fortifications of the *polis* thanks to the bravery of Bishop George, who, after overseeing the evacuation of the villages of the territory of Amastris, threw himself into battle against the invaders (*Vita Georgii ep. Amastridos*: 38–43, § 24–26; Crow 2017b). Adam Izdebski's (2013: 83) suggestion that the hagiographer's decision to include this event in his account indicates that it was unusual is hard to accept: in the turbulent years of the seventh and eighth centuries, such cases of emergency were not unusual. The passages in both Andrew of Crete and George of Amastris' *Vitae* reflect the growing importance of the bishop, who in this period was the main local and lifelong representative of authority.

But what happened in the absence of a brave bishop? In this case the army probably played an important role in the protection of the rural population. Perhaps the only text in which the concern for the protection of rural populations pervades is the *De velitatione bellica*, a tenth-century text on guerrilla warfare attributed to Nikephoros Phokas. The text records the defensive tactics of the Byzantine army in its eastern borders. Several passages give specific instructions on how to evacuate the villages located in areas suffering from Arab raids. The task of the evacuation was the responsibility of the *strategos*. The army's evacuation specialists (*ekspilatores*) organized the transfer of villagers and their herds to fortified places, called *ochyromata* but also *kastra* (*Skirmishing* 1986: 39 §1.5–8, 51–53 §1.2–5, 77 §1.11–12, 79, §5.40–41, 121 §1.2–6).

Polyrrhenia was not a *polis* like Amastris, Gortyn, or Eleutherna. However, the area of Polyrrhenia enclosed by the extensive circuit can be compared to that of a *polis*. Technically, Polyrrhenia was a *kômopolis*. Malalas reports that many Syrian *kômopoleis* were fortified in the mid-fourth century by Theodosius, and that large *kômai* in Cappadocia were fortified by Anastasius (Malalas: 268.11–14, 333.6–7; Dagron 1979: 44, Crow 2017a: 94).

Polyrrhenia is probably an example of a fortified space intended for the protection not only of its own inhabitants, but also of the neighboring villages and countryside. As a place that offered security and refuge, it could be considered a *kastron* (Haldon 1999: 10–18). Future archaeological research could determine whether military forces were present at Polyrrhenia

Figure 7.10. Kastelos Varypetrou, south section of the fortification: (left) semi-circular tower of the Middle Byzantine period; (right) polygonal tower of the Early Byzantine period.

or not. Either way, Polyrrhenia's strategic position is also confirmed by the reinforcement of its fortifications in the Middle Byzantine period, which is not the case at Gortyn or Eleutherna.

Polyrrhenia's case is not unique. The fortification at Kastelos Varypetrou is mostly known for its Middle Byzantine phase, but is, in fact, a multi-phase construction, parts of which were rebuilt before and after the Arab conquest. The site is situated inland, in hilly terrain, eight km southwest of Kydonia. The estimated enclosed area is approximately 5.6 ha (altitude: 365 m ASL). On the southern side of the enclosure two monumental towers of different type dominate: a compact, polygonal tower of the Early Byzantine period and a semi-circular tower of Middle Byzantine date (Figure 7.10). Nikos Gigourtakis demonstrated that the fortified cities of West Crete in the Middle Byzantine period were strategically chosen because they communicate visually, an indication of central planning; the fortress of Polyrrhenia has visual contact with that of Malathyro, whereas both have visual contact with the fortress of Roka, which has visual contact with the fortress at Kastelos Varypetrou (Gigourtakis 2011, 2011–2013). This network of visual communication, which connects fortified sites, indicates a dynamic system of control of the land and sea. It remains to be seen whether, in addition to Polyrrhenia and Kastelos Varypetrou, the Middle Byzantine sites of Malathyro and Roka were already fortified in the Early Byzantine period.

The fortifications of Gortyn, Eleutherna, and Polyrrhenia were strong and expensive structures. Their construction indicates the presence of the army on the island, since this was the only body with the engineering skills and resources to design and execute such large-scale projects. According to Maurice's *Strategikon*, fortresses were built in three to four months by able craftsmen with the help of the infantry. The same text gives precise instructions on how to build cisterns (*Strategikon*: 346.7–10, 350.45–62). It is commonly accepted that military presence on the island increased after the creation of the Theme of Crete. However, there is no consensus as to when this Theme was created. Most scholars date it to the reign of Leo III, as part of the radical reformation of the Byzantine defense system. According to the Life of Saint Stephen the Younger (*BHG* 1666), a text by Stephen the Deacon dating to 807/809, the iconophile monk Paul was questioned and tortured in the praetorium of Gortyn by the island's *archisatrapes* Theophanes Lardotyros (*Vita Stephani Junioris:* 160, §58). The text refers to Lardotyros twice as *strategos*—although he obviously also fulfilled judicial functions—providing evidence for the establishment of the Theme of Crete before A.D. 767, the year of Saint Stephen's martyrdom (Herrin 1986; Yannopoulos 1995; Kountoura-Galake 2017; cf. Živković 2005–2007; Brubaker and Haldon 2011: 734–739). However, before the establishment of the Theme of Crete, and possibly for a period of time after, Crete, like other border regions and islands (e.g., Dalmatia, Dyrrachium, Cyprus, Crimea, and Chaldia), enjoyed the special status of *archontia*, possibly to face invasions more efficiently. Seven lead seals of the *archontes Kritis* recording the offices of imperial *protospatharios* and *spatharios* date from approximately the end of the eighth century to the early decades of the ninth century (Tsougarakis 1990: 146–147, nos. 16–20, 22, 23). The seal of *Ioannes, archon* and *parafylax Kritis*, dates to the first half of the eighth century (cf. Tsougarakis 1990: 146, no. 21; Baldini et al. 2012: 245–246). The seal of *Ioulianos genikos kommerkiarios apothikis Kritis* (668–690) and those of the *vassilika kommerkia Kritis* (730–741) prove that the island was integrated into the *kommerkiarioi-apothekai* system, which supplied and equipped the army (Ragia 2011). At the same time, Crete was a naval station for the Byzantine fleet, as suggested by the narrative of the failed Byzantine campaign to reconquer Carthage in A.D. 697 (*Chronicle of Theophanes*, vol. I: 567; Kountoura-Galake 2017).

The particularly high percentage of coins of the emperors Heraclius and Constans II indicates the strengthening of a military presence on the island earlier in the seventh century. More particularly, the bronze issues of Constans II constitute the majority of numismatic finds both at Eleutherna (Sidiropoulos 2000a: 850–851, figures 6 and 7; 2000b: 273, table C; Tsigonaki 2007: 286–288) and Gortyn (Garraffo 2004: 32, table 1). The same applies to Rhodes (Kasdagli 2000: 270–271, tables 1 and 4) and Pergamon (Otten 2010: 17, figure 12). The concentration of coins of Constans II at Athens led Michael Hendy (1985: 661) to argue for the role of the state and its organs as a direct distributary mechanism behind coinage. Cécile Morrisson also argued that peaks in coin finds in the cities of Asia Minor are to be associated with military events rather than with settlement history (Morrisson 2017: 75).

Seventh-century Crete does not appear to be different from other regions of the Empire in terms of military presence and communication with the central administration. In the case of Eleutherna, I dated the fortification, which I believe to be an integral part of the acropolis district that it protected, to the seventh century (Tsigonaki 2007), a date that I still support. Even though we are not in a position to date the wall's construction precisely, we can reasonably assume that the defensive upgrades of Gortyn, Eleutherna, and Polyrrhenia were part of a comprehensive plan to shield the island implemented during the first period of the Arab expansion in the Mediterranean. The dating of Crete's fortifications should not be associated with the creation of the Theme of Crete in the eighth century. The island's place in the military planning of the Byzantine state changed dramatically after the Arab conquest of Alexandria and the Byzantine defeat at the Battle of Phoenix in the mid-seventh century.

All the transformations in the appearance and structure of the cities and important settlements described so far were part of top-down processes. Seventh- and eighth-century seals of high officials found on the island also argue in favor of the direct involvement of imperial administration in Crete. Particularly noteworthy are two seals from the Gortyn and Knossos acropoleis, the former belonging to Antiochos *koubikoularios* and *basilikos chartoularios* (seventh century) (Rizza and Santa Maria Scrinari 1968: 118–119, figure 198, 3; Tsougarakis 1990: 148, no. 30), the latter of Ioannes *vestitor* and *protonotarios* of the Imperial Treasury (first decades of the ninth century) (Dunn 2004).

The Life of Andrew of Crete contains one reference that demonstrates yet another aspect of the defense of Crete and its connection to the capital. Andrew built a church dedicated to the Theotokos of Blachernae in Gortyn (*Vita Andreae Cretensis:* 176.4–7), thus contributing to the establishment of the worship of the Virgin not only with his rich body of written works, but also with the construction of a church (he also atoned for his temporary adherence to the doctrine of Monothelitism). Theotokos of Blachernae was the protector *par excellence* of Constantinople. It is she who, according to seventh century sources, saved Constantinople from the Avar attack of A.D. 626; she also protected the city against the Arabs in 676–678 and 717/718.

The introduction at Gortyn of the Constantinopolitan worship of the Theotokos Blachernitissa by Andrew, whom Constantinople, and not Rome, had appointed Metropolitan of Crete, offers itself for multiple readings. Firstly, it can be seen as an effort to lift the morale of the city's inhabitants. Furthermore, it was probably also an attempt to reinforce the connection between the island's population and the authority of Constantinople. Written sources relate two more instances of churches dedicated to the Theotokos of Blachernae in the Early Byzantine period: one at Ravenna (Agnellus of Ravenna: 286–287) and another at Cherson in Crimea (*Narrationes*: 220.1–8; Romancuk 2005: 84–85). Both cities were located on the Empire's border, isolated from the rest of the Empire. Both churches, as at Constantinople, were located outside of the city walls.

The diffusion of the worship of the Theotokos of Blachernae constitutes an official act of imperial and ecclesiastical propaganda. As the Arab raids and Byzantine military presence made life on Crete grimmer by the day, it is only natural that the central authority would seek to complement its defense program by "framing" both landscape and mindscape using the period's super-weapon: the Theotokos of Blachernae.

Acknowledgments

I owe many thanks to my friend and collaborator Ioannis Theodorakopoulos, who introduced me to the world of Byzantine hagiography. I am most grateful to Roxani Margariti for her help with Arab written sources, as well as Werner Seibt and Alexandra-Kyriaki Vassileiou-Seibt for helping me read and date the seals relevant to Crete. My collaborators Kostantinos Roussos and Gianluca Cantoro accompany me during difficult explorations of the Cretan mountains. Nikos Gigourtakis kindly provided me with the photo of the towers at Kastelos Varypetrou.

Notes

1. According to Roxani Margariti the Arabic source is ambiguous at the point where it refers to the attack on Crete by Junādah. Hitti's translation could be rendered as follows: Junādah led a razzia against Crete. When the era of al-Walīd came, a part of it was conquered ("was opened"), then it was lost ("was closed").

2. The identification and documentation of the fortifications fulfilled one of the goals of the research program "Recapturing the Dynamics of the Early Byzantine Settlements in Crete: Old problems – New Interpretations through an Interdisciplinary Approach" that took place in 2013–2015. This investigation continues through the program "In Times of Crisis: Fortified Places in Crete (7th–9th centuries)", part of the research action METOPO – Mediterranean Cultural Landscapes (Institute for Mediterranean Studies / Foundation for Research and Technology-Hellas).

3. A question to be addressed by future research is whether the *asty* of Gortyn was also protected by fortification. A dedicatory inscription, known only from old drawings, was found out of its context near the temple of Pythian Apollo, in an area called *Viglai*. The text commemorates the renovation of a wall (*toichos*) at the time of the archbishop Theodoros and the proconsul Helios in the consulship of Flavius Apion. Anastasius Bandy, who dated the inscription to 539, considers it not unlikely that the text actually refers to the city wall renovation (Bandy 1970: 58–61, no. 31).

References

Primary Sources

Al-Balādhurī
 1916   *The Origins of the Islamic State, Being a Translation from the Arabic, Accompanied with Annotations, Geographic and Historic Notes of the Kitâb fûtuḥ al-bâldan of al-Imâm abu-l Abbâs, Aḥmad ibn-Jâbir al-Balâḥdhuri* by Philip Khûri Ḥitti. New York Columbia University, London.

Agnellus of Ravenna
 2004   *The Books of Pontiffs of the Church of Ravenna.* Translated with an introduction and notes by Deborah Mauskopf Deliyannis. The Catholic University of America Press, Washington D.C.

Chronicle of Theophanes
 1883   *Theophanis Chronographia,* edited by Carl de Boor, Vol. 1. Teubner, Leipzig.

Genesios
 1978   *Iosephi Genesii regum libri quattuor,* edited by Anni Lesmüller-Werner and Hans Thurn. Corpus Fontium Historiae Byzantinae vol. 14. De Gruyter, Berlin.

Khalīfa b. Khayyāṭ
 2015   *Khalifa ibn Khayyat's History on the Umayyad Dynasty (660–750).* Translated by Carl Wurtzel and prepared for publication by Robert G. Hoyland. Translated Texts for Historians vol. 63. Liverpool University Press, Liverpool.

Malalas
 2000   *Ioannis Malalae: Chronographia,* edited by Hans Thurn. Corpus Fontium Historiae Byzantinae vol. 35. De Gruyter, Berlin.

Michael the Syrian
 1901   *Chronique de Michel le Syrien, Patriarche Jacobite d'Antioche (1166–1199),* edited by Jean-Baptiste Chabot, tome II. Leroux, Paris.

Miracula S. Theodori Tironis
 1909   *Vita et Miracula S. Theodori Tironis.* In Hippolyte Delehaye, *Les légendes grecques des saints militaires,* pp. 183–201. Picard, Paris.

Narrationes
 2006   *Narrationes de exilio sancti papae Martini.* Edited and translated by Bronwen Neil, *Seventh-Century Popes and Martyrs: The Political Hagiography of Anastasius Bibliothecarius.* Brepols, Turnhout.

On Strategy
 1985   *The Anonymous Byzantine Treatise on Strategy.* In *Three Byzantine Military Treatises.* Edited and translated by George T. Dennis. Corpus Fontium Historiae Byzantinae vol. 25, pp. 1–137. Dumbarton Oaks, Washington D.C.

Skirmishing
 1986   *Le traité sur la guérilla (De velitatione) de l'Empereur Nicéphore Phocas (963–969),* edited by Gilbert Dagron and Haralambie Mihăescu. Centre National de la Recherche Scientifique, Paris.

Strategikon of Maurice
 1981   *Das Strategikon des Maurikios,* edited by George T. Dennis and Ernst Gamillscheg. Corpus Fontium Historiae Byzantinae vol. 17. Verlag der Österreichischen Akademie der Wissenschaften, Wien.

al-Ṭabarī

1987   *The History of al-Ṭabarī Vol. 18: Between Civil Wars: The Caliphate of Muʿawiyah A.D. 661–680/A.H. 40–60.* Translated and annotated by Michael G. Morony. State University of New York Press, Albany.

1989   *The History of al-Ṭabarī Vol. 30: The ʿAbbasid Caliphate in Equilibrium: The Caliphates of Musa al-Hadi and Harun al-Rashid A.D. 785–809/A.H. 169–193.* Translated by C. E. Bosworth. State University of New York Press, Albany.

1990   *The History of al-Ṭabarī Vol. 15: The Crisis of the Early Caliphate: The Reign of ʿUthman A.D. 644–656/A.H. 24–35.* Translated and annotated by R. Stephan Humphreys. State University of New York Press, Albany.

Theophanes Continuatus

2015   *Chronographiae quae Theophanis Continuati nomine fertur Libri I–IV*, edited by Michael Featherstone and Juan Signes Codoñer. Corpus Fontium Historiae Byzantinae vol. 53. Walter de Gruyter, Boston/Berlin.

Vita Andreae Cretensis

1898   Βίος τοῦ ἐν ἁγίοις πατρός ἡμῶν Ἀνδρέου τοῦ Ἱεροσολυμίτου, edited by Athanasios Papadopoulos-Kerameus. In *Analekta Hierosolymitikis Stachyologias* vol. 5, pp. 169–179, 422–424. St. Petersburg.

Vita Georgii ep. Amastridos

1893   Βίος σὺν ἐγκωμίῳ εἰς τόν ἐν ἁγίοις πατέρα ἡμῶν καὶ θαυματουργὸν Γεώργιον τὸν ἀρχιεπίσκοπον Ἀμάστριδος, edited by Vasily Vasil'evskij. *Russko-vizantijkie issledovanija* 2: 1–73 (St. Petersburg).

Vita Stephani Junioris

1997   *La Vie d'Étienne le Jeune par Étienne le Diacre.* Introduction, edited and translated by Marie-France Auzépy. Birmingham Byzantine and Ottoman Monographs 3. Variorum, Aldershot.

Secondary References

Allegro, Nuzio, and Maria Ricciardi

1999   *Gortina IV: Le Fortificazioni di età ellenistica.* Monografie della Scuola Archeologica Italiana di Atene 10. Padova, Italy.

Andrianakis, Michalis

2012   Η πρωτοβυζαντινή Ακρόπολη των Χανίων. *Η οχυρωματική αρχιτεκτονική στο Αιγαίο και ο μεσαιωνικός οικισμός Αναβατού Χίου, Χίος 26–28 Σεπτεμβρίου 2008, Πρακτικά Διεθνούς Συμποσίου*, edited by Aristea Kavvadia and Panagiotis Damoulos, pp. 75–90. Y.PAI.TH. P.A., Chios, Greece.

Auzépy, Marie-France

1995   La carrière d'André de Crète. *Byzantinische Zeitschrift* 88: 1–12.

Baldini, Isabela, Salvatore Cosentino, Enzo Lippolis, Enrica Sgarzi, and Giulia Marsili

2012   Gortina, Mitropolis e il suo episcopato nel VII e nell'VIII secolo: Ricerche preliminari. *Annuario della Scuola archeologica di Atene* 90: 239–308.

Bandy, Anastasius

1970   *The Greek Christian Inscriptions of Crete. Vol. X, part I: IV-IX A.D.* Christian Archaeological Society, Athens.

Brubaker, Leslie, and John Haldon
2011   *Byzantium in the Iconoclast Era, c. 680–850: A History.* Cambridge University Press. Cambridge, New York.

Canard, Marius
1971   Iḳrīṭish. *Encyclopedia of Islam*, second edition, vol.3, edited by Peri Bearman, Thierry Bianquis, Clifford E. Bosworth, E.J. van Donzel, and Wolfhart Heinrichs, pp. 1082–1086. Brill, Leiden.

Christides, Vassilios
1984   *The Conquest of Crete by the Arabs (ca. 824): A Turning Point in the Struggle between Byzantium and Islam.* Academy of Athens, Athens.

Christodoulakos, Yannis
2015   Στερέωση – ανάκτηση επιλεγμένων πύργων των Ελληνιστικών τειχών της αρχαίας Πολυρρήνιας Ν. Χανίων. *Archaeological Work in Crete 3, Proceedings of the 3rd Meeting, Rethymnon, 5–8 December 2013*, edited by Pavlina Karanastasi, Anastasia Tzigounaki, and Christina Tsigonaki, vol. 2, pp. 147–154. Faculty of Letters Publications, University of Crete / Ministry of Culture and Sports – Ephorate of Antiquities of Rethymnon, Chania, Greece.

Coutsinas, Nadia
2013   *Défenses crétoises: Fortifications urbaines et défense du territoire en Crète aux époques classique et hellénistique.* Publications de la Sorbonne, Paris.

Crow, James
2017a   Fortifications. In *The Archaeology of Byzantine Anatolia: From the End of Late Antiquity until the Coming of the Turks,* edited by Philipp Niewöhner, pp. 90–108. Oxford University Press, New York.
2017b   Amastris. In *The Archaeology of Byzantine Anatolia: From the End of Late Antiquity until the Coming of the Turks,* edited by Philipp Niewöhner, pp. 389–394. Oxford University Press, New York.

Dagron, Gilbert
1979   Entre village et cité: la bourgade rurale des IVᵉ-VIIᵉ siècles en Orient. Κοινωνία 3: 29–52.

Detorakis, Theocharis
1969   Αι αραβικαι επιδρομαι εις αγιολογικα κείμενα. *Kritika Chronika* 21: 119–129.

Di Vita, Antonino
2010   *Gortina di Creta: Quindici secoli di vita urbana.* «L'Erma» di Bretschneider, Rome.

Fois, Piero
2014   Peut-on dégager une stratégie militaire islamique propre aux îles de la Méditerranée aux VIIᵉ–VIIIᵉ siècles? In *Les dynamiques de l'islamisation en Méditerranée centrale et en Sicile: nouvelles propositions et découvertes récentes,* edited by Annliese Nef and Fabiola Ardizzone, pp. 15–24. Ecole française de Rome, Rome-Bari.

Garraffo, Salvatore
2004   Problemi della circolazione monetaria a Gortina in età romana e protobizantina. *Creta romana e protobizantina: atti del congresso internazionale (Iraklion, 23–30 settembre 2000)*, edited by Monica Livadiotti and Ilaria Simiakaki, vol. I, pp.181–192. Bottega d'Erasmo, Padova.

Gerola, Giuseppe
   1905   *Monumenti Veneti nell'isola di Creta: Ricerche e descrizione fatte dal dottor Giuseppe
             Gerola per incarico del R. Istituto Veneto di scienze, lettere ed arti,* Vol. 1. Venice.
Gigourtakis, Nikos M.
   2011   Οχυρώσεις στην Κρήτη κατά τη Β΄ Βυζαντινή περίοδο. *Proceedings of the
             10th International Cretological Congress, Chania, 1–8 October 2006,* edited by
             Eratosthenis Kapsomenos, Maria Andreadaki-Vlazaki and Michalis Andrianakis,
             Vol. A', pp. 363–380. "Chrysostomos" Literary Society, Chania, Greece.
   2011–2013 Η οχυρωμένη Βυζαντινή Ακρόπολη της Λύκτου. *Kritiki Estia* 14: 49–64.
Haldon, John
   1999   The Idea of the Town in the Byzantine Empire. In *The Idea and Ideal of the
             Town between Late Antiquity and the Early Middle Ages,* edited by Gian Pietro
             Brogiolo and Bryan Ward-Perkins, pp. 1–13. Brill, Leiden.
Haldon, John, Hugh Elton, and James Newhard
   2017   Euchaïta. In *The Archaeology of Byzantine Anatolia: From the End of Late
             Antiquity until the Coming of the Turks,* edited by Philipp Niewöhner, pp.
             375–388. Oxford University Press, New York.
Hendy, Michael
   1985   *Studies in the Byzantine Monetary Economy c. 300–1450.* Cambridge University
             Press, Cambridge.
Herrin, Judith
   1986   Crete in the Conflicts of the Eighth Century. In Αφιέρωμα στον Νίκο
             Σβορώνο, vol. 1, pp. 113–126. Ekdoseis Panepistimiou Kritis, Rethymnon,
             Greece.
Izdebski, Adam
   2013   *Rural Economy in Transition: Asia Minor from Late Antiquity into the Early Middle
             Ages.* The Journal of Juristic Papyrology Supplement 18. Warsaw, Poland.
Ivanišević, Vujadin
   2017   Main Patterns of Urbanism in Caričin Grad. In *New cities in Late Antiquity:
             Documents and Archaeology,* edited by Efthymios Rizos, pp. 221–232.
             Bibliothèque de l'Antiquité Tardive vol. 35. Brepols, Turnhout.
Kalpaxis, Athanasios
   2004   Οι Ακροπόλεις της Ελεύθερνας. Κεντρικός Ανασκαφικός Τομέας II. In
             Eleutherna: Polis – Acropolis – Necropolis, edited by Nicholas Chr. Stampolidis,
             pp. 104–115. Ekdoseis Panepistimiou Kritis, Athens.
Kasdagli, Anna-Maria
   2000   Χριστιανικά νομίσματα από τη Ρόδο. Μια πρώτη προσέγγιση, *Deltion tis
             Christianikis Archaiologikis Etaireias* 21: 267–274.
Kiourtzian, Georges
   2013   L'incident de Cnossos (fin septembre/début octobre 610). In *Constructing the
             Seventh Century,* edited by Constantin Zuckerman. *Travaux et Mémoires* 17:
             173–196.
Kountoura-Galake, Eleonora
   2017   The Byzantine and Arab Navies in the Southern Aegean and Crete: Shipping,
             Mobility and Transport (7th–9th c.). *Graeco-Arabica* 12: 171–234.

Laourdas, Vassilios
  1949   Ανδρέου αρχιεπισκόπου Κρήτης του Ιεροσολυμίτου, Εγκώμιον εις τους
            Αγίους Δέκα και καλλινίκους μάρτυρας. *Kritika Chronika* 3: 85–117.

Lévi-Provençal, Évariste
  1956   *Une description arabe inédite de la Crète.* In *Studi orientalistici in Onore di Giorgio
            Levi della Vida,* vol. 2, pp. 49–57. Istituto per l'Oriente, Rome.

Markoulaki, Stavroula, and Dimitra Goula
  2015   Ανασκαφικές έρευνες και αποτελέσματα στο πλαίσιο του έργου "Στερέωση –
            ανάκτηση επιλεγμένων πύργων των Ελληνιστικών τειχών της αρχαίας
            Πολυρρήνιας Ν. Χανίων". *Archaeological Work in Crete 3, Proceedings of the
            3rd Meeting, Rethymnon, 5–8 December 2013,* edited by Pavlina Karanastasi,
            Anastasia Tzigounaki, and Christina Tsigonaki, vol. 2, pp. 135–145. Faculty of
            Letters Publications, University of Crete / Ministry of Culture and Sports –
            Ephorate of Antiquities of Rethymnon, Chania, Greece.

Markoulaki, Stavroula, and Yannis Christodoulakos
  2014–2018 Η αρχαία Πολυρρήνια και το σύστημα ύδρευσής της. *Kritiki Estia* 15: 75–140.

Morrisson, Cécile
  2017   Coins. In *The Archaeology of Byzantine Anatolia: From the End of Late Antiquity
            until the Coming of the Turks,* edited by Philipp Niewöhner, pp. 71–81. Oxford
            University Press, New York.

Otten, Thomas
  2010   Das Byzantinische Pergamon – Ein Uberblick zu Forschungsstand und
            Quellenlage. In *Byzanz – das Römerreich im Mittelalter,* edited by Falko
            Daim and Jörg Drauschke, vol. 2.2, pp. 809–830. Römisch-Germanischen
            Zentralmuseums Monographien 84. Verlag des Römisch-Germanischen
            Zentralmuseums, Mainz.

Panayotakis, Nikolaos
  1961–1962 Ζητήματα της κατακτήσεως της Κρήτης από των Αράβων. *Proceedings of
            the First International Cretological Congress, Herakleion, 22–28 September 1961,*
            Vol. B', pp. 9–41. Herakleion, Greece.

Pashley, Robert
  1837   *Travels in Crete.* Cambridge University Press, London.

Perna, Roberto
  2012   *L'Acropoli di Gortina. La tavola "A" della carta archeological della città di Gortina.*
            Ichnia (Second Series) 6. Macerata, Italy.

  2017   Indagini recenti nel quartiere delle Case bizantine di Gortina: lo scavo
            dell'Edificio Sud (campagne 2007–2015). *Annuario della Scuola archeologica di
            Atene* 94: 107–132.

Poulou-Papadimitriou, Natalia
  2005   Les plaques-boucles byzantines de l'île de Crète (fin VIe –IXe siècle). In *Mélanges
            Jean-Pierre Sodini, Travaux et Mémoires* 15: 687–704.

Ragia, Efi
  2011   The Geography of the Provincial Administration of the Byzantine Empire (ca.
            600–1200), I.2: Apothekai of the Balkans and of the Islands of the Aegean Sea
            (7th–8th c.). *Byzantinoslavica* 69: 86–113.

Rizza, Giovanni, and Valnea Santamaria Scrinari

1968   *Il Santuario sull'Acropoli di Gortina*, vol. I. Monografie della Scuola Archeologica Italiana di Atene e delle Missioni Italiane in Oriente Vol. II. Istituto poligrafico dello Stato, Rome.

Romancuk, Alla

2005   *Studien zur Geschichte und Archäologie des byzantinischen Cherson*. Colloquia Pontica vol. 11. Leiden, Brill.

Savignoni, Luigi, and Gaetano de Sanctis

1901   Esplorazione archeologica delle province occidentali di Creta. *Monumenti Antichi* 11: 285–550.

Sidiropoulos, Kleanthis

2000a   Münzfunde und Münzumlauf im spätrömischen und protobyzantinischen Kreta. *XII. Internationaler Numismatischer Kongress Berlin 1997: Akten II*, edited by Bernd Kluge and Bernhard Weisser, pp. 840–852. Staatliche Museen zu Berlin, Berlin.

2000b   Νομισματικά ευρήματα. In *Πρωτοβυζαντινή Ελεύθερνα, Τομέας Ι, Δεύτερος τόμος,* edited by Petros Themelis, pp. 263–287. Ekdoseis Panepistimiou Kritis, Athens.

Spratt, T. A. B.

1865   *Travels and Researches in Crete,* vols. I–II. Van Voorst, London.

Stavrinidis, Nikolaos

1961–1962 Ειδήσεις αράβων ιστορικών περί της αραβοκρατίας εν Κρήτη. *Proceedings of the First International Cretological Congress, Herakleion, 22–28 September 1961,* pp.74–83. Herakleion, Greece.

Sythiakaki, Vassiliki, Eleni Kanaki, and Chara Mpilmezi

2015   Οι παλαιότερες οχυρώσεις του Πρακλείου: Μια διαφορετική προσέγγιση με βάση τα νεότερα ανασκαφικά δεδομένα. *Archaeological Work in Crete 3, Proceedings of the 3rd Meeting, Rethymnon, 5–8 December 2013,* edited by Pavlina Karanastasi, Anastasia Tzigounaki and Christina Tsigonaki, vol. 1, pp. 395–410. Faculty of Letters Publications, University of Crete / Ministry of Culture and Sports – Ephorate of Antiquities of Rethymnon, Chania, Greece.

Themelis, Petros (editor)

2009   *Ancient Eleutherna, Sector I*, vol. 1. University of Crete, Athens.

Theophanidis, Vassilios

1942–1944 Ανασκαφικαί Έρευναι και τυχαία ευρήματα ανά την Δ. Κρήτη. Επαρχία Κισσάμου. Β´ Ανασκαφαί Πολυρρήνιας. *Archaeologiki Ephimeris*:17–31.

Tsigonaki, Christina

2007   Les villes crétoises aux VIIe et VIIIe siècles: l'apport des recherches archéologiques à Eleutherna. *Annuario della Scuola archeologica di Atene* 84: 263–297.

2012   Πόλεων ἀνελπίστοις μεταβολαῖς: ιστορικές και αρχαιολογικές μαρτυρίες από τη Γόρτυνα και την Ελεύθερνα της Κρήτης (4ος – 8ος αι.). In *Οι βυζαντινές πόλεις (8ος –15ος αιώνας). Προοπτικές της έρευνας και νέες ερμηνευτικές προσεγγίσεις,* edited by Tonia Kiousopoulou, pp. 73–100. Faculty of Letters Publications, University of Crete, Rethymno.

2015   Οι ανασκαφές του Πανεπιστημίου Κρήτης στην Ακρόπολη της Ελεύθερνας (Τομέας ΙΙ, Κεντρικός). *Archaeological Work in Crete 3, Proceedings of the*

3rd Meeting, Rethymnon, 5–8 December 2013, edited by Pavlina Karanastasi, Anastasia Tzigounaki, and Christina Tsigonaki, vol. 2, pp. 391–406. Faculty of Letters Publications, University of Crete / Ministry of Culture and Sports – Ephorate of Antiquities of Rethymnon, Chania.

Tsigonaki, Christina, and Apostolos Sarris

2016   Recapturing the Dynamics of the Early Byzantine Settlements in Crete: Old problems – New Interpretations through an Interdisciplinary Approach. *Third International Landscape Archaeology Conference 2014, Rome, 17th –20th September 2014,* pp. 1–11. Academia Press of the University of Amsterdam, Amsterdam. doi.10.5463/lac.2014.5.

Tsigonaki, Christina, and Anastasia Yangaki

2015   Οι αρχαιολογικές έρευνες του Τομέα II στις Δεξαμενές της Ελεύθερνας και η μαρτυρία της κεραμικής. *Archaeological Work in Crete 3, Proceedings of the 3rd Meeting, Rethymnon, 5–8 December 2013,* edited by Pavlina Karanastasi, Anastasia Tzigounaki, and Christina Tsigonaki, vol. 2, pp. 429–448. Faculty of Letters Publications, University of Crete / Ministry of Culture and Sports – Ephorate of Antiquities of Rethymnon, Chania.

Tsougarakis, Dimitrios

1988   *Byzantine Crete: From the 5th Century to the Venetian Conquest.* Basilopoulos, Athens.

1990   The Byzantine Seals of Crete. In *Studies in Byzantine Sigillography, vol. 2,* edited by Nicolas Oikonomides, pp. 137–152. Dumbarton Oaks Research Library and Collection, Washington, D.C.

1991   Παρατηρήσεις στον χαρακτήρα των οικισμών της Βυζαντινής Κρήτης. *Proceedings of the Sixth International Cretological Congress, Chania 1986,* vol. 2, pp. 591–619. "Chrysostomos" Literary Society, Chania, Greece.

Vailhé, Siméon

1902   Saint André de Crète. *Echos d'Orient* 5: 378–387.

Yangaki, Anastasia

2005   *La céramique des Ive–VIIIe siècles ap. J.-C. d'Eleutherna: sa place en Crète et dans le bassin égéen.* Ekdoseis Panepistimiou Kritis, Athens.

Yannopoulos, Panayotis

1995   Ορισμένα προβλήματα από την ιστορία της μεσοβυζαντινής Κρήτης προ της αραβικής κατοχής. *Proceedings of the 7th International Cretological Congress, Rethymnon 1991,* Vol. B' 1, pp. 175–192. Rethymnon, Greece.

Zanini, Enrico

2017   Indagini archeologiche nell'area del quartiere bizantino del *Pythion* di Gortina: sesta relazione preliminare (campagne 2011–2015). *Annuario della Scuola archeologica di Atene* 94: 133–139.

Živković, Tibor

2005–2007   Uspenskij's Taktikon and the Theme of Dalmatia. *Symmeikta* 17: 49–85.

Islands and Resilience: Christianization Processes in the Cyclades

Rebecca J. Sweetman

Commonly perceived as pawns in wider imperial machinations, the Cyclades have often been side-lined as peripheral due to their assumed seclusion. Conversely, even a brief analysis of the archaeological evidence indicates that these islands had groups of resident Christian communities, and experienced the monumentalized manifestation of Christianity, much earlier than their mainland counterparts to the west. To establish why this is the case, it is necessary to shed the bias of preconceived notions of insularity. In so doing, this allows identification of the significant variety of communication networks that the islands had. Evidence of Christianization is seen in the spread of churches throughout the islands. The earliest churches were founded through strategic or organic processes; that is to say as a consequence of, for example, imperial or ecclesiastical intentionality, or as indirect results of contact through movement of people for purposes such as trade or craft. As such, it represents processes of complexity. Furthermore, it is suggested that a natural resilience of the islands meant that the impact of Christianity was minimal on daily life.

Introduction

For millennia, writers and historians have dismissed the Roman and Late Antique Cyclades as isolated and peripheral—for example, Catullus (*Carmen* 4): "And [the boat] denies that the shore of the menacing Adriatic denies this, or the Cyclades awkward [to navigate], or noble Rhodes". When they are mentioned, it is largely in terms of their insularity—as havens for pirates, places of exile, or targets for invasions. Therefore, it is not surprising that the Cyclades have become a trope for danger: "This year has been to me like steering through the Cyclades in a storm without a rudder; I hope to have a less dangerous and more open sea the next ..." *Thomas Sheridan to his friend Dean Jonathon Swift (1735–36)* (Swift 1768: 153). It is worth

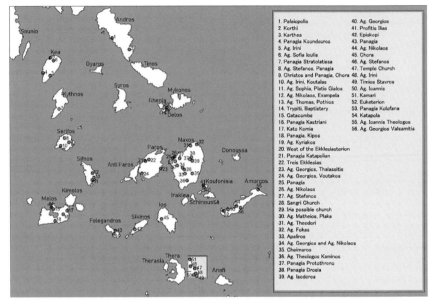

Figure 8.1. Map of the Cyclades showing location of the churches.

noting that those who write in negative terms about the islands tend not to be from islands themselves, while island writers are often more sympathetic to their homeland. For example, Paros' famous poet, Archilochus, seems to have written favorably about his island (he mentions figs and seafaring). The opposite is not always true: some well-famed island authors such as Peig Sayers wrote endless tracts about the misery of life on the Blasket Islands, off the Kerry coast in Ireland.

In recent years, there has been something of an adjustment in the way islands are perceived in scholarship, particularly as positive views of resilience and adaptability begin to underpin interpretations. This is paralleled in literature; where once islands signified remoteness, as mobility across the world has increased, the idea of the quiet island has become a positive (Myres 2011). Crucially, an analysis of the archaeology of the Cyclades in the Roman and Late Antique periods indicates more the optimistic view of life on the islands, rather than the gloom-laden one purported in the literary data. In a sense, the lived experience is the resilient and dynamic one, while the notional one is conservative and isolated. It is unquestionable that the islands faced significant challenges, including the collapse of Delos, the Cyclades' major trade and religious hub, with ensuing changes in networks and economy, as well as wars being played out in their waters. In spite of such setbacks, the islands seem to have rebounded, continued to thrive, and remained well-networked into wider socio-political and religious systems. This is shown by the fact that islands such as Amorgos, Paros, and Thera were some of the earliest in the Greek provinces to have Christian churches and is indicative of resilience and complexity seen on the islands today (Figure 8.1). In this chapter, I address the central question of why the apparently isolated Cycladic islands were among the first in the Greek provinces to be Christianized and how these processes occurred. By taking a diachronic approach, some of the bias of expectation of change with the adoption of a new religion will be challenged. Within this context of a positive approach, the chapter focuses on portable material culture and the topography of the churches. Through comparative data and application of theoretical approaches, I argue that there are natural and engineered tendencies for islands to be resilient and open to new ideas that encompass theories of complexity for understanding Christianization processes.

Christianization Processes

Recent analysis of the topography and architecture of Late Antique churches has contributed to understanding the spread of Christianity within the Eastern provinces (Sweetman 2010; 2015a; 2015b; 2017). In some cases, it has been possible to postulate reasons why certain places were Christianized at particular times (for example, through pilgrimage or trade), and the next stage is to examine the practicalities of how this happened. Islands are a particularly good place to embark on such a study, in part because insular spaces represent dichotomies: they are isolated yet central, and innovative yet traditional. In travelers' tales, islands are commonly present in mythic and/ or real circumstances. They are seen as representative of the journey but are also depicted in contradictory ways: as welcoming and threatening, as places of calm and agitation, or as wild and civilized (Chamberlin 2013: xiii). Just as individual islands have seemingly contrary characteristics, so too do groups of islands. The Cyclades are often discussed in terms of being a monolithic group, with the consequence that individual islands are lost in generalizations of isolation. However, as we will see here, certain islands played different roles within the wider networks of trade, tourism, and pilgrimage, while others may not have participated directly, but rather indirectly through other islands. In this respect, a diachronic view of the Cyclades shows that they conform to processes of dialectical change, where apparent paradoxes are incorporated into society.

Islands have a considerable reputation as being resilient, particularly in terms of battles with climate change, and especially issues with rising sea levels.[1] As Dahlberg (2015: 543) has noted, there are widely varying definitions of resilience. Across most disciplines, however, there is fundamental agreement that it signifies "to rebound" and the ability to absorb and adapt to change (although in common parlance the phrase tends to be used in the more negative sense of resisting). A similar issue exists with the use of the word "adaptation" that is central to island resilience: "Adaptation has been framed in terms of identifying what is to be preserved and what is expendable, rather than what can be reformed or gained" (Pelling 2010: 9).

Ecologists were some of the first to apply the concept of resilience to understand how swift disasters, as well as long-term events, are dealt with (Rose 2017: 19). Several disciplines now work with theories such as individual and community resilience, and also resilience as a process. But as Cutter et al. (2008: 598) note, it is still difficult to assess and quantify the role of community or individual resilience. Further complexities arise when trying to ascertain whether repeated incidents (both natural and manufactured) resulted in an acquired resilience or, rather, made islands more vulnerable: "Vulnerability is the pre-event, inherent characteristics or qualities of social systems that create the potential for harm" (Cutter et al. 2008: 599).

The application of these theories is even more complicated when relating them to past societies. An advantage of examining an archipelago, however, is that it might be possible to identify vulnerabilities and resiliences of different islands, leading to a deeper understanding of how they adapted to change. Islands have a robustness that that makes them strong enough to absorb change without impacting the security of their own identity. This may come from the sense of uncertainty with which island communities naturally live, giving them a sense of readiness and, arguably, a natural resilience. In fact, when examining islands that face challenges of climate change, what can be seen is a strong community involvement and, in many cases, even the banding together of diverse islands in the face of a common threat. For example, the SIDS (Small Island Developing States) group consists of islands from the Caribbean, Pacific and Indian Oceans that do not share a common culture but consider themselves like-minded in the face of climate change induced by larger, more powerful countries. Resilience, Petzold (2017: 25) notes, does not imply passivity or conservatism, and in fact a complex system needs constant change and 'non-linear' behavior. Furthermore, different agents (local and global) can be identified in building resilience (Olwig 2012: 112). This is particularly pertinent in the Cyclades, which were part of a wider imperial system, but maintained strong community identities.

Resilience and Complexity Theory

Complexity theory identifies a process of sharing ideas used to initiate change, which is manifested through adaptive behavior where the change is quickly taken on (Sweetman 2015: 289). There are elements of both intended and organically instigated changes. If there is sufficient complexity within a region, new ideas may emerge that are not necessarily predictable. So while there may be processes of planned change (for example, the desire to build a church), their outcomes may be unintended. With complexity theory in mind, it is easy to see how island communities are among the earliest to build churches, while the elements of unintended consequences mean that there is a diversity of effects.

In earlier work on Christianization processes, I have identified three different means for the spread of church building: complexity, social movement and tipping point (Sweetman 2015b). Although the processes happen sequentially, they are not tied to specific time-periods and I have argued that the earliest churches were constructed through complexity. Complexity processes led to the earliest churches in the Peloponnese being constructed at the edges of sanctuaries or in major port towns, where there was a high volume of traffic and multiple networks already in existence. In these areas, the population was used to new ideas and therefore adapted quickly to change (Sweetman 2015a: 289–290). Furthermore, those islands that were already more culturally diverse were perhaps among the first to hear of new trends, as well as being chosen to have strategically-placed churches because of their high level of traffic.

Despite the potential for using islands as a means of understanding a range of issues—from political structuring processes to social interaction, as well as continuity and change—islands in the Late Antique period remain an under-utilized resource. With the benefit of a long-term perspective, what can be seen on the islands is acceptance of significant socio-political and religious transformations, as well as adaptations to them that resulted in changes that would probably not be perceptible within a generation.

The Christianization of the Cyclades was not a sudden process; in fact, the outcomes should be traced to much earlier in the period, when the Cyclades were part of the Roman Empire. Just as contemporary ancient sources and modern scholars emphasize the isolation of the islands, they also tend to treat them erroneously as a unified archipelago. In the Hellenistic period, the Cyclades were the center of religious and economic movements in the Eastern Mediterranean. But once Delos, a major hub, was taken out, the network collapsed and the Cyclades changed. When the Cyclades were navigated in the Roman period, ships sailed east–west through the islands as fast as they could, rarely stopping unless it was necessary to do so (Le Quéré 2015a: 58–59). Opportunities and weaknesses came into play for different islands: Melos, for example, became a more significant player in terms of trade, but many of the other islands, such as Tinos, were self-sufficient and did not attract much external attention (Sweetman 2016).

Throughout the Roman period, many of the Cycladic islands played a variety of roles within the wider imperial networks. Levels of participation varied, depending on willingness and resources of the individual islands, as well as a degree of involvement by requirement. For example, with a desire to make the most of its mineral resources, Melian communities made a number of safe harbors around the islands available to move its alum off the island in as efficient a manner as possible (Photos-Jones and Hall 2014: 68–73). The distribution of Melian amphorae as far as northern Italy is indicative of the success of its adaptation to new trading potentials after the collapse of Delos (Quiri and Spagnolo Garziola 2015). Andros, Thera, Paros, and Naxos also appear to have maintained reasonable trade links for their agricultural and marble supplies. Islands such as Tinos and Delos continued to be the focus of religious tourism and others (such as Serifos, Kythnos, and Amorgos) were commonly used for exiles and, as such, different and less enduring connections were made with the imperial network (Sweetman 2016).

The third and early fourth century was a period of fluctuation, in terms of the changing Roman Empire and the foundation of Constantinople. Giardina (2007: 74) argues that significant economic changes occurred between the reigns of Marcus Aurelius and Diocletian, when there was a decrease in population, agricultural production and tax increases. Debasing of coinage did not help to combat this, but to a degree the expansion of imperial-owned properties did make a difference. Where

Figure 8.2. Melos, Catacombs.

Figure 8.3. Amorgos, Eukterion.

once the Late Antique economy was seen as a decline, it is increasingly being seen as a period of diversity and prosperity (Giardina 2007: 75). The assumption of swift and significant social changes during the period of the rise of Christianity is also being re-evaluated (Sweetman 2015b), and the archaeology of the Cyclades also indicates that evidence for change is less perceptible than supposed. Diocletian created the province of the islands (*Provincia Insularum*), which was part of the Diocese of Asia under the Prefecture of the East, with Rhodes as its capital. This situation lasted from

Figure 8.4. Thera, Agia Irini.

Figure 8.5. Paros, Katapoliani.

around A.D. 293 to 563 when the islands became part of the *quaestura exercitus* under Justinian. The Cyclades came under religious jurisdiction from the East. The extent to which religious authority played a role in the impact of Christianization processes, however, appears to be negligible (Sweetman 2017). Through an examination of how Christianity spread, we can assess the evidence (or not) for change on the islands themselves, especially in terms of wider networks such as religious and economic ones. Giardina's (2007: 75) questioning of terminology is a useful addition to the discussion. He notes that terms such as "decline" and "continuity" are often replaced with "transition". Although the word is meant to be neutral, he believes that it does not allow enough emphasis on continuity.

Early Christian Material

The majority of the evidence for Early Christian communities on the islands comes from the churches constructed between the late fourth and seventh centuries (Figure 8.1), yet evidence for Christian communities active from the second century is plentiful. Most striking are the Christian catacombs on Melos which were in use from the second to the fourth centuries (Figure 8.2). A combination of traditions is used in some of these burials: for example, the use of a coin to pay Charon on a Christian burial, and an inscription threatening a curse in the name of the 'guardian angel' on any attempts to include non-family members in the grave (Sweetman 2019). A diverse group of communities lived in the Cyclades in the Roman and Late Antique periods. In addition to Christian and polytheistic groups, Valeva and Vionis (2015: 343) note the evidence for Jewish communities in Thera, Naxos, Paros, and Melos. Epigraphic data is not especially revealing for the fourth century, save for some epitaphs from the Melian catacombs and epigrams from Keos (Kiourtizan 2000: 83–96). A significantly larger number of inscriptions is found in the fifth and sixth centuries, including the names of individual priests and deacons from Melos, Naxos, Paros, and Delos, and graffiti from Syros (Kiourtizan 2000). The Ecumenical Councils record the attendance of a number of Cycladic bishops: for example, bishops from Paros and Naxos attended the 3rd and 4th Councils. Bishoprics are known from islands such as Amorgos and Thera. It can be no coincidence that the earliest churches constructed in the Cyclades have been identified on Amorgos, Kalotaritissa Bay (Figure 8.3), Thera, Perissa (Agia Irini) (Figure 8.4) and Paros Parikia (Katapoliani) (Figure 8.5). In each case, the earliest church foundations at these sites appear to be from the late fourth century or possibly the early fifth. This is at least a generation earlier than most churches in the province of Achaea and, with the exception of the KMF basilica in Knossos, earlier than most of the churches in Crete as well.

Previously (Sweetman 2016), I argued that the foundations were a result of imperial input (Empress Helena, in the case of Katapoliani), trade or contact with Asia Minor (Amorgos), and trade or Jewish communities (Thera). However, I have yet to explore these suppositions in terms of the practical means for these connections, via analysis of evidence of contact through trade (pottery, lamps, and numismatics) and individual travel (epigraphy). From the fourth century, the majority of the Cyclades appear to have been self-sufficient but lacking in the capability to produce a sufficiently significant surplus to attract external buyers. Even the role the Cyclades played in *annona* provision is difficult to define, although Diamanti (2016: 693) suggests that the number of sixth-century amphorae that the Parians were producing indicates a role as part of the *quaestura exercitus*. Before this period, however, the extent to which large-scale merchants were willing to travel to the islands remains in contention. In addition to Diamanti (2016), Empereur and Picon (1985) have published evidence for significant amphora production on Paros and Naxos. Current exploration of Naxos' south coast is revealing new evidence for small harbors and extensive indications of amphorae.[2] Following his study of the imported ceramics at Karthaia on Keos in the Late Antique period, Zachos suggested that ships called into Keos as a regular stop from the East before heading into Piraeus. He noted evidence of African Red Slip and table wares, along with beehives and amphorae (Zachos 2010: 788–789). This evidence in combination with that from Melos suggests that Kiourtizan's (2000: 17) hypothesis that the Cyclades more generally played a role in the redistribution of goods throughout the Aegean carries weight. This is not a unique situation. Olesen and Hohlfelder (2011: 818) distinguish international harbors such as Portus or Carthage from smaller examples such as Aperlae in Lycia. They suggest that although deepwater freighters could not access the harbor, smaller vessels were able to do so. Aperlae could have redistributed goods to and from the larger nearby harbor at Andriaki.

The issue at hand, however, is identifying where these redistribution points might be. It is important to note the work undertaken by Caraher and Pettegrew (2016: 169) who suggest that evidence of large quantities of amphorae imply wide-scale and state-controlled trade, but that imported fine wares indicate evidence of local tastes and preference. Yet, as they note, fine wares are not as readily visible on surveys, and coarse wares are over-represented in the archaeological record. They also note that the changes in import types may correspond to a specific event in time and are not necessarily a long-term trend (Caraher and Pettegrew 2016: 190–191).

Kingsley and Decker (2001: 3) question the prevailing view propagated in literary sources, such as Libanius, that Constantinople suppressed private commerce between the fourth and fifth centuries. They further note that in the East there is little evidence of any one particular import dominating pottery distribution in the Aegean East. Contrary to the sources that primarily provide evidence for state and high-level trade, Kingsley and Decker (2001: 5) argue that there was an expectation that local populations would produce their own food, while transformation of ship construction in Late Antiquity created cheaper and more efficiently built ships enabling local, independent business people to set up their own trading ventures. Patterns of internal connections between the Cyclades are further attested by epigraphic data. Religious tourism appears to have been focused more on a local rather than international market, according to the epigraphic data. Overall, as the epigraphic data from Syros suggests, the majority of known visitors come from neighbouring islands and locations such as Andros, Gyaros, Melos, Naxos, Paros, and Thera (Kiourtizan 2000: 25) (Figure 8.1). External visitors to Syros came from Hydra, Miletus, Pinara (Lycia), Peluse (Egypt), and Tyre, but their numbers are fewer than those from neighbouring islands. Examples of the more extraordinary traveller tend to make a greater impression in sources such as St Jerome and Empress Helena (Kiourtizan 2000: 25), although in both of these cases at least they appear to have been accidental pilgrims at the mercy of Cycladic storms.

The question remains of how the first churches came to be constructed on the islands. Thera and Naxos are worth exploring in a little more detail for analysis of the lamps found at a number of sites there. Bournias (2014: 792) concluded that the import profile of the lamps shows a concentration of connections with Asia Minor, Syria, and Cyprus in the Late Antique period. In addition to locally produced lamps at sites such as Gyroulas and Naxos town, there were imports from the Levant and Palestine; there were also copies of Syro-Palestinian lamps which may have been made on site too. Importantly, Bournias noted a complete absence of Athenian third- to fifth-century lamps, which is an unusual feature in the Aegean islands. The presence of imported lamps, as well as the copies, indicates either a direct connection with the Holy Land or possibly indirect connections via Cyprus. As such, these communications with the Holy land illustrate a conduit for the spread of Christianity to the islands. The fact that it was so successful comparatively early is a result of strategic planning in terms of church location and melding of tradition, as well as the openness and resilience of the Cyclades.

Spread of Christianity

Religion spreads through a number of means, such as migration, organized missions or more informal and personal connections (Stump 2008: 20). In

Figure 8.6. Sikinos, Episkopi from the south coast.

some respects, Christianity faced more of a challenge for gaining followers, since it was such a completely new spiritual option, with little connection to older religions (Stump 2008: 39). In light of this, it is possible to see why place was such a fundamental element in conversion processes. It is clear from the location of the Cycladic churches, on routes throughout the islands and places visible from the sea, for example Sikinos (Figures 8.6 and 8.7), that a primary means of conversion was through advertising the church itself. Stump (2008: 21) further notes how the impact of adoption of a new religion is more likely to be noticed in places where there are few existing religious institutions. As such, the fact that it was a supposedly seamless transition is helped by the concentration of cult buildings already on the islands.

As is to be expected from these culturally complex islands, there is significant religious diversity in the Cyclades throughout the Roman period. Although Delos was no longer as religiously significant as it had been in the Hellenistic period, the island had a panoply of sanctuaries which included ones to Egyptian gods (Isis and Serapis), more traditionally Greek sanctuaries (Apollo and Artemis), as well as those with local epithets (Sanctuary of Kynthian Zeus), and new cults like Agathe Tyche. Throughout the Roman period there were many imperial dedications such as those to Augustus, Livia, and Julia Domna. Agrippa and Hadrian attempted (unsuccessfully) to reinvigorate the Delian cult. As both Le

Figure 8.7. Sikinos, Episkopi closer view from the south coast.

Quéré (2015a: 109) and Morales (2016: 146) note, the dedications are indicative of a continued Athenian interest in the island during the Early Imperial period, rather than direct connections with Rome. Assimilation of the Emperors into the Delian cult and the Sanctuary of Apollo was a cultural and religious move that was part of the political propaganda of Athens. There is literary evidence for a Jewish population on Delos (I Maccabees 15: 15–23; Josephus, *Antiquities* 14: 213–216). Many scholars have argued that building GD80 on Delos was a synagogue (Plassart 1914: 23; Bruneau 1982). Trümper (2004) suggested that the building was a diaspora synagogue and Hudson McLean (1996) believes it to have been a Samaritan synagogue. Others such as Mazur and Sukenik (White 1987: 137) argue that the building is both too early and different in form to be considered a synagogue at all. The most recent consensus is that it is a synagogue and likely a diaspora one.

Delos was not alone in its diversity. The wide variety of religion and cult of Palaiopolis, the main city of Andros, is also evident primarily from the epigraphic remains. While the festival of Dionysus was renowned, and recorded by Pliny, there were also the cults of Eileithyia, Estia Voulaia, Apollo, Zeus, Artemis, Nemesis, Isis, and Mithras. There was also imperial

Figure 8.8. Thera, Agios Stefanos.

cult, with a heavy emphasis on worship of Hadrian. It is likely that, as a well-watered and fertile island, Andros was thoroughly networked to other islands in the Cyclades and the dedications by citizens and military certainly indicate connections with the wider imperial network. A similar situation can be seen at the *polis* of Thera, where the profile of the sanctuaries reflects its Hellenistic diversity, with the Sanctuary of Apollo Karneios, Hermes and Herakles, Temple of Dionysus, and Temple of Egyptian gods joining the more traditional Temple of Apollo Pythios.

Widespread architectural evidence for cult practice is not as well-known on islands such as Paros and Naxos, although in each case significant sanctuaries have been investigated. On Naxos, the sanctuaries of Demeter and Dionysus appear to continue in use at least until the third century and both have evidence for a Christian presence (the sanctuary of Demeter is one of the few examples of the conversion of a temple into a church). On Paros, while the temple of Delian Apollo went out of use in the Hellenistic period, it is likely that the sanctuaries of Asclepius and Pythian Apollo continued to be used, possibly even during the period of the building of the Katapoliani church to the southwest.

Figure 8.9. Delos, Agia Kyriaki.

Location of the Churches

The Christianization of the Cyclades was a successful process in part because the islands were adaptable and used to change, and in part because there were strategic choices made about the location of the first churches, including relationship to earlier cult buildings as well as visibility.

The earliest churches in the Cyclades are all constructed by good harbors. In the case of Thera and Paros, the churches were constructed near or in existing cemeteries on the edge of town, within good sight of incoming vessels to the harbor. The Amorgos church is an interesting example, as it is not actually within the main harbor town of Katapola, but instead in a small harbor on the southwest coast. This gives weight to the suggestion that it functioned more as a *eukterion* or house shrine rather than a public church (Gikoles and Pallas 2014: 377, no. 591). Although establishing the chronology of church foundation in the Cyclades is as problematic as it is across the Empire, it is possible to ascertain that following the first church constructions, a small number of churches were built in the course of the fifth century—for example, at Palaiopolis on Andros, Panayia Kipos on Melos, Agios Stefanos on Thera (Figure 8.8), and Agios Kyrikos on Delos (Figure 8.9) (Sweetman et al. 2018). As with other provinces such as Crete and Achaea, the majority of Late Antique churches in the Cyclades date to the sixth century. This includes Treis Ekklesies on Paros; the churches at

Figure 8.10. Folegandros, Agios Nikolaos.

Portaria and the Sanctuary of Demeter, as well as Agios Stefanos, Fraron and Panagia Drosiani on Naxos; Agios Ioannis Theologos on Amorgos; and possibly two churches at Karthaia on Keos (Sweetman et al. 2018). Dating issues stem from the lack of well-preserved stratigraphic contexts (with the exception of Treis Ekklesies on Paros, and Sangri and Agios Stefanos on Naxos), and many churches have either been cleared to reveal earlier buildings (Portaria on Naxos) or incorporated into later buildings (Agios Georgios Valsamitis on Amorgos).

As noted elsewhere (Sweetman 2015b), locations for the new Christian churches capitalized on visibility and drew on existing social patterns (traditions and memories) to help situate the church without stress on the local community. In the majority of cases, the new churches were built in existing cemeteries (e.g. Katapoliani on Paros; Figure 8.5), approaches to towns (Agios Stefanos on Thera; Figure 8.8), or other gathering spaces such as holy springs like those at Agios Giorgios Valsamitis on Amorgos or Panagia Kipos on Melos. The mausoleum (Episkopi) on the lower slopes of Agia Marina on Sikinos was probably located in the cemetery of the ancient hilltop town (Figures 8.6 and 8.7); this too became the site of a Late Antique church. On other islands also, churches were located on natural route-ways both in rural and peri-urban spaces: for example, a late fifth- or early sixth-century church was excavated on the approach to Karthaia from the interior of the island via the Vathypotamos valley (Graindor 1905: 352). On Folegandros, the church of Agios Nikolaos incorporates a number of earlier architectural fragments and it is likely to have been the site of a previous church. This is located on a natural route through the central hills of the island between Chora and the coast (Figure 8.10).

There is little evidence for temple closure or destruction. Those churches that directly re-use temple space in varying ways (particularly the Temple of Demeter and the Temple of Dionysus and Portaria on Naxos) are likely to have been built only after the temple had already gone out of use. A number of other churches on the islands are located close to earlier cult sites—for example, the church above the temples of Apollo and of the Egyptian gods on Thera. Other examples, such as Treis Ekklesies on Paros and Agios Matthaios on Naxos, contain architectural elements of earlier cult buildings in their superstructures. As with other provinces, the location of the churches and their relationship to earlier cult buildings by and large suggests a strategic process of Christianization undertaken to encourage participation in the new religion through visibility and availability. That does not preclude individual expressions of Christian ideals. For example, a grave relief of a poet or philosopher now in the Andros Museum had a Christian cross carved into it at a later date.

Location of the Settlements

A significant issue with the study of the Cyclades (and in fact many other places) is the expectation of change because of a known event (such as the spread of Christianity). However, what is abundantly clear from the Cyclades is that, although there is a religious change, there are significant amounts of continuity in settlement patterns. The Cyclades in the Late Antique period are still primarily known through the evidence of the churches and cemeteries. In recent years, however, more attention has been given to secular material from the period. The evidence revealed through rescue excavations and by surveys on land and underwater is indicative of a largely unchanged urban landscape. It is more difficult to assess the rural situation, but we will examine the data to see what can be gleaned.

In terms of the archipelago, the islands that seem to have been of significance in the wider structures of the Empire, such as Melos, Thera, Paros, and Andros, continued to play similar roles throughout the Roman and Late Antique periods. There are certainly changes: for example, Tinos does not appear to have attracted the same kind of external visitors as it did in the Early Imperial period. However, it is arguable that this change occurred in the third century and not as a result of Christian input. Unless an island had specific resources (such as Melos and Paros) or food (Theran wine) or could be used as a center for redistribution (Amorgos), it is unlikely they would have attracted a multitude of different visitors who would leave clear evidence of their presence on the island.

The majority of settlement evidence for the Late Antique period comes from urban spaces. Of the primary sites that have been investigated, such as Paliopolis on Andros, Parikia on Paros, Chora on Naxos, and Perissa on Thera, there is little to indicate significant changes in the topography of the city from the Roman to Late Antique periods. In fact, excavations in these urban areas have indicated long-term continuity in domestic and industrial spaces (Sweetman 2013). Surveys have been undertaken on Kea, Melos, and Naxos; and, although it is more difficult to identify chronologically well-defined rural settlement distributions, there seems to be continuity and increase in the number of rural sites from Roman through Late Antique (Cherry et al. 1991; Renfrew and Wagstaff 1982). It is possible, as I suggest elsewhere, that some islands may have grown in importance throughout the Late Antique period (Sweetman 2019). Amorgos, Thera, and Naxos seem to have been significant hubs in the Late Antique period, marked by several large settlements on each island. More significant changes in settlement evidence in the Cyclades can be identified during the seventh century, when a large number of hill-top settlements on Naxos (Apalirou), Andros, and Kythnos (Kastro) grow and become the major centers at this time. Bournias (2014: 792) suggests that there was little impact of the seventh-century Slavic raids in terms of Cycladic trade patterns and that it was the Arab raids that were more disruptive, leading to recession and growing regionalism.

The lack of change in settlement evidence until the seventh century suggests that the impact of Christianization was minimal and that this is reflective of a high level of resilience. It was a slow-paced change and one engineered to incorporate existing social processes and tradition as much as possible. The visibility of the churches in highly visited space meant that there was always a subtle remainder of the promise of the new religion. The islands that were among the first to have Christian churches built on them were those that were already well networked with a diversity of existing cults, including traditional polytheistic cults as well as the Jewish diaspora. Once the first churches were constructed on Amorgos, Thera, and Paros, the motivation for further church-building is seen first in ports of the other islands such as Melos, Andros, and Delos, before the interior areas of those original islands. This further emphasizes the significant role well-connected port towns played in the process on the islands, both in terms of being open to accepting new ideas and actually hearing about them first. Christianization processes are not identical on all the islands; for example, a Late Antique church has yet to be identified on Tinos, while Deligannakis has noted Naxos as being different, with the foundation of two churches on earlier cult spaces

(Dionysus and Demeter). Once the momentum for church-building spreads to other islands, there is significant internal variation in how churches are subsequently distributed, based on a range of factors including topography, and both local and imperial choice.

To examine this in a little more detail, it is worth comparing two larger islands, Crete and Cyprus. On Crete, the earliest churches are found in the largest towns on the island, Knossos and Gortyn (Sweetman 2017: 10). Unlike in the Cyclades, the busiest and most cosmopolitan towns were not necessarily coastal. Following these suburban constructions, churches were built along busy routes through the Cretan mountains—for example, along the Amari Valley from Agia Galini in the south to Panormou in the north (Sweetman 2017: 16–17). In contrast, the earliest Cypriot churches were built at coastal locations with an emphasis on towns, particularly in the south and west, throughout the Late Antique period. It has been argued that this was a strategic move to maximize the potential for passing and visiting pilgrims (Sweetman 2017: 23). For both Crete and Cyprus, it is arguable that the urban topography changed over the course of the Late Antique period in order to adapt to the new religious focus in the city—namely, the church (Sweetman 2004: 352). This is not so obviously the case with the cities of the Cycladic islands. What all these islands have in common is the importance of the visibility of the earliest churches. In the case of Crete and Cyprus, the valley and pilgrim routes were marked and arguably used for wayfinding. The same might be the case for the Cycladic islands without the early churches. In these examples, churches such as Episkopi on Sikinos (Figures 8.6 and 8.7), Agia Anagyri on Anafi, Kastro on Kythnos, Chora on Serifos, and Kastro on Sifnos would have acted as landmarks for sailors, some of them more visible from the sea than the land. Like Crete, there are churches on internal routes, such as Agios Nikolaos on Folegandros and Agios Stefanos on Serifos. There are clear elements in common between the islands in terms of the Christianization processes: primary among them is the swift adoption of the new religion without significant disruption to everyday life. The paradox of isolation and connection, as well as continuity and change, is central to a sense of island-ness.

Conclusion

Braudel (1972) argued that Mediterranean unity, the connectivity through objects and landscapes, superseded any impact of change from structuring systems such as the Empire or even unified religion. Although Horden and Purcell (2000) with their emphasis on human agency moved away from the rather deterministic views of Braudel, they all defined the Mediterranean as something of a single entity, connected physically and conceptually by environment (Concannon and Mazurek 2016: 5). I would argue, however, that it was not so much Mediterranean unity which enabled a buffering from the impact of Christianization, but rather levels of resilience on the individual islands at a particular period. Diversity of island communities is seen with archipelagos and between different islands in terms of Christianization processes. Furthermore, resilience is not necessarily a constant; it is a temporal phenomenon dependent on a range of factors, including how often their levels of resilience are tested.

Islands by their nature will experience change and adopt new ideas faster than mainland locations, but only if the islands are already part of a network or benefitted from phase transition from other islands. Once the initial, strategic, decision to construct a church had been taken, the impetus for further church-building and community use was more organic. In these respects, the Christianization of the Cyclades foreshadows the process on the Greek mainland. The state of being islands has an impact on how early they were Christianized. The consequences of the foundation of the churches and conversion to Christianity on secular life on the islands was, on the whole, quite low-key, with significant continuity in domestic and mortuary contexts. This is what typifies the island-ness of the Cyclades: the successful co-existence of sets of dichotomies.

Acknowledgements

I would like to thank the organizers, Miguel Ángel Cau Ontiveros and Catalina Mas Florit, as well as colleagues at Brown University, for bringing together scholars from across the Mediterranean and organizing such a stimulating conference.

Notes

1. https://www.wilsoncenter.org/event/islands-champions-resilience
2. https://archaeologynewsnetwork.blogspot.co.uk/2017/11/underwater-survey-on-south-coast-of.html#GVc3Hrr8p5FBzlQR.97

References

Bonnin, Grégory, and Enora Le Quéré (editors)

    2014   *Pouvoirs, îles et mer: ormes et modalités de l'hégémonie dans les Cyclades antiques (VIIe s. a.C–IIIe s. p.C.).* Scripta Antiqua 64. Ausonius Editions, Bordeaux.

Bournias, Leonidas

    2014   Roman and Early Byzantine Lamps from the Island of Naxos in the Cyclades. In *LRCW 4. Late Roman Coarse Wares, Cooking Wares and Amphorae in the Mediterranean: Archaeology and Archaeometry. The Mediterranean: A Market without Frontiers,* edited by Natalia Poulou-Papadimitriou, Eleni Nodarou and Vassilis Kilikoglou, pp. 787–794. Archaeopress, Oxford.

Braudel, Fernand
 1972   *The Mediterranean and the Mediterranean World in the Age of Philip II.* Translated by Siân Reynolds. Fontana/Collins, London and New York.

Bruneau, Philippe
 1982   Les Israélites de Délos et la juiverie délienne. *Bulletin de correspondance hellénique* 106: 465–504.

Caraher, William, and David K. Pettegrew
 2016   Imperial Surplus and Local Tastes: A Comparative Study of Mediterranean Connectivity and Trade. In *Across the Corrupting Sea: Post-Braudelian Approaches to the Ancient Eastern Mediterranean,* edited by Cavan Concannon and Lindsay A. Mazurek, pp. 165–192. Ashgate, Farnham.

Catullus
 1894   *Carmena.* Translated by Sir Richard Francis Burton. Privately Published, London.

Chamberlin, J. Edward
 2013   *Island: How Islands Transform the World.* Elliott and Thompson, London.

Cherry, John F., Jack L. Davis, and Eleni Mantzourani (editors)
 1991   *Landscape Archaeology as Long-Term History: Northern Keos in the Cycladic Islands from Earliest Settlement until Modern Times.* Monumenta Archaeologica 16. University of California at Los Angeles, Los Angeles.

Concannon, Cavan, and Lindsay A. Mazurek (editors)
 2016   *Across the Corrupting Sea: Post-Braudelian Approaches to the Eastern Mediterranean.* Routledge, New York.

Cutter, Susan L., Lindsey Barnes, Melissa Berry, Christopher Burton, Elijah Evans, Eric Tate, and Jennifer Webb
 2008   A Place-based Model for Understanding Community Resilience to Natural Disasters. *Global Environmental Change* 18(4): 598–606.

Dahlberg, Rasmus
 2015   Resilience and Complexity: Conjoining the Discourses of Two Contested Concepts. *Culture Unbound* 7: 541–557.

Diamanti, Charikleia
 2016   The Late Roman Amphora Workshops of Paros Island in the Aegean Sea: Recent Results. *Rei Cretariæ Romanæ Favtorvm Acta* 44: 691–697.

Empereur, Jean-Yves, and Maurice Picon
 1986   Des ateliers d'amphores à Paros et à Naxos. *Bulletin de correspondance hellénique* 110: 495–511.

Giardina, Andrea
 2007   The Transition to Late Antiquity. In *The Cambridge Economic History of the Greco-Roman World,* edited by Walter Scheidel, Ian Morris, and Richard P. Saller, pp. 743–768. Cambridge University Press, Cambridge.

Gkioles, Nikolaos, and Giorgos Pallis (editors)
 2014   *Atlas of the Christian Monuments of the Aegean: From the Early Christian Years to the Fall of Constantinople.* Secretariat General for the Aegean and Island Policy, Athens.

Graindor, Paul
  1905   Fouilles de Karthaia (Ile de Kéos). *Bulletin de correspondance hellénique* 29: 329–361.
Horden, Peregrine, and Nicholas Purcell
  2000   *The Corrupting Sea: A Study of Mediterranean History*. Blackwell, Oxford.
Josephus
  2006   *Antiquities*. Translated by William Whiston. Wordsworth Editions, Ware.
Karagiorgou, Olga
  2001   LR2: A Container for the Military *Annona* on the Danubian Border? In *Economy and Exchange in the East Mediterranean during Late Antiquity*, edited by Sean Kingsley and Michael Decker, pp. 129–166. Oxbow Books, Oxford.
Kingsley, Sean, and Michael Decker
  2001   New Rome, New Theories on Inter-Regional Exchange: An Introduction to the East Mediterranean in Late Antiquity. In *Economy and Exchange in the East Mediterranean during Late Antiquity*, edited by Sean Kingsley and Michael Decker, pp. 1–27. Oxbow Books, Oxford.
Kiourtzian, Georges
  2000   *Recueil des inscriptions grecques chrétiennes des Cyclades: de la fin du IIIᵉ au VIIᵉ siècle après J.-C.* Travaux et Mémoires du Centre de Recherche d'Histoire et Civilisation de Byzance, Monographies 12. Centre de Recherche d'Histoire et Civilisation de Byzance, Paris.
Le Quéré, Enora
  2015a   *Les Cyclades sous l'empire romain: histoire d'une renaissance*. Presses Universitaires de Rennes, Rennes.
  2015b   The 'Opportunistic Exploitation' of Melos: A Case Study of Economic Integration and Cultural Change in the Roman Cyclades. In *Processes of Cultural Change and Integration in the Roman World*, edited by Saskia T. Roselaar, pp. 222–238. Brill, Leiden.
McLean, B. Hudson
  1996   The Place of Cult in Voluntary Associations and Christian Churches on Delos. In *Voluntary Associations in the Graeco-Roman World*. edited by John S. Kloppenburg and Stephen G. Wilson, pp. 191–195. Routledge, London.
Morales, Fabio Augusto
  2016   The Monument of Roma and Augustus on the Athenian Acropolis: Imperial Identities and Local Traditions. In *Imperial Identities in the Roman World*, edited by Wouter Vanacker and Arjan Zuiderhoek, pp. 141–162. Routledge, London.
Mylonopoulos, Joannis
  2008   The Dynamics of Ritual Space in the Hellenistic and Roman East. *Kernos* 21: 49–79.
Myres, Ben
  2011   Why Writers Treasure Islands. *The Guardian* 31 May, 2011. https://www.theguardian.com/books/booksblog/2011/may/31/writers-islands-fiction.
Oleson, John P., and Robert L. Hohlfelder
  2011   Ancient Harbors in the Mediterranean. In *The Oxford Handbook of Maritime Archaeology*, edited by Alexis Catsambis, Ben Ford, and Donny L. Hamilton, pp. 809–833. Oxford University Press, Oxford.

Olwig, Mette F.
   2012   Multi-sited Resilience: The Mutual Construction of "Local" and "Global"
                Understandings and Practices of Adaptation and Innovation. *Applied Geography*
                33 (April): 112–118.

Pelling, Mark
   2010   *Adaptation to Climate Change: From Resilience to Transformation.* Routledge,
                London.

Petzold, Jan
   2017   *Social Capital, Resilience and Adaptation on Small Islands: Climate Change on the
                Isles of Scilly.* Springer, Basel.

Photos-Jones, Effie, and Alan J. Hall
   2014   *Eros, Mercator and the Cultural Landscape of Melos in Antiquity.* Archaeopress,
                Oxford.

Plassart, André
   1914   La synagogue juive de Délos. *Revue Biblique* 23: 523–534.

Quiri, Elena, and Giuseppina Spagnolo Garzoli
   2015   Imports of Alum from Milos to Novara. In *Per Terram Per Mare: Seaborne Trade
                and the Distribution of Roman Amphorae in the Mediterranean*, edited by Stella
                Demesticha, pp. 181–188. Studies in Mediterranean Archaeology and Literature,
                Pocketbook 180. Åström, Uppsala.

Renfrew, Colin, and Malcolm Wagstaff (editors)
   1982   *An Island Polity: The Archaeology of Exploitation in Melos.* Cambridge University
                Press, Cambridge.

Rose, Adam
   2017   *Defining and Measuring Economic Resilience from a Societal, Environmental and
                Security Perspective.* Springer, Singapore.

Stump, Roger W.
   2008   *The Geography of Religion: Faith, Place and Space.* Rowman and Littlefield,
                Lanham.

Sweetman, Rebecca J.
   2004   Late Antique Knossos. Understanding the City: Evidence of Mosaics and
                Religious Architecture. *Annual of the British School at Athens* 99: 315–354.

   2010   Christianization of the Peloponnese: The Topography and Function of Late
                Antique churches. *Journal of Late Antique Studies* 3(2): 203–261.

   2013   Religion and Culture in Late Antique Greece. *Archaeological Reports* 59: 103–112.

   2015a   The Christianization of the Peloponnese: The Case for Emergent Change.
                Annual of the British School at Athens 110: 285–319.

   2015b   Memory, Tradition and Christianization of the Peloponnese. *American Journal
                of Archaeology* 119(4): 501–531.

   2016   Networks: Exile and Tourism in the Roman Cyclades. In *Beyond Boundaries:
                Visual Culture in the Roman Provinces*, edited by Susan E Alcock, Mariana Egri,
                and James F. D. Frakes, pp. 46–61. Getty Publications, Malibu.

   2017   Networks and Church Building in the Aegean: Crete, Cyprus, Lycia and the
                Peloponnese. *Annual of the British School at Athens* 112: 207–266.

2019   Community, Church, and Conversion in the Prefecture of Illyricum and the
                Cyclades. In *The Oxford Handbook of Early Christian Archaeology*, edited by David
                K. Pettegrew, William R. Caraher, and Thomas W. Davis. Oxford University
                Press, Oxford. (forthcoming) doi: 10.1093/oxfordhb/9780199369041.013.27

Sweetman, Rebecca J., Alice Devlin, and Nefeli Pirée Iliou

2018   The Cyclades in the Late Antique Period: Churches, Networks and
                Christianization. In *Cycladic Archaeology and Research: New Approaches and
                Discoveries,* edited by Erica Angliker and John Tully, pp. 215–238. Archaeopress,
                Oxford.

Swift, Jonathan

1768   *Letters Written by the Late Jonathan Swift, Dean of St. Patrick's Dublin and Several
                of his Friends. T. Davies; R. Davis; L. Davis, and C. Reymers; and J. Dodsley,*
                London.

Trümper, Monika

2004   The Oldest Original Synagogue Building in the Diaspora: The Delos Synagogue
                Reconsidered. *Hesperia* 73: 513–598.

Valeva, Julia, and Athanasios K. Vionis.

2014   The Balkan Peninsula. In *Early Christianity in Context: An Exploration Across
                Cultures and Continents,* edited by William Tabbernee, pp. 315–378. Baker
                Academic, Grand Rapids.

White, L. Michael

1987   The Delos Synagogue Revisited: Recent Fieldwork in the Graeco-Roman
                Diaspora. *Harvard Theological Review* 80(2): 133–160.

Zachos, Georgios A.

2010   Keos in Late Roman Context. In *Κεραμική της Ύστερης Αρχαιότητας από τον
                Ελλαδικό Χώρο (3ος–7ος αι. μ. Χ.). Επιστημονική Συνάντηση, Θεσσαλονίκη,*
                12–16 Νοεμβρίου 2006, edited by Demetra Papanikola-Mpakirtzi and Ntina
                Kousoulakou, pp. 782–794. Δημοσιεύματα Αρχαιολογικού Ινστιτύτου
                Μακεδονικιών και Θραικίων σπουδών, Thessaloniki.

The Christianization of Island Landscapes in Late Antiquity and the Early Middle Ages: New Perspectives from Naxos in the Aegean

Sam Turner and Jim Crow

To understand the impact of religious change in the landscapes of the early Middle Ages (about A.D. 600–900) is a significant challenge for scholars in many parts of Europe and the Mediterranean. Our knowledge of the structure and experience of sacred space after Late Antiquity is not only restricted by the difficulty of identifying sacred sites, but also by our relatively limited understanding of contemporary settlements and land-use patterns. Across much of the eastern Mediterranean, few documentary sources for daily life survive, and the narrative and hagiographical sources which do exist often suggest desolate landscapes. Previous generations of archaeologists have sometimes accepted this picture uncritically, leading them to assume that island landscapes were depopulated until some time in the Middle Byzantine period. The difficulty of identifying characteristic material remains such as ceramics, and the resulting apparent absence of finds, was taken to confirm the abandonment suggested by the documentary sources.

Careful examination of the documentary record and the archaeological evidence yields hints of a more complex history. Recent collaborative fieldwork on Naxos in the Cyclades has begun to unravel previously unsuspected complexities through case-studies in the central parts of the island. Naxos provides exceptional opportunities to explore the nature of Christianization in the Early and Middle Byzantine periods. This paper presents some interim results from research on Naxos through examples which illustrate the Christianization of both rural and urban space between the seventh and the tenth centuries.

Introduction

Understanding the Christianization of landscapes is key to defining many aspects of Early Medieval European society. During the centuries before A.D. 1000, Christianity became integral to the developing power structures of states and kingdoms across the continent: mapping the distribution and organization of ecclesiastical institutions sheds much light on both political and social structures. But individual and group experiences of religious practices were also fundamental to the everyday personal and emotional lives of people. When we try to account for the number and density of church foundations, their organization and relationships, and their size, architecture, accessibility, and decoration, we seek to illuminate not only the connections between rulers and ruled, but also the everyday experience of Early Medieval people and the ways their social interactions were shaped and mediated through sacred spaces.

This paper addresses the process of Christianization in the island landscapes of the eastern Mediterranean. We use interim results from ongoing fieldwork on Naxos in the Cyclades to illustrate a case study of the establishment of churches in both rural and urban landscapes during the early Middle Ages. Although the paper includes a brief outline of developments in Late Antiquity, it is not primarily concerned with the initial conversion to Christianity but rather with the systemic Christianization of society that followed from around A.D. 600 to 900, a period that has conventionally been termed a Byzantine "Dark Age" (Decker 2016: 28–37).

In common with many other parts of Europe, relatively few documentary sources survive from this period that shed light on daily life in the Aegean islands. Lists of delegates to sporadic church councils show that there were bishops on the larger islands, and inscriptions and seals occasionally provide the titles of imperial officials or other administrative details, but the information is sparse and even the overarching structures of the Byzantine empire in the region remain uncertain (Roussos 2017: 37–45). Byzantine writers' accounts of destructive incursions by Arab raiders from the eighth century and the saintly isolation encountered in sporadic hagiographical texts helped to establish an historical view that Aegean landscapes were desolate places in the Early Middle Ages (as shown by Magdalino 2018). Historical archaeologists have often accepted such interpretations, with the result that the absence of (historical) evidence has been taken as evidence of (historic) absence. In apparent corroboration of the picture taken from the historical sources, many archaeological survey projects report a precipitous decline in evidence for settlement activity during the Early Middle Ages (Decker 2016: 124–134). However, a growing number of studies from the Aegean suggest that better methodological control and more careful examination of material from field survey may reveal much more activity than scholars have previously realized (Poulou 2018).

Understanding the relationship between the sacred topography established in Late Antiquity and that of the Early Middle Ages remains a challenge. In Greece and across the Mediterranean, early churches—often basilicas—

were established under the Late Roman Empire and during Late Antiquity in both urban and rural landscapes. Major churches displayed the imperial patronage of the church from the fourth century onwards, whilst the gradual re-dedication of temples from pagan deities to Christian figures underlined the new religion's increasingly central role in society. In recent research on southern Greece, Sweetman (2015) has argued that the foundation of basilicas followed a spatial logic that underpinned the gradual Christianization of urban and rural landscapes from marginal but strategic locations in the suburbs. The architecture of Late Roman churches is frequently monumental and relatively easy to identify as *spolia* in later fabric. Where Late Roman churches can be identified, their Early Medieval successors often seem to have been more modest in character. It is possible that in regions like the Peloponnese, where most Byzantine churches are conventionally dated to the Later Medieval period, Early Medieval predecessors have disappeared without leaving easily-detectable traces.

The extent to which there was a disjuncture between the pattern of churches in Late Antiquity and that of the Early Byzantine empire remains unclear. Although there have been many archaeological excavations of basilica churches, the chronology of their abandonment or destruction is often uncertain. While the reuse of sites for later buildings hints at continuous use, there are few certain examples and the construction of subsequent churches on earlier sites is frequently hard to date. In part this is because the Medieval churches built on the sites of Late Antique basilicas were often small and simple buildings with relatively little decoration or other features such as inscriptions that can be easily dated. If material culture from associated rural settlements could be identified and characterized it might provide strong indications of the abandonment or continuity of sites, but unfortunately the interpretation of the evidence is strongly skewed towards the earlier part of the period. Publications presenting the results of intensive pedestrian surveys frequently identify large volumes of material as Late Roman, suggesting that rural settlements were plentiful in the fifth and sixth centuries (Vionis 2017). By contrast, surveyors have been much less confident in identifying Early Medieval ceramics, to the extent that few projects offer any substantial evidence of settlements dating to the second half of the first millennium A.D. (Poulou 2018; Roberts et al. 2018). Although some sites were likely abandoned in the seventh century, it is also possible that the difficulty of identifying Early Medieval ceramics has reinforced the impression of widespread abandonment derived from the historical sources.

These difficulties mean there have been few attempts to characterize the evolution of Early Medieval landscapes in any detail across the islands of the eastern Mediterranean. Recent syntheses clearly illustrate how few sites have

been firmly assigned to the period between the seventh and ninth centuries—
for example, Kostas Roussos' survey of the evidence from Paros (Roussos
2017: 160; Crow 2014). New evidence from landscape survey, however, is
beginning to suggest a different picture, at least in some places. In particular,
recent research on the island of Naxos provides evidence for a landscape that
was progressively Christianised throughout the Early Middle Ages, not only
in rural areas, but also in urban centers and large villages.

An Island Landscape: Naxos in the Early Middle Ages

Naxos is the largest of the Cycladic Islands. It lies at the center of the
southern Aegean region, roughly equidistant from the Peloponnese and
southern Turkey (Figure 9.1). Its physical landscape is topographically varied,
with a high, central mountainous ridge rising to 1000 m above sea-level and
fertile plains watered by small rivers, both in the central part of the interior
and towards the western and south-western coasts.

The Classical and historical capital of the island was at Chora, which has
remained the chief town up to the present day (Figure 9.2). In Late Antiquity,
the town extended from the Classical center along the shore to the north, as
demonstrated by the remains which lie below the present suburbs of Grotta

Figure 9.1. Naxos in the Aegean (map: Alex Turner).

Figure 9.2. Chora, Naxos, looking northwest; the coastline of Paros is visible in the distance (photo: Jim Crow).

and Aplomata. More than 100 years of excavations have revealed different types of houses, ranging from modest structures, such as workshops, to suburban villas with impressive mosaic floors which continued to be occupied into the eighth century (Roussos 2017: 173–179). Research on the town's ancient aqueduct shows that it also continued to function into the Early Middle Ages, perhaps as late as the 700s (Lambrinoudakis 2018; Roussos 2017: 179–183); its use is believed to have ceased when it became blocked with sinter. The presence of several very large (albeit undated) cisterns within the kastro suggests residents might have then developed alternative strategies for water management and storage.

Although epigraphy indicates that there were churches in the Late Antique town of Naxos, their locations remain uncertain and little can be deduced about the Christianization of this urban space (Roussos 2017: 178–179). By contrast, previous studies in the environs of the town and further afield have yielded evidence for a number of Late Antique basilica churches, some newly established and others reusing the sites of earlier Classical temples. Closest to the urban center was the church inserted into an ancient temple on the islet of Palatia/Portara, just offshore to the north. Other temple-church conversions include one at Yria in the fertile plain to the south of Chora, and another at Gyroulas near the village of Ano Sangri (Dimitrokallis 2000; Lambrinoudakis and Ohnesorg 2019). It is possible that the sites at Palatia and Gyroulas witnessed small-scale adaptations to accommodate Christian liturgy in the fifth century before more comprehensive reconstructions took place in the sixth century (Deligiannakis 2011: 333).

The majority of the 11 known Early Christian basilicas dating to Late Antiquity were also likely constructed during the sixth century. An example is the excavated church at Phraron, on the line of the aqueduct around 1.5 km northeast of Chora. The three aisles of this large apsidal basilica were separated by two colonnades and the structure included a quantity of reused ancient masonry believed to have been transported from Paros. Some time after the life of the first building ended, the site was reused for a Middle Byzantine cross-in-square church. The problem for understanding the Early Medieval Christianization of the landscape is that here, as in many other examples, it remains unclear how much time elapsed between these two events.

In 1968, George Dimitrokallis published a short article in the *American Journal of Archaeology* noting the significance and extent of the architectural and artistic remains from early churches on the island, including reference to a number of other basilicas similar to the one at Phraron. Those in urban or suburban locations are in the minority: more stand in coastal and rural situations like the examples of Agios Matthaios on the western coast of the island, or Cheimarrou, adjacent to a Hellenistic tower on the southeastern shoulders of the central mountains. These buildings of the fifth and sixth centuries are frequently discussed as though they are in a distinct category from the churches of the Early Middle Ages (A.D. 600–900), separated in the minds of scholars by a conceptual "Dark Age", a view which is reinforced by an apparent lack of historical and material evidence. As we have discussed elsewhere, this classification scheme is likely to overemphasize the changes of the seventh century (Crow and Turner 2018). Some well-known examples, such as the Protothronos church in the central village of Chalki, provide evidence of buildings erected in Late Antiquity and remodeled through the Early Middle Ages. In this case, the Early Christian basilica was reshaped as a centrally-domed, long-axis, three-aisled building, and the earliest decoration in the apse was replaced with aniconic paintings (Zias 1989: fig. 28). The Protothronos church stands today in a large village at the center of a fertile and productive plain and it seems likely that it could have been a continuous focus for settlement since its construction.

Besides the colonnaded basilicas with accepted Late Antique origins, there are also a number of simpler three-aisled basilicas. These are comparable in size and basic plan but distinguished by the use of piers rather than columns between the nave and side aisles and sometimes the appearance of apses at the end of the north and south aisles. Many similar churches are known from Late Antique settlements in nearby parts of southern Asia Minor and on Cyprus (Hill 1996; Varinlioğlu 2008; Stewart 2010; Crow and Turner 2018). Some such buildings on Naxos may also belong to this early period, for example the well-preserved basilicas of Agios Isidoros and Taxiarchis Rachi just to the west of Chalki, which contain potentially early fragments of sculpted decoration and painting, respectively (Dimitrokallis 2000). Such examples suggest the possibility that the establishment, use, and alteration of churches was a broadly continuous process on Naxos, and not one interrupted by a significant break in the seventh and eighth centuries.

Research in other parts of Europe has highlighted the importance of knowing basic information about the number and density of churches in the landscape at any particular time. For example, in Ireland a thick scattering of thousands of tiny churches seems to have been rapidly established in the sixth and seventh centuries, with the result that in some areas the distance between churches was only 2–3 km (Boazman 2016; Gleeson and Ó Carragáin 2016). In Anglo-Saxon England, by contrast, there were far fewer churches and each one controlled a much larger territory (Blair 2005). The principal difference between these two regions appears to be the scale of political organization: in Ireland there were around 200 small kingdoms with relatively autonomous elites who were able to found and support their own churches; in the much larger Anglo-Saxon kingdoms, rulers and their most important nobles seem to have controlled the process of church foundation more tightly, linking it in ideological, administrative, and spatial terms to the mechanisms of royal power (Turner et al. 2013). Different agents' ability (and willingness) to build churches varied in different contexts. The number, size, and location of church buildings reflect both the political ability to found them and the social value of doing so. Accurate identification and dating of the monuments and related archaeological sites could therefore provide the basis for more profound reflections on the nature of Early Medieval society.

Recent syntheses have identified around 150 medieval churches on Naxos (Mastoropoulos 2006; Aslanidis 2014; 2018). Of these, more than 20 contain so-called "aniconic" wall paintings, believed to date to the period of Byzantine iconoclasm (or just after it) in the eighth and ninth centuries (Crow and Turner 2015). Aniconic decoration is known from a range of building types, most commonly single-aisled churches, often with domes (for example, Agios Ioannis at Adissarou, Agios Artemios at Stavros, and Agia Kyriaki Kalonis near Apeiranthos (Chatzidakis 1989; Aslanidis 2014)). Whilst aniconic decoration was presumably created at the time that some churches were first built, in other cases it was added to existing buildings (as at the Protothronos in Chalki). In addition, there are many examples of buildings *without* aniconic decoration that are closely comparable in form to those where it does survive; it seems possible that where evidence for such painting has not been recognized, the churches' simple form and continuous reuse may have led researchers to discount the potential for Early Medieval origins (Crow and Turner 2018). The already large number of churches on the island thought to date to the Early Middle Ages (about 50) may therefore be an underestimate.

A rapid field survey undertaken by Athanasios Vionis for the Greek Ministry of Culture in the early 2000s was designed to assess whether any relationship existed between a series of these Early Medieval churches and contemporary settlements. Its tentative conclusion, based on the distribution of ceramic finds from a radius of about 200 m around each church, suggested that in many cases a relationship probably did exist (e.g. Agia Kyriaki Kalonis) (Figure 9.3). Vionis's work highlighted key questions about the chronology of Late Antique and Early Medieval settlements and the character of churches in the landscape, which remain largely unanswered. Key objectives must be to understand the number of churches in the Early Middle Ages and, if possible, to assess the timescales of their foundation. Understanding the links between Early Medieval churches and any associated settlements is also crucial: were they always integrated into villages or hamlets, or were they (as today) sometimes in relatively isolated positions in the landscape? Similar questions are pertinent in urban contexts: were churches established in Medieval urban centers from an early date, or do the many churches nestling in the streets of today's Aegean towns owe their foundation to the later Middle Ages? By understanding more about the contexts for church foundation, we may be able to understand better who were the principal agents of Christianization. Michel Kaplan (1990) noted that the initiative for church foundation and clergy sponsorship might rest either with local communities and small-

Figure 9.3. A view towards Agia Kyriaki Kalonis, looking northeast (photo: Sam Turner).

Figure 9.4. A Naxos landscape: The Early Medieval church of Agios Ioannis Adissarou with the mountain of Apalirou Kastro in the distance to the southeast (photo: Sam Turner).

scale landowners or with powerful actors such as bishops. In the absence of significant historical records, it is through interpretation of the archaeological evidence that we must seek answers to such questions.

The landscape of Naxos provides an unusually rich assemblage for historical studies, including not only the many surviving Medieval churches, but also hundreds of archaeological sites and thousands of kilometers of historic features such as roads and terraces (Figure 9.4). We used a method called historic landscape characterization (HLC) in an initial attempt to assess the potential of this landscape (Turner and Crow 2010). HLC is a qualitative but formalized method whose aim is to interpret and represent the historic processes behind the development of the landscape. Its outputs are GIS data which map the whole landscape as a series of HLC "types" (Crow et al. 2011). On Naxos, our pilot HLC included different categories ranging from fields and terraces to rough grazing and woodland. The HLC enabled us to locate known Early Medieval churches in relation to the historic patterns that survive in today's cultural landscape. This analysis illustrated that churches are sited in a variety of locations, ranging from historic village centres (e.g., Protothronos, Chalki) and fertile arable land (e.g., Agios Ioannis at Adissarou), to the margins of the mountains where terraced olive groves meet rough pasture (e.g., Taxiarchis Rachi). The data underpinning our pilot HLC did not, however, allow us to make firm interpretations about the date of terraces, field systems and most other landscape types, because it relied on remote sensing data to build a simple retrogressive analysis of related landscape features. Nevertheless, in combination with the results of research by Vionis and others, it has helped us to shape a research strategy which is currently addressing those questions through more intensive fieldwork.

The opportunity to begin fieldwork arose through a collaboration with the University of Oslo and the Cycladic Ephoreia of the Greek Ministry of Culture. The strategy for this research is to create a detailed characterization of the development of the historic landscape from ancient times to the present. Our approach embraces not only the identification and mapping of conventional archaeological sites, but also documentary and oral history, analysis of recent settlement, and historical ecology. Our archaeological fieldwork entails intensive pedestrian field survey, 3D analysis of historic buildings using digital methods, analytical survey of structural and earthwork remains, and the application of innovative geoarchaeological methods to date the development of landscape features, especially terraces (for discussion of key methods used in the 2015–2017 seasons, see Manolopoulou et al. 2018; Turner et al. 2018).

Our study area lies in the southwest of Naxos, focused on the fortified mountaintop settlement of Apalirou Kastro. Just beyond our study area to the northwest, extensive excavations at the ancient temple site of Gyroulas have identified an important Late Antique and Early Medieval settlement around the basilica which succeeded the Classical sanctuary (Simantoni-Bournia 2001; Lambrinoudakis and Ohnesorg 2019). As Kostas Roussos has noted, the erection of several Early Medieval churches in the surrounding plain of Lathrino suggests that people continued to inhabit this productive agricultural region. Several of these churches, such as Agios Giorgios and Nikolaos, contain masonry fragments that appear to be from Early Christian basilicas (Roussos 2017: 205–208). In the early 2000s, this was also one of the sites surveyed by Athanasios Vionis for the Ministry of Culture that yielded evidence for settlement in Late Antiquity. Within our Apalirou Environs Survey's study area around the flanks of the mountain, several other churches thought to date to the Early Middle Ages also contain ancient *spolia*. The nearby church of Agios Ioannis Adissarou fetchingly sports the stump of a fluted ancient column on its dome; it also contains some of the most extensive surviving aniconic decoration in the area (Chatzidakis 1989; Martiniani-Reber 2015) (Figure 9.5). Vionis's survey identified ceramic evidence for ancient and medieval activity here, suggesting that the site remained a focus for settlement from Late Antiquity onwards; tentative results from our recent survey corroborate these conclusions.

To the south of Apalirou lies the small plain of Marathos, its gentle farmland ringed with hills on all sides but the southwest. Here, further intensive survey yielded similar results, with evidence for episodes of Classical

Figure 9.5. Agios Ioannis Adissarou, Naxos. The image is based on data captured in 2015 using a terrestrial laser scan; it shows the structure and internal decoration (image: Alex Turner).

and Late Antique settlement to the south and west of the church of Agios Stephanos (Aslanidis 2014: 88–90). Like several of the churches in Lathrino, Agios Stephanos also contains marble fragments and spolia and our recent laser-scan survey of the building makes it clear that it has a complex history (Figure 9.6). Close inspection suggests that the structure shrank from a two- or three-aisled basilica over the course of several Early Medieval phases; the surviving fabric of the apse preserves the remains of an earlier phase which probably dates to Late Antiquity. Intensive ceramic survey has identified the remains of a focused Early Medieval settlement around the church. This is significant because our survey shows that in much of the surrounding plain there is little sign of Early Medieval material. As at Agios Ioannis Adissarou, this evidence suggests the church was a continuing focus for settlement in the form of a small village throughout the Early Middle Ages. Rather than abandoning the island in the seventh century, the evidence from Naxos probably indicates that Early Medieval communities continued to thrive across the island. In fact, compared to other rural landscapes in Europe, the evidence for both churches and settlements in Early Medieval Naxos seems exceptionally strong. Although the dating remains uncertain, the density of *surviving* Early Medieval churches compares favorably with evidence for *all* known churches in parts of Ireland such as County Kerry, which is itself considered exceptional; it far exceeds the frequency of churches in places like

Figure 9.6. The Early Medieval church of Agios Stephanos in the plain of Marathos, Naxos. The site of Kastro Apalirou is visible to the north, on top of the mountain on the left of the image (photo: Sam Turner).

Anglo-Saxon England or Merovingian Gaul (Ó Carragáin and Turner 2016). In several places, as at Agios Stephanos, churches appear to have been adapted and rebuilt progressively, presumably to suit the changing needs of their congregations. The foundation and maintenance of so many small churches suggest that local community actors are likely to have been responsible, rather than external agents such as the bishop or imperial administration. Current evidence from field survey suggests such churches were commonly associated with small settlements.

Survey on the mountain above the plain of Marathos suggests a different situation at Kastro Apalirou. Here a team from the University of Oslo led by Prof. Knut Ødegård has mapped a carefully-planned walled town of around two hectares, with many streets, houses, cisterns and other structures, including an elaborate system for distributing water (Hill et al. 2017). Intensive ceramic survey across the site suggests that it was probably founded in the seventh century and abandoned no later than the early thirteenth century: it is therefore an unusual example of a town founded in the Early Middle Ages that does not have a Classical predecessor. Although more than 100 buildings have been surveyed to date, only two churches have been identified. At the southern end of the town, close to the peak of the mountain, a small church complex made up of two parallel naves has recently been studied: the dating of the ceramics integrated into the structure suggests it was built in the seventh century (Ingtjerd 2018). Towards the northern end of the mountain ridge stands the ruinous complex known as Agios Giorgios. This church was clearly developed and extended over time: the earliest apsidal structure was subdivided with an arcade and additional naves or *parekklesia* were built on both the north and south sides. In terms of the provision of churches, there is a striking contrast between the dense urban settlement on the mountain-top and the plains below. Whereas only two churches are known within the walls, there are many small churches scattered amongst the lower settlements. It seems likely that in the town, the opportunity to found churches was limited—perhaps controlled by episcopal or imperial interests—whereas the residents of the settlements below were free to invest in religious buildings. The scale and complexity of the mountain-top town suggest it was established on imperial authority when it was founded in the seventh century. Kastro Apalirou was a new center for the island that was dropped onto an existing pattern of settlements and the churches that were integral parts of them.

Settlement on the mountain at Kastro Apalirou is not limited to the walled area. Immediately outside it to the southwest lies another church with substantial ancillary structures. On the west side of the mountain, however, there are also the remains of a village or suburb which extends for several hundred meters below the Kastro. The plan-form of this settlement, which we have called Kato Choria, is less regular than the town above, but it is still relatively dense. In the south part of the site, some of the houses are approximately square and laid out in rows; to the north there are traces of long houses with internal subdivisions. Unlike the buildings in the kastro, all the houses in this area are built in dry-stone or clay/soil bonded, with no evidence for lime mortar. There is no evidence for cisterns either associated with or below the houses. Altogether, we have been able to survey at least 50 individual structures and it seems likely that further work will add many more to this number. A preliminary assessment of ceramic finds from field survey suggests that this unfortified settlement was occupied between the later-sixth and tenth centuries, with a terminal date significantly earlier than the kastro above. Four or five churches in total are known from this area, a significantly higher density than in the kastro. Given the relatively short life of this early suburban settlement, it seems likely that the churches here were established over a fairly short space of time. The evidence from Kato Choria suggests that churches were integral to developing Early Medieval (sub) urban settlements. It also hints that individuals or community groups were able to sponsor new religious buildings here in a way that was not possible in the kastro. Their presence would have shaped the everyday religious and social experiences of ordinary people in the seventh and eighth centuries and throughout the Early Middle Ages.

Conclusion

After the Bronze Age, Naxos's main center of population was on the west coast at Chora close to the sea (Roussos 2017: 172–174). In Classical times, the entrance to the harbor was dominated by a striking temple set out on a rocky islet at Palatia, now connected by a causeway to the mainland. This was converted by the fifth to sixth century into a new basilical church marking the transition from a pagan to a Christian empire (Roussos 2017: 178). Like the new church of Katapoliani on the neighbouring island of Paros and the massive Lechaion basilica at the harbor of Corinth (Ćurčić 2010: 127, 236), the church at Palatia was positioned in a port, acting as an ideological beacon for the new era. The exact fate of the temple-basilica at Palatia is not known and, although there is some evidence for early churches in Chora in the period that follows, from the seventh to the tenth centuries the overwhelming evidence is for churches built in rural settings. In many instances it is apparent that these churches—some continuing from Late Antiquity and others newly constructed—may be associated with small settlements, although in cases such as Protothronos at Chalki it is quite likely that there was a larger settlement which is now concealed by the modern village. What remains unclear is how far this pattern of settlement is distinct from the Classical landscape of the island, since before our current surveys there had been little attempt to undertake an extensive diachronic survey in any of the island's districts.

In trying to assess the changing patterns of landscape use and settlement between Classical times and the Early Medieval period on Naxos, we are struck with the major reconfiguration of the main administrative settlement on the island at Kastro Apalirou. Here, there is a sizeable settlement within the walled hill-top, with a more widespread unenclosed settlement below. It is notable that within the walled town, only two church complexes have so far been identified (Ingtjerd 2018), with another perched on the shoulder of the hillside just outside the walls. It seems likely that a substantial church such as Agios Giorgios (Ødegård 2018; Aslanidis 2018: fig. 20), which is located in a prominent position at the heart of the town and would have been visible for miles around, was founded on imperial or episcopal authority rather than by local patrons. In the lower settlement of Kato Choria, by contrast, four or five small churches lie scattered amongst the dry-stone houses. The churches appear to be coeval with the domestic buildings and would have provided foci for the spiritual and communal routines of the settlement. This concentration of religious buildings anticipates the frequency of small urban churches encountered in Middle Byzantine and later urban settlements in the Aegean.

In the landscape around Kastro Apalirou lies what might be described as an extended network of rural churches and settlements, including Agios Stephanos in Marathos, Agios Giorgios and Agios Nikolaos, and the aniconic decorated church of Agios Ioannes Adissarou. The latter displays some of the most impressive examples of aniconic decoration and reveals the sophisticated choices made by patrons and painters in the Early Medieval period, as well as providing an example of how some of the now-ruinous churches in the area were probably decorated. Agios Ioannes Adissarou is not unique, however, since across the island there are more than 20 examples of aniconic decoration (Achiemastou-Potamianou 1986; Masteropoulos 2006; Crow and Turner 2018). While their chronology remains disputed, these decorative programs deliberately avoid sacred figural images, preferring an extensive selection of natural motifs (e.g., the hens and fish represented at Agia Kyriake Kalonis). Much of the discussion of these decorations has focused on their chronology, but equally they reveal a common and distinctive Christian visual culture. The emerging evidence from Naxos shows that rural communities could thrive on the islands of the eastern Mediterranean from Late Antiquity through the Early Middle Ages, where they created sacred landscapes that have endured to the present day.

References

Acheimastou-Potamianou, Myrtali

1986   Νέος ἀνεικονικὸς διάκοσμος ἐκκλησίας στὴ Νάξο. Οἱ τοιχογραφίες τοῦ Ἁγίου Ἰωάννου στ᾽ Ἀδησαροῦ. *Δελτίον τῆς Χριστιανικῆς Ἀρχαιολογικῆς Ἑταιρείας* 12(4): 329–382.

Aslanidis, Klimis

2014   Βυζαντινή Ναοδομία στη Νάξο. Η μετεξέλιξη από την παλαιοχριστιανική στη μεσοβυζαντινή αρχιτεκτονική. PhD thesis, University of Patras, Greece. (http://hdl.handle.net/10889/8392).

2018   The Evolution from Early Christian to Middle Byzantine Church Architecture on the Island of Naxos. In *Naxos and the Byzantine Aegean*, edited by Jim Crow and David Hill, pp. 311–337. Norwegian Institute in Athens, Oslo.

Boazman, Gill

2016   Hallowed by Saints, Coveted by Kings: Christianisation and Land Tenure in Rathdown, c. 400–900. In *Making Christian Landscapes in Atlantic Europe: Conversion and Consolidation in the Early Middle Ages,* edited by Tomás Ó Carragáin and Sam Turner, pp. 21–53. Cork University Press, Cork.

Blair, John

2005   *The Church in Anglo-Saxon Society.* Oxford University Press, Oxford.

Chatzidakis, Manolis (editor)

1989   *Byzantine Art in Greece: Naxos, Mosaics Wall Paintings.* Melissa, Athens.

Crow, Jim

    2014   Perspectives on the Archaeology of Byzantine Greece 600–1000 A.D. *Pharos* 20(1): 291–311. doi: 10.2143/PHA.20.1.3064545

Crow, Jim, and Sam Turner

    2015   L'archéologie des églises aniconiques de Naxos. In *L'aniconisme dans l'art religieux byzantin. Actes du colloque de Genève (1–3 Octobre 2009),* edited by Matteo Campagnolo, Paul Magdalino, Marielle Martiniani-Reber, and André-Louis Rey, pp. 193–204. La Pomme d'Or, Geneva.

    2018   The Archaeology of the Aniconic Churches of Naxos. In *Naxos and the Byzantine Aegean,* edited by Jim Crow and David Hill, pp. 223–237. Norwegian Institute in Athens, Oslo.

Crow, Jim, Athanasios Vionis, and Sam Turner

    2011   Characterizing the Historic Landscapes of Naxos. *Journal of Mediterranean Archaeology* 24(1): 111–137. doi: 10.1558/jmea.v24i1.111

Ćurčić, Slobodan

    2010   *Architecture in the Balkans from Diocletian to Süleyman the Magnificent.* Yale University Press, New Haven.

Decker, Michael

    2016   *The Byzantine Dark Ages.* Bloomsbury, London.

Deligiannakis, Giorgos

    2011   Late Paganism on the Aegean Islands and the Processes of Christianisation. In *The Archaeology of the Late Antique "Paganism",* edited by Luke Lavan and Michael Mulryan, pp. 311–345. Brill, Leiden.

Dimitrokallis, Giorgios

    1968   The Byzantine Churches of Naxos. *American Journal of Archaeology* 72(3): 283–286.

    2000   Βυζντινή Ναόδομια στήν Νάξο (Byzantine Churches in Naxos). Privately published, Athens.

Gleeson, Patrick, and Tomás Ó Carragáin

    2016   Conversion and Consolidation in Leinster's Royal Heartland. In *Making Christian Landscapes in Atlantic Europe: Conversion and Consolidation in the Early Middle Ages,* edited by Tomás Ó Carragáin and Sam Turner, pp. 75–108. Cork University Press, Cork.

Hill, Stephen

    1996   *The Early Byzantine Churches of Cilicia and Isauria.* Variorum, Aldershot.

Hill, David, Knut Ødegård, and Håkon Roland

    2017   Kastro Apalirou, Naxos: A 7th-Century Urban Foundation. In *New Cities in Late Antiquity,* edited by Efthymios Rizos, pp. 281–292. Bibliothèque de l'antiquité tardive 35. Brepols, Turnhout.

Ingtjerd, Hallvard

    2018   Ceramics as (Datable) Building Material at Kastro Apalirou: Preliminary Observations, in *Naxos and the Byzantine Aegean,* edited by Jim Crow and David Hill, pp. 145–154. Norwegian Institute at Athens, Athens.

Kaplan, Michel

    1990   Le village byzantin: naissance d'une communauté chrétienne. In *Villages et villageois au Moyen-Age. Actes des 21 congrès de la Société des historiens médiévistes de l'enseignement supérieur public*, pp. 15–25. Histoire ancienne et médiévale 26. Publications de la Sorbonne, Paris. doi: 10.3406/shmes.1990.1572

Lambrinoudakis, Vassilios

2018   Naxos in Imperial and Early Christian Times. In *Naxos and the Byzantine Aegean*, edited by Jim Crow and David Hill, pp. 3–17. Norwegian Institute at Athens, Athens.

Lambrinoudakis, Vassilios, and Aenne Ohnesorg (editors)

2019   *Das Heiligtum von Gyroulas bei Sangri auf Naxos*. Melissa Books, Athens.

Magdalino, Paul

2018   The Historical Context of Settlement Change on Naxos in the Early Middle Ages. In *Naxos and the Byzantine Aegean*, edited by Jim Crow and David Hill, pp. 19–27. Norwegian Institute at Athens, Athens.

Manolopoulou, Vicky, Stelios Lekakis, Mark Jackson, and Sam Turner

2018   Microcosm to Landscape: The Church called Theoskepasti and the Environs of Apalirou. In *Naxos and the Byzantine Aegean*, edited by Jim Crow and David Hill, pp. 239–254. Norwegian Institute at Athens, Athens.

Martiniani-Reber, Marielle

2015   Textiles et décors peints aniconiques. In *L'aniconisme dans l'art religieux byzantin. Actes du colloque de Genève (1–3 Octobre 2009),* edited by Matteo Campagnolo, Paul Magdalino, Marielle Martiniani-Reber, and André-Louis Rey, pp. 75–84. La Pomme d'Or, Geneva.

Masteropoulos, Giorgios.

2006   Νάξος:Το άλλο κάλλος. Περιηγήσεις σε βυζαντινά μνημεία / Naxos: Byzantine Monuments. Ελληνικές ομοιογραφικές εκδόσεις, Athens.

Ó Carragáin, Tomás, and Sam Turner

2016   Introduction: Making Christian Landscapes in the Early Medieval Atlantic World. In *Making Christian Landscapes in Atlantic Europe: Conversion and Consolidation in the Early Middle Ages,* edited by Tomás Ó Carragáin and Sam Turner, pp. 1–17. Cork University Press, Cork.

Ødegård, Knut

2018   The Churches of Apalirou, In *Naxos and the Byzantine Aegean*, edited by Jim Crow and David Hill, pp. 123–136. Norwegian Institute at Athens, Athens.

Poulou, Natalia

2018   The Aegean during the 'Transitional' Period of Byzantium: The Archaeological Evidence. In *Naxos and the Byzantine Aegean*, edited by Jim Crow and David Hill, pp. 29–50. Norwegian Institute at Athens, Athens.

Roberts, Neil, Marica Cassis, Owen Doonan, Warren Eastwood, Hugh Elton, John Haldon, Adam Izdebski, and James Newhard

2018   Not the End of the World? Post-Classical Decline and Recovery in Rural Anatolia. *Human Ecology*. doi: 10.1007/s10745–018–9973–2

Roussos, Konstantinos

2017   *Reconstructing the Settled Landscape of the Cyclades: The Islands of Paros and Naxos during the Late Antique and Early Byzantine Centuries*. Leiden University Press, Leiden.

Simantoni-Bournia, E. (editor)
 2001   Νάξος: Το αρχαίο ιερό του Γύρουλα στο Σαγκρί. Ministry of the Aegean,
             Athens.

Sweetman, Rebecca
 2015   The Christianisation of the Peloponnese: The Case for Strategic Change. *Annual
             of the British School at Athens* 110: 285–319.

Stewart, Charles A.
 2010   The First Vaulted Churches of Cyprus. *Journal of the Society of Architectural
             Historians* 69(2): 162–189.

Turner, Sam, and Jim Crow
 2010   Unlocking Historic Landscapes in the Eastern Mediterranean: Two Pilot Studies
             using Historic Landscape Characterisation. *Antiquity* 84(323): 216–229. doi:
             10.1017/S0003598X00099889

Turner, Sam, Jordi Bolòs, and Tim Kinnaird
 2018   Changes and Continuities in a Mediterranean Landscape: A New Interdisciplinary
             Approach to Understanding Historic Character in Western Catalonia. *Landscape
             Research* 43(7): 922–938. doi: 10.1080/01426397.2017.1386778

Turner, Sam, Sarah Semple, and Alex Turner
 2013   *Wearmouth and Jarrow: Northumbrian Monasteries in an Historic Landscape.*
             University of Hertfordshire Press, Hatfield.

Varinlioğlu, Günder
 2008   Living in a Marginal Environment: Rural Habitat and Landscape in Southeastern
             Isauria. *Dumbarton Oaks Papers* 61: 287–317.

Vionis, Athanasios K.
 2017   Understanding Settlements in Byzantine Greece: New Data and Approaches for
             Boeotia, Sixth to Thirteenth Century. *Dumbarton Oaks Papers* 71: 127–173.

Zias, Nicos
 1989   Panagia Protothrone at Chalki. In *Byzantine Art in Greece: Naxos, Mosaics Wall
             Paintings*, edited by Manolis Chatzidakis, pp. 30–49. Melissa, Athens.

The Islands of the Southern Aegean from Late Antiquity to the Early Middle Ages: The Archaeological Evidence

Natalia Poulou

The Aegean Sea connects mainland Greece with the western coast of Asia Minor and demarcates the maritime routes leading from the Mediterranean (east and west) to Propontis (i.e., the Sea of Marmara) and through it to Pontus Euxinus (i.e., the Black Sea). In 324 Constantine the Great founded Constantinople and transferred there the capital of the Roman Empire, thus strengthening the eastern part of his empire, which progressively became Byzantium. After the fourth century the Aegean islands became political and economic foci in the Eastern Mediterranean under the influence of the new capital.

Three centuries later the advent of the Arabs brought a series of changes in the Aegean with subsequent transformations in settlement patterns, sea routes, and in the overall dynamic of sea trade. In this contribution we examine the archaeological evidence reflecting the changes that occurred in the islands of the southern Aegean, with emphasis on major sites in the Cyclades, the Dodecanese, and Kythera, the latter situated on the sea route between the western and eastern Mediterranean. The issues addressed comprise changes in human activity and settlement patterns, contacts with neighboring and distant areas, and sea routes and trade networks during a period of transformation leading from the Late Roman period to the Early Middle Ages.

Introduction

The Aegean Sea and its islands are located between the west coast of Asia Minor and the Greek mainland. It is one of the seas that constitute the Mediterranean which the Byzantines called *pelagos* (πέλαγος), as they considered that it was for them the sea *par excellence* (Ahrweiler 1966, 1987: 63). The Aegean Sea has numerous larger and smaller islands, while its southern limit is an important island, Crete. Geographical proximity and cultural similarities link these islands with Asia Minor and the Greek coastline. The Aegean islands are autonomous units, but at the same time they act as communication bridges with each other and with the nearest shores. So we can accept that, as the Byzantines used to say, the sea unites rather than divides (συνάπτει μᾶλλον ἡ τέμνει) (Ahrweiler 1987: 63). Their ports, harbors, bays, or even coves were useful in ensuring a safe journey for every ship belonging to the merchant marine, the fishing fleet, or the navy.

Until the early fourth century, the majority of products produced in the provinces headed to Rome. Although ships were crossing the entire Mediterranean and of course also the Aegean Sea, the major commercial sea routes led to the Italian peninsula (Wickham 2005: 76, 708–709). In A.D. 324 Constantine the First founded Constantinople, "as a new Roman capital, which by the fifth century was a city with a population of around half-a-million" (Wickham 2005: 29). This act, the transfer of the capital, strengthened the eastern part of the Roman Empire, which was slowly transformed into the Byzantine empire. The other important factor contributing to this transformation was the new religion, Christianity.

The presence of the Arabs in the Mediterranean by the mid-seventh century, and in the Aegean in particular, created conditions which imposed major changes in important sectors of administration, defense, the character of commerce, and the security of communications (on this period see: Haldon 1997; 2012: 99–122; 2016; McCormick 2001; Wickham 2005; Brubaker and Haldon 2011). Within this historical context, it is interesting to examine the archaeological evidence indicating the changes that occurred in cities and in larger or smaller settlements of the Aegean islands and their communities.

The archaeological evidence presented in this chapter comes mainly from islands in the Dodecanese, some islands in the Cyclades, and the island of Kythera—in other words, islands of the southern Aegean (Figure 10.1). During the transitional period, Crete was the southern frontier of Byzantium bordering the Aegean islands. This situation renders Crete a very important island for control of the maritime network; but other contributions to this volume deal with Crete.

The Dodecanese

We start with the two important islands of the Dodecanese, Rhodes and Cos. The city of Rhodes, along with the city of Cos, was the most important city in this insular complex in the southeastern Aegean. Rhodes' harbor was important for ships on the maritime road leading to and from the east Mediterranean to Constantinople and the Black Sea (Michailidou 2013: 241–242).

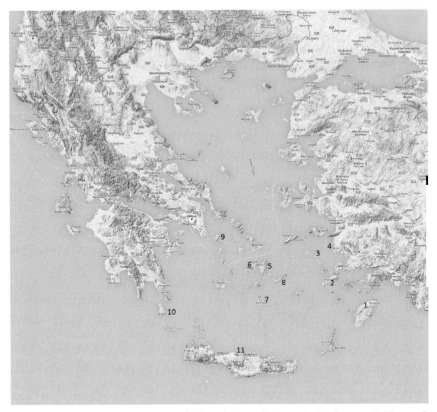

Figure 10.1. Map of the Aegean: 1) Rhodes, 2) Cos, 3) Lipsi, 4) Agathonisi, 5) Naxos, 6) Paros, 7) Thera, 8) Amorgos, 9) Kea, 10) Kythera, 11) Crete.

Archaeological investigation has shown that the ancient town was in continuous use during Late Antiquity (Figure 10.2); the city's main roads conducting from the countryside to the town were more or less respected. Large Christian basilicas were built in the town from the late fifth to the sixth century (Kollias 2000: 301). It is noteworthy that during the seventh century a new defensive wall was built on the north side of the town. An Arab source allows us to deduce that this strong defensive system was in place by the second half of the seventh century (Kollias 2000: 303–307; Michailidou 2013: 244–245). During the seventh and eighth centuries settlement extended beyond the Early Byzantine walls, but the inhabitants could take refuge within the walls at times of danger. The enlarged town did receive its own considerable fortifications, possibly sponsored by the state, after the ninth century and perhaps in the late eleventh or early twelfth century (Kollias 2000: 305–306). Two gates existed on the south side, and another on the side by the main harbor of Emporio, in continuous use from antiquity to the present day, as the latest research has shown. We should not forget the existence of a second harbor at Mandraki, also in use during this period (Manousou-Ntella 2012: 21–36).

On the island of Cos, excavations have revealed a large part of the ancient city and many smaller settlements in the countryside. The city of Cos was founded on a natural harbor along the same important maritime route from the southeastern Mediterranean to the north Aegean. The ancient city had a regular urban plan with public and private spaces. Residential areas were located mainly in the southern and eastern part of the city, while public buildings surrounded the acropolis (Rocco 2015: 2, fig. I.1.1.1). Archaeological research demonstrates continuity in the use of the main roads, the *fora* and the buildings through the Early Byzantine period (Figure 10.3) (Baldini 2015a: 12–17, fig. I.1.2.1). We can observe the successive transformations of public space in Late Antiquity. The vast *agora* of Cos preserved its ancient character until the fourth century (Rocco and Livadiotti 2011), but it seems that, from the fifth century onwards, the use of this area gradually changed: some of the shops continued to be used and at the same time a glass workshop was installed there (Livadiotti 2015: 32). The port was restored after the devastating earthquake of the mid-sixth century; the commercial area near the harbor, the old *emporium*, was frequented during this period and for many centuries after that. The Medieval name of the area as *Porta tou Forou* and that of a church as *Panagia tou Forou* testify to the use of this area for a very long period (Livadiotti 2015: 33–34).

Although an Episcopal seat is documented from the fourth century, the construction of the Christian basilicas is dated to the fifth century: for instance, a large basilica occupies the ancient sanctuaries that were in the harbor (Baldini 2015a: 19–20; Pellacchia 2015: 37–38). Nevertheless, under the *Odeion*, a number of statues in good condition, related to the cult of Asclepius, were gathered for safekeeping (Baldini 2015a: 17, Fig.I. 1.2.3). This is a deliberate pagan action that indicates continuity of the cult of Asclepius during the fourth and early fifth centuries, despite the prevalence of the new religion (Figure 10.4).

The archaeological investigations in an important area of the city, next to the *cardo* and near the crossroad with the *decumanus*, allow us to follow the successive transformations of the thermal complex through the centuries. The area of the baths was soon transformed into the Episcopal palace of the city. This impressive complex remained important at least until the eighth century, as inscriptions inform us (Baldini 2015a: 23–25; Cosentino 2015a: 115–116; 2015b: 240–245).

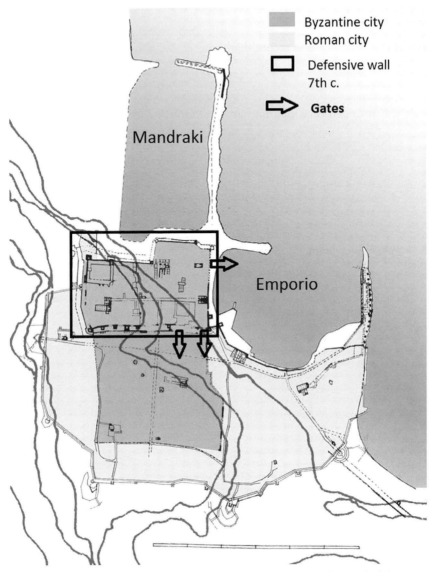

Figure 10.2. The Byzantine fortification and the harbors on Rhodes (after Michailidou 2013, with additional annotations by the present author).

It seems that the effects of the earthquakes of the sixth century did not cause drastic breaks in the life of the city; furthermore, the Arab raids of the seventh century did not cause a radical interruption of human activity. The reduction of the city seems to occur after the seventh century (Didioumi 2015). We observe that

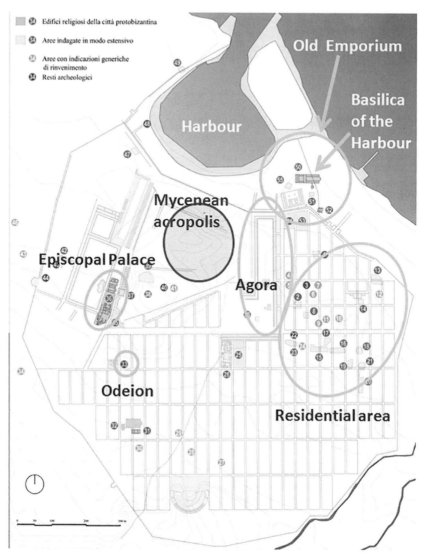

Figure 10.3. The city of Cos during the Early Byzantine period (after Baldini 2015a, with additional annotations by the present author).

there are two factors contributing to the prosperity and blossoming of the city of Cos during the Late Roman and the Early Byzantine period: the maintenance of its commercial role along the maritime routes and the survival of a social elite of the Byzantine state (Baldini 2015: 13; Cosentino 2015b; Pellacchia 2015: 53).

Figure 10.4. The statues under the Odeion on Cos during the excavation (after Baldini 2015b).

In the countryside, surveys across the island have produced a very interesting picture: a lot of rural settlements and workshop installations have been found, mostly close to the sea. The fact that most of them are located near the coastline is an outcome of the fact that archaeological research has focused on these areas, due to intensive modern construction there. Rural settlements, such as those of Kephalos, Kardamaina, and Mastichari, are small nuclei of habitation near the basilicas, easily reached from the sea, and it is worth noting that these Late Roman settlements are established on or near those of previous periods. Interestingly, in at least one case—the settlement of Kephalos—a warehouse of a simple type, probably a state warehouse, dating from the late sixth to the ninth century, has been identified (Didioumi 2011: 106–108). Moreover, pottery workshops have been extensively investigated

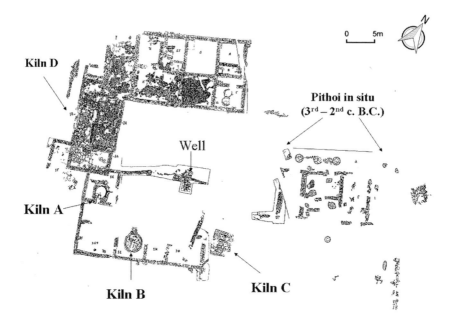

Figure 10.5. The pottery workshop at Mastichari on Cos (after Poulou and Didioumi 2015).

at Mastichari and Kardamaina (Poulou-Papadimitriou and Didioumi 2010: 741–749; 2015: 401–403) (Figure 10.5). The local production of transport vessels presupposes the existence of significant production and export of agricultural products at least until the ninth century (Poulou-Papadimitriou 2018).

Archaeological research has uncovered further evidence from all the islands of the Dodecanese; however, here I present the results of just two archaeological investigations that I consider very important. An amphora workshop is known from excavations on Lipsi, a tiny island in the eastern Aegean (Papavassileiou et al. 2014: 159–168). These transport vessels, dated in our opinion to the eighth century, belong to Hayes' Saraçhane type 45 (called "survivals" of the LRA1 type as well) (Poulou-Papadimitriou 2018: 32); amphorae of the same type have been uncovered in the Bozburun and Yenikapı 12 shipwrecks, dated to the ninth century (Hocker and Yamini 1998: 3–13; Denker et al. 2013: 204, no. 237). Moreover, on another small island, Agathonisi, a large vaulted complex at the site of Tholoi has been interpreted as a big granary or *horreum* dating to the seventh–eighth centuries (Figure 10.6). The existence of low pillars (*suspensurae*) for supporting a wooden floor, a characteristic feature of such warehouses,

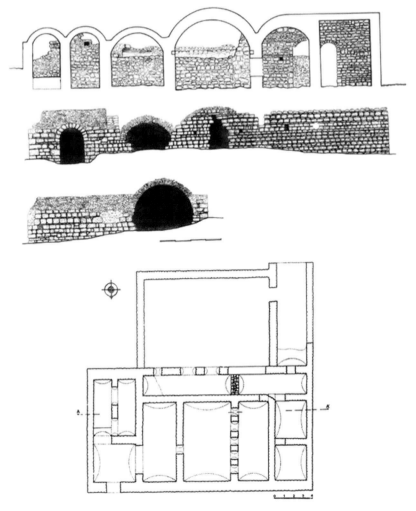

Figure 10.6. The warehouse on Agathonisi (after Triantafyllidis 2006).

reinforces the characterization of the building as a granary (Triantafyllidis 2006: 186–192). Similar elements have been identified in a warehouse unearthed in Achaia in the Peloponnese, dated to the late sixth/seventh centuries (Koumousi and Theodoropoulou 2015: 93–107). These warehouses must have been integrated as part of a well-organized system supervised by state officials.

The Cyclades

The island group of the Cyclades, lying at the center of the Aegean, was extremely valuable for the free movement of the Byzantine fleet and the passage of people and goods to and from Constantinople (Poulou-Papadimitriou 2018: 34).

The island of Naxos with its large agricultural output continued to be of great significance in the following centuries as well. The major importance of Naxos at this time is revealed first by defensive structures such as the fortress of Apalirou (Hill et al. 2017: 281–291; 2018: 83–87). From this fortress, which includes churches and water cisterns, it is possible to overlook almost the whole seascape between the islands of Naxos, Paros, Ios, Amorgos, and the small islands of Heraklia, Schinousa, and Keros, while this position offers a view over the island's territory as well (Poulou-Papadimitriou 2018: 35; Roussos 2017: 163–278). Residential developments must have been important as well, to judge from the considerable number of churches with interesting aniconic wall paintings (Acheimastou-Potamianou 1984: 329–382). Concerning architecture, recent research has shown that the church of Taxiarchis, in its first phase dated to the seventh/eighth centuries, was a three-aisled basilica with piers (Tsafou and Delaporta 2017: 150). This picture is complemented by earlier discoveries such as the eighth-century residential structure at Aplomata, where a *solidus* of Constantine V (741–775) was found, or the eighth/ninth-century workshops at Grotta, with a cistern and the remains of a tannery, together with the find of a *miliaresion* of Leo V (813–820) (Lambrinoudakis 1982: 254–55; 1993: 162–63; 2018: 6–9; Penna 2001: 403–4; 2018: 51–60).

On Paros, excavations at the cove of Zoodochos Pighi, situated in the northeast of Naoussa bay, were able to identify a potter's workshop (Diamanti 2016: 691–697, fig. 2, 8–9). The amphorae produced there, during the early eighth century, belong to two different types: the Byzantine globular amphora (BGA) and the type we have recognized as Hayes' Saraçhane 45 (called also "survival" of the LRA1) (Poulou 2018; Poulou-Papadimitriou and Nodarou 2014: 875–878). The stamps found on the Byzantine globular amphorae indicate that there was a system of control in place (Diamanti 2016: 691–697). This archaeological investigation provides us with new information on the handling of agricultural production in the early eighth century.

Discoveries on Thera (Santorini) are also very important. The excavations at Perissa have revealed a three-aisled basilica, in which three phases were distinguished. In the third phase, during the eighth and ninth centuries, the church was reduced in size and a two-aisle vaulted church was constructed

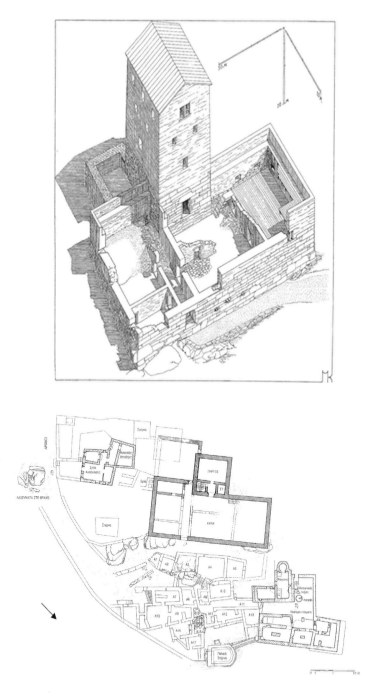

Figure 10.7. The Pyrgos of Agia Triada on Amorgos (after Marangou 2005; drawing of the tower by M. Korres).

in the eastern part of its middle aisle (Gerousi 2010). The finds—pottery and coins—date to the seventh, eighth, and ninth centuries (Poulou-Papadimitriou 2018: 35–36). During the same period there was activity in the area of ancient Thera: it is worth mentioning that a hoard of 29 *miliaresia* of the emperor Theophilus was found there, while recent research in this area has unearthed buildings and pottery—in particular, amphorae dated to the eighth and ninth centuries, similar to those from the ninth-century Yenikapı 12 and Bozburun shipwrecks (Denker et al. 2013: 204, no. 237; Gerousi-Bendermacher 2018; Hocker and Yamini 1998: 3–13; Poulou-Papadimitriou 2018: 35–36). This archaeological evidence may be explained by some small port installation in the natural harbor of Perissa in the eighth and ninth centuries, which would have been in direct contact with a larger settlement in the island's interior, such as the settlement at ancient Thera. The island had probably recovered quickly after the catastrophic eruption of A.D. 726, regaining its important position on the sea routes (Poulou-Papadimitriou 2018: 36).

The remainder of the Cyclades yields little information. Nevertheless, we have evidence about continuity of human activity and its nature on other islands. The island of Amorgos looks like it housed a regular naval station; the hoard hidden on the acropolis of Arkesini along with material of the seventh to ninth centuries (pottery and bronze belt buckles), unearthed in the Pyrgos (Tower) of Agia Triada (Figure 10.7), indicate a military presence on the island during this period (Marangou 2005: 59, 67, figures 58.3, 66.6–7; Penna 2001: 408, n. 40; Poulou-Papadimitriou 2018: 36–37; Touratsoglou 1999: 351–352). It seems that ancient towers on Amorgos and on other Cycladic islands such as Sifnos, Kea, and Serifos were probably used as watch-posts and/or as storehouses at this time (Pennas 2002: 44–45; see also Malamut 1988: 214); some of these constructions, strengthened by small fortifications, probably housed a military unit and played a defensive role (Poulou-Papadimitriou 2018: 37). It is worth noting that on Kea there was a naval base for the *Karabisianoi* in 680 and a safe harbor later in the eighth century (Ahrweiler 1966: 26; Malamut 1988: 105, 539).

The Island of Kythera

Kythera lies in the southwestern Aegean, between Crete and the Peloponnese, occupying the southwestern entrance to the Aegean sea; its position has been of high importance from prehistoric times until today (Figure 10.8). The sites on the east coast in particular—Palaiopolis (Skandeia), Avlemon (Agios Nikolaos), Agios Georgios sto Vouno, and Agios Georgios tis Kolokythias—played an important role for the island's rulers.

Figure 10.8. Left: map of Kythera showing sites mentioned in the text; right: the view from the site of Agios Georgios sto Vouno (photo by the author). Key to sites: 1. Ag. Georgios sto Vouno; 2. Kastri; 3. Palaiopolis; 4. Avlemon; 5. Ag. Georgios Kolokythias; 6. Chora (photo by the author).

The ancient city of Skandeia (modern Palaiopolis) is located on the east coast. During the sixth century a very important fortification, Kastri, was built on the southwestern side of the small peninsula (Herrin 1972: 43). Its towers, ruined today, were described and drawn by Ciriaco de Pizzicolli (also known as Cyriac of Ancona) during the fifteenth century (Bodnar 1960; Chadzidakis 2017). Excavation shows that Skandeia was inhabited from the Early Bronze Age until the early Middle Byzantine period (Huxley 1972: 33–40). Atop a hill a short distance north of this coastal settlement is the site of Agios Georgios sto Vouno, a very important Minoan peak sanctuary during the prehistoric period (Sakellarakis 2011) with uninterrupted use as a sanctuary in the following centuries (Poulou-Papadimitriou 2013: 168–184). During the seventh century A.D., a fortified settlement with a church and a water cistern was established on the hilltop, and smaller-sized constructions were also built on the south slopes (Figure 10.9). All these architectural remains were constructed in the seventh century and remained in use during the eighth, ninth, and tenth centuries, as evidenced by ten *folles* of Heraclius and ten *folles* of Constans II, an eighth-century lead seal, and a *follis* of Leo V (Penna 2013: 421–456), as well as by pottery found during the excavation (Poulou-Papadimitriou 2013: 34–57, 64–159, 168–170, 185–191). The site seems to have functioned as a point of control for the harbors of Palaiopolis and Avlemon: from this hilltop it is possible at the same time to oversee almost the whole seascape between Crete and Kythera, i.e., from the western Mediterranean into the Aegean (Poulou-Papadimitriou 2013: 184).

The fortification of Kolokythia, on the northeastern coast of the island, was built and used during the same period (eighth to tenth centuries). We

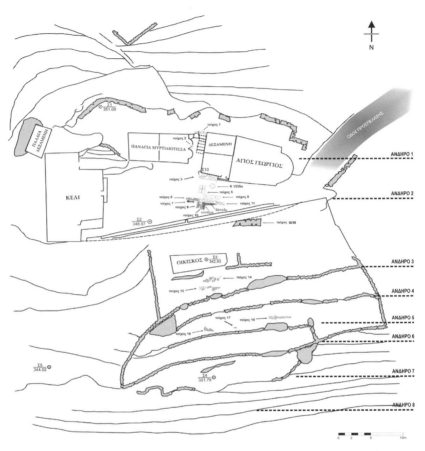

Figure 10.9. The site of Agios Georgios sto Vouno on Kythera (after Poulou-Papadimitriou 2013).

believe that this construction served as a point of control for the important maritime route between Kythera and the Peloponnese (Papadimitriou 2011; Poulou-Papadimitriou 2013: 160, 177).

The Arabs in the Aegean

And what about the Arabs? Is there material evidence of an Arab presence in the southern Aegean during the eighth century, as the written sources indicate? The presence of Arab graffiti dating to the eighth century, found in many islands and on the coast of Asia Minor, prove that the Arabs constituted a real threat in the heart of the Aegean. They have been found on two columns in the *extra muros* religious complex of Agios Gabriel in Cos (Beghelli and Di Branco 2011: 61,

Figure 10.10. The Arab graffiti at Ag. Gabriel on Cos (photograph by Isabela Baldini).

figure I.4.2; Cosentino 2015a: 112–114; Imbert 2014: 731–760), on architectural members of the Stoa of Philippus V in the ancient port of Delos (Vallois 1923: 166–168, figure 232), on a marble cover of a Roman pilaster in secondary use in the basilica at Tsoutsouros on the south coast of Crete (Epitropakis 2006; Poulou-Papadimitriou 2011: 443, n. 103), but also on architectural members in Cnidus, the Cilician coast, and Cyprus. All these graffiti talk about soldiers who thank God for their victory (Imbert 2014: 731–760) (Figure 10.10). We believe that Arab garrisons were established in these sites for a short period during the eighth century.

Conclusions

All this evidence leads us to formulate certain hypotheses and interpretations. As in other regions of the Empire, the islanders continued to live in the same cities as in the Hellenistic and Roman periods. The main roads were more or less respected. However, we can observe successive transformations of public spaces and public buildings in Late Antiquity. The shrinking of these ancient cities seems to occur after the seventh century. The presence of the Arabs in the Mediterranean, by the mid-seventh century, and in the Aegean in particular, created conditions which imposed major changes in important sectors of administration, defense, the character of commerce and the security of communications.

The mid-seventh century saw the construction or reinforcement, in whole or in part, of existing urban fortifications in many Aegean islands and in Crete; most Byzantine fortifications in Crete date back to this period (seventh to eighth centuries A.D.) (Poulou-Papadimitriou 2011: 384–387; Poulou 2018). During this same period we observe an increase in coastal settlements across the Aegean, as a means of control on behalf of the state over sea routes and sea trade. The discovery of warehouse facilities, along with the increase of ceramic workshops manufacturing transport amphorae, in many islands and islets of the Aegean, reflects an active agricultural economy and trade networks linking Constantinople with the east and the west via the Aegean Sea. These goods were shipped to Constantinople or to other regions (Poulou-Papadimitriou 2014:127–152), even as far as Sicily (Laiou 2002: 708, n. 50). Byzantium seems to have been taking advantage of the geographical position of the Aegean islands, incorporating them into the globalized trade system that characterizes this transitional period.

References

Acheimastou-Potamianou, Myrtali

1984   Νέος ανεικονικός διάκοσμος εκκλησίας στη Νάξο. Οι τοιχογραφίες του Αγίου Ιωάννη του Θεολόγου στ' Αδησαρού. *Deltion tis Christianikis Archaiologikis Etaireias* 12: 329–82.

Ahrweiler, Hélène

1966   *Byzance et la mer: la marine de guerre, la politique et les institutions maritimes de Byzance aux VIIe–XVe siècles.* Presses Universitaires de France, Paris.

1987   The Importance of the Sea in the Byzantine Period. In *Greece and the Sea*, edited by Angelos Delivorrias, pp. 63–72. Cosmopress, Athens.

Baldini, Isabella

2015a   La città cristiana. In *Archeologia protobizantina a Kos: la città e il complesso episcopale,* edited by Isabella Baldini and Monica Livadiotti, pp. 12–27. Bonona University Press, Bologna.

2015b   Il complesso episcopale: sviluppo architettonico e modelli. In *Archeologia protobizantina a Kos: la città e il complesso episcopale,* edited by Isabella Baldini and Monica Livadiotti, pp. 154–172. Bonona University Press, Bologna.

Beghelli, Michelle, and Marco Di Branco

2011   Kos durante le invasioni musulmane. In *Archeologia protobizantina a Kos: la basilica di S. Gabriele* edited by Isabella Baldini and Monica Livadiotti, pp. 59–67. Ante Quem, Bologna.

Brubaker, Leslie, and John F. Haldon

2011   *Byzantium in the Iconoclast Era c. 680–850: A History.* Cambridge University Press, Cambridge.

Bodnar, Edward W.

 1960   *Cyriacus of Ancona and Athens.* Latomus 43. Revue d'Études Latines, Brussels

Chatzidakis, Michail

 2017   *Cyriac of Ancona and the Rediscovery of Greece in the Fifteenth Century.* Franz
             Philipp Rutzen, Petersberg; Michael Imhof Verlag, Mainz.

Cosentino, Salvatore

 2015a   Episcopato e società a Kos tra IV e VIII secolo. In *Archeologia protobizantina
             a Kos: la città e il complesso episcopale,* edited by Isabella Baldini and Monica
             Livadiotti, pp. 105–116. Bonona University Press, Bologna.

 2015b   La documentazione epigrafica. In *Archeologia protobizantina a Kos: la città e
             il complesso episcopale,* edited by Isabella Baldini and Monica Livadiotti, pp.
             240–245. Bonona University Press, Bologna.

Denker, Asuman, Feza Dermikök, Gülcan Kongaz, Mine Kiraz, Özlem Korkmaz Kömürcü,
and Tuğçe Akbaytogan

 2013   YK 12. In *Stories from the Hidden Harbour: Shipwrecks of Yenikapı,* edited by Zeynep
             Kiziltan and Gülbahar Baran Çelik, pp. 198–209. Koç University Press, Istanbul.

Diamanti, Charikleia

 2016   The Late Roman Amphora Workshops of Paros Island in the Aegean Sea: Recent
             Results. *Rei Cretariae Romanae Fautorum Acta* 44: 691–697.

Didioumi, Sophia

 2011   Νεότερα ευρήματα για την πρωτοβυζαντινή Κω από τις σωστικές ανασκαφές
             στο νησί. In *Archeologia protobizantina a Kos: la basilica di S. Gabriele* edited
             by Isabella Baldini and Monica Livadiotti, pp. 87–115. Ante Quem, Bologna.

 2015   Kos: The Material Culture and the Ecclesiastic Productions. In *Archeologia
             protobizantina a Kos: la città e il complesso episcopale,* edited by Isabella Baldini
             and Monica Livadiotti, pp. 12–27, 95–104. Bonona University Press, Bologna.

Epitropakis, Periandros

 2006   Παλαιοχριστιανική βασιλική Τσούτσουρου: τα πρώτα ανασκαφικά
             αποτελέσματα. *Περιλήψεις Ι' Διεθνούς Κρητολογικού Συνεδρίου,* pp. 154–155
             Φιλολογικός Σύλλογος «Ο Χρυσόστομος», Chania.

Gerousi, Eugenia

 2010   Η παλαιοχριστιανική βασιλική της Αγίας Ειρήνης στην Περίσσα Θήρας. Μία
             πρώτη προσέγγιση. *Deltion tis Christianikis Archaiologikis Etaireias* Δ': 17–31.

Gerousi-Bendermacher, Eugenia

 2018   In Search of Social and Economic Activities in the Cyclades Islands in the 8th
             Century. In *The 8th Century: Patterns of Transition in Economy and Trade
             throughout the Late Antique, Early Medieval and Islamicate Mediterranean in
             Multidisciplinary Perspectives.* Millennium: Yearbook on the Culture and History
             of the First Millennium A.D. De Gruyter, Berlin (forthcoming).

Haldon, John F.

 1997   *Byzantium in the Seventh Century.* Second edition. Cambridge University Press,
             Cambridge.

 2012   Commerce and Exchange in the Seventh and Eighth Centuries: Regional Trade
             and the Movement of Goods. In *Trade and Markets in Byzantium,* edited by
             Cécile Morrisson, pp. 99–122. Dumbarton Oaks Byzantine Symposia and

Colloquia. Dumbarton Oaks Research Library and Collection, Washington D.C.

2016   *The Empire That Would Not Die: The Paradox of Eastern Roman Survival, 640–740.* Harvard University Press, Cambridge MA.

Hayes, John W.

1992   *Excavations at Saraçhane in Constantinople: The Pottery.* Princeton University Press, Princeton NJ.

Herrin, Judith

1972   Byzantine Kythera. In *Kythera: Excavations and Studies Conducted by the University of Pennsylvania Museum and the British School at Athens,* edited by John N. Coldstream and George L. Huxley, pp. 41–51. British School at Athens, London.

Hill, David, Håkon Roland, and Knut Ødergård

2017   Kastro Apalirou, Naxos: A 7th Century Urban Foundation. In *New Cities in Late Antiquity: Documents and Archaeology,* edited by Efthymios Rizos, pp. 281–291. Bibliothèque de l'Antiquité tardive. Brepols, Turnhout.

2018   The Kastro Apalirou Project. In *Naxos and the Byzantine Aegean: Insular Responses to Regional Change,* edited by James Crow and David Hill, pp. 83–87. Papers and Monographs from the Norwegian Institute at Athens 7. Norwegian Institute at Athens, Athens.

Hocker, Frederick M., Sara W. Yamini, and George O. Yamini

1998   Bozburun Byzantine Shipwreck Excavation: The Final Campaign 1998. *The INA Quarterly* 25 (4): 3–13.

Huxley, George L.

1972   The History and Topography of Ancient Kythera. In *Kythera: Excavations and Studies Conducted by the University of Pennsylvania Museum and the British School at Athens,* edited by John N. Coldstream and George L. Huxley, pp. 33–40. British School at Athens, London.

Imbert, Frédéric

2014   Graffiti arabes de Cnide et Kos: premières traces épigraphiques de la conquête musulmane en mer Égée. *Constructing the Seventh Century,* edited by Constantin Zuckerman. Travaux et Mémoires 17: 731–760.

Kollias, Ilias

2000   Η παλαιοχριστιανική και βυζαντινή Ρόδος. Η αντίσταση μιας ελληνιστικής πόλης. In *Ρόδος 2.400 χρόνια,* edited by Evangelia Kypraiou, pp. 299–308. Υπουργείο Πολιτισμού και Αθλητισμού, Athens.

Koumousi, Anastasia, and Theodoropoulou, Maria

2015   *Ζαχλωρίτικα Αιγιαλείας: συμβολή στην ιστορική γεωγραφία της περιοχής κατά την πρωτοβυζαντινή περίοδο.* Υπουργείο Πολιτισμού και Αθλητισμού, Εφορεία Αρχαιοτήτων Αχαΐας, Patras.

Laiou, Angeliki E.

2002   Exchange and Trade, Seventh–Twelfth Centuries. In *The Economic History of Byzantium,* vol. 2: *From the Seventh Through the Fifteenth Century,* edited by Angeliki E. Laiou, pp. 697–770. Dumbarton Oaks, Washington D. C.

Lambrinoudakis, Vassilios

1982   Ανασκαφή Νάξου. *Praktika tis en Athinais Archaiologikis Etaireias*: 253–259.

1993   Ανασκαφή Νάξου. *Praktika tis en Athinais Archaiologikis Etaireias*: 162–163.

2018   Naxos in Imperial and Early Christian Times. In *Naxos and the Byzantine Aegean: Insular Responses to Regional Change*, edited by James Crow and David Hill, pp. 3–17. Papers and Monographs from the Norwegian Institute at Athens 7. Norwegian Institute at Athens, Athens.

Livadiotti, Monica

2015   Le aree pubbliche. In *Archeologia protobizantina a Kos: la città e il complesso episcopale,* edited by Isabella Baldini and Monica Livadiotti, pp. 28–34. Bonona University Press, Bologna.

Malamut, Elisabeth

1988   *Les îles de l'empire byzantin (VIIIᵉ–XIIᵉ siècles).* Publications de la Sorbonne, Paris.

Manousou-Ntella, Katerina

2012   Μνημειακή τοπογραφία του βόρειου άκρου της πόλης της Ρόδου. *Deltion tis Christianikis Archaiologikis Etaireias* 33: 21–36.

Marangou, Lila

2005   *Αμοργός II. Οι αρχαίοι πύργοι.* Βιβλιοθήκη της εν Αθήναις Αρχαιολογικής Εταιρείας 239. Η εν Αθήναις Αρχαιολογική Εταιρεία, Athens.

McCormick, Michael

2001   *Origins of the European Economy: Communications and Commerce A.D. 300–900.* Cambridge University Press, Cambridge.

Michailidou, Maria

2013   The City of Rhodes. In *Heaven and Earth: Countryside in Byzantine Greece,* edited by Albani Jenny and Chalkia Eugenia, pp. 240–251. Hellenic Ministry of Culture and Sports and Benaki Museum, Athens.

Papadimitriou, Marina

2011   Η οχυρωματική θέση στον Άγιο Γεώργιο Κολοκυθιάς Κυθήρων. In *Defensive Architecture in the Peloponnese, 5th-15th Century, International Conference, Novenber 2011.* Abstracts: http://defensivearchitecture.blogspot.com/

Papavassileiou, Eleni, Konstantinos Sarantidis, and Eirini Papanikolaou

2014   A Ceramic Workshop of the Early Byzantine Period on the Island of Lipsi in the Dodecanese (Greece): A Preliminary Approach. In *LRCW 4, Late Roman Coarse Wares, Cooking Wares and Amphorae in the Mediterranean: Archaeology and Archaeometry. The Mediterranean: A Market without Frontiers,* edited by Natalia Poulou-Papadimitriou, Eleni Nodarou, and Vassilis Kilikoglou, pp. 159–167. British Archaeological Reports International Series 2616, vol. 1. Archaeopress, Oxford.

Pellacchia, Debora

2015   Il quartiere del porto. In *Archeologia protobizantina a Kos: la città e il complesso episcopale,* edited by Isabella Baldini and Monica Livadiotti, pp. 35–53. Bonona University Press, Bologna.

Penna, Vassiliki

2001   Νομισματικές νύξεις για τη ζωή στις Κυκλάδες κατά τους 8ο και 9ο αιώνες.
        In *Οι σκοτεινοί αιώνες του Βυζαντίου (7ος–9ος αι.)*, edited by Eleonora
        Kountoura-Galaki, pp. 399–410. Διεθνή Συμπόσια 9. Εθνικό Ίδρυμα
        Ερευνών, Ινστιτούτο Βυζαντινών Ερευνών, Athens.

2010   Κοινωνία και οικονομία στο Αιγαίο κατά τους βυζαντινούς χρόνους (4ος–
        12ος αι.). In *Το νόμισμα στα νησιά του Αιγαίου, Οβολός* 9, edited by Panagiotis
        Tselekas, pp. 11–42. Οι Φίλοι του Νομισματικού Μουσείου, Athens.

2013   Μαρτυρία των νομισμάτων και των σφραγίδων**.** In *Άγιος Γεώργιος στο
        Βουνό. Το μινωϊκό ιερό κορυφής. Τα ευρήματα 3*, edited by Yannis Sakellarakis,
        pp. 420–462. Βιβλιοθήκη της εν Αθήναις Αρχαιολογικής Εταιρείας 282. Η
        εν Αθήναις Αρχαιολογική Εταιρεία, Athens.

2018   Monetary Circulation in the Cyclades during the Dark Ages: An Updated
        Approach. In *Naxos and the Byzantine Aegean: Insular Responses to Regional
        Change*, edited by James Crow and David Hill, pp. 51–60. Papers and
        Monographs from the Norwegian Institute at Athens 7. Norwegian Institute
        at Athens, Athens.

Pennas, Charalampos

2002   Η ιστορία των αρχαίων *πύργων*. Επίμετρο στη σπουδή για τη Βυζαντινή
        Σίφνο. In *Σπουδή για τη Βυζαντινή Σίφνο,* edited by Pennas Charalampos, pp.
        44–45. Υπουργείο Πολιτισμού και Αθλητισμού, 2η Εφορεία Αρχαιοτήτων
        Κυκλάδων και Αργοσαρωνικού, Athens.

Poulou, Natalia

2019   Sailing in the Dark: Human Activity, Trade Networks and Commercial
        Interaction between Crete and the Aegean Islands in a Period of Transition.
        In *The 8th Century: Patterns of Transition in Economy and Trade throughout the
        Late Antique, Early Medieval and Islamicate Mediterranean in Multidisciplinary
        Perspectives,* edited by Stefan Esders, Frederic Krueger, Silvia Polla, Tonio
        Sebastian Richter, and Chris Wickham. Millenium. De Gruyter, Berlin–New
        York (forthcoming).

Poulou-Papadimitriou, Natalia

2011   Τεκμήρια υλικού πολιτισμού στη βυζαντινή Κρήτη: από τον 7ο έως το
        τέλος του 12ου αιώνα. In *Πεπραγμένα Ι' Διεθνούς Συνεδρίου (Χανιά 2006),
        vol. Α, Στρογγυλή Τράπεζα, 1. Μεσοβυζαντινή Κρήτη,* edited by Kapsomenos
        Eratosthenis, Maria Andreadaki-Vlazaki, and Michalis Andrianakis, pp. 381–
        447. Φιλολογικός Σύλλογος «Ο Χρυσόστομος», Chania.

2013   Άγιος Γεώργιος στο Βουνό. Η βυζαντινή και η πρώϊμη ενετική περίοδος. In
        Άγιος Γεώργιος στο Βουνό. Το μινωϊκό ιερό κορυφής. Τα ευρήματα 3, edited by
        Yannis Sakellarakis, pp. 25–266. Βιβλιοθήκη της εν Αθήναις Αρχαιολογικής
        Εταιρείας, 282. Η εν Αθήναις Αρχαιολογική Εταιρεία, Athens.

2014   Θαλάσσιοι δρόμοι στο Αιγαίο κατά την *πρωτοβυζαντινή* περίοδο: η
        μαρτυρία της κεραμικής. In *Αρχαιολογία και Τέχνη στα Δωδεκάνησα
        κατά την Ύστερη Αρχαιότητα, Ευλιμένη* 2, edited by Nektarios Zarras and
        Emmanouil Stefanakis, pp. 127–152. Μεσογειακή Αρχαιολογική Εταιρεία,
        Rethymnon.

2018   The Aegean during the 'Transitional' Period of Byzantium: The Archaeological
            Evidence. In *Naxos and the Byzantine Aegean: Insular Responses to Regional
            Change*, edited by James Crow and David Hill, pp. 29–50. Papers and
            Monographs from the Norwegian Institute at Athens 7. Norwegian Institute
            at Athens, Athens.

Poulou-Papadimitriou, Natalia, and Sophia Didioumi

2010   Nouvelles données sur la production de l'atelier céramique protobyzantin à
            Kardamaina (Cos-Grèce). In *LRCW3. Late Roman Coarse Wares, Cooking Wares
            and Amphorae in the Mediterranean: Archaeology and Archaeometry. Comparison
            between Western and Eastern Mediterranean*, edited by Simonetta Menchelli, Sara
            Santoro, Marinella Pasquinucci, and Gabriella Guiducci, pp. 741–749. British
            Archaeological Reports International Series 2185, vol. 2. Archaeopress, Oxford.

2015   Two Pottery Workshops in the Island of Cos (Greece). In *Tourner autour du pot:
            Les ateliers de potiers médiévaux du Ve au XIIe siècle dans l'espace européen*, edited
            by Freddy Thuillier and Étienne Louis, pp. 401–418. Presses universitaires de
            Caen, Caen.

Poulou-Papadimitriou, Natalia, and Eleni Nodarou

2014   Transport Vessels and Maritime Routes in the Aegean from the 5th to the 9th c.
            A.D. Preliminary Results of the EU funded 'Pythagoras II' Project: The Cretan
            Case Study. In *LRCW 4, Late Roman Coarse Wares, Cooking Wares and Amphorae
            in the Mediterranean: Archaeology and Archaeometry. The Mediterranean: A
            Market without Frontiers,* edited by Natalia Poulou-Papadimitriou, Eleni
            Nodarou, and Vassilis Kilikoglou, pp. 873–883. British Archaeological Reports
            International Series 2616, vol. 1. Archaeopress, Oxford.

Rocco, Giorgio

2015   L'impianto greco-romano. In *Archeologia protobizantina a Kos: la città e il
            complesso episcopale,* edited by Isabella Baldini and Monica Livadiotti, pp.1–11.
            Bonona University Press, Bologna.

Rocco, Giorgio, and Monica Livadiotti

2011   The Agora of Kos: The Hellenistic and Roman Phases. In *Η Αγορά στη Μεσόγειο
            από τους ομηρικούς έως τους ρωμαϊκούς χρόνους. Διεθνές Επιστημονικό
            Συνέδριο. Κως, 14–17 Απριλίου 2011*, edited by Aggeliki Giannikouri, pp.383–
            423. Αρχαιολογικό Ινστιτούτο Αιγαιακών Σπουδών, Athens.

Roussos, Konstantinos

2017   *Reconstructing the Settled Landscape of the Cyclades: The Islands of Paros and Naxos
            during the Late Antique and Early Byzantine centuries.* Leiden University Press,
            Leiden.

Sakellarakis, Yannis

2011   *Κύθηρα. Το μινωϊκό ιερό κορυφής στον Άγιο Γεώργιο στο Βουνό. 1: Τα
            προανασκαφικά και η ανασκαφή.* Βιβλιοθήκη της εν Αθήναις Αρχαιολογικής
            Εταιρείας 271. Η εν Αθήναις Αρχαιολογική Εταιρεία, Athens.

Touratsoglou, Ioannis

1999   εν οστράκω θαλασσίω...Ο "Θησαυρός" της Αρκεσίνης Αμοργού. In *Φως
            Κυκλαδικόν. Τιμητικός τόμος στη μνήμη του Νίκου Ζαφειρόπουλου*, edited by
            Nikolaos Stampolidis, pp. 348–359. Idryma Nikolaou P. Goulandri, Athens.

Triantafyllidis, Pavlos
    2006   Ιστορικά και αρχαιολογικά Αγαθονησίου. *Αρχαιολογικά Ανάλεκτα εξ Αθηνών* 39: 175–191.

Tsafou, Maria, and Aikaterini Delaporta
    2017   Στερέωση-Συντήρηση Βυζαντινών Μνημείων Νάξου. Παναγία Ορφανή στο Σαγκρί, Ταξιάρχης στα Μονοίτσια. In *Το Αρχαιολογικό Έργο στα νησιά του Αιγαίου, Διεθνές Επιστημονικό Συνέδριο, Ρόδος, 27 Νοεμβρίου – 1 Δεκεμβρίου 2013,* vol. A, edited by Pavlos Triantafyllidis, pp. 135–152. Υπουργείο Πολιτισμού και Αθλητισμού, Εφορεία Αρχαιοτήτων Λέσβου, Mytilene.

Vallois, René
    1923   *Les portiques au Sud du Hiéron* 1: *Le portique de Philippe.* Exploration archéologique de Délos VII. École française d'Athènes, Paris.

Wickham, Chris
    2005   *Framing the Early Middle Ages: Europe and the Mediterranean, 400–800.* Oxford University Press, Oxford.

Economic Landscapes and Transformed Mindscapes in Cyprus from Roman Times to the Early Middle Ages

ATHANASIOS K. VIONIS AND GIORGOS PAPANTONIOU

The concept of island insularity can be examined both as a world of isolation and as one of integration; that is, both as environments separated and bordered by sea in the Braudelian sense of the word, and as "stepping stones" of interregional and intercultural contact between neighboring islands and mainlands. In a more recent approach, Mediterranean islands have also been discussed in the context of the theoretical frameworks of fragmented topography and connectivity, where "globalism", "regionalism" and "localism" coexist.

This paper focuses on Cyprus, one of the largest Mediterranean islands, and examines transformed landscapes and mindscapes during times of growth and crisis, suggesting an interpretative framework based on a pendulum from administrative segmentation to unification and back again. The analysis of Cypriot economic landscapes and mindscapes becomes a significant interlocutor, which stimulates understanding of the broader cultural and socio-political space, bringing the various approaches of landscape archaeology into a closer dialogue.

We first discuss the economic and sacred landscapes of the periods under consideration, setting out the framework of a case-study-based analysis. Then, we move to the discussion of the economic and settled landscapes of the island, based primarily on archaeological evidence from our surface survey project in the Xeros river valley in Larnaca District, entitled Settled and Sacred Landscapes of Cyprus *(SeSaLaC). Finally, archaeological evidence, indicating transformations in economy and settlement patterns in the Early Middle Ages, is placed in a wider Mediterranean and European context, highlighting local responses to global phenomena during the passage from Antique to Early Medieval lifeways and mentalities.*

Introduction

Inter-island and island–mainland relations, maritime connectivity of things and people, insular definitions of centrality and marginality, ideological values, and islanders' views of their insularity and identity, are crucial in rethinking island cultures in relation to social change, colonization, and interaction (Broodbank 2000: 1). One of the most important features of islands is their diversity and, as Broodbank (2000: 7) notes, this is the reason why we need plurality in interpretative approaches. Scholars have periodically characterized islands as predominantly bounded, conservative, and closed systems (Evans 1973), open and receptive to outside ideas (Kirch 1986), or between involution and cosmopolitanism, archaism, and innovation (Braudel 1972: 149–150). As Broodbank (2000: 32) has suggested, "a brightest future surely lies in the development of an island archaeology… that explores how island space, environment, time and culture can be most convincingly woven together into island history".

The relatively recent work of Knapp (2008) has attempted at systematically bringing together issues of identities, insularities, and Mediterranean connectivities with special reference to prehistoric and protohistoric Cyprus. Also, scholars such as Iacovou (2007; 2013), Papantoniou (2012; 2013a; 2016), Counts and Iacovou (2013), and Gordon (2012; 2016) have touched upon the issues of identities, insularities, and connectivities with special references to the whole range of what we term "ancient Cyprus". As far as can be determined, however, later periods in Cyprus (Late Antiquity to Late Ottoman), remain relatively uninformed by such processes. Cyprus, a large and self-contained island in terms of natural resources, may differ from other smaller island societies (such as those discussed in Broodbank 2000) or other islands and island-groups where "insularity" is determined by distance from mainland coasts and other islands (Patton 1996; Vogiatzakis et al. 2017). As Cyprus' culture has traditionally been seen mainly in terms of "acculturation" and "emulation", we need to shift our focus from current interpretative paradigms, largely characterized by adaptive models and simple, static concepts of insularity, towards more complex and culturally-driven perspectives that recognize "the extent to which islanders have consciously fashioned, and refashioned, their own identities and worlds" (Broodbank 2000: 1).

Despite the fact that Mediterranean islands share in most cases particular characteristics with neighboring islands and continents (in terms of flora, fauna, climate, and culture), we need to stress the role that the sea (Vogiatzakis et al. 2017) and the special natural and/or anthropogenic features of each island, be that mining and cultivation practices, dialects or languages (Rackham 2012:

89), played in shaping their particularity, individuality, and distinct identity. It is true that neo-Malthusian population cycles, demographic pressure, and the straining of natural resources have long dominated settlement archaeology and economic studies of the pre-modern periods (Le Roy Ladurie 1974; Bintliff 1996; Vionis 2016). Although such explanations have become unfashionable lately (Curtis 2014: 2), one cannot underestimate the effects of human interference with the natural environment and its resources. Environmental determinism, on the other hand, still offers a valid explanatory framework to crisis and resilience for specific parts of the globe (Curtis 2014: 7–10), such as the drought and famines, accompanied by cold weather conditions, recorded for the period from the later sixth into the eighth centuries in the Levant and Asia Minor (Haldon et al. 2014: 126, 138). Last but not least, the turn-around of politico-economic factors and the manifestation of the 'sacred' seem to have played a pivotal role in the expression of power and ideology (Papantoniou 2012), shaping settled and sacred landscapes accordingly, as well as determining settlement recovery and resettlement of abandoned or semi-abandoned micro-regions (Papantoniou and Vionis 2017).

Previous studies have attempted to define geographically the terrestrial boundary of the coastal zone, describing the relationship between the sea, the coastline, the landward buffer, and the landscape beyond, based on a combination of Landscape Character Assessment and Seascape Assessment (Vogiatzakis et al. 2017). The archaeological case-study discussed below is located within the "landward buffer" (within a zone of 10 km inland from the coastline) of Cyprus and provides a highly promising micro-region through which we examine processes of change and resilience on this sizable island between Roman times and the Byzantine Early Middle Ages (Figure 11.1). The aim is to contextualize settlement change and evaluate it within a multi-layered explanatory framework, as exemplified above (i.e., environmental, politico-economic, ideational, and computational). As we have recently illustrated (Papantoniou and Vionis 2017), landscape archaeology, and in particular the concept of sacred landscapes, can offer an improved interpretative framework to address the aforementioned issues.[1]

The Sacred and Economic Landscapes of Cyprus in Roman and Late Roman times

By the Roman period, many Cypriot extra-urban sanctuaries were deserted and only a few of them were remodelled and enlarged (Papantoniou 2013b: 50). While excavation and survey activities confirm that *ex novo* foundation of sanctuaries is rare in the Roman period (see also Given and Knapp 2003: 313), the use of pre-existing, extra-urban sanctuary sites is visibly reduced.

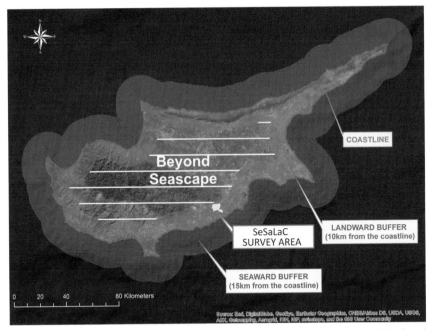

Figure 11.1. The location of the SeSaLaC survey area in relation to the seascape and landward buffer of Cyprus (after Vogiatzakis et al. 2017: figure 1, modified by A.K. Vionis).

It seems that the Romans invested in rebuilding and temple constructions, usually at those same primarily urban sites as their Ptolemaic predecessors. The transition from polytheism to Christianity during the Late Antique era in the late fourth and fifth centuries A.D. eventually resulted in major transformations in the island's social and cultural identities (Vionis and Papantoniou 2017: 253). Any effort to understand continuity and abandonment from Roman times to Late Antiquity needs to be inserted within the framework of a macro-historic and geographically contextual landscape approach.

As one of us has argued at length elsewhere (Papantoniou 2012: 92–93; 2013b), the multiplication of extra-urban sanctuaries in early Archaic times represents the climax of a process that started within the Geometric period, and relates to the consolidation of the many Cypriot city-kingdoms and their territories. Excavation of extra-urban shrines of the Archaic and Classical periods in the past has produced evidence which is also confirmed by more recent excavation activity (Smith 1997), and which highlights the role of the Cypriot Iron Age sanctuary as a focus of wealth disposal and economic networks (cf. Beer 1992; Fischer 2001). The distribution of these sanctuaries across the landscape served as a map for a socio-political system providing a mechanism

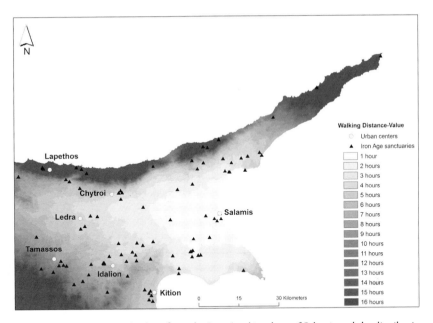

Figure 11.2. Cost-Distance Analysis from the Iron Age kingdom of Salamis and the distribution of identified Iron Age sanctuaries in the wider territory (digital data courtesy of the Geological Survey Department, Republic of Cyprus; map drafted by V. Trigkas, UnSaLa-CY).

for the centralized Archaic and Classical city-kingdom authorities to organize and control their peripheries (Papantoniou 2012: 95; 2013b: 41). In addition, environmental and Geographic Information System (GIS) analyses employed recently in the context of the UnSaLa-CY project (Papantoniou et al. 2015; Papantoniou and Vionis 2017; Papantoniou 2019), reinforce this argument about the territoriality of Iron Age Cypriot sanctuaries, placing them at the same time in economic routes related to the island's copper industry and arable land for agricultural production (Figure 11.2).

The transformation of Hellenistic political topographies, and the passing of Cyprus from segmented to unitary, colonial administration under a foreign general, the *strategos,* brought a marked urban and extra-urban change. In a unified state that offered unlimited access to inland resources, official emphasis was put primarily on urbanized and strongly 'hellenized' coastal centers for political, military, and economic reasons. The coastal cities of Nea Paphos, Marion-Arsinoe, Kourion, Amathus, Soloi, and Salamis undoubtedly mirror Ptolemaic strategic interests in coastal port bases and settlements, as well as maritime activity and power (Marquaille 2001: 139).

The gravitation of people towards these coastal cities was of greater historical significance. Several surface surveys on the island have noted a dense settlement pattern in the Hellenistic and Roman countryside, followed by a general contraction during the second through the fourth centuries A.D. (Rautman 2001). According to Rautman, rural settlement began to decline around the second century A.D.; evidence of Severan prosperity, which possibly represents the apogee of Roman Cyprus, is overwhelmingly urban and may have come about at the expense of the countryside (Papantoniou and Vionis 2017; Rautman 2001). Settlement patterns in transitional phases, however, are not entirely consistent; thus, new regional survey projects need to address such issues by exploring potential pastoral, agricultural, and other economic activities, and how these may relate to the various political situations and to the siting of sanctuaries.

Nonetheless, we would observe that the widespread abandonment of the extra-urban shrines, no less than the elaboration of public cults in the cities, set the stage for profound social and religious reassessments that go back to the Hellenistic period and have to be studied within the context of the transition from segmented to unitary government and administration (Papantoniou 2012; 2013b). Changing economic conditions within the Cypriot cities under a unitary government and administration also entailed some significant changes in financing and, as a result, in the sociological structure of their religion. In the Hellenistic, and especially in the Roman periods, financial management eventually shifted from the city-state to a more unified and centralized control. The most important bearer of a unifying ideology should have been played by the *Koinon Kyprion* (Union of Cypriots), dedicated to the promotion of the Ptolemaic, and later the imperial cult.

Following the Severan period, we know very little regarding Cypriot sacred space during the third and fourth centuries A.D. The stratigraphy, material culture, and architecture related to post-Severan sacred landscapes remains to be identified, published, and sufficiently analyzed. By the mid-fourth century A.D., the social transformations taking place throughout the eastern Mediterranean led to the gradual decline and abandonment of polytheistic temples in various urban centers of Cyprus, mainly due to constrained state funds to maintain them (Rautman 2001). By the early fifth century, a dense network of 15 bishoprics was established on the island (Rapp 2014: 30), while the growing power of Cypriot bishops is confirmed by the sacralization of urban space at Paphos, Amathus, Kourion, and Salamis/Constantia (Rautman 2001). It is noteworthy that after the Church of Cyprus gained its autocephaly at the Council of Ephesus in A.D. 431, the role of the bishops and the clergy in church investment and community leadership began to take off. Archaeological surface surveys in Cyprus have confirmed not only the successful Christianization of the island by the fifth century through the construction of basilicas in cities and the countryside, but also a tremendous boom in rural settlement, industrial activity, and commercial expansion down to the mid-seventh century (Caraher et al. 2014; Given et al. 2013; Rautman 2000). This a crucial period in the development of Cypriot sacred landscapes as, again, like the beginning of the Archaic period and the consolidation of the Iron Age polities, we move from a "half-empty" to a "full" sacred landscape.

We believe that one should address the transformation processes that took place during Late Antiquity at two different levels: first, within the urban fabric itself and, second, within the broader landscape of the island, attempting to connect urban centers or bishoprics and countryside. We feel that the spatial approach that the UnSaLa-CY and SeSaLaC projects are currently undertaking and promoting has great potential. In addition, environmental, geographical, and statistical approaches, currently in progress in the context of these projects, will further clarify the role of early Christian basilicas.

A number of factors contributed to the gradual conversion of sacred space in the urban centers of the island. The official establishment of Christianity, the economic prosperity that Cyprus started enjoying, and the shift of political control (at the local level) from imperial families to Christian elites and bishops contributed to the transformation of the sacred townscapes and landscapes of Cyprus (Chrysos 1993: 5; Caraher et al. 2014: 294; Rautman 2014: 51). Iconographic and epigraphic evidence is nicely illustrative of these arguments. As Nicolaou (2001) and Daszewski and Michaelides (1988) have convincingly argued for the cases of the mosaic floors in the secular buildings of the House of Eustolios at Kourion, the Villa of Theseus (Bath of Achilles), and the House of Aion at Nea Paphos, for example, one can clearly read the interaction between the artistic and literary forms of Late Roman and Early Christian spirits, especially as the latter were still creating their own. Naturally, the propaganda of the new religion may have been partly created through the traditional pagan means of expression; and, as recent studies on the transition from polytheism to Christianity have shown, scholars are encouraged to read the two traditions in terms of connectivity and co-existence, rather than in clash or opposition (cf. Horster et al. 2017).

More than 60 Christian basilicas have been identified in towns and countryside throughout the island, a number of them encroaching on civic public space or replacing pre-Christian sanctuaries, others erected in the periphery of cities and along major communication axes, close to city walls and gates or near ports and nearly always on prominent locations, comprising important landmarks of sacred space (Vionis 2017a: 145). It would be expectable that large cities, being important administrative and economic centers on the island (e.g. Salamis/Constantia, Amathus, Kourion, and Paphos), would preserve a significant degree of monumentality. The grand architectural expressions of basilicas hinted at capital and the rank of the lay patrons, and were recognized as special places for the community (Yasin 2009: 286–290; Leone 2013: 22). In towns of lesser status, expression of monumentality in basilica churches was shaped accordingly, perhaps not in terms of size, but certainly in terms of luxury. Cyprus, being an island lacking marble and other fine stone, could not but express its religiosity or Christian identity through the monumental scale of basilicas on the one hand, and through promoting the cult of celebrated personalities on the other (Rautman 2001; Kyriakou 2019). Moreover, Cyprus did not claim a tradition in the cult of martyrs; thus, early bishops and foreign saints (e.g., Auxibios of Soloi, Spyridon of Tremithus, Herakleidios of Tamassos, Triphyllios of Ledra) were sanctified and comprised local cults, attracting pilgrims, promoting secular and religious pride, and consequently boosting the towns' economy (Brandes and Haldon 2000: 144; Maguire 2012: 21; Vionis and Papantoniou 2017: 253–254; Kyriakou 2019).

As already noted above, the city gathered administrative, economic, and cultural/cultic functions for a surrounding countryside, as intermediary to superior centers (Koder 1986: 157). On the basis of a more recent and synthetic study of the archaeology of Late Antique urban environments, however, the situation seems more complex: provincial cities/towns of the empire acquired a more "central place" role, functioning as "primary local centers" or "local first-rank" settled spaces (Vionis 2017b: 138–139). Despite the fact that we do not know the extent of city territories in Late Antique Cyprus, archaeological evidence confirms thriving cities and a busy countryside throughout much of the fifth, sixth, and early seventh centuries (Mitford 1980; Rupp and Sørensen 1993; Rautman 2014: 43). The erection of new basilicas in the Cypriot countryside testifies to the agricultural and population explosion in rural areas and reveals the spread of Christianity into the countryside, redefining the island's religious and economic landscapes (Rautman 2000: 318; Caraher et al. 2014: 294; Kyriakou 2019).

Preliminary GIS analyses of the churches[2] in relation to the road networks and arable land aim to reveal the function of these countryside basilicas in the context of economic and symbolic landscapes. The analyses confirm that Christian basilicas are found in association with rural establishments (e.g., villages), local central places (e.g., towns, agro-towns, and ports or coastal *emporia*), and other significant economic and communication nodes (e.g., road networks, rivers, and agriculturally rich areas) (Figure 11.3). According to Rautman (2014: 43), and as we will see below in the case of the Xeros valley, what is archaeologically evident is that, along with the thriving cities,

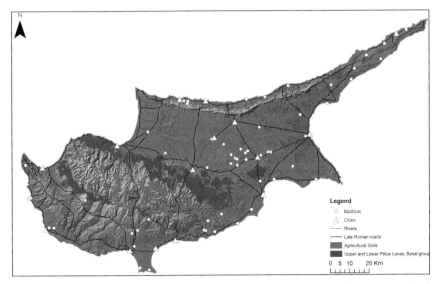

Figure 11.3. Distribution of basilica churches throughout Cyprus and their topographical relation to the Roman road network, agricultural lands and copper sources. (Digital data courtesy of the Geological Survey Department, Republic of Cyprus; map drafted by N. Kyriakou, UnSaLa-CY.)

the exploitation of the countryside in Late Roman Cyprus was phenomenal. The Kalavasos-Kopetra basilicas, for example, built on a hill in the middle of the Vasilikos valley, were the most tangible expressions of continuing investment of wealth generated in the valley, and acted as regional economic nodes at a central point for the collection and distribution of imported and local products (Rautman 2003: 38, 241–242, 318). It is clear that, as in earlier periods of Cypriot antiquity, at the transition from the Roman to the Late Antique period, we move from a "half-empty" to a "half-full" and later to a "full" sacred landscape. This is a much-celebrated phase of Cypriot religiosity extending well beyond the limits of monocausal explanations.

The Settled and Economic Landscapes of Cyprus in Late Antiquity: A Case Study

The application of "Community Area Theory" (Kuna 1991) aims to recognize shifts in the location of the main settlements within each "settlement chamber" or "micro-region"—also known as *Siedlungskammer*—and indicates a "continuity" of settlement at or beside the occupation of the previous phase. This sort of "continuity" or location and relocation of settlement at or beside the occupation of the previous phase within the same micro-region of the Xeros valley in Cyprus is not a unique phenomenon

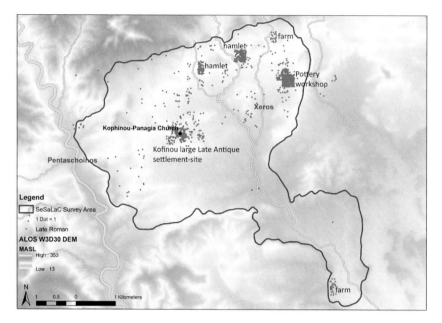

Figure 11.4. The distribution of Late Antique pottery identified in the Xeros Valley: the large settlement site of Kofinou Panagia and other Late Antique sites in the SeSaLaC survey area (digital data courtesy of the Geological Survey Department, Republic of Cyprus; map drafted by H. Paraskeva, SeSaLaC).

in settlement archaeology. Large areas of land with natural boundaries and desirable resources sustained nucleated communities and remained occupied for almost every period. Indeed, the largest archaeological site we have identified to date is located in the approximate center of our survey area, east of the present-day village of Kofinou (Figure 11.4). This is a site with evidence for continuous occupation and use from the Late Bronze Age to the end of the Ottoman period, within an area of 25 ha around the standing Byzantine church of Panagia. Panagia is a compressed cross-in-square church-type with a dome, dated to the early eleventh century. Excavations carried out around Panagia in 2011 revealed the foundations of a three-aisled basilica of the sixth or early seventh century, upon the central aisle of which the eleventh-century church of Panagia was erected (Procopiou 2014: 228) (Figure 11.5). We were able to identify the remains of two more churches in different parts of the same site during the course of our field survey, one of them possibly dated to the sixth or seventh century (Figure 11.6).

The occupational phase of the site in Late Antiquity, especially in the sixth and seventh centuries, is represented by the most satisfactory of all

Figure 11.5. The Byzantine domed church of Panagia built over the central aisle of a Late Antique basilica (aerial photograph by courtesy of the Department of Antiquities, Cyprus).

our ceramic assemblages, clear in its date and distribution. The spatial distribution of pottery dated to this period gives the impression of a thriving rural establishment, some 13 ha in size. The pottery distribution map suggests that the built-up area was focused within a radius of 200 m around the church of Panagia. Thus, it is worth examining whether the extensive settlement of the sixth to seventh centuries in the Xeros valley actually comprises the main settlement of its micro-region, what its agricultural and economic potential was, on which regional central place or city it was dependent, whether other minor satellite establishments can be identified in the same region, and what role its basilica played in the symbolic, religious, social and economic sphere.

What is striking about this rather large Late Antique inland site is the fact that nearly half of the ceramic assemblage represents tiles, storage and transport jars, and large *pithoi*, made of local clays, and intended for roofing and everyday household use. This does not come as a surprise: during the 2017 field season, we identified a Late Antique ceramic workshop 2 km northeast of Kofinou (Figure 11.4), and next to the River Xeros, through a thick concentration of wasters, over-fired pottery, and kiln furniture. The workshop, located very close to a major junction of the Roman road-

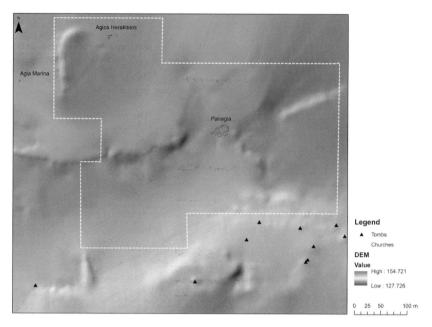

Figure 11.6. Digital Elevation Model (DEM) of the settlement site of Kofinou Panagia (showing its extent in Late Antiquity) with the church of Panagia and the ruins of the chapels of Agios Herakleios and Agia Marina (GIS mapping by N. Kyriakou).

network on the island (linking Nicosia and the interior of the island with the coastal places of Larnaca and Limassol), produced almost every class of domestic ceramics, from roof-tiles and water pipes, to *pithoi*, smaller storage and transport jars, jugs, and basins. About a quarter of the total ceramic assemblage is made up of transport amphorae. As in the case of the neighboring site of Kalavasos-Kopetra (Rautman 2014), considering that most of the amphorae in our assemblage are Cypriot, it is likely that they were used to redistribute or export goods, while those remaining at the site document a lively consumer economy.

The ceramic evidence, the presence of a monument of Christian worship, topographic parameters, extensive surrounding agricultural territory, and comparative evidence from other excavated and surveyed sites suggest that in Late Antiquity the site of Kofinou, around the church of Panagia, played a central role within its "settlement chamber" or micro-region, coincidentally overlapping with our survey area (Vionis and Papantoniou 2017). Looking at population figures based on excavation and survey evidence, the extent of the site of Kofinou suggests that the settlement should have accommodated approximately 250–300 families during its maximum size in the sixth and seventh centuries A.D. (when the built space around the basilica, according to surface ceramic scatters, reached almost 13 ha). The excavated basilica must have functioned as the focal point of the settlement, standing at its approximate center, dominating its immediate environs and marking a primary approach to the site. All the aforementioned parameters point to the status of Kofinou as a second-rank settlement, and as the main habitation site of the micro-region of the Xeros valley. Such secondary settlements in the countryside had a major role to play as local centers—that is, as important loci within the territory of their "settlement chamber", acquiring an important role in agricultural production, processing and distribution of goods, and sometimes administrative functions as well. If, then, Kofinou comprised a second-rank settlement, which we would define here as an "agro-town", one needs to identify the closest primary center, or regional central place, and other minor rural establishments. Although this remains guesswork at this stage, the region's primary center should have been the city and bishopric of Kition, present-day Larnaca, 23 km northeast. In this context, it is worth looking at similar examples elsewhere in Cyprus.

In the neighboring region of Kalavasos-Kopetra, 12 km southwest of Kofinou, excavations have unearthed the remains of a prosperous rural settlement of 4 ha, home to 100 families, together with three churches, serving as physical and social landmarks for local residents. According to the excavator (Rautman 2005: 456–458), the churches and other archaeological evidence in Kalavasos reflect the economic success of this Cypriot community, identified as a "market village" and its control of transport and exchange on a sub-regional level. The second example concerns the site of Pyla-Koutsopetria, 32 km northeast of Kofinou, where a surface survey has identified an enormous coastal site of 40 ha, with plentiful ceramic evidence confirming the agricultural and quarrying activities at that locality, but most importantly, engagement in maritime trade (Caraher et al. 2014). Moreover, monumentality is also present at the site. Excavations by the Department of Antiquities in the past have revealed a basilica with *opus sectile* floors, while the results of recent geophysical prospection by the University of North Dakota indicate the existence of more churches at the site (Caraher et al. 2008: 82; 2014: 4). Thus, Pyla-Koutsopetria functioned as an *emporion* in Late Antiquity, involved in the inter-regional distribution of Cypriot goods.

It goes without saying that every respectful second-rank settlement (in our case the agro-town of Kofinou) should be the focus and local center of a series of satellite minor rural establishments, such as hamlets, villas, and farmsteads. Indeed, four smaller loci of ceramic concentrations northeast and southeast of the large settlement of Kofinou, comprising mainly roof tiles and transport and storage vessels, have been interpreted as hamlets and farms, housing a number of farming families closer to their fields. Hamlets, farmsteads and villa estates are amongst the commonest rural sites identified in Cyprus and beyond (from Spain and Italy, to the Levant) throughout Late Antiquity. Previous survey work on the island (e.g., in the territory of Kourion) has revealed that farmsteads were usually small in size (ranging between 0.01 and 0.4 ha), had access to fresh water, and were located in prominent positions overlooking the surrounding countryside and the sea (Mavromatis and Swiny 2000).

The pattern that emerges when one focuses on archaeological evidence from our site dated to the Late Antique era is of particular importance here. The micro-region of the Xeros valley, very much as in the micro-region of Kalavasos-Kopetra, was characterized by the presence of a main settlement with associated basilicas. Thus, the presence of one or more basilicas at these places possibly indicated the settlement's status as a local center, with churches supervising agricultural, processing, distribution, and sometimes industrial activities. These secondary places may have varied in size and function. Pyla-Koutsopetria, of some 40 ha, must have functioned as an *emporion* distributing goods inter-regionally; Kofinou, an agro-town of 13 ha participated in intensive agricultural production, storage, and distribution of goods to nearby cities and port-towns; Kalavasos-Kopetra, a village of 4 ha, functioned as a principal market for local products (Vionis and Papantoniou 2017: 259). The primary center or regional central place, towards which these second-rank settlements were oriented, is always a nearby city, usually with a bishop, such as Kition to the east of Kofinou and Amathus to the west. Finally, third-rank settlements were satellite minor farming establishments *without* a church, or settlements occupied seasonally by a labor force residing in cities, port-towns, agro-towns, and market-villages, and commuting seasonally between secondary settlements and their farms.

This settlement hierarchy for Cyprus is always adapted by SeSaLaC according to the period under investigation, and is primarily based on deterministic factors of what makes central and secondary places. It should be borne in mind, however, for periods about which archaeological data or textual evidence are limited or lacking, that central-place functions might be dispersed between a variety of sites and places, while a central person might be as important as a central place (Vionis 2017b: 159). It is evident that there is clearly much more going on in the case of the Xeros valley (and other fertile and well-populated regions in Cyprus) than a three-level settlement hierarchy and dots on the map, as can be illustrated by land capacity and population estimates for the period.

Taking Kofinou as a secondary settlement in Late Antiquity, one wonders whether the land available in its micro-region and the approximate number of people that lived in the settlement were actually compatible. Although the immediate surroundings of the Christian basilica at Kofinou nowadays give the impression of a rich and intensively cultivated landscape, the *Soil Atlas of Europe* shows that the best and most fertile soils within our survey area and the Kofinou settlement chamber amount to 1,510 ha (Figure 11.7). Interestingly, the Late Antique settlement itself lies in the middle of less fertile soils, a very wise choice on the part of its inhabitants, making use of less productive areas for their settlement's built space, as well as for less demanding types of cultivation, such as vegetable gardens and olive groves, or as pastureland. More demanding crops, such as wheat and vines, would have been cultivated in the areas with the best soils, lying 800 m away from the settlement. Considering that approximately 300 families were living in Kofinou, and taking into account that 3.6 ha of land were required per family to meet their subsistence needs in pre-industrial times (Shiel and Stewart 2007: 107), we arrive at the figure of 1,080 ha needed for feeding the population of Kofinou. That means that the remaining 430 ha would be reserved for sustaining the population of hamlets and farmsteads and, of course, for the export of a significant surplus that would bring in the necessary cash for the community to meet its tax obligations.

The above exercise demonstrates that the agro-town of Kofinou was the main settlement and the only basilica of its micro-region, within reach of an agricultural territory that was able to sustain no more than the population of the main settlement and its satellite rural establishments, as well as provide a surplus for export. Cost-Distance analysis shows that the farmers of Late Antique Kofinou would need no more than 40 minutes to walk or ride to the limits of their community's territory and within their "settlement chamber", also overlapping with our survey area. This is actually the average time that pre-modern populations needed to commute between home and their fields on a daily basis (Bintliff and Snodgrass 2007: 137). We can identify the exact same pattern for other neighboring settlements and micro-regions, at least in the case of those for which we have archaeological evidence (Figure 11.8). If nothing else, this implies an extremely organized settlement and agricultural plan in Late Antique Cyprus. It becomes evident that basilica churches mark monumental space and feature prominently within settlements of some status in Late Antique Cyprus and beyond. Just as with the ancient sanctuaries, Late Antique basilicas played an important role in inscribing social memory, territorial significance, and economic activities on the landscape. Last, but not least, one of the roles that basilicas in rural environments seem to have assumed was that of supervisor of industrial, processing, and storage activities.

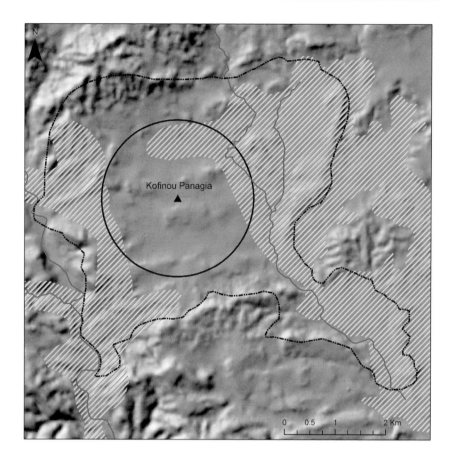

Legend

---·---· Survey_Area

☐ Kofinou Panagia Buffer

▨ Potential Agricultural Soils

Dem25m50k

Value

High : 1943.18

Low : -11.2607

Figure 11.7. Best agricultural soils in the Xeros Valley according to the Soil Atlas of Europe (digital data courtesy of the Geological Survey Department, Republic of Cyprus; map drafted by N. Kyriakou, SeSaLaC).

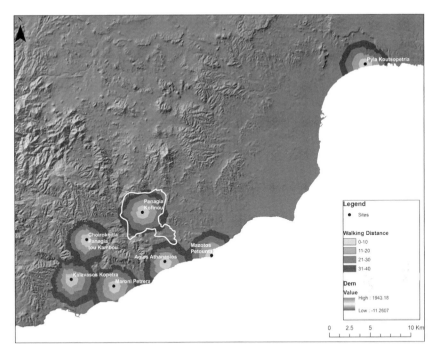

Figure 11.8. Cost-Distance Analysis from known basilicas (including Panagia in the SeSaLaC survey area) associated with Late Antique settlement and/or industrial/processing/storage activity along the south coast of Cyprus (digital data courtesy of the Geological Survey Department, Republic of Cyprus; GIS mapping and analysis by N. Kyriakou, SeSaLaC).

Transformations in Economy and Settlement Patterns in the Early Middle Ages

We should note that we ought to view the sacred landscapes of Cyprus in the framework of an insular scheme relating to the transition from segmented to unitary administration (or politico-economic and ideological orientations) and *vice versa*. Ancient extra-urban sanctuaries acted as symbolic, territorial (even *liminal* in some instances, in the case of the so-called frontier sanctuaries), and economic nodes within and/or between urban centers, second-rank settlements, villages, and farmsteads. Similarly, Early Christian basilicas in the Cypriot countryside also acted as important symbolic and economic nodes within and/or between urban centers, second-rank agro-towns, market villages, or monastic centers in close proximity to regional central places or cities/bishoprics, and satellite farm estates. As we also noted above, this is a much-celebrated phase of Cypriot religiosity, extending well beyond the limits of monocausal explanations. However, what happens in the Byzantine Early Middle Ages, between the mid-seventh and ninth centuries A.D.?

Turning to issues of urban and rural abandonment and resilience in the Byzantine Early Middle Ages, it should be noted that the "idea of the city" did not necessarily collapse overall, but the role of previous "local/regional centers" may have survived in an altered form after the conventional end of Late Antiquity in the seventh century. Although we do recognize that major changes occurred during the period in question, we would rather detach our views and approaches to the issue of "continuity" or "discontinuity" of *civitates* and urban life in the Byzantine Early Middle Ages from the established traditionalists' and non-traditionalists' theories in the existing scholarship (Kazhdan and Cutler 1982). Similarly, we can better understand the notion of "abandonment" or "decline" through comparison between previous monumental centers and their surrounding countryside.

Archaeological surveys outside Cyprus, such as that in the territory of Sagalassos in southwest Asia Minor, have concluded that after the traditional collapse of a complex urban life from the late sixth century onwards, the countryside went back to being a landscape organized around peer villages. By that time, rural communities had established ways of becoming self-sufficient. In the seventh to ninth centuries, villages may have remained in use, but rural communities were rather smaller. The landscape was still occupied, however, and exploited continuously between the seventh and ninth centuries. Unfortunately, the nature of this use was such that it left less visible archaeological traces (Vanhaverbeke et al. 2009: 186–187). Our ongoing field survey in the Xeros valley reveals a similar picture, where a booming Late Antique countryside of village and agro-towns, such as Kofinou, transformed into village-communities, dispersed and scattered into a cluster of small sites in the open country during the Byzantine Early Middle Ages (Figure 11.9).

The pattern emerging through archaeological surveys may indicate, based on counted and statistically-weighted surface ceramic concentrations, a rather pessimistic view of a downward "city-curve" after the late sixth century, but a surprisingly optimistic steady "countryside-curve". This visualization testifies to the fact that the economic crisis and the overall changing situation after the end of Late Antiquity should have a greater effect on the fate of the city and its urban population, while it must have been little felt by pre-industrial rural populations living in an environment that allowed them agricultural autarky (Vanhaverbeke et al. 2009: 187).

This pattern, however, inevitably emerges through the limited distribution of ceramic wares in different parts of the eastern Mediterranean, and on

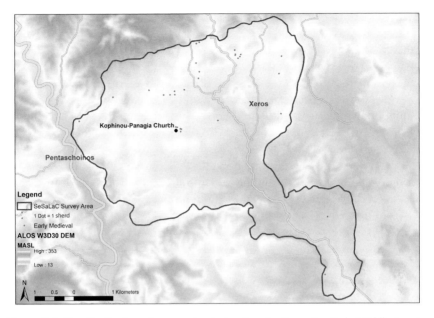

Figure 11.9. The distribution of pottery sherds dated to the Byzantine Early Middle Ages in the Xeros Valley (digital data courtesy of the Geological Survey Department, Republic of Cyprus; map drafted by H. Paraskeva, SeSaLaC).

archaeologists' ability to recognize the pottery of this period. Although more classes of ceramics are gradually being recognized, our knowledge is still confined to a few different types of amphorae, undecorated jugs, and handmade cookware (Vionis et al. 2009; Vionis 2017c: 364–366). One does not necessarily need to consider hand-made kitchenware solely as a result of a general decline in trade, rural and/or urban life, but rather, as a local response to a general changing economic system and an emerging local pottery tradition based on household-organized production and exchange (Vionis et al. 2009: 161). The shift from the Roman mass-produced and customized wares (that started to disappear from the market) to non-specialized local/regional production (that started to satisfy basic household needs) need not have been a sudden one. Cyprus is a characteristic case, where hand-made cooking wares first appear in early seventh-century contexts and its tradition continued almost without break into the second half of the twentieth century. Evidence for this transition to the manufacture of hand-made domestic pottery in the Early Middle Ages in Cyprus (and elsewhere) suggests that it had become small scale and at village- and household-level, probably as a result of a number of economic, historical and environmental factors, as in much of post-Roman western Europe previously (Rautman 1998: 92–93).

An interesting parallel can be made with another island—Naxos in the Aegean—where pottery at several sites dated to the late seventh, eighth, and ninth centuries testifies to the existence of small and large settlements associated with contemporary ecclesiastical monuments, not merely restricted to the interior of the island, but also a short distance from the coast (Vionis 2013a: 29–31; 2017d: 174–176). The ceramic record itself provides direct evidence for the economic links between the island and other parts of the eastern Mediterranean, as well as with Constantinople, thanks to securely dated amphorae of the LRA1 variant-types and of Hayes' (1992: 71) "Saraçhane type 36" (Vionis 2013a: 30–31). The picture of settlement during the period of the Arab raids in the Aegean, emerging through the corroborating evidence, contradicts previous historical views (Malamut 1988: 67–68) about the desolation of coastal regions and retreat of populations to the mountains and into island interiors. A fascinating picture, similar to Naxos, is currently emerging though excavations in various parts of Cyprus: ceramic evidence dated to the transitional Early Middle Ages in the eighth and ninth centuries has been unearthed in coastal sites, such as Kofinou, Akrotiri, Paphos, and Agios Kononas, as well as inland, such as Nicosia. The Early Medieval ceramic assemblage from the above-mentioned sites in Cyprus include globular amphorae, undecorated jugs, pattern-burnished and handmade wares, and Constantinopolitan Glazed White Ware.

Interestingly, an evaluation of the material culture of this period (i.e., ceramics and numismatic evidence) from Constantinople, the Aegean islands, the coasts of mainland Greece, and Asia Minor, Crete, and Cyprus, reveals another ceramic *koine* and testifies to the presence of the Byzantine army in the Aegean and to the existence of a regional network of communication with the imperial center (Vionis et al. 2009: 154–156; Vionis 2013b: 114–115, 2017d: 174) (Figure 11.10). It is unclear how such a pattern could have emerged if the two antagonistic powers of the period—Arabs and Byzantine islanders—were not communicating, compromising, or even collaborating in some fashion. On the level of everyday life, it is interesting that in Cyprus, during the so-called "condominium years" in the Byzantine Early Middle Ages, Arabs and Byzantines lived together in peace and harmony in cities such as Paphos and Salamis/Constantia, as witnessed by Willibald, an English pilgrim who visited the island in A.D. 723 and paid his respects in the church of Saint Epiphanios at Salamis/Constantia (Talbot 1954: 161).

We would argue that Cyprus, very much like certain Aegean islands, may be recognized as belonging to a "peripheral" or "buffer" zone between the Byzantine imperial center and the growing Arab sovereignty in the eastern Mediterranean, enjoying a degree of freedom from central state control. The evidence from the material culture of the island, scanty textual references,

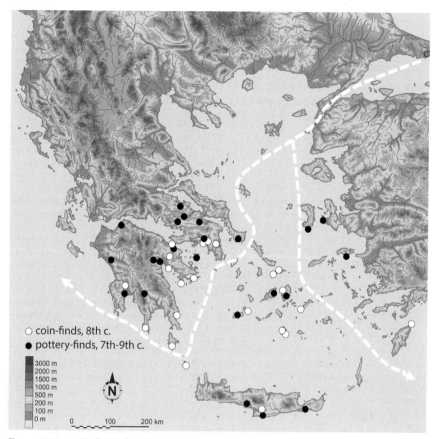

Figure 11.10. An Early Medieval ceramic *koine* in the Aegean, along the major communication axes connecting Constantinople with the Aegean, southern Italy and Cyprus (map drafted by A.K. Vionis).

visual art, and mechanisms supporting contact continuity between Cyprus and other regions in the eighth and ninth centuries, can only point to two insular responses towards the imperial center and the newcomers. The first response points to material connectivity and religious affiliation with Constantinople, resulting in maintaining traditional ties with the imperial center. The second points to an intense encounter with new people, resulting in economic stability and/or resilience. The afore-mentioned evidence reinforces the argument that the islands acted as the frontier between the Arabs and the world of Byzantine sovereignty (and did not fit exactly into the profile of islands under central control), having become a zone of cross-imperial interaction, rather than a cultural barrier between antagonistic empires (Vionis 2013b: 116–117; 2017d: 175–176).

On a final note, concerning "abandonment" and/or resilience between Late Antiquity and the Early Middle Ages, it is worth mentioning that a number of recent studies have focused on the examination of climatic and environmental conditions in the first millennium A.D. and how these may have affected human societies and political systems (McCormick et al. 2012; Haldon et al. 2014). Both proxy data and the Byzantine documentary sources agree that in the period known as the "Dark Ages Cold Period" (after A.D. 730 and until 900), droughts and famines became more frequent and were accompanied by severe winters with frosts and snow (Haldon et al. 2014: 126). These climatic fluctuations may partly explain downward demographic trends and the militarization of the empire, and may have affected agricultural patterns throughout the Early Middle Ages, from the cultivation of vines and olives, to less "risky" investments, such as cereal production and livestock raising (Haldon et al. 2014: 139).

Notes

1. Our collaboration is based on two interconnected projects: (a) the *Unlocking the Sacred Landscapes of Cyprus (UnSaLa-CY)* research project (funded by the Cyprus Research Promotion Foundation: EXCELLENCE/1216/0362), functioning in the framework of the *Unlocking Sacred Landscapes Network (UnSaLa)*, an official collaboration between the University of Cyprus, Trinity College Dublin, and the Institute for Mediterranean Studies in Crete; and (b) our ongoing *Settled and Sacred Landscapes of Cyprus* Surface Survey Project (*SeSaLaC*) in the Xeros river valley (Larnaca District).
2. Undertaken by Niki Kyriakou, in the context of the *UnSaLa* and *SeSaLaC* projects

References

Beer, Cecilia
　　1992　　Ethnic Diversity and Financial Differentiation in Cypriot Sanctuaries. In *Economics of Cult in the Ancient Greek World. Proceedings of the Uppsala Symposium 1990*, edited by Tullia Linders and Brita Alroth, pp. 73–84. Boreas: Uppsala Studies in Ancient Mediterranean and Near Eastern Civilizations 21. Acta Universitatis Upsaliensis, Uppsala.

Bintliff, John L.
　　1996　　The Mountain Peoples of Ancient Greece: The Relevance of World-Systems Theory and Neo-Malthusianism to their Development. In *Stuttgarter Kolloquium zur historischen Geographie des Altertums* 5, 1993, edited by Eckart Olshausen and Holger Sonnabend, pp. 105–141. Geographica historica 8. Hakkert, Amsterdam.

Bintliff, John, L., and Anthony Snodgrass
　　2007　　The Sites and Their Setting: Distribution, Chronology and Function. In *Testing the Hinterland: The Work of the Boeotia Survey (1989–1991) in the Southern Approaches to the City of Thespiae*, edited by John L. Bintliff, Phil Howard, and

Anthony Snodgrass, pp. 129–169. Cambridge University McDonald Institute Monographs, Cambridge.

Brandes, Wolfram, and John Haldon

2000   Towns, Tax and Transformation: State, Cities and their Hinterlands in the East Roman World, ca. 500–800. In *Towns and their Territories: Between Late Antiquity and the Early Middle Ages*, edited by Gian Pietro Brogiolo, Nancy Gauthier, and Neil Christie, pp. 141–172. Brill, Leiden.

Braudel, Fernand

1972   *The Mediterranean and the Mediterranean World in the Age of Philip II*, Vol. I. Translated by S. Reynolds. Collins, London.

Broodbank, Cyprian

2000   *An Island Archaeology of the Early Cyclades*. Cambridge University Press, Cambridge.

Caraher, William, R. Scott Moore, and David K. Pettegrew

2008   Surveying Late Antique Cyprus. *Near Eastern Archaeology* 71: 82–89.

2014   *Pyla-Koutsopetria* I: *Archaeological Survey of an Ancient Coastal Town*. American Schools of Oriental Research Archaeological Reports 21. American Schools of Oriental Research, Boston.

Chrysos, Evangelos

1993   Cyprus in Early Byzantine Times. In *The Sweet Land of Cyprus: Papers Given at the Twenty-Fifth Jubilee Spring Symposium of Byzantine Studies, Birmingham, March 1991*, edited by Anthony M. Bryer and Georgios S. Georghallides, pp. 3–14. Cyprus Research Centre, Nicosia.

Counts, Derek B., and Maria Iacovou

2013   New Approaches to the Elusive Iron Age Polities of Ancient Cyprus: An Introduction. *Bulletin of the American Schools of Oriental Research* 370: 1–13.

Curtis, Daniel R. (editor)

2014   *Coping with Crisis: The Resilience and Vulnerability of Pre-Industrial Settlements*. Routledge, London.

Daszewski, Wiktor A., and Demetrios Michaelides

1988   *Guide to the Paphos Mosaics*. Bank of Cyprus Cultural Foundation, Nicosia.

Evans, John D.

1973   Islands as Laboratories for the Study of Culture Process. In *The Explanation of Culture Change: Models in Prehistory*, edited by Colin Renfrew, pp. 517–520. Duckworth, London.

Fischer, Bettina

2001   Le rôle des sanctuaires dans l'économie chypriote. *Cahier du Centre d'Études* 31: 51–58.

Given, Michael, and A. Bernard Knapp (editors)

2003   *The Sydney Cyprus Survey Project: Social Approaches to Regional Archaeological Survey*. Monumenta Archaeologica Series 21. Cotsen Institute of Archaeology, University of California, Los Angeles

Given, Michael, A. Bernard Knapp, Jay Noller, Luke Sollars, and Vasiliki Kassianidou

2013   *Landscape and Interaction: The Troodos Archaeological and Environmental Survey Project. Methodology, Analysis and Interpretation*, Vol. I. Levant Supplementary Series 14. Council for British Research in the Levant, Oxford.

Gordon, Jody M.

2012   Between Alexandria and Rome: A Postcolonial Archaeology of Cultural Identity in Hellenistic and Roman Cyprus. Unpublished Ph.D. dissertation, University of Cincinnati.

2016   To Obey by Land and Sea: Empires, the Mediterranean, and Cultural Identity in Hellenistic and Roman Cyprus. In *Across the Corrupting Sea: Post-Braudelian Approaches to the Ancient Eastern Mediterranean*, edited by Cavan Concannon and Lindsey A. Mazurek, pp. 133–164. Routledge, London.

Haldon, John, Neil Roberts, Adam Izdebski, Dominik Fleitmann, Michael McCormick, Marica Cassis, Owen Doonan, Warren Eastwood, Hugh Elton, Sabine Ladstätter, Sturt Manning, James Newhard, Kathleen Nicoll, Ioannes Telelis, and Elena Xoplaki

2014   The Climate and Environment of Byzantine Anatolia: Integrating Science, History, and Archaeology. *Journal of Interdisciplinary History* 45(2): 113–161.

Hayes, John W.

1992   *Excavations at Saraçhane in Istanbul*, Vol. II: *The Pottery*. Princeton University Press, Princeton.

Horster, Mariette, Doria Nicolaou, and Sabine Rogge (editors)

2017   *Church Building in Cyprus (4th to 7th Centuries): A Mirror of Intercultural Contacts in the Eastern Mediterranean*. Schriften des Instituts für Interdiziplinäre Zypern-Studien 12. Waxmann, Münster/New York.

Iacovou, Maria

2007   Advocating Cyprocentricism: An Indigenous Model for the Emergence of State Formation on Cyprus. In *"Up to the Gates of Ekron": Essays on the Archaeology and History of the Eastern Mediterranean in Honor of Seymour Gitin*, edited by Sidnie White Crawford, Amnon Ben-Tor, J.P. Dessel, William G. Dever, Amihai Mazar, and Joseph Aviram, pp. 461–475. The W.F. Albright Institute of Archaeological Research/The Israel Exploration Society, Jerusalem.

2013   Historically Elusive and Internally Fragile Island Polities: The Intricacies of Cyprus's Political Geography in the Iron Age. *Bulletin of the American Schools of Oriental Research* 370: 15–47.

Kazhdan, Alexander, and Anthony Cutler

1982   Continuity and Discontinuity in Byzantine History. *Byzantion* 52: 429–478.

Kirch, Patrick V.

1986   Exchange Systems and Inter-Island Contact in the Transformation of an Island Society: the Tikopia Case. In *Island Societies: Archaeological Approaches to Evolution and Transformation*, edited by Patrick V. Kirch, pp. 33–41. Cambridge University Press, Cambridge.

Koder, Johannes

1986   The Urban Character of the Early Byzantine Empire: Some Reflections on a Settlement Geographical Approach to the Topic. *The 17th International Byzantine Congress: Major Papers*, 155–187. Caratzas, New York.

Knapp, A. Bernard

2008   *Prehistoric and Protohistoric Cyprus: Identity, Insularity and Connectivity*. Oxford University Press, Oxford.

Kuna, Martin

1991   The Structuring of Prehistoric Landscape. *Antiquity* 65: 332–347.

Kyriakou, Niki

2019   Sacred Landscapes in Late Roman Cyprus: Cityscapes and Peripheries in Context. In *Spatial Analysis of Ritual and Cult in the Mediterranean*, edited by Giorgos Papantoniou, Christine Morris, and Athanasios K. Vionis, forthcoming. Åström Editions, Uppsala.

Leone, Anna

2013   *The End of the Pagan City: Religion, Economy, and Urbanism in Late Antique North Africa*. Oxford University Press, Oxford.

Le Roy Ladurie, Emmanuel

1974   L'histoire immobile. *Annales* 29: 673–692.

Maguire, Richard

2012   Late Antique Basilicas on Cyprus: Sources, Contexts, Histories. Unpublished Ph.D. dissertation, University of East Anglia.

Malamut, Elizabeth

1988   *Les Iles de l'Empire Byzantine, VIIIe-XIIe Siècles*, Vol. I. Publications de la Sorbonne, Paris.

Marquaille, Céline

2001   The External Image of Ptolemaic Egypt. Unpublished Ph.D. dissertation, King's College, University of London.

Mavromatis, Christopher, and Stuart Swiny

2000   Land behind Kourion: Results of the 1997 Sotira Archaeological Project Survey. *Report of the Department of Antiquities, Cyprus* 2000: 433–452.

McCormick, Michael, Ulf Büntgen, Mark A. Cane, Edward R. Cook, Kyle Harper, Peter Huybers, Thomas Litt, Sturt W. Manning, Paul Andrew Mayewski, Alexander F. M. More, Kurt Nicolussi, and Willy Tegel

2012   Climate Change during and after the Roman Empire: Reconstructing the Past from Scientific and Historical Evidence. *Journal of Interdisciplinary History* 43(2): 169–220.

Mitford, Terence B.

1980   Roman Cyprus. In *Aufstieg und Niedergang der römischen Welt*, edited by Hildegard Temporini, pp. 1285–1384. De Guyter, Berlin/New York.

Nicolaou, Ino

2001   The Transition from Paganism to Christianity as Revealed in the Mosaic Inscriptions of Cyprus. In *Mosaic: Festschrift for A.H.S. Megaw*, edited by Judith Herrin, Margaret Mullett, and Catherine Otten-Froux, pp. 13–17. British School at Athens Studies 8. British School at Athens, London.

Papantoniou, Giorgos

2012   *Religion and Social Transformations in Cyprus: From the Cypriot 'Basileis' to the Hellenistic 'Strategos'*. Mnemosyne Supplement 347. Brill, Leiden.

2013a   Cypriot Autonomous Polities at the Crossroads of Empire: The Imprint of a Transformed Islandscape in the Classical and Hellenistic Periods. *Bulletin of the American Schools of Oriental Research* 307: 169–205.

2013b   Cyprus from Basileis to Strategos: A Sacred-Landscapes Approach. *American Journal of Archaeology* 117(1): 33–57.

2016   Cypriot Ritual and Cult from the Bronze to the Iron Age: A *longue-durée* Approach. *Journal of Greek Archaeology* 1: 73–108.

2019   Unlocking Sacred Landscapes: The Applicability of a GIS Approach to the Territorial Formation of the Cypro-Archaic and Cypro-Classical Polities. In *Spatial Analysis of Ritual and Cult in the Mediterranean*, edited by Giorgos Papantoniou, Christine E. Morris, and Athanasios K. Vionis, forthcoming. Studies in Mediterranean Archaeology. Åström Editions, Uppsala.

Papantoniou, Giorgos, Niki Kyriakou, Apostolos Sarris, and Maria Iacovou

2015   Sacred Topography in Iron Age Cyprus: The Case of Vavla-Kapsalaes. In *Archaeological Research in the Digital Age. Proceedings of the 1st Conference on Computer Applications and Quantitative Methods in Archaeology: Greek Chapter (CAA-GR), Rethymno, Crete, 6–8 March 2014*, edited by Constantinos Papadopoulos, Eleftheria Paliou, Angeliki Chrysanthi, Eleni Kotoula, and Apostolos Sarris, pp. 70–75. Institute for Mediterranean Studies – Foundation of Research and Technology, Rethymno.

Papantoniou, Giorgos, and Athanasios K. Vionis

2017   Landscape Archaeology and Sacred Space in the Eastern Mediterranean: A Glimpse from Cyprus. *Land* 6: 40.

Patton, Mark

1996   *Islands in Time: Island Sociogeography and Mediterranean Prehistory*. Routledge, Abingdon-on-Thames.

Procopiou, Eleni

2014   Η Αρχιτεκτονική του Ναού της Παναγίας Κοφίνου. In *Ευμάθιος Φιλοκάλης: Ανάδειξη Βυζαντινών Μνημείων Κρήτης και Κύπρου*, edited by Eleni Procopiou and Nikoleta Pyrrou, pp. 220–238. Hellenic Ministry of Culture, Rethymno.

Rackham, Oliver

2012   Island Landscapes: Some Preliminary Questions. *Journal of Marine and Island Cultures* 1: 87–90.

Rapp, Claudia

2014   Christianity in Cyprus in the Fourth to Seventh Centuries: Chronological and Geographical Frameworks. In *Cyprus and the Balance of Empires: Art and Archaeology from Justinian I to the Coeur de Lion*, edited by Charles A. Stewart, Thomas W. Davis, and Annemarie Weyl Carr, pp. 29–38. American Schools of Oriental Research Archaeological Reports 20, CAARI Monograph Series 5. American Schools of Oriental Research, Boston.

Rautman, Marcus

1998   Handmade Pottery and Social Change: The View from Late Roman Cyprus. *Journal of Mediterranean Archaeology* 11(1): 81–104.

2000   The Busy Countryside of Late Roman Cyprus. *Report of the Department of Antiquities, Cyprus* 2000: 317–331.

2001   From Polytheism to Christianity in the Temples of Cyprus. In *Ancient Journeys: A Festschrift in Honour of Eugene Numa Lane*. Stoa consortium. Electronic document, http://www.stoa.org/hopper/text.jsp? doc=Stoa: text:2001.01.0014, accessed November 14, 2017.

2003   *A Cypriot Village of Late Antiquity: Kalavasos–Kopetra in the Vasilikos Valley.* Journal of Roman Archaeology Supplementary Series 52. Journal of Roman Archaeology, Portsmouth, Rhode Island.

2005   The Villages of Byzantine Cyprus. In *Les Villages dans l'empire byzantin*, edited by Jacques Lefort, Cécile Morrisson, and Jean-Pierre Sodini, pp. 453–463. Réalités byzantines 11. Lethielleux, Paris.

2014   The Troodos in Twilight: A Provincial Landscape in the Time of Justinian. In *Cyprus and the Balance of Empires: Art and Archaeology from Justinian I to the Coeur de Lion*, edited by Charles A. Stewart, Thomas W. Davis, and Annemarie Weyl Carr, pp. 39–56. American Schools of Oriental Research Archaeological Reports 20. CAARI Monograph Series 5. American Schools of Oriental Research, Boston.

Rupp, David W., and Lone W. Sørensen
1993   *The Land of the Paphian Aphrodite. The Canadian Palaipaphos Survey Project: Artifact and Ecofactual Studies*, Vol. II. Studies in Mediterranean Archaeology 104. Åström Editions, Goteborg.

Shiel, Robert S., and Andrew Stewart
2007   The Soils and Agricultural Potential of the Thespiai Area. In *Testing the Hinterland: The Work of the Boeotia Survey (1989–1991) in the Southern Approaches to the City of Thespiae*, edited by John L. Bintliff, Phil Howard, and Anthony Snodgrass, pp. 95–109. Cambridge University McDonald Institute Monographs, Cambridge.

Smith, Joanna S.
1997   Preliminary Comments on a Rural Cypro-Archaic Sanctuary in Polis-Peristeries. *Bulletin of the American Schools of Oriental Research* 308: 77–98.

Talbot, Charles H.
1954   *The Anglo-Saxon Missionaries in Germany, Being the Lives of SS. Willibrord, Boniface, Leoba and Lebuin together with the Hodoepericon of St. Willibald and a Selection from the Correspondence of St. Boniface.* Sheed and Ward, New York.

Vanhaverbeke, Hannelore, Athanasios K. Vionis, Jeroen Poblome, and Marc Waelkens
2009   What Happened after the 7th Century AD? A Different Perspective on Post-Roman Rural Anatolia. In *Archaeology of the Countryside in Medieval Anatolia*, edited by Tasha Vorderstrasse and Jacob J. Roondenberg, pp. 177–190. PIHANS 113. Netherlands Institute for the Near East, Leiden.

Vionis, Athanasios K.
2013a   Considering a Rural and Household Archaeology of the Byzantine Aegean: The Ceramic Spectrum. In *Pottery and Social Dynamics in the Mediterranean and Beyond in Medieval and Post-Medieval Times*, edited by John L. Bintliff, and Marta Caroscio, pp. 25–40. British Archaeological Reports International Series 2557. British Archaeological Reports, Oxford.

2013b   Reading Art and Material Culture: Greeks, Slavs and Arabs in the Byzantine Aegean. In *Negotiating Co-Existence: Communities, Culture and 'Convivencia' in Byzantine Society*, edited by Barbara Crostini and Sergio La Porta, pp. 103–127. Wissenschaftlicher Verlag Trier, Trier.

2016   A Boom-Bust Cycle in Ottoman Greece and the Ceramic Legacy of Two Boeotian Villages. *Journal of Greek Archaeology* 1: 353–384.

2017a   Sacred Townscapes in Late Antique Greece: Christianisation and Economic Diversity in the Aegean. *Journal of Mediterranean Archaeology* 30(2): 141–165.

2017b   Understanding Settlements in Byzantine Greece: New Data and Approaches for Boeotia, Sixth to Thirteenth Centuries. *Dumbarton Oaks Papers* 71: 127–173.

2017c   The Byzantine to Early Modern Pottery from Thespiai. In *Boeotia Project,* Vol. II. *The City of Thespiai: Survey at a Complex Urban Site*, edited by John L. Bintliff, Emeri Farinetti, Božidar Slapšak, and Anthony Snodgrass, pp. 351–374. Cambridge University McDonald Institute Monographs, Cambridge.

2017d   Imperial Impacts, Regional Diversities and Local Responses: Island Identities as Reflected on Byzantine Naxos. In *Imperial Lineages and Legacies in the Eastern Mediterranean: Recording the Imprint of Roman, Byzantine and Ottoman Rule*, edited by Rhoads Murphey, pp. 165–196. Routledge, London/New York.

Vionis, Athanasios K., and Giorgos Papantoniou

2017   Sacred Landscapes as Economic Central Places in Late Antique Naxos and Cyprus. *Antiquité tardive* 25: 263–286.

Vionis, Athanasios K., Jeroen Poblome, and Marc Waelkens

2009   The Hidden Material Culture of the Dark Ages. Early Medieval Ceramics at Sagalassos (Turkey): New Evidence (ca AD 650–800). *Anatolian Studies* 59: 147–165.

Vogiatzakis, Ioannis N., Maria Zomeni, and Antoinette M. Mannion

2017   Characterizing Islandscapes: Conceptual and Methodological Challenges Exemplified in the Mediterranean. *Land* 6: 14.

Yasin, Ann Marie

2009   *Saints and Church Spaces in the Late Antique Mediterranean: Architecture, Cult, and Community*. Cambridge University Press, Cambridge.

— 12 —

Islands in Context, A.D. 400–1000

DAVID ABULAFIA

> No man is an island entire of itself; every man
> is a piece of the continent, a part of the main.
> (John Donne)

I

For those examining past societies, insularity is a concept full of contradictions. The image of island societies as self-sufficient, autonomous, isolated (to use the obvious word) is by and large a fantasy. One or two possible exceptions come to mind—Neolithic Malta appears to have developed a distinctive culture that owed little to neighbors in Africa or Sicily, and may not have traded much with either place. The Berber inhabitants of the Canary Islands, prior to European conquest, had lost the art of navigation and seem not even to have made contact from island to island—and the other eastern Atlantic islands, Madeira, the Azores, and Cape Verde, were uninhabited before the Portuguese arrived in the fifteenth century. At the opposite side of the world, Rapa Nui (Easter Island), once settled, seems to have maintained no links with the outside world; but it was exceptionally remote from any neighbor, which cannot be said for any island within the closed and relatively narrow space of the Mediterranean. Within the Mediterranean, a few islands stand apart physically: the Balearics (though Ibiza was easily accessible from the coastline of Valencia), Sardinia (although a route past Corsica could lead ships to the Tuscan shore without losing sight of land), Crete (standing halfway to Africa), and Cyprus (although on a clear day southern Turkey is visible from Kyrenia).

Understanding the ancient and medieval societies of Mediterranean islands therefore depends on our understanding of the balance between influences from the nearby mainland, from neighboring islands (particularly within island chains such as the Cyclades), and from further afield in cases where islands became stopping-points along extended trade routes, or were conquered by mainland powers: in the period under consideration here, notable empires embracing Mediterranean islands were those of the Vandals, Byzantines, and the Arabs. On the other hand, within the period of this volume, none of the Mediterranean islands actually became the capital of what might be called a thalassocracy, an imperial network, based on the exercise of sea-power through powerful navies. The Vandals, it is true, did manage to use Carthage as the control center for operations that took their fleets to Sicily, Sardinia, Corsica, the Balearics and even western Greece, but Sicily only became the seat of a major thalassocracy in the twelfth century, with the foundation of the Norman Kingdom of Sicily by Roger II. To describe the Vandal territories as an island empire is to forget that these conquerors installed themselves on the edges of the largest Mediterranean islands, without, so far as can be seen, exercising rule over their entirety—quite apart from the fact that their capital lay on the north African mainland at Carthage. Another candidate for an island thalassocracy might be Byzantium in the age of Justinian, though the same reservations apply concerning the location of its capital, this time on the extreme edge of Europe. An island network, a sort of "route of the isles", connected Constantinople via the Aegean with territories in Sicily, Sardinia, and the Balearics, as a means of maintaining some sort of communication with the small Byzantine enclave on the southeastern coast of Spain. The emperor's aim was not so much mastery over the wide spaces of the Mediterranean, as the re-establishment of Roman imperial authority in Italy and Spain. As Poulou (Ch. 10), Tsigonaki (Ch. 7) and other contributors to this volume make plain, the Byzantine empire came to depend increasingly on trade networks within the Aegean, and saw Crete as an important line of defense or barricade holding Arab navies and armies at bay. This may well have stimulated the economy of the Early Medieval Aegean, during the seventh to tenth centuries, despite the temporary loss of Crete.

In the increasingly fragmented Late Roman world, the process of commercial and political integration that had held the Mediterranean together since the time of Augustus slowed to a halt. Already characterized, as Horden and Purcell (2000) have rightly insisted, by very considerable regional variation, distinctive local features led to very different outcomes in areas not far from one another. One could find intensification in some Greek islands, perhaps the result of demand from the relatively new capital at Constantinople, while others lost their role in intra-Mediterranean exchanges and slipped into relative obscurity. On a large scale, this differentiation is best visible in the contrast between the western and the eastern Mediterranean around the start of the sixth century, with the east, taken as a whole, showing greater resilience, and the west, more heavily affected by Germanic and other invasions, witnessing the disintegration of the old order as the so-called barbarian kingdoms took charge on the mainland—but not necessarily in the Balearic islands, where the Byzantine presence was still felt alongside that of the rival Franks up to the Islamic conquest in the early tenth century. In Sardinia (examined by Spanu in Ch. 3), Byzantine influence was still felt until the Pisans and Genoese became masters of much of the island in the eleventh century. What this term "influence" denotes varied over time: the lingering Byzantine connection is a very interesting example of insularity, as it declined from physical presence (Mas Florit and Cau in Ch. 1 note the discovery of a Byzantine seal in Menorca) into notional sovereignty (as in the case of the early Sardinian *giudicati*, "judgeships" that developed in time into petty kingdoms under the rule of competing native dynasties). Something remained of the old ecclesiastical order, linked to the Greek Church, until the penetration of Sardinia by monks and other clergy from Pisa, Genoa, and also Provence.

This serves as a reminder that it is important to insert within this framework the role of religious change. Broadly, the period of this volume begins with the adoption of Christianity within the Late Roman empire and ends with the conquest of much of the southern Mediterranean by the forces of Islam. How communities responded to the arrival of Christianity is documented in Turner and Crow's analysis of Naxos (Ch. 9) and in Sweetman's account of the Cyclades (Ch. 8). The speed with which the new faith spread within the Cyclades is striking. That Christianity spread by sea can be established easily enough: the evidence is there in the career of Paul of Tarsus. Whether small islands were easier to Christianize is an interesting question. Judging from the extraordinary account of the conversion of the Jews of Menorca to Christianity around A.D. 400, written by Bishop Severus, the leaders of a community played an essential role in convincing their followers to change religion. Individual choice was important (in the Menorcan case, some Jews resisted conversion, but apparently gave way after thinking further or even experiencing a miracle); but often it was suppressed as a whole group converted *en masse*.

We can imagine similar outcomes in, for instance, Delos, with its many pagan cults dedicated to Apollo and other gods, in the great age of Cycladic church-building following the conversion of Constantine. Nor should one forget the extraordinary religious history of the peninsula of Akté on which Mount Athos sits—not a true island, but an island to the extent that the mountain has remained carefully isolated from surrounding lands, beginning with Byzantine imperial decrees of the end of the ninth century that created a reserved area for monks; besides, access to the Holy Mountain is almost invariably by boat. Even so, this was by no means a one-way process. Castiglia and Pergola (Ch. 2) point out that fears were being expressed around A.D. 600 that paganism had revived in Corsica (insofar as the Catholic Church had been able to strike deep roots in an island whose mountainous character made its interior less accessible to outside influences than other western Mediterranean islands).

II

The fate of the islands cannot, then, be understood without taking into account the wider picture of economic, social, and political developments around the shores of the Mediterranean. As the grain trade of Alexandria was redirected to fourth-century Constantinople, Rome became dependent on the granaries of North Africa. This had a significant effect on the islands, as the Aegean became a more closely integrated trading zone (a point made by Poulou in Ch. 10). But to make fuller sense of developments in the islands a brief look at the wider picture is required, in which developments within the islands themselves are borne in mind. Without addressing issues such as demographic decline and climate change across the whole region, the islands would be left floating loose in an open sea.

The centuries between A.D. 400 and 1000 have traditionally been regarded as a low point in the history of the Mediterranean. What that means is that population had declined precipitately; that trade across the sea was at a very low ebb, compared to earlier centuries; that the towns which had been feeding that trade had shrunk or even disappeared; that the high culture of the Roman empire had been eroded by the less sophisticated cultures of the barbarian peoples who had already been entering the empire for centuries, and who now stood on the very shores of the Mediterranean, in Italy, Spain, North Africa, and so on. Inevitably, this view has been challenged by new schools of historians who speak more of the continuity from a Roman imperial past that was never forgotten, and that provided the basis for a political revival first in the years around A.D. 800, under Charlemagne, and then in the tenth century, when a Saxon dynasty claimed the crown of the western Roman empire—I think here of Chris Wickham's decision to entitle his Penguin history of Early Medieval Europe *The Inheritance of Rome* (2010).

This critique turns, at least implicitly, on the assumption that one should not disparage the culture of the Germanic and other peoples who took charge of large tracts of the empire by the sixth century. But defining a high culture is not in fact very difficult. Demand for luxury goods such as spices and perfumes was intense, not just at the top level of Roman society. Truly massive quantities of pepper were stored in the *horrea* of Rome, imported from India by way of the Red Sea and Egypt; this was flavoring for the upper and lower middle class, as well as for the Roman elites. The Roman city, with its public baths, its drainage systems, its arcaded markets, not to mention the high level of artistic production at the top end of the scale, looked and felt very different from the habitat of the incoming peoples. That said, these incoming peoples were keen to learn from the Romans and, in some areas such as Ostrogothic Italy, they were anxious to become patrons of the arts and builders, as one can still see in the remains of Ravenna. Carthage had flourished greatly under Roman imperial rule, becoming one of the major centers of trade, industry, and agriculture in the Mediterranean (despite its supposed annihilation in 146 B.C.). The arrival of the Vandals at the start of the fifth century was marked as much by the invaders' determination to keep alive Roman theatre and other signs of classical culture, as it was by revolution—which mainly affected the Church, as the Vandals were Arian Christians who began an active persecution of Roman Catholics, dumping many in Sardinia. Eastern amphorae arrived in the newly-renovated harbor of Carthage in considerable quantities, along with eastern silks and Byzantine coins. No longer supplying Rome with local grain, which was then plentiful, North African merchants could make their own choices about where to trade for a profit. And the Vandal rulers, like the Visigoths in Spain (who were very attentive to Roman law codes in the sixth century), still proudly preserved their Germanic personal names, for Romanization had its limits.

The real problem with the image of a Roman Empire in steep decline after A.D. 400 is of a different order. The nature of change varied significantly from region to region. Whereas the town of Luni, in northwestern Italy, disappeared off the map, Naples continued to play a significant role in Mediterranean trade throughout the Early Middle Ages. As Molinari (Ch. 4) shows, the largest Mediterranean island, Sicily, experienced decline from the late seventh century onwards, with a drastic fall in African imports by the eighth century (though this would naturally be reversed following the Islamic conquest in the ninth century). Her suggestion that the fortunes of Sicily might be linked to an arid period in the Mediterranean between the eighth and the fourteenth century needs to be considered further; in the twelfth century the island had restored its reputation as one of the great granaries of the Mediterranean, but one could argue that this was a relative success, since the chief victim of the arid period may well have been Tunisia, a former Roman bread-basket that became dependent on Sicilian wheat from about A.D. 1100 onwards. So too Vionis and Papantoniou (Ch. 11), looking at Cyprus, speak of a "Dark Ages Cold Period" between A.D. 730 and 900, and thought needs to be given to the ways in which some territories adapted agrarian production to cope with such changes (it is arguable that this happened in another cold period, the seventeenth century, when Crete moved away from grain production and towards wine production, although there were also political factors at work).

Certainly, some new centers of trade emerged, destined for bright futures in later centuries. Yet the situation in the eastern Mediterranean was in significant respects different to that in the western Mediterranean, since the greater degree of urbanization in the east and the less dramatic impact of invasions (which certainly occurred, nonetheless) permitted a reasonably vibrant economy to operate further east. Economic specialization in town and country, with exchanges of foodstuffs for textiles, and the inflow of eastern spices and perfumes by way of the Red Sea and the Persian Gulf, gave a different character to the lands that remained under the direct rule of the Roman emperors, based since the fourth century at New Rome, Constantinople. (The Red Sea route went into relative recession in the sixth century, but some traffic continued to ply back and forth.)

Coastal ports such as Gaza were important centers of trade, tying the eastern Mediterranean to elongated routes that penetrated far beyond the eastern boundaries of the Roman empire. Imperial rule extended as far as Sicily, despite the attacks on the island by the Goths and the Vandals. This position was maintained despite very severe blows: the Slav invasions, which overwhelmed large areas of the Balkans and reached down into Greece; the arrival of what we now know to have been bubonic plague in the sixth century, from A.D. 541 onwards, when the Emperor Justinian was attempting to restore Roman imperial rule, with a degree of success, as far west as Spain and the Maghrib. The analysis of atmospheric pollutants found in the Colle Gnifetti glacier in the Swiss Alps indicates that the plague was preceded and perhaps in some way prompted by a massive volcanic eruption in A.D. 536, followed by a further eruption on the very eve of the arrival of the plague. The eruptions occurred far away in Iceland, but a vast plume of ash spread southeastwards and enveloped much of Europe—crops failed in Ireland (as two sets of Irish annals testify), the Middle East, and even (assuming this too is connected) in China. It was as if the world was enveloped in a great fog. The Byzantine historian Prokopios wrote: "the sun gave forth its light without brightness" throughout the whole year. A series of very cold years followed, apparently the coldest decade for 2,000 years. Michael McCormick very plausibly identifies the eruptions and the plague as the moments when the Mediterranean economy entered a deep recession, from which it did not begin to emerge until 100 years later; and even then, the economy of large parts of the Mediterranean, especially in the west, remained sluggish for several more centuries. Although attempts are being made to show that the Justinianic plague was a milder affair than has been assumed, rather than a precursor of the Black Death, it is very hard to escape from the evidence that, as in the fourteenth century, a major demographic calamity and an extraordinary climatic event reshaped the economy of the Early Medieval Mediterranean (Eisenberg and Mordechai 2019). But how it did so, with so much less evidence available than in the Late Middle Ages, is for now an unresolved problem which archaeologists are best placed to answer.

The mid-sixth century appears to be the crucial moment. From this perspective the studies of Crete in this volume, by Zanini (Ch. 6) and Tsigonaki (Ch. 7), and of Cyprus, by Vionis and Papantoniou (Ch. 11), offer very valuable qualifications of the assumption that the eastern Mediterranean had greater resilience. What Zanini describes as "brutal change" within the cities of Crete followed a period of urban prosperity for, as Tsigonaki points out, Gortyn had been a grand metropolis up to the mid-sixth century. Here extraneous factors may account for decline: the heavy cost of Justinian's ambitious wars, leading to economic exhaustion, and the still uncalculated effects of the great plague, and the volcanic eruptions mentioned above. In Cyprus there is evidence of prosperity in small agro-towns such as Kofinou during the sixth and seventh centuries, even though drought and famine afflicted the lands bordering the eastern Mediterranean at this time; but one person's impoverishment can be another person's economic opportunity, particularly when one looks at the production of vital foodstuffs. That was certainly the response to the great plague of the fourteenth century.

The great question for economic historians, ever since Henri Pirenne wrote his celebrated book *Mahomet et Charlemagne* (1936), has been whether the Islamic invasions, or the earlier barbarian ones, played a greater role in the sundering of trade links within the Mediterranean, and the apparent isolation of the northwestern Mediterranean from Byzantium and the Middle East. He pointed to the disappearance of gold from western coinage, notably under Charlemagne, who pursued a policy of silver monometallism; and he described the decline in pepper imports from India, which had been of quite astonishing quantities in the Roman imperial period, but shrank to a small fraction in the fifth and sixth centuries; he also stressed that the lack of availability of papyrus left the western Europeans without the writing paper they needed, pushing them towards reliance on parchment instead, which was costly and cumbersome to produce—and this itself speaks for a decline in record-keeping and therefore of government efficiency, though both certainly expanded by the late eighth century, under Charlemagne.

Pirenne did overstate his case. There is enough evidence to show that in the sixth century there were still markets for eastern luxuries in the western Mediterranean, some of which arrived by way of the Provençal abbey of

Fos. However, it is important to distinguish between the rights that this abbey possessed to import substantial quantities of goods such as pepper, and daily reality; it is quite possible that this pepper was a distant memory. Michael McCormick has shown that trans-Mediterranean traffic continued in the eighth and ninth centuries, carrying pilgrims to the Holy Land and ambassadors to Constantinople, while a slave-trade bringing captives out of eastern Europe as far as Spain was already in existence, although many of the slaves came overland by way of centers such as Prague and never had sight of the sea (McCormick 2001). One should not confuse dozens of references to intermittent sea travel during the eighth and ninth centuries with the idea that regular and profitable trade existed between east and west. Indeed, the Byzantine emperors carefully controlled the movement of prestige goods.

In the case of Byzantium, the most prestigious export was silk, some obtained from the Far East by way of the intermittent Silk Road to China or by way of the active maritime trade routes across the Indian Ocean. By the tenth century the Byzantines knew perfectly well how to weave fine silks, and placed a ban on the export of top-quality purple dyed silk, which was reserved for the imperial court—the ambassador of the German emperor Otto I, Liudprand of Cremona, confessed in his reports that he had managed to smuggle some of this out of Constantinople. It is also important to qualify the loose use of the term "west" in what has been said so far. The real economic power-houses in Spain lay in the south, in al-Andalus, where the courts of Abd ar-Rahman II and III in the ninth and tenth centuries and of several of the local kings who ruled southern Spain in the eleventh century were places of great magnificence, modelled on what was known of the Abbasid court in Baghdad.

The best way to describe trade at this time, within and beyond the Mediterranean, is as "pedlar trade", characterized by the movement of merchants carrying high-value goods in small quantities, often across very long distances. The Arabic writer ibn Khurradidbih described the Radhanites, a name no one has satisfactorily deciphered (it may refer to the River Rhône, and hence to Provençal merchants). Around A.D. 800 they were travelling by land and sea routes as far as Persia and even, it seems, China. They were Jews, although one should not take that statement too literally, as the western European sources tended to refer to "Jews" and "Syrians", meaning by those terms "merchants" rather than people of one particular religion or origin. Whether they were organized in companies and derived their working capital from sedentary investors is unknown, but it seems unlikely. Some enjoyed the protection of the Merovingian and Carolingian rulers of Gaul, whom they were able to supply with jewels and other luxury items.

Within the Islamic Mediterranean, on the other hand, the Jewish presence in trade became more and more visible in the tenth and eleventh centuries, to judge from the remarkable collection of commercial letters preserved for centuries in a synagogue in Old Cairo. The rise of this merchant community reflected the success of the Shi'ite Fatimids in challenging Abbasid power in the Islamic heartlands, so we cannot assume that these traders were active in similar fashion before the record begins in the tenth century. In one direction, the Cairo merchants travelled as far as India in search of spices and other exotica; in the other direction they were very active on the coast of Tunisia, at the important new town of Mahdia, and in Sicily, conquered by the Muslims in the ninth century. Some reached Spain as well. They were experts in the silk trade, treating silk as an investment, as well as an article of trade. Knowledge was the key to success—which explains the letters with the very latest information about the price of pepper at Palermo, or the movement of friendly and enemy shipping in the Mediterranean. Many also had the knowledge of languages that enabled them to cross boundaries and conduct business without misunderstanding. It was a lively world of commerce that survived until about A.D. 1150, by which time new forces—the Genoese, Pisans, and Venetians—were taking command of the spice trade within the Mediterranean. The relatively light limitations on the Jews (and Christians) in most Islamic lands should also be noted: some extra taxes, but no coercion to convert and a general acceptance by Muslim princes that they ruled over an ethnically and religiously diverse population.

How the West heaved itself out of the trough of commercial depression is still a mystery. Although most historians would point to the twelfth century as the time when expansion became particularly vigorous, there were important antecedents, mainly in Italy. Here too islands played a crucial role, but these were islands close to the mainland with a very distinctive character. Venice emerged out of the muddy silt of the northern Adriatic. At the start, it was a community of fishermen and salt manufacturers, but the profits from these enterprises led the Venetians further afield, to the shores of Dalmatia (studied in this volume by Jurković); then they penetrated ever deeper into the Byzantine Empire, receiving a trading privilege from the Byzantine emperor in the late ninth century. Jurković (Ch. 5) demonstrates the importance of the frontier status of the Adriatic at this time: an attack on the lagoon by the Carolingians at the end of the eighth century encouraged the inhabitants of scattered islets to gather at a single defensible point, the *Rivo Alto* or "High Bank", which became "Rialto" in Venetian dialect. The Venetians proved remarkably successful in playing off first the Carolingians and then the Ottonians against their Byzantine rivals. Even so, early Venice was not one place but several, an island state with a multiplicity of bishops and communities, from Grado in the north to Chioggia in the south. Keeping up vestigial political ties with Constantinople ensured that the citizens of Venice could develop their own commercial network without too much interference; notionally the *dux* was a Byzantine official, but over time this idea faded, to be replaced by the constant reminder, in the mosaics and other accoutrements of Venetian churches, that these islands formed part of the cultural rather than the political world of Byzantium. Increasingly, this network encompassed the settlements that dotted the fragmented coastline of Dalmatia, some on islands, others, like Dubrovnik (Ragusa) and Kotor, on promontories or in bays. Indeed, Dubrovnik may have originally consisted of a small island disconnected from the mainland; the present-day main street, known as Stradun or Placa, was quite possibly a watery channel, later filled in to connect the island to the mainland; in some historians' scenario, the Latin settlement of Ragusa became joined to the Slav settlement of Dubrovnik, whose name seems to mean "wooded area".

Much the same applies to the other town that earned a reputation as a center of trade between east and west at this period, Amalfi, by which must be understood not just the minute town of that name, but its close neighbors Maiori, Minori, Ravello, Cetara, and so on, which together formed a fragmented city that outsiders saw as a significant commercial community. As in the case of Athos, the inaccessibility by land of the little towns of the Sorrentine peninsula made this area into a *de facto* island, connected to its neighbors mainly by sea. Here too the duke, like the Venetian doge, was technically an official of the Byzantine emperor; here too the emperors would occasionally bestow grandiloquent titles of honor, but in practice the relationship was a very loose one—still close enough to win the Amalfitans trading rights on the Golden Horn. Amalfi also developed close relations with the Muslims in Sicily and Tunisia and provided a channel through which the luxuries of Byzantium and the Islamic world reached the papal court in Rome and the wealthy abbey of Montecassino not far away, whose agents the Amalfitans were. They minted a gold coinage, proof that they were able to tap into the flow of gold that reached North Africa and Byzantium. But the fact that "Saracen" raiders had become a scourge for the inhabitants of southern Italy seems not to have worried them greatly; indeed, they were accused of collaboration with the Muslims.

After A.D. 1100 Amalfi was to be overtaken by north Italian cities—not just Venice, but Pisa and Genoa. The Pisans were already proving themselves at sea around A.D. 1000, helping to keep Sardinia clear of the Muslim pirates from Spain who were trying to conquer the island (a vain hope in reality).

However, the other great naval power of the future, Genoa, had much more modest beginnings. It had been a Byzantine base until the middle of the seventh century, but the region was experiencing severe enough economic difficulties for the leading historian of early Genoa to call the area "Dark Age Liguria" (Balzaretti 2003) Around 1000 the Genoese were still tending to look inwards at the valleys and mountainsides of a region that could produce little apart from the oil, nuts and herbs that make up its most famous product, pesto. Much the same can be said of Barcelona, which experienced a flash-in-the pan period of wealth in the eleventh century, and then relapsed into relative insignificance until about a.d. 1200. By a.d. 1000, then, there were glimmers of recovery in the west, but not yet the bright light of full-scale expansion. Very slowly the Mediterranean was coming together as an integrated trading area, but the most successful areas were still those under Islamic or Byzantine rule.

III

It has become increasingly obvious to historians of the Mediterranean that it is only possible to understand what Braudel called the "rhythms" of its trade when one takes into account what was happening further along the maritime trade routes—routes which, ultimately, linked Alexandria and other Levantine ports to the spice islands of the Far East. So-called Roman merchants (more often Egyptian Greeks) had made extensive use of sea-routes towards India since the time of Augustus. The Red Sea lost and regained primacy during the Early Middle Ages, because a rival passage-way, the Persian Gulf, also flourished for a while, following the rise of Abbasid power in Baghdad. Which of the two narrow seas was the more important depended on the political convulsions that were taking place within the Middle East, but the really significant point is that the sea-route, whether it passed Aden bound for Egypt or the Straits of Hormuz bound for Iraq and Iran, remained busy, functioning not just as a channel along which fine goods from east and west were passed, but as an open duct along which religious and other cultural influences flowed. How these influences affected the islands of the Mediterranean was determined by all sorts of factors: the political regime within the islands; their accessibility; their ability to offer desirable products; their position along the most manageable sea-routes across the Mediterranean. But at one point or another, the individual islands engaged with a much larger world, even if at other times depopulation, ruralization and desiccation led to their relative isolation. The history of islands is, by and large, a history of variety and, to repeat an over-used term, connectivity.

References

Balzaretti, Ross
  2003   *Dark Age Liguria: Regional Identity and Local Power, c. 400–1020*. Bloomsbury, London.
Eisenberg, Merle, and Lee Mordechai
  2019   Rejecting Catastrophe: The Case of the Justinianic Plague. *Past and Present* 244 (August 2019).
Horden, Peregrine, and Nicholas Purcell
  2000   *The Corrupting Sea: A Study of Mediterranean History*. Blackwell, Oxford.
McCormick, Michael
  2001   *Origins of the European Economy: Communications and Commerce, AD 300–900*. Cambridge University Press, Cambridge.
Pirenne, Henri
  1937   *Mahomet et Charlemagne*. Nouvelle Société d'Éditions, Brussels.
Wickham, Chris
  2010   *The Inheritance of Rome: A History of Europe from 400 to 1000*. Penguin Books, London.

Index

Figures in *italics*; n refers to note